Crime

Its Causes and Remedies

Cesare Lombroso

Alpha Editions

This edition published in 2019

ISBN : 9789353977139

Design and Setting By
Alpha Editions
email - alphaedis@gmail.com

THE MODERN CRIMINAL SCIENCE SERIES

Published under the Auspices of

THE AMERICAN INSTITUTE OF CRIMINAL LAW AND CRIMINOLOGY

Crime
Its Causes and Remedies

By CESARE LOMBROSO, M. D.

Professor of Psychiatry and Criminal Anthropology in the University of Turin

Translated by

HENRY P. HORTON, M. A.

WITH AN INTRODUCTION BY MAURICE PARMELEE, PH. D.

Assistant Professor of Sociology in the University of Missouri

Author of "Principles of Criminal Anthropology," etc.

BOSTON

LITTLE, BROWN, AND COMPANY

1918

GENERAL INTRODUCTION TO THE MODERN CRIMINAL SCIENCE SERIES.

At the National Conference of Criminal Law and Criminology, held in Chicago, at Northwestern University, in June, 1909, the American Institute of Criminal Law and Criminology was organized; and, as a part of its work, the following resolution was passed:

"*Whereas*, it is exceedingly desirable that important treatises on criminology in foreign languages be made readily accessible in the English language, *Resolved*, that the president appoint a committee of five with power to select such treatises as in their judgment should be translated, and to arrange for their publication."

The Committee appointed under this Resolution has made careful investigation of the literature of the subject, and has consulted by frequent correspondence. It has selected several works from among the mass of material. It has arranged with publisher, with authors, and with translators, for the immediate undertaking and rapid progress of the task. It realizes the necessity of educating the professions and the public by the wide diffusion of information on this subject. It desires here to explain the considerations which have moved it in seeking to select the treatises best adapted to the purpose.

For the community at large, it is important to recognize that criminal science is a larger thing than criminal law. The legal profession in particular has a duty to familiarize itself with the principles of that science, as the sole means for intelligent and systematic improvement of the criminal law.

Two centuries ago, while modern medical science was still young, medical practitioners proceeded upon two general assumptions: one as to the cause of disease, the other as to its treatment. As to the cause of disease, — disease was sent by the inscrutable will of God. No man could fathom that will, nor its arbitrary operation. As to the treatment of disease, there were believed to be a few remedial agents of universal efficacy. Calomel and blood-letting, for example, were two of the principal ones. A larger or smaller dose of calomel, a greater or less quantity of bloodletting, — this blindly indiscriminate mode of treatment was regarded as orthodox for all common varieties of ailment. And so his calomel pill and his bloodletting lancet were carried everywhere with him by the doctor.

Nowadays, all this is past, in medical science. As to the causes of disease, we know that they are facts of nature, — various, but distinguishable by diagnosis and research, and more or less capable of prevention or control or counteraction. As to the treatment, we now know that there are various specific modes of treatment for specific causes or symptoms, and that the treatment must be adapted to the cause. In short, the individualization of disease, in cause and in treatment, is the dominant truth of modern medical science.

The same truth is now known about crime; but the understanding and the application of it are just opening upon us. The old and still dominant thought is, as to cause, that a crime is caused by the inscrutable moral free will of the human being, doing or not doing the crime, just as it pleases; absolutely free in advance, at any moment of time, to choose or not to choose the criminal act, and therefore in itself the sole and ultimate cause of crime. As to treatment, there still are just two traditional measures, used in varying doses for all kinds of crime and all kinds of persons, — jail, or a fine (for death is now employed in rare cases only). But modern science, here as in medicine, recognizes that crime also (like disease) has natural causes. It need not be asserted for one moment that crime is a disease. But it does have natural causes, — that is, circumstances which work to produce it in a given case. And as to treatment, modern science recognizes that penal or remedial treatment cannot possibly be indiscriminate and machine-like, but must be adapted to the causes, and to the man as affected by those causes. Common sense and logic alike require, inevitably, that the moment we predicate a specific cause for an undesirable effect, the remedial treatment must be specifically adapted to that cause.

Thus the great truth of the present and the future, for criminal science, is the individualization of penal treatment, — for that man, and for the cause of that man's crime.

Now this truth opens up a vast field for re-examination. It means that we must study all the possible data that can be causes of crime, — the man's heredity, the man's physical and moral make-up, his emotional temperament, the surroundings of his youth, his present home, and other conditions, — all the influencing circumstances. And it means that the effect of different methods of treatment, old or new, for different kinds of men and of causes, must be studied, experimented, and compared. Only in this way can accurate knowledge be reached, and new efficient measures be adopted.

All this has been going on in Europe for forty years past, and in limited fields in this country. All the branches of science that can help have been working, — anthropology, medicine, psychology, economics, sociology, philanthropy, penology. The law alone has abstained. The science of law is the one to be served by all this. But the public in general and the legal profession in particular have remained either ignorant of the entire subject or indifferent to the entire scientific movement. And this ignorance or indifference has blocked the way to progress in administration.

The Institute therefore takes upon itself, as one of its aims, to inculcate the study of modern criminal science, as a pressing duty for the legal profession and for the thoughtful community at large. One of its principal modes of stimulating and aiding this study is to make available in the English language the most useful treatises now extant in the Continental languages. Our country has started late. There is much to catch up with, in the results reached elsewhere. We shall, to be sure, profit by the long period of argument and theorizing and experimentation which European thinkers and workers have passed through. But to reap that profit, the results of their experience must be made accessible in the English language.

The effort, in selecting this series of translations, has been to choose those works which best represent the various schools of thought in criminal science, the general results reached, the points of contact or of controversy, and the contrasts of method — having always in view that class of works which have a more than local value and could best be serviceable to criminal science in our country. As the science has various aspects and emphases — the anthropological, psychological, sociological, legal, statistical, economic, pathological — due regard was paid, in the selection, to a representation of all these aspects. And as the several Continental countries have contributed in different ways to these various aspects, — France, Germany, Italy, most abundantly, but the others each its share, — the effort was made also to recognize the different contributions as far as feasible.

The selection made by the Committee, then, represents its judgment of the works that are most useful and most instructive for the purpose of translation. It is its conviction that this Series, when completed, will furnish the American student of criminal science a systematic and sufficient acquaintance with the controlling doctrines and methods that now hold the stage of thought in Continental Europe.

Which of the various principles and methods will prove best adapted to help our problems can only be told after our students and workers have tested them in our own experience. But it is certain that we must first acquaint ourselves with these results of a generation of European thought.

In closing, the Committee thinks it desirable to refer the members of the Institute, for purposes of further investigation of the literature, to the "Preliminary Bibliography of Modern Criminal Law and Criminology" (Bulletin No. 1 of the Gary Library of Law of Northwestern University), already issued to members of the Conference. The Committee believes that some of the Anglo-American works listed therein will be found useful.

COMMITTEE ON TRANSLATIONS.

Chairman, JOHN H. WIGMORE,
Professor of Law in Northwestern University, Chicago.

ERNST FREUND,
Professor of Law in the University of Chicago.

MAURICE PARMELEE,
Professor of Sociology in the State University of Missouri.

ROSCOE POUND,
Professor of Law in Harvard University.

ROBERT B. SCOTT,
Formerly Professor of Political Science in the State University of Wisconsin.

WM. W. SMITHERS,
Secretary of the Comparative Law Bureau of the American Bar Association, Philadelphia, Pa.

INTRODUCTION TO THE ENGLISH VERSION

THE treatment of the criminal up to the latter part of the nineteenth century was dominated by the theories of the classical school of criminology. This school was based upon the thought of the eighteenth century philosophers. Its chief founder was the distinguished Italian criminologist, Cesare Beccaria. In his great work entitled "Crimes and Punishments," published in 1764, he condemned the almost unlimited power which judges frequently had in determining the punishment of criminals. This power frequently led to inhuman and unjust treatment of the criminal. Filled with the humanitarian feeling and dominated by the democratic ideas of the time, Beccaria insisted that no punishment should be greater than the crime warranted, and that all men should be equal in the eyes of the law. Thus the fundamental principle of the classical school was that the treatment of a criminal should be determined by the character of the crime that he had committed. In each criminal case it was to be determined what crime had been committed, and then the penalty designated by the penal code was to be applied regardless of the personality of the criminal.

We can now discern many variations in the treatment of the criminal from the principle laid down by the classical school. Criminals guilty of the same crime are very frequently not subjected to the same penalty, and the variations in their treatment are not usually due to differences in their social standing as was frequently the case previous to the time of the classical school. The treatment of the criminal is being based more and more upon his own characteristics rather than upon the character of the crime he has committed. How has this great change come about? The largest credit for it is undoubtedly due to the great Italian criminal anthropologist, Cesare Lombroso, who died in October, 1909. Few men have suffered the amount of criticism and abuse that Lombroso experienced during his lifetime. But if the degree of interest and difference of opinion aroused by his ideas, and the extensive literature devoted to the discussion of them, are any indications of his influence, Lombroso is certainly the most important figure in criminological science since Beccaria. Let us see what were the characteristics of his teachings which gave them so great an influence.

Lombroso was one of the group of great thinkers of the nineteenth century who had the courage and the wisdom to apply the positive, inductive method of modern science to the study of human and social phenomena. He was not the first one to search for the causes of human conduct in the physiological and mental characteristics of the individual, for others, such as Galenus, Gall, and Morel, had preceded him in this study. But no one of these had carried his analysis very far and the methods used were not always very scientific. Lombroso devoted his whole life to his study and used thoroughly inductive methods. His teachings immediately aroused great opposition; in the first place, because of the prejudice which existed against attributing human conduct to natural causes. But much of this opposition was also due to the fact that in his first writings he attributed criminal conduct almost entirely to the characteristics of the criminal himself. That, however, he recognized later on the social causes of crime is indicated by this book in which ample weight is given to these social causes.

Lombroso commenced his studies by spending several years in studying the characteristics of the criminals in the Italian penitentiaries. In 1876 he published the first edition of his "L'Uomo Delinquente." In this book he set forth his theory that crime is caused almost entirely by the anthropological characteristics of the criminal. But in later editions of the same work he gave more and more weight to the social causes of crime, and ultimately published the work of which the present volume is a translation. While several of his less important books have been translated into English, neither of his two principal works have ever before been translated. Thus it is that the English-speaking world is acquainted with his theories largely through hearsay.[1] The Committee on European Translations of the American Institute of Criminal Law and Criminology has chosen the second of his great works for translation in the belief that his theories should be better known in this country. The Institute is devoting itself to the work of applying science in the administration of the criminal law, and we are glad to know that Lombroso approved of its work in the following words written shortly before his death:[2]

"I beg to express my satisfaction at learning of the call for the National Conference on Criminal Law and Criminology, to take place in Chicago. It will mark a new era in the progress of criminal law. If I could offer any suggestion to so competent a body of men, it would be to emphasize the importance of apportioning penalties, not according to the offense, but according to the offender. To this end the probation system, which it is the great credit of America to have introduced, should be extended so as to suit the offender's type and individuality. It is futile to fix a term of imprisonment for the born criminal; but it is most necessary to shorten to the minimum the term for the emotional offender, and to modify it for the occasional offender, and to place the latter under the supervision of a judge, and not to let his fate be so fixed that it amounts merely to a modern form of slavery."

The present volume discusses in the main the social causes of crime. It has seemed well to the Committee that in this introduction there should be given a critical summary of Lombroso's theory as to the anthropological causes of crime as set forth in his great work on Criminal Man.[3]

[1] A summary of his "Criminal Man" is now published in America (by Messrs. Putnam's Sons), under the editorship of his daughter, Signora Gina Lombroso-Ferrero and Professor Ferrero. The present Introduction covers the ground of that Summary.

[2] Extract from a letter to Professor John H. Wigmore, first President of the American Institute of Criminal Law and Criminology, dated Turin, May 3, 1909.

It is interesting to learn that Dr. Lombroso, in May, 1908, was visited by Mr. Wigmore with the purpose of tendering him the nomination as Harris Lecturer at Northwestern University in 1909–10, his subject to be "Modern Criminal Science," and that Dr. Lombroso expressed a deep interest but was prevented by his advanced age from making any engagements to leave Italy.

Dr. Lombroso's death occurred a few months after the above letter was written.

[3] The following summary is taken in the main from the writer's "Principles of Anthropology and Sociology in their Relations to Criminal Procedure," The Macmillan Company, New York, 1908, pages 25–78.

A quotation from Lombroso's opening speech at the Sixth Congress of Criminal Anthropology at Turin in April, 1906, will give the key to the first stage in the development of his theory:

"In 1870 I was carrying on for several months researches in the prisons and asylums of Pavia upon cadavers and living persons, in order to determine upon substantial differences between the insane and criminals, without succeeding very well. At last I found in the skull of a brigand a very long series of atavistic anomalies, above all an enormous middle occipital fossa and a hypertrophy of the vermis analogous to those that are found in inferior vertebrates. At the sight of these strange anomalies the problem of the nature and of the origin of the criminal seemed to me resolved; the characteristics of primitive men and of inferior animals must be reproduced in our times. Many facts seemed to confirm this hypothesis, above all the psychology of the criminal; the frequency of tattooing and of professional slang; the passions as much more fleeting as they are more violent, above all that of vengeance; the lack of foresight which resembles courage and courage which alternates with cowardice, and idleness which alternates with the passion for play and activity." [1]

His first conception of the criminal, which was greatly modified later on, was, then, that the criminal is an atavistic phenomenon reproducing a type of the past. In order to find the origin of this atavistic phenomenon he goes back not only to savage man but also to animals and even to plants. Crime and criminals are, strictly speaking, human phenomena and are, therefore, not to be found outside of human society. But when a criminal displays a strong tendency towards crime which results from abnormal or pathological, physiological, and psychological characteristics it is necessary to search in the lower species for characteristics which correspond to those of the criminal. The acts which result from these characteristics Lombroso called the equivalents of crime. Among plants he finds such equivalents in the habits of the insectivorous plants. It is questionable, however, if the so-called "murders" of insects by these plants can be considered as equivalents of crime, since they are

[1] In the "Archives d'anthropologie criminelle," Lyons, June, 1906.

committed by one species against another and belong in the same category with man's habit of eating animals and plants. But among animals are to be found veritable equivalents of crime in acts contrary to the general habits and welfare of a species by one of its members. Cannibalism, infanticide, and parricide frequently occur, while murder, maltreatment, and theft are used to procure food, to secure command, and for many other reasons. In the past the idea that crimes are committed by animals was so strong that in ancient times and in the Middle Ages animals were frequently condemned according to juridical forms for acts harmful to man. Various causes for these equivalents of crime among animals have been noted, as, for example, congenital anomalies of the brain. Veterinary surgeons recognize these anomalies and give them as the causes for the misbehavior of horses. Other causes are antipathy causing murder, old age resulting in ill-temper, sudden anger, physical pain, etc.

Not only the equivalents of crime but those of punishment, also, have been noted among the lower species. Many cases are on record of a group of animals having torn to pieces one of its members who had committed an act contrary to the welfare of the group or had failed in performing its duties towards the group. In this blind act of vengeance we see the embryo of the form of social reaction called punishment.

There are, also, many habits of the lower species which, because they are natural and normal, cannot be called the equivalents of crime, but which when reproduced among civilized men become criminal. The same is true of many habits of savages. For example, homicide is frequently practised under social sanction, such as infanticide, murder of the aged, of women, and of the sick, religious sacrifices, etc., while cannibalism is prevalent in many tribes. Theft also exists under social sanction, though it is not so common, because the institution of private property is not highly developed among savages. The veritable crimes among savages are those against usage in which an established custom or religious rite is violated.

In like manner, as among the savages, characteristics are to be found in the child in a normal fashion which would be criminal in an adult, such as anger, vengeance, jealousy, lying, cruelty, lack of foresight, etc. For the first year or more of its life a child lacks a moral standard and its development is determined largely by its surroundings. There are, furthermore, many abnormal children in whom a tendency to crime manifests itself early.

It was the consideration of these facts with regard to the lower species, savages, and children which led Lombroso to formulate his first theory that crime is atavistic in its origin. This theory, as we shall see, he modified greatly later on. He discusses the atavistic origin of crime in the first part of his work, and then proceeds to the study of the constitution which the criminal inherits. This we will now briefly summarize.

The first series of the characteristics of the criminal is the anatomical. The study of 383 skulls of criminals gives him the results which he sums up in the following words:

"On considering the results that these 383 skulls give us it is found that the lesions most frequent are: great prominence of the superciliary arches, 58.2 per cent; anomaly in the development of the wisdom teeth, 44.6 per cent; diminution of the capacity of the skull, 32.5 per cent; synostosis of the sutures, 28.9 per cent; retreating forehead, 28 per cent; hyperostosis of the bones, 28.9 per cent; plagiocephaly, 23.1 per cent; wormian bones, 22 per cent; simplicity of the sutures, 18.4 per cent; prominence of the occipital protuberance, 16.6 per cent; the middle occipital fossa, 16 per cent; symbolic sutures, 13.6 per cent; flattening of the occipital, 13.2 per cent; osteophytes of the clivus, 10.1 per cent; the Inca's or epactal bone, 10.5 per cent."[1]

A union of many of these anomalies is to be found in the same skull in a proportion of 43 per cent, while 21 per cent have single anomalies. But these figures would have little value if not compared with corresponding figures for non-criminals. Such a comparison results in destroying the significance of some of these anomalies, since they prove to exist in about the same proportion among the latter.

"But there are others, on the contrary, which are present in a double or triple proportion in the criminals. Such are,

[1] "Homme Criminel," Paris, 1895, I, 155.

for example, sclerosis, the epactal bone, asymmetry, the retreating forehead, exaggeration of the frontal sinus and the superciliary arches, oxycephaly, the open internasal suture, anomalous teeth, asymmetries of the face, and above all the middle occipital fossa among males, the fusion of the atlas and the anomalies of the occipital opening." [1]

Comparison with the skulls of the insane shows that criminals surpass the insane in most of the cranial anomalies. Comparison with savage and pre-historic skulls shows the atavistic character of some of these anomalies.

"Atavism, however, does not permit us to explain either the frequent obliquity of the skull and of the face, or the fusion and welding of the atlas with the occipital, or the plagiocephaly, or the exaggerated sclerosis, anomalies which seem to be the result of an error in the development of the fœtal skull, or a product of diseases which have slowly evolved in the nervous centers." [2]

As to the significance of the cranial anomalies, he says:

"Is it possible that individuals afflicted with so great a number of alterations should have the same sentiments as men with a skull entirely normal? And note that these cranial alterations bear only upon the most visible modifications of the intellectual center, the alterations of volume and of form." [3]

A study of the convolutions of the brains of criminals reveals many anomalies, of which he says:

"It would be too rash to conclude that at last have been found with certainty anomalies peculiar to the cerebral circumvolutions of criminals; but it can very well be said already that in criminals these anomalies are abundant and are of two orders: some which are different from every normal type, even inferior, as the transverse grooves of the frontal lobe, found by Flesch in some cases, and so prominently that they do not allow the longitudinal grooves to be seen; others are deviations from the type, but recall the type of lower animals, as the separation of the calcarine fissure from the occipital, the fissure of Sylvius which remains open, the frequent formation of an operculum of the occipital lobe." [4]

[1] *Op. cit.*, I, 161.
[2] *Op. cit.*, I, 168.
[3] *Op. cit.*, I, 174.
[4] *Op. cit.*, I, 185.

The histology of the criminal brain also shows many anomalies due in most cases to arrested development. Anomalies of the skeleton, heart, genital organs, and stomach are also noted.

He then passes to the study of the anthropometry and physiognomy of 5907 criminals examined by himself and about a dozen other criminologists. In the anthropometric measurements it may be noted that the type usually reproduces the regional type, that the reach from finger tip to finger tip with the arms outstretched is usually superior to the height, frequent left-handedness, the prehensile foot in which the great toe is mobile and is removed an unusually long distance from the other toes, precocious wrinkles, absence of baldness, a low and narrow forehead, large jaws, etc. In the physiognomy he discusses peculiarities of the hair, iris, ears, nose, teeth, etc., noting differences between different kinds of criminals.

"In general, many criminals have outstanding ears, abundant hair, a sparse beard, enormous frontal sinuses and jaws, a square and projecting chin, broad cheekbones, frequent gestures, in fact a type resembling the Mongolian and sometimes the Negro."[1]

In summarizing the anatomical study of the criminal he says:

"The study of the living, in short, confirms, although less exactly and less constantly, this frequency of microcephalies, of asymmetries, of oblique orbits, of prognathisms, of frontal sinuses developed as the anatomical table has shown us. It shows new analogies between the insane, savages, and criminals. The prognathism, the hair abundant, black and frizzled, the sparse beard, the skin very often brown, the oxycephaly, the oblique eyes; the small skull, the developed jaw and zygomas, the retreating forehead, the voluminous ears, the analogy between the two sexes, a greater reach, are new characteristics added to the characteristics observed in the dead which bring the European criminals nearer to the Australian and Mongolian type; while the strabism, the cranial asymmetries and the serious histological anomalies, the osteomates, the meningitic lesions, hepatic and cardiac, also show us in the criminal a man abnormal before his birth, by arrest of development or by disease acquired from different organs,

[1] *Op. cit.*, I, 222.

above all, from the nervous centers, as in the insane; and make him a person who is in truth chronically ill."[1]

The study of the anatomical characteristics of the criminal enabled him to separate the born criminal from the criminal of habit, of passion, or of occasion who is born with very few or no abnormal characteristics. Leaving aside for the moment the latter classes of criminals he takes up the biological and psychological characteristics of the born criminals, the first being the psychological characteristic of tattooing.

"One of the most characteristic traits of primitive man or of the savage is the facility with which he submits himself to this operation, surgical rather than æsthetic, and of which the name even has been furnished to us by an Oceanic idiom."[2]

By means of the statistics of 13,566 individuals of which 4,376 were honest, 6,347 criminal and 2,943 insane, he shows that tattooing is quite common in some of the inferior classes of society, but is most common among criminals.

"It may be said that, for these last, it constitutes on account of its frequency a specific and entirely new anatomico-legal characteristic."[3]

He cites many causes for tattooing, such as religion, imitation, carnal love, vengeance, idleness, vanity, and above all atavism.

"But the first, the principal cause which has spread this custom among us, is, in my opinion, atavism, or this other kind of historic atavism called tradition. Tattooing is in fact one of the essential characteristics of primitive man and of the man who is still living in a savage state."[4]

After noting peculiarities of the molecular exchange as indicated in the temperature, pulse, and urine he discusses the general sensibilities of the criminal.

"The special taste of criminals for a painful operation so long and so full of danger as tattooing, the large number of wounds their bodies present, have led me to suspect in them

[1] *Op. cit.*, I, 262.
[2] *Op. cit.*, I, 266.
[3] *Op. cit.*, I, 266.
[4] *Op. cit.*, I, 295.

a physical insensibility greater than amongst most men, an insensibility like that which is encountered in some insane persons and especially in violent lunatics."[1]

Numerous experiments have revealed obtuseness in the sensibility of many parts of the body. Peculiarities have been noted in the visual acuteness and visual field, in the smelling, the taste, and the hearing, in the motility, in the reaction to various external influences, and in the vaso-motor reflexes.

"From all of these facts it could be deduced that nearly all the different kinds of sensibility, tactile, olfactory, and of the taste, are obtuse in the criminal; even in the occasional criminal as compared with the normal man; while in the criminal as in the insane and hysterical the sensibility to metals, to the magnet, and to the atmosphere is exaggerated. Their physical insensibility recalls quite forcibly that of savage peoples, who can face, in the initiations to puberty, tortures which a man of the white race could never endure."[2]

From this study showing the marked analgesia of the criminal he passes to his affective sensibility.

"In general, in criminal man, the moral insensibility is as great as the physical insensibility; undoubtedly the one is the effect of the other. It is not that in him the voice of sentiment is entirely silent, as some literary men of inferior ability suppose; but it is certain that the passions which make the heart of the normal man beat with the greatest force are very feeble in him. The first sentiment which is extinguished in these beings is that of pity for the suffering of another, and this happens just because they themselves are insensible to suffering."[3]

He then discusses various psychological characteristics of the criminal showing his instability, vanity, lasciviousness, laziness, lack of foresight, etc. He shows that his intelligence varies greatly among the different classes of criminals. He discusses at some length the *argot* or professional slang of criminals.

"Atavism contributes more to this than any other thing. They talk differently from us because they do not feel in the same way; they talk like savages because they are veritable savages in the midst of this brilliant European civilization."[4]

[1] *Op. cit.*, I, 310.
[2] *Op. cit.*, I, 346.
[3] *Op. cit.*, I, 356.
[4] *Op. cit.*, I, 497.

In a similar manner he studies the hieroglyphics, writing, and literature of criminals.

In the first volume of this work Lombroso describes the characteristics of the born criminal who, as we shall see, he believes represents a distinct anthropological type. In the second volume he takes up first certain analogies which he believes exist between the born criminal and certain other abnormal types, and then deals with the other classes of criminals. And first he deals with the analogy and indeed the identity which he believes exists between congenital criminality and moral insanity. "The characteristics of the born criminal that we have studied in the first volume are the same as those of the moral imbecile."[1] Under the name of moral imbecile psychiatrists have classified the insane, whose most prominent pathological characteristic is a complete or almost complete absence of moral feeling and of moral ideas. The famous English alienist, Henry Maudsley, has described this class in the following words:

"Notwithstanding prejudices to the contrary, there is a disorder of the mind, in which, without illusion, delusion, or hallucination, the symptoms are mainly exhibited in a perversion of those mental faculties which are usually called the active and moral powers—the feeling, affection, propensities, temper, habits, and conduct. The affective life of the individual is profoundly deranged, and his derangement shows itself in what he feels, desires, and does. He has no capacity of true moral feeling; all his impulses and desires, to which he yields without check, are egoistic; his conduct appears to be governed by immoral motives, which are cherished and obeyed without any evident desire to resist them. There is an amazing moral insensibility. The intelligence is often acute enough, being not affected otherwise than in being tainted by the morbid feeling under the influence of which the persons think and act; indeed they often display an extraordinary ingenuity in explaining, excusing, or justifying their behaviour, exaggerating this, ignoring that, and so coloring the whole as to make themselves appear the victims of misrepresentation and persecution."[2]

[1] *Op. cit.*, II, 1.
[2] "Responsibility in Mental Disease," London, 1874, 171–172.

Such a person may very easily become a criminal.

"A person who has no moral sense is naturally well fitted to become a criminal, and if his intellect is not strong enough to convince him that crime will not in the end succeed, and that it is, therefore, on the lowest grounds a folly, he is very likely to become one."[1]

Moral insanity may be caused by various abnormal or pathological mental characteristics, congenital or acquired in the individual. Whenever one of these characteristics destroys the capacity for moral feeling and for comprehending moral ideas the individual becomes a moral imbecile. Moral insanity, therefore, is not a morbid entity in the sense that it arises out of one pathological mental characteristic or state of mind. It is, on the contrary, as Baer has said, a symptom common to various cerebral diseases. Lombroso, however, apparently regarded it as such an entity, for he frequently spoke of it as if it were a distinct disease, and, furthermore, he identified it with the born criminal whom he considered a distinct type. He cites a good deal of evidence in support of this identification.

"One of the things which prove indirectly the identity of moral insanity and of crime, and which at the same time explains to us the doubts with which the alienists have been possessed up to this day, is the extreme rarity of the first in the insane asylums, and its great frequency, on the contrary, in the prisons."[2]

After supporting this statement with statistics he demonstrates many likenesses between the moral imbecile and the born criminal, with regard to the weight, the skull, the physiognomy, the analgesia, tactile sensibility, tattooing, vascular reaction, affectibility, etc. By contending that there is an identity between the moral imbecile and the born criminal, he does not, however, mean that every moral imbecile is a criminal. For that matter not every person born with a criminal temperament becomes a criminal, for external circumstances may resist and overcome the innate criminal tendencies. But he believes

[1] Maudsley, *Op. cit.*, 58.

[2] *Op. cit.*, II, 3-4.

that in physical constitution and mental characteristics the two are fundamentally alike.

This identity of the moral imbecile with the born criminal is, he believes, still more conclusively proved by a similar likeness which he finds between the criminal and the epileptic.

> "The objection has justly been made against this fusion that the cases of true moral insanity that I have been able to study are too restrictive in number. That is true; but it is after all very natural; for, precisely because moral imbeciles are born criminals, they are not found as frequently in the asylum as in the prison; and it is also for that reason that it is not easy to establish a comparison. But there exists in epilepsy a uniting bond much more important, much more comprehensible, which can be studied upon a great scale, that unites and bases the moral imbecile and the born criminal in the same natural family."[1]

As in the case of the analogy between the moral imbecile and the born criminal he demonstrates many likenesses between the epileptic and the born criminal, in height, weight, the brain, the skull, the physiognomy, the flat and prehensile foot, the sensibility, the visual field, motility, tattooing, etc.

> "Criminality is therefore an atavistic phenonenon which is provoked by morbid causes of which the fundamental manifestation is epilepsy. It is very true that criminality can be provoked by other diseases (hysteria, alchoholism, paralysis, insanity, phrenastenia, etc.), but it is epilepsy which gives to it, by its frequency, by its gravity, the most extended basis."[2]

But while all born criminals are epileptics, according to Lombroso, not all epileptics are born criminals. In all three, congenital criminality, moral insanity, and epilepsy, we find the irresistible force which results in crime or similar irresponsible acts.

> "The perversion of the affective sphere, the hate, exaggerated and without motive, the absence or insufficiency of all restraint, the multiple hereditary tendencies, are the source of irresistible impulses in the moral imbecile as well as in the born criminal and the epileptic."[3]

[1] *Op. cit.*, II, 49–50. [2] *Op. cit.*, II, 120. [3] *Op. cit.*, II, 125.

These two analogies between the born criminal and the moral imbecile and the epileptic mark the second stage in the development of his theory.

"The studies which form the first part of this volume accord admirably with those which have been developed in the second and third parts of the first volume to make us see in the criminal a savage and at the same time a sick man."[1]

In other words, he no longer sees in the born criminal only an atavistic return to the savage, but also arrested development and disease, thus making the born criminal both an atavistic and a degenerate phenomenon.

He now passes to the treatment of the classes of criminals other than the born criminal. The first of these is the criminal by passion.

"Among the criminals there is a category which is distinguished absolutely from all others; it is this of the criminals by passion, who ought rather to be called criminals by violence, because as we have seen, and as we shall see better still in their ætiology, all these crimes have for substratum the violence of some passion."[2]

These criminals are quite rare, are usually young, have few anomalies of the skull, a good physiognomy, honesty of character, exaggerated affectibility as opposed to the apathy of the born criminal, and frequent repentance after the crime, sometimes followed by suicide or reformation in prison. A larger percentage of them are women than among other criminals.

"The passions which excite these criminals are not those which rise gradually in the organism, as avarice and ambition, but those which burst forth unexpectedly, as anger, platonic or filial love, offended honor; which are usually generous passions and often sublime. On the other hand, those which predominate in ordinary criminals are the most ignoble and the most ferocious, as vengeance, cupidity, carnal love, and drunkenness."[3]

But in them as in ordinary criminals are found sometimes traces of epilepsy and impulsive insanity, shown by the impetu-

[1] *Op. cit.*, II, 135. [2] *Op. cit.*, II, 153. [3] *Op. cit.*, II, 165–166.

osity, suddenness, and ferocity of their crimes. The frequency of suicide among criminals by passion also indicates a pathological state of mind.

A special kind of criminal by passion is the political criminal.

"In nearly all political criminals by passion we have noticed an exaggerated sensibility, a veritable hyperesthesia, as in the ordinary criminals by passion; but a powerful intellect, a great altruism pushed them towards ends much higher than those of the latter: it is never wealth, vanity, the smile of woman (even though often eroticism is not lacking in them, as in Garibaldi, Mazzini, Cavour) which impel them, but rather the great patriotic, religious, scientific ideals."[1]

Statistics show a much higher proportion than the average of insane persons among criminals, and therefore Lombroso deals next with insane criminals as a special class of criminals.

"A study made upon one hundred insane criminals, chosen by preference from those who had become insane before the crime, with the exception of the epileptics, has shown to me the frequency of the criminal type (that is to say, the presence of five to six characteristics of degeneracy, and especially outstanding ears (*oreilles à anse*), frontal sinuses, a voluminous jaw and zygoma, a ferocious look or strabism, a thin upper lip) in the proportion of 44 per cent."[2]

This fact, however, does not lead him to identify the insane criminal with the born criminal, but he finds numerous analogies between the two in the weight, height, skull, tattooing, etc., and also many psychological analogies in the manner of committing a crime. He connects certain kinds of crime with certain kinds of insanity.

"I have just mentioned the existence of certain kinds of insanity which reproduce each of the sub-species of criminality, so that to the juridical figure of incendiarism, of homicide, can be opposed the psychiatric figure of pyromania, homicidal monomania, paradoxical sexuality, etc."[3]

Thus he opposes to the juridical figure of theft the psychiatric figure of kleptomania; to habitual drunkenness, dipsomania:

[1] *Op. cit.*, II, 217. [2] *Op. cit.*, II, 254 [3] *Op. cit.*, II, 290.

to rape and pederasty, sexual inversion; to crimes of lust, satyriasis and nymphomania; to idleness and vagabondage, neurasthenia. He then discusses the psychological differences between the born criminal and the insane criminal with respect to the different kinds of mental maladies, and to the differences in motives for crimes and in the manner of committing them. He finishes the study of the insane criminal with the study of three special kinds, — the alcoholic criminal, the hysterical criminal, and the criminal mattoid.

The last part of his work is devoted to the occasional criminal. Of this study he says:

> "If I have been forced to delay for several years the publication of this book, it has been on account of this part in particular; for, although in possession of numerous documents, direct contact with the facts failed me in the measure that I was trying to approach myself to them. The abundance of the facts also, their excessive variety, constituted for me a cause of uncertainty which prevented me from reaching a conclusion."[1]

The first group with which he deals is that of the pseudo-criminals. These criminals are those who commit crimes involuntarily, who commit acts which are not perverse or prejudicial to society but which are called crimes by the law, who commit crimes under very extraordinary circumstances, such as in defense of the person, of honor, or for the sustenance of the family. These crimes are "rather juridical than real, because they are created by imperfections of the law rather than by those of men; they do not awaken any fear for the future, and they do not disturb the moral sense of the masses."[2]

The next group is that of the criminaloids. "Here the accident, the all-powerful occasion, draws only those who are already somewhat predisposed to evil."[3] The occasions out of which these crimes arise are the temptation to imitate, the constant opportunities offered by the commercial profession for fraud, abuse of confidence, etc., the associations of the prison, a passion less intense than in the criminal by passion which draws an honest man slowly to crime, the criminal couple, the stronger

[1] *Op. cit.*, II, 463. [2] *Op. cit.*, II, 484. [3] *Op. cit.*, II, 485.

member of which having evil tendencies perverts the weaker, epidemic allurement, etc.

"These are individuals who constitute the gradations between the born criminal and the honest man, or, better still, a variety of born criminal who has indeed a special organic tendency but one which is less intense, who has therefore only a touch of degeneracy; that is why I will call them *criminaloids*. But it is natural that in them the importance of the occasion determining the crime should be decisive, while it is not so for the born criminal, for whom it is a circumstance with which he can dispense and with which he often does dispense, as, for example, in cases of *brutal mischievousness*."[1]

This position of the criminaloid between the born criminal and the honest man is in harmony with all natural phenomena, "where the most striking phenomena are in continuity with a series of analogous phenomena less accentuated";[2] just as in the moral sphere we have genius, talent, intelligence, etc., and in the pathology of degeneracy the cretin, the cretinous, the sub-cretin, the idiot, the mattoid, the imbecile, etc.

The third group of occasional criminals is that of the habitual criminal.

"The greatest number of these individuals is furnished by those who — normal from birth and without tendencies for a peculiar constitution for crime — not having found in the early education of parents, schools, etc., this force which provokes, or, better said, facilitates the passage from this physiological criminality — which we have seen belongs properly to an early age — to a normal, honest life, fall continually lower into the primitive tendency towards evil."[3]

So that these individuals without an abnormal heredity are led not by one circumstance offering the occasion for crime, but by a group of circumstances conditioning their early life into a career of crime.

Associations of criminals, such as those of brigands, *mafia*, and *camorra* in Italy, and the "black hand" in Spain, etc., contain many members drawn into crime by their associates. In the classes in which on account of wealth, power, etc., the condi-

[1] *Op. cit.*, II, 512. [2] *Op. cit.*, II, 513. [3] *Op. cit.*, II, 534.

tions are against the commission of crime, the criminal tendencies of those born with such tendencies remain latent or manifest themselves in other ways. Finally, there is a class of epileptoids in whom there is a substratum of epilepsy which sometimes forms the basis for the development of criminal tendencies.

In the first edition of his work Lombroso gave excessive weight to his anatomical and anthropometric data which was not very surprising, since they were the most obvious and the most easily obtainable. This excessive emphasis laid upon the anatomical characteristics of the criminal led him to distinguish but one type, — the criminal as an atavistic phenomenon. This immediately called forth the charge of unilaterality. The idea still exists that Lombroso recognized but one type of criminal who is the result of a single cause, namely, atavism. But the brief summary of his work which I have so far given is sufficient to disprove this. We have seen that in addition to studying the anatomical characterictics of the criminal he makes a lengthy study of his biological and psychological characteristics as well. In the later editions of his work he rejected in part the atavistic theory of crime, no longer considering atavism as the only cause of crime, and adopted the theory of degeneracy as one of its causes.

"In this edition I have demonstrated that in addition to the characteristics truly atavistic there are acquired and entirely pathological characteristics; facial asymmetry, for example, which does not exist in the savage, strabism, inequality of the ears, dischromatopsy, unilateral paresia, irresistible impulses, the need of doing evil for the sake of evil, etc., and this sinister gayety which is noticeable in the professional slang of criminals and which, alternating with a certain religiousness, is found so often in epileptics. There may be added meningitis and softening of the brain, which certainly do not result from atavism."[1]

In his studies of moral imbecility and epilepsy he has demonstrated the analogies between these two and congenital criminality. Though his identification of the moral imbecile with the born criminal and of the born criminal with the epileptic may be disproved, his demonstration of the pathological like-

[1] *Op. cit.*, I, xi–xii.

nesses of the three to each other is incontestible. In his study of the insane criminal he has exposed the characteristics of another very abnormal criminal type. He has demonstrated the abnormality of certain of the criminals by passion. In the criminaloid he has shown a criminal partially abnormal, who, however, will not commit a crime until a good opportunity presents itself. The habitual criminal, though born without criminal tendencies, has them developed in him by the circumstances of his early life. Finally, in some of the criminals by passion and in the pseudo-criminal we find entirely normal persons who have committed crimes under very exceptional circumstances. Thus we see how very synthetic is his study of the characteristics of the criminal, since it ranges from the most abnormal to the perfectly normal, and there borders upon the study of the social causes of crime, which he takes up at great length in the work of which the present volume is a translation.

The theory which is most closely connected with the name of Lombroso is that of the criminal anthropological type, that is to say, his theory that there is an anthropological type which corresponds to habitual criminal conduct. This has been the most contested idea in criminal anthropology and the one that has received the largest amount of discussion in books, congresses, etc. Though this idea of a criminal type had been suggested several times in the past, it was fully developed for the first time by Lombroso. We have already summarized his conception of the born criminal who constitutes for him a distinct criminal type. A quotation from his speech at the Congress of Criminal Anthropology at Turin in 1906 has shown that his early studies led him to regard the criminal as an atavistic type, as reproducing the characteristics of lower races and species. This theory, offered in his early works as an explanation of congenital criminal tendencies, was severely attacked on account of its unilaterality. These criticisms and his further researches led him, as we have seen, to modify his theory and to recognize degeneracy as the cause of congenital criminality. He even came to regard atavism as a form of degeneracy, as where he speaks of the criminal type as "the presence of five

[1] *Op. cit.*, II, 254.

or six characteristics of degeneracy and especially: outstanding ears (*oreilles à anse*), frontal sinuses, jaw and zygomas voluminous, a ferocious look or strabism, thin upper lip."[1] This recognition of degeneracy as a cause of crime has made Lombroso's doctrine more catholic, so that it is much easier to connect the criminal with the social and physical conditions out of which he has evolved, but it is questionable, as we shall see, whether degeneracy can be regarded as a form of atavism.

In order to make more distinct his conception of the criminal type he discusses the character of a type in general, as follows:

> "In my opinion, one should receive the *type* with the same reserve that one uses in estimating the value of *averages* in statistics. When one says that the average life is thirty-two years and that the most fatal month is December, no one understands by that that everybody must die at thirty-two years and in the month of December."[1]

The type is, therefore, an abstract conception including the characteristics which are most common in a certain group of individuals. But this does not mean that every individual in the group must have all these characteristics. As Isidore G. Saint-Hilaire has said:

> "The type is a sort of fixed point and common centre about which the differences presented are like so many deviations in different directions and oscillations varied almost indefinitely, about which nature seems to play, as the anatomists used to say."[2]

Applying this general conception of a type, it is evident that every criminal representing this type need not have all its characteristics. In fact, it is doubtful if any one criminal ever did have all these characteristics.

Furthermore, he discusses what percentage of criminals represent the criminal type. This number he places at about 40 per cent. The objection has been made that it is impossible to talk about a criminal type when 60 per cent of the criminals do not represent it, to which he replies as follows:

[1] *Op. cit.*, I, ix. [2] Quoted in Lombroso, *op. cit.*, I, 237.

"But, in addition to the fact that the figure of 40 per cent is not to be disdained, the . . . insensible passage from one character to another manifests itself in all organic beings; it manifests itself even from one species to another; with more reason is it so in the anthropological field, where the individual variability, increasing in direct proportion to improvement and to civilization, seems to efface the complete type." [1]

We can give no more space to this summary of Lombroso's theory, but must now make certain comments and criticisms. Strange to say, Lombroso seems to have been somewhat ignorant of biology, and especially of the theory of heredity. This is indicated, for example, by the loose way in which he uses the term "atavism." It is true that biologists recognize that atavism, or reversion, as they usually call it, takes place when there reappear in an individual of the present day characteristics of earlier types, if this reappearance is the result of hereditary forces. That is to say, if earlier characteristics which have long remained dormant reassert themselves in the germ plasm at the time of conception there is a true case of reversion. But it is very evident that many of the criminal characteristics which Lombroso calls atavistic are not hereditary in their origin, but are cases of arrested development either before or after birth. This is the case when he speaks of degeneracy as a form of atavism, for it is very evident that most if not all the characteristics he has in mind are not congenital. The fact that the individual has them at birth does not indicate necessarily that they are congenital, for they may be the result of arrested development during the ante-natal period of the life of the individual. In other cases he calls characteristics atavistic which are simply habits which have been transmitted by social means. For example, he seems to regard the habit of tattooing as an atavistic trait, but tattooing is no more than a habit, which could not possibly be transmitted by hereditary means. This indicates that Lombroso may have believed in the hereditary transmission of acquired characteristics, though he nowhere explicitly states his opinion as to this point. But he again and again speaks as if habits or the effects of habits are transmitted by

[1] *Op. cit.*, I, ix.

hereditary means. The consensus of opinion of biologists to-day is that no acquired characteristics can be transmitted by hereditary means, therefore Lombroso was very much in error in this respect.

Lombroso believed that there is a criminal anthropological type, or rather that there are several such types which correspond to habitual modes of criminal conduct. Here again he seems to be holding the belief that acquired characteristics are inheritable, for otherwise it is inconceivable that any anthropological type necessarily possesses certain habits. Such a type may possess congenital tendencies which make it more likely to acquire certain habits, but this is not necessarily the case. It is true that Lombroso recognized that environmental forces might prevent the individual from expressing these inborn tendencies to certain kinds of action in acts. But he laid too much emphasis upon the extent to which the habits of a person are determined by hereditary forces.

But whatever may have been his faults, Lombroso was the great pioneer whose original and versatile genius and aggressive personality led in the great movement towards the application of the positive, inductive methods of modern science to the problem of crime, and who stimulated, more than any other man, the development of the new science of criminology. The breadth of his treatment of the subject of crime is nowhere illustrated better than in the present volume, in which a large number of the complex causes of crime are discussed. It is therefore to be hoped that through this volume the English-speaking world will acquire an adequate idea of his genius and of the great services he rendered to the study and treatment of crime.

MAURICE PARMELEE.

THE AUTHOR'S PREFACE

To Max Nordau.

TO you, as the ablest and best beloved of my brothers in arms, I dedicate this book. In it I attempt by means of facts to answer those who, not having read my "Criminal Man" (of which it is the necessary complement), nor the works of Pelmann, Kurella, Van Hamel, Salillas, Ellis, Bleuler, and others, accuse my school of having neglected the economic and social causes of crime, and of having confined itself to the study of the born criminal, thus teaching that the criminal is riveted irrevocably to his destiny, and that humanity has no escape from his atavistic ferocity.

Now, if this charge were true, the unfortunate nature of the facts revealed could not be urged against the school which discovered them. But the truth is that, while the old jurists had nothing to propose for the prevention of crime more efficacious than the cruel and sterile empiricism of the prison and deportation system, and while the most practical peoples have arrived at good results only sporadically and as the chance outcome of unsystematic gropings, my school has devised a new strategic method of proceeding against crime, based upon a study of its ætiology and nature.

In the first place, the distinction which we have made between the criminaloid, the occasional criminal, the criminal by passion, and the born criminal, as well as the study of the more important causes of crime, enables us to determine with precision the individuals to whom we can apply our curative processes, and the method appropriate to each case.

With the born criminal, to be sure, only a palliative treatment is possible. This is what I have called "symbiosis," the attempt to utilize the criminal's evil propensities by diverting the course of the criminal instinct. The measures for the attainment of this object, however, can only be individual.

But with criminaloids,[1] whose evil propensities are not so deep seated, we may often hope for better results. Here again it is necessary to commence the treatment in early youth by what I should call moral nurture, which would withdraw the young criminals from the influence of depraved parents and from that of the streets, and place them on farms and in the colonies.

In this matter legislation and social influences are of great importance. Thus emigration from overpopulated countries toward those less thickly settled wards off one of the worst influences, that of a dense population; divorce prevents adulteries, poisonings, etc.; while the war made upon drunkenness by religious associations and temperance societies, and through the enforcement of penalties, prevents much brawling and violence. All this has been established by statistics.

These directly preventive measures, it is true, do not always suffice. Since it is a need of cerebral stimulation that leads men to drink, and since this need grows with the progress of civilization, it is necessary to get at the root of the evil, and satisfy this need by means less dangerous than drink, such as shows, coffee-rooms, etc.

But here another difficulty arises; namely, that nearly all the physical and moral causes of crime present a double aspect, often contradictory. Thus there are crimes which are favored by density of population, like rebellion; and others, like brigandage and homicide, which are occasioned by sparseness of population. So also while there are crimes caused by poverty, there are almost as many which are encouraged by extreme wealth. The same contradiction is observed when we pass from one country to another. Thus, while homicide decreases in Italy with the increase of population and wealth, in France this crime increases with the increase of these two factors, — a fact which is to be explained by the great influence of alcoholism and of foreign immigration.[2]

Religion, which among Protestants appears to prevent many crimes, in many Catholic countries multiplies them, or at least

[1] See my "Homme Criminel," II, 485–539.
[2] See sections 31, 54, and 60 of the present work.

fails to prevent their increase. And if education appears to be useful in preventing homicide, theft, assault, etc., it very often, when too advanced, seems to encourage fraud, false testimony, and political crime.[1]

The difficulty is increased still more by the fact that, even if we find effective methods of combating the influence of environment, it is not easy to apply them. It is possible, for example, to counteract the effect of heat upon the frequency of crimes of violence and immorality, by means of cold baths; but it is not easy to bring a whole section of the people to the bath-houses or to the sea, as was done in ancient Rome, and as the practice still is in Calabria.

The statesman, then, who wishes to prevent crime ought to be eclectic and not limit himself to a single course of action. He must guard against the dangerous effects of wealth no less than against those of poverty, against the corrupting influence of education not less than against that of ignorance. In this labyrinth of contradictions the only safe guide is the study of the criminal combined with the study of the ætiology of crime.

From all this we can understand the uncertainty and embarrassment to which these contradictions expose our public officials, and can see why men whose trade is law-making find that their most obvious recourse is the modification of a few pages of the penal code. This is why the prison, the worst of all remedies (if we can call it a remedy at all, and not a poison), will always be applied as the simplest and most practical means of safety. It has antiquity and custom on its side, and these are points of great importance for the ordinary man, who finds it easier always to apply the same remedy than to find a number of different remedies suited to differences of age, sex, and education.

I have traced above only the outlines of the system of criminal therapeutics which I intend to set forth in this book. But, to tell the truth, it is not a system that is entirely new.

It has been stated that certain practical nations, less smoth-

[1] See sections 51, 52, and 160 of the present work.

ered than our own under a too glorious past, and for that reason less infatuated with the ancient codes, have already here and there arrived empirically, without knowing a word of criminal anthropology, at several of the reforms that I shall suggest. The asylum for the criminal insane, the truant schools, the "ragged schools," the societies for the protection of children, and the asylums for alcoholics, are institutions which, without being a part of the criminal code, have been applied more or less completely in North America, England, and Switzerland. For these are happy countries, where religion is less a mass of dogmas and rites than an ardent war against crime, so that in these lands, and especially in London itself, where wealth, density, and immigration would naturally favor crime, the conquering march of criminality has been checked.

These attempts, however, being partial, scattered, and without coördination, lack the effectiveness in the eyes of the world which proceeds from a complete demonstration, at once theoretical and practical. Yet they have a great value, because partial applications always precede and prepare for a scientific codification; and also because, for timid spirits, they give to our reforms the most convincing sanction, — that of experience.

What now lies before us is to complete and systematize these reforms in a final way, in accordance with the data of biology and sociology. It is this that I attempt to do in this book.

C. Lombroso.

Turin, 1906.

TRANSLATOR'S NOTE

WHILE the present work is based upon Professor Lombroso's French version, the German translation of Dr. Kurella and Dr. Jentsch has been found a valuable commentary upon certain passages, and has been followed in the omission of some few notes and other details interesting to Italians only. The French work was published in Paris in 1899, and appears to have been embodied by the author in his "L'Uomo Delinquente" as the third volume in its latest Italian edition. The German translation was published in 1902.

HENRY P. HORTON.

COLUMBIA, MISSOURI,
November, 1910.

CONTENTS

Part One

ÆTIOLOGY OF CRIME

Part Two

PROPHYLAXIS AND THERAPEUSIS OF CRIME

Part Three

SYNTHESIS AND APPLICATION

CRIME:

ITS CAUSES AND REMEDIES

Part One

ÆTIOLOGY OF CRIME

CHAPTER I

METEOROLOGICAL AND CLIMATIC INFLUENCES — MONTHS — HIGH TEMPERATURES

§ 1. Meteorological and Climatic Influences

EVERY crime has its origin in a multiplicity of causes, often intertwined and confused, each of which we must, in obedience to the necessities of thought and speech, investigate singly. This multiplicity is generally the rule with human phenomena, to which one can almost never assign a single cause unrelated to others. Every one knows that cholera, typhus, and tuberculosis have specific causes, but no one would venture to maintain that meteorological, hygienic, and psychic factors have nothing to do with them. Indeed, the best observers often remain undecided as to the true specific cause of any given phenomenon.

§ 2. Extremes of Temperature

Among the determining causes of all biological activity are reckoned meteorological phenomena, and among these is heat. Thus the leaves of *Drosera rotundifolia*, after having been immersed in water at 110° F., become inflected and more sensitive to the action of nitrogenous substances;[1] but at 130° F.

[1] Darwin, "Insectivorous Plants."

they no longer show any inflection, and the tentacles are temporarily paralyzed, not regaining their mobility until immersed in cold water.

Physiology and statistics show that most human functions are subject to the influence of heat.[1] It is to be expected, then, that excessive heat will have its effect upon the human mind.

History records no example of a tropical people that has not fallen into subjection. Great heat leads to overproduction, which in turn becomes the cause, first, of an unequal distribution of wealth, and then, as a consequence, of great inequality in the distribution of political and social power. In the countries subject to great heat the mass of the people count for nothing; they have neither voice nor influence in the government; and though revolutions may often occur, these are but palace-revolutions, never uprisings of the people, who attach no importance to them.[2] Buckle, among other reasons, finds an explanation in the fact that the dwellers in hot countries need less food, clothing, and fuel, and hence do not possess the powers of resistance which dwellers in colder countries acquire in their contest with nature. On this account tropical peoples are more inclined to inertia, to the use of narcotics, to the passive meditation of the Yogi, and to the extravagant asceticism and self-torture of the fakir. The inertia brought on by the heat and the constant feeling of weakness that follows it, renders the constitution more liable to convulsions, and favors a tendency to vague dreaming, to exaggerated imagination, and, in consequence, to fanaticism at once religious and despotic. From this condition of things flows naturally excessive licentiousness, alternating with excessive asceticism, as the most brutal absolutism alternates with the most unrestrained anarchy.

In cold countries the power of resisting hardship is greater, owing to the expenditure of energy necessary in procuring food, clothing, and fuel; but just for that reason a visionary and unstable character is less frequent, the excessive cold making the imagination inactive, the mind less irritable and less inconstant.

[1] Lombroso, "Pensiero e Meteore," Milan, 1878.
[2] Buckle, "Hist. of Civilization," I, 195–196.

The contest with the cold consumes energy that would otherwise have been available for the social and personal activity of the individual. From this fact, and from the depressing effect which the cold exercises directly upon the nervous system, proceed the placidity and mildness of the inhabitants of the polar regions. Dr. Rink depicts certain Eskimo tribes as so pacific and placid that they have not even a word for "quarrel," their strongest reaction to an affront being merely silence. Larrey notices that on the retreat from Moscow the snows of Russia made weaklings and even cowards of soldiers whom, up to that time, neither danger, wounds, nor hunger had been able to shake. Bove relates that among the Chukchi at 40° below zero there are no quarrels, acts of violence, or crimes. Preyer, the bold polar traveler, notes how at the same temperature his will became paralyzed, his senses dulled, and his speech embarrassed.[1]

This explains why, not only despotic Russia, but also the liberal Scandinavian countries, have rarely experienced revolutions.

§ 3. Influence of Moderate Temperatures

The influence which is most apt to produce a disposition toward rebellion and crime is that of a relatively moderate degree of heat. This is confirmed by a study of the psychology of the peoples of southern Europe, which shows us that they tend to be unstable, and to subordinate the interests of the community and state to the individual. This is doubtless because heat excites the nervous centers as alcohol does, without, however, arriving at the point of producing apathy; and further because the climate, without removing human needs entirely, reduces them by increasing the productivity of the soil and at the same time diminishing the necessity for food, clothing, and alcoholic drinks. In the dialect of Parma the sun is called the "Father of Ragamuffins."

Daudet, who has written an entire novel ("Nouma Roumestan") to depict the great influence of the climate of southern Europe upon conduct, says:

[1] Petermann, "Mitteilungen," 1876.

"The Southerner does not love strong drinks; he is intoxicated by nature. Sun and wind distil in him a terrible natural alcohol to whose influence every one born under this sky is subject. Some have only the mild fever which sets their speech and gesture free, redoubles their audacity, makes everything seem rosy-hued, and drives them on to boasting; others live in a blind delirium. And what Southerner has not felt the sudden giving way, the exhaustion of his whole being, that follows an outburst of rage or enthusiasm?"

Neri Taufucio ("Napoli a Colpo d'Occchio") remarks that inconstancy is a characteristic of the southern peoples.

"One at first considers them naïve, until suddenly one perceives that they are finished rascals. They are at the same time industrious and lazy, sober and intemperate; in short, their character, at least among the lower classes, has such different aspects and changes so rapidly, that it is impossible to fix it. The climate favors the loss of modesty. The people are prolific; the thought of the future of their children does not terrify them. The lazzarone steals when he has a chance, but never when there is any risk to be incurred. A boaster, he promises ten things, and performs one. If he falls into a quarrel, he shouts and gesticulates to arouse fear, although he is afraid himself; he tries to avoid actual fighting, but becomes wild if it comes to actual blows. Jealous, he slashes his wife's face if he doubts her. Independent, he can endure neither hospitals nor asylums. When he has work, he does it well. He feels a strong affection for his family, contents himself with little, and does not become intoxicated. Crafty, mendacious, and timid, his existence is a series of petty frauds, deceits, and acts of beggary. To get a few cents in alms he is capable of kissing your shoes without feeling himself humiliated thereby. His science is superstition. Meeting a hunchback or a blind man conveys a quite definite augury. His ideas move in the small circle of God, devil, witches, evil eye, Holy Trinity, honor, knife, theft, ornaments, and — Camorra. The masses fear this last, but respect it. For they feel that this despotic power protects them against the other despots. It is the only authority from which they can hope for anything that resembles justice."

§ 4. Crimes and Seasons

The influence of heat upon certain crimes is then quite comprehensible.

It is brought out in Guerry's statistics that the crime of rape occurs in England and France oftenest in the hot months; and Curcio has observed the same thing in Italy.

	Rapes committed in		
	England (1834–56)	France (1829–60)	Italy (1869)
	Per cent	Per cent	Total number
January	5.25	5.29	26
February	7.39	5.67	22
March	7.75	6.39	16
April	9.21	8.98	28
May	9.24	10.91	29
June	10.72	12.88	29
July	10.46	12.95	37
August	10.52	11.52	35
September	10.29	8.77	29
October	8.18	6.71	14
November	5.91	5.16	12
December	3.08	4.97	15

In England, according to Guerry, and in Italy, according to Curcio, the maximum number of murders falls in the hottest months. There occurred:

	England (1834–56)	Italy (1869)
July	1043	307
June	1071	301
August	928	343
May	842	288
February	701	254
March	681	273
December	651	236
January	605	237

Poisoning also, according to Guerry, occurs oftenest in May. The same phenomenon is to be observed in the case of rebellions. In studying (as I have in my "Political Crime") the 836 uprisings that took place in the whole world in the period between 1791 and 1880, one finds that in Asia and Africa the greatest number falls in July. In Europe and America the greater prevalence of rebellions in the hot months could not be more clearly marked. In Europe the maximum proved to be in July, and in South America in January, which are respectively the two hottest months. The minimum falls in Europe in December and January, and in South America in May and June, which again correspond in temperature.

If now we pass from the whole of Europe to the particular countries, we still find the greatest number of uprisings in the hot months. July leads in Italy, Spain, Portugal, and France; August, in Germany, Turkey, England, and (with March) in Greece. March leads in Ireland, Sweden, Norway, and Denmark; January, in Switzerland; September, in Belgium and the Netherlands; April, in Russia and Poland; and May, in Bosnia, Herzegovina, Servia, and Bulgaria. From this the influence of the hot months would seem to be greatest in the countries of the South.

§ 5. Seasons

Bringing together by seasons the data of uprisings in Europe during a hundred years, we get the following:

	Spain	Italy	Portugal	Turkey in Europe	Greece	France	Belgium and the Netherlands	Switzerland	Bosnia, Herzegovina, Servia, and Bulgaria	Ireland	England and Scotland	Germany	Austria-Hungary	Sweden, Norway, and Denmark	Poland	Russia in Europe
Spring .	23	27	7	9	6	16	7	6	7	6	5	7	3	4	6	3
Summer	38	29	12	11	7	20	8	5	3	3	9	11	6	4	1	0
Autumn	18	14	4	5	3	15	6	3	1	3	5	4	7	2	2	2
Winter .	20	18	6	3	3	10	2	10	4	3	4	3	2	2	1	1

From this it appears that summer holds the first place in the case of five nations, among them all those of the South. In the case of four, including the most northerly, it is spring that leads; in one case (Austro-Hungary) it is autumn; and in one other (Switzerland) it is winter. We find, further, that five times, and principally in the hottest countries, the winter has more revolutions than the autumn; eight times it has fewer, and three times an equal number.

If we consider America, especially South America (remembering that January there corresponds to our July, and February to our August) we shall find:

	America	Europe
Spring	76	142
Summer	92	167
Autumn	54	94
Winter	61	92

We see, then, that in both hemispheres summer takes the first place, while spring always surpasses both autumn and winter, doubtless, as with crimes, because of the first heat, but also because of the diminution of the food supply. Autumn and winter, on the contrary, differ little in the number of revolutions, winter giving in America seven more than autumn, and in Europe two fewer.

With regard to crimes, also, spring and summer stand plainly in the first rank. Guerry gives the following figures for the occurrence of crimes against persons:

	In England	In France
In winter	17.92%	15.93%
In spring	26.20%	26.00%
In summer	31.70%	37.31%
In autumn	24.38%	20.60%

Benoiston de Chateneuf points out that duels in the army are more frequent in the summer.[1]

I have proved that the same influence manifests itself in the case of men of genius.[2]

[1] Corre, "Crimes et Suicides," 1891, 628.
[2] "Man of Genius," Part I.

§ 6. Hot Years

Ferri, in his "Crime in its Relation to Temperature," has proved from a study of the French criminal statistics from 1825 to 1878 that one can deduce an almost complete parallelism between heat and criminality, not only for the different months, but also for years of different degrees of heat. The influence of the temperature on crime from 1825 to 1848 appears to be very pronounced and constant, and is often even greater than that exercised by agricultural production. Since 1848, notwithstanding the more serious agricultural and political disturbances, the coincidence between temperature and criminality becomes from time to time plainly apparent, especially in the case of homicide and murder. This coincidence is to be noted especially in the years 1826, 1829, 1831–32, 1833, 1837, 1842–43, 1844–45, 1846, 1858, 1865, 1867–68.

The connection comes out much more plainly, however, in the statistics of rape and offenses against chastity, which follow to an even greater degree the annual variations in temperature. This may be seen from the following table:

Year	Temperature	Cases of	
1830	89° F.	430	Homicide
1832	95°	520	
1848	89°	435	
1850	91°	560	
1848	89°	380	Rape
1852	95°	640	
1871	90°	550	
1874	100°	850	

As regards crimes against property there is a marked increase in the winter (theft and forgery being most abundant in January), while the other seasons differ little from one another. Here the influence of the weather is entirely different. Needs increase, while the means of satisfying them diminishes.

§ 7. Criminal Calendars

Lacassagne, Chaussinaud, and Maury, in confirmation of this contention, have constructed, with the aid of the statistics of each individual crime, real criminal calendars upon the model of the botanists' calendars of flora.

Among the crimes against persons, infanticide holds the first place in the months of January, February, March, and April (647, 750, 783, 662); which corresponds to the greater number of births taking place in the spring. This number falls off somewhat in May, and considerably in June and July, to increase again in November and December, through the influence of the Carnival. In the months named we find illegitimate births occurring with great frequency (1100, 1131, 1095, 1134), as well as abortions. Homicides and assaults [1] reach their maximum in July (716). Parricides,[2] on the contrary, are more numerous in January and October.

June is the month in which appears the greatest influence of the temperature upon the number of rapes practiced upon children, May, July, and August coming after it (2671, 2175, 2459, 2238). The minimum falls in December (993), followed by the other cold months; while the monthly average is 1684. Rapes upon adults do not follow the same course. Their maximum is in June (1078), the minimum in November (534); they increase in December and January (584), apparently as a result of the Carnival; they remain stationary in February (616) and increase in March and May (904), while the monthly average is 698.

Assaults are distributed irregularly because they are least influenced by the climate; they increase in February (931), decrease during the following months (840–467), to rise again in May (983), June (958), going down in July (919), rising once more in August (997) and September (993), to undergo a new decrease in November and December (886).

In the case of crimes against property the variations are not so pronounced, though they are more numerous by 3000 cases

[1] To avoid awkwardness of expression the term *assault* will be used for assaults other than those peculiarly against women, the original being about equivalent to our "assault and battery." — Transl.

[2] The French *parricide*, like the Italian *parricidio*, includes the murder of near relatives other than antecedents. As the argument will not be affected, however, the English cognate will be used throughout this translation. — Transl.

in December and January (16,879 and 16,396) and in the cold season generally, than in April (13,491) and in the hot season. (The monthly average is 14,630.) Plainly it is not here a question of the direct effect of the cold, but rather of an increase of needs in winter and a diminution of the means of satisfying them, so that the motives for theft are more abundant.

From the investigations of Maury,[1] it is possible to arrive at the following conclusions with regard to the individual months: In March infanticide holds the first place, accounting for 1193 crimes out of 10,000; then come in order, rape (1115 cases), substitution of children and concealment of birth (1019), kidnapping (1054), and threatening letters (997).

In May, vagrancy comes first (1257), then rapes and offenses against chastity (1150); then comes poisoning (1144), and finally rape of minors (1106). This last crime, under the influence of the heat, rises abruptly to the fourth place in May, having been only thirty-fifth in March and tenth in April, and reaches the second place in June, with 1303 cases. In June the first place is held by the analogous crime of rape upon adults (1313). The fourth place, also, belongs to a sexual offense, abortion (1080), while parricide occupies the third place (1151).

In July, rape of minors rises to the first place (1330), and the other most numerous crimes are of a similar kind, — kidnapping (1118) and offenses against chastity (1093). In the third place come bodily injuries to blood relatives, with 1100 cases. In August, sexual crimes recede to the third place, yielding the first to crop-burning. This, however, is caused not so much by the temperature as by the opportunity; for at the harvest time it is easiest for the workman to revenge himself upon the landlord. However, as Maury rightly observes, the heat is not without its responsibility for the appearance of this passionate tendency. These crimes may be responsible for the fact that perjury becomes rarer than subornation of minors.

In September, brutal passions become less violent, sexual assaults upon children move to the fifteenth place, and those upon adults to the twenty-fifth; while theft and breach of trust take the fourth place.

[1] "Le Mouvement Moral de la Société," 1860.

Embezzlement and bribery have the first place in September and October, for in those months rents fall due and accounts are settled. The numerous substitutions and concealments of new-born children correspond to the greater number of births.

From October to January, murder, parricide, and highway robbery are more frequent, since the nights are long and the fields deserted. In November, business resumes its full activity, and, as a consequence, falsification of accounts and bribery increase.

In January, the passing of counterfeit money and the robbing of churches take the first place, apparently on account of the dark days. In February, infanticide and the concealment of birth break out again, corresponding to the increased birth-rate.

Sexual crimes, having fallen in October to the twenty-eighth place, and rapes upon adults to the twenty-ninth, rise in November to the twenty-fourth and twenty-sixth places respectively.

There can be no doubt of the influence of heat upon crimes of passion. I have proved this in another way: first, by consulting the registers of five great Italian prisons, where the punishments inflicted were for rioting, fighting, and violence against persons; and, secondly, from the observations made by Virgilio in the penal institution at Aversa during a period of five years. The following figures show that acts of violence are much more numerous in the hot months:

May	346	October	368
June	522	November	364
July	503	December	352
August	433	January	362
September	508	February	361

One obtains similar figures in insane asylums by keeping account of the acute attacks of the insane.

	1867	1868
The maximum in September	460	191
" " " June	452	207
" " " July	451	298
" minimum " November	206	206
" " " February	205	121
" " " December	245	87
" " " January	222	139

§ 8. Excessive Heat

Excessive heat, on the contrary, especially when coupled with humidity, exercises a slighter influence. Corre observed with regard to the crimes of the Creoles in Guadaloupe that when the maximum temperature is reached (July 5th, 85°) there is the minimum of crime, especially against persons; while in March (with a temperature of 62°) there is the maximum number of criminals. We have here, then, an inversion like that which too great heat produces in the case of revolutions, and this because moist heat, when excessive, acts as a depressant, while moderate cold, on the contrary, acts as a stimulant.

There were:

	In the hot season	In the cool season
Crimes against property	51	53
" " persons	23	48

Corre observes also that the month of June furnishes the largest number of crimes against persons, and January the smallest.

§ 9. Other Meteorological Influences

Superintendents of prisons have generally observed that the inmates are more excited when storms are approaching, and during the first quarter of the moon. I myself have not sufficient data to prove this; but as the insane, who have numerous points of contact with criminals, are very sensitive to the influence of temperature and respond quickly to the variations of the barometer and of the moon, it is therefore very probable that the same is true of criminals.[1]

One fact, however, has proved to me that organic influences are at work at the same time as meteorological. For several years I have noted day by day the criminals received into the jails of Turin, and have always found that upon corresponding days in different years there have entered a remarkable number of individuals (10 to 15) with the same bodily peculiarity, persons who had hernia, or were asymmetric, blonde or brunette,

[1] See "Pensiero e Meteore" (C. Lombroso, Milan, 1878).

though often coming from different provinces. Entirely different groups were to be found within the days of the same week, when, therefore, there was no significant change in the influence of the temperature.

In recent years economic and political influences have come to the front and have reduced meteorological causes to the second rank. Thus, in France, the effect of the mean annual temperature upon revolts, evident in the past, has decreased in the last few years; while northern Europe (Russia, Denmark), on the other hand, although under the same climatic conditions, has had several uprisings. But, nevertheless, the effect of the weather cannot be doubted.

§ 10. Crimes and Rebellions in Hot Countries

In all this the preponderant influence of temperature is plainly evident, even if it is not exclusive; and this may be seen still better from the geographical distribution of crimes and political rebellions.

In the southern parts of Italy and France there occur many more crimes against persons than in the central and northern portions. We shall return to this fact again in speaking of brigandage and of the Camorra. Guerry has shown that crimes against persons are twice as numerous in southern France (4.9) as in central and northern France (2.7 and 2.9). *Vice versa*, crimes against property are more frequent in the north (4.9), than in the central and southern regions (2.3).

In Italy there occur —

For each 100,000 Inhabitants

	Indictments for crime	Homicides, highway robberies with homicide	Aggravated theft
Northern Italy	746	7.22	143.4
Central Italy	862	15.24	174.2
Southern Italy	1094	31.00	143.3
Insular Italy	1141	30.50	195.9

Liguria, simply because of its warmer climate, shows a greater number of crimes against persons than the rest of north Italy. In the period from 1875–84 the maximum number of crimes was furnished by Latium, and the next highest number by the islands. The minimum occurred in the north, with 512 crimes to the 100,000 inhabitants in Piedmont and 689 in Lombardy, while Latium showed 1537, Sardinia, 1293, and Calabria, 1287. We find the greatest number of homicides exclusively in the south, and upon the islands. In Russia, infanticide and stealing from churches are most numerous in the southeast, while homicide, and especially parricide, occurs with a frequency that increases as one goes from the northeast to the southwest (Anutschin). Holtzendorff[1] estimates that murder is fifteen times as frequent in the southern States of North America as it is in the northern States; so in the north of England there is one homicide to 66,000 inhabitants, and in the south one homicide to from 4000 to 6000 inhabitants. In Texas, according to Redfield, in 15 years there were 7000 homicides to 818,000 inhabitants. Even the school children were frequently provided with dangerous weapons.

In studying the distribution of simple and aggravated homicides in Europe, we find the highest figures in Italy and the other southern countries, and the lowest in the more northerly regions, England, Denmark, Germany. The same can be said of political uprisings in all Europe.[2] We see, in fact, that the number of crimes increases as we go from north to south, and in the same measure as the heat increases. We find the maximum in Greece, which, with a population of ten millions, shows ninety-five revolutions; and the minimum in Russia, for which, on the basis of the same population, the number would be only .8. We note that the smallest number is to be found in the northern countries, England and Scotland, Germany, Poland, Sweden, Norway, and Denmark; and the largest in the southern countries, Portugal, Spain, Turkey in Europe, and southern and central Italy; and intermediate numbers in the regions lying between. Grouping the figures in this way we find:

[1] Das Verbrechen des Mordes und die Todesstrafe," Berlin, 1875.
[2] See the charts in my "Crime Politique," 1889.

In northern Europe about 12 revolts to 10,000,000 inhabitants
In central " " 25 " " 10,000,000 "
In southern " " 56 " " 10,000,000 "

Considering Italy separately we find:

In northern Italy, 27 revolts to 10,000,000 inhabitants
In central " 32 " " 10,000,000 "
In southern " 33 " " 10,000,000 "
(Including 17 in Corsica, Sardinia, and Sicily)[1]

Arranging these crimes by degrees of latitude and figuring their ratio to the population we arrive at the following table:

Degrees of latitude	Spain — To 100,000 inhabitants — Number of crimes committed: Revolts against officers of the law	Spain — Number of crimes committed: Crimes against persons	Italy — Number of indictments for crime: Resistance to officers	Italy — Number of indictments for crime: Homicides
From 36° to 37°	14	74.3	...	...
" 37° " 38°	12	112.1	36.7	39.9
" 38° " 39°	9	58.5	42.0	32.8
" 39° " 40°	3	48.4	30.6	30.0
" 40° " 41°	11 (1)	72.4	37.8 (3)	31.9
" 41° " 42°	9 (2)	39.7	36.8 (4)	28.7
" 42° " 43°	6	31.2	32.7	20.9
" 43° " 44°	5	29.7	18.7	14.1
" 44° " 45°	...	...	19.8	9.2
" 45° " 46°	...	...	19.2	5.8
" 46° " 47°	...	...	16.2	5.8

From this table the influence of the climate is plainly to be seen; it is modified only by the influence of the capital (1 and 2) and other great cities (3 and 4). Aggravated theft occurs in Spain in the north (Santander, Leon), in the south, and in the center with nearly equal frequency; as often in Cadiz

[1] These facts as to homicides and revolts both are confirmed in the "Statistique Decennale de la Criminalité en Italie," published by Bodio, and in the "Stat. Crim. de l'Année,1884, pour l'Espagne," published by the Spanish minister of justice, Madrid, 1885.

as in Badajos, Caceras, and Salamanca, because this crime depends less upon climate than upon opportunity. For the same reason infanticide and parricide are more numerous in the central provinces (where the capital is) and in the north. The same is true in France and Italy and in Europe generally. In Italy we see from the investigations of Ferri that in all southern Italy and the islands, with the exception of Sardinia, the influence of the heat is dominant in the number of simple homicides, and, with the added exception of Forli, in the case of aggravated homicides also. So, likewise, murders increase in southern Italy and the islands, with the exception of the regions colonized by the Greeks, the provinces of Apulia, Catania, Messina, etc. Assaults also vary according to the same law, except in the case of Sardinia, where they are less numerous than would be expected, and of Liguria, where they are more so. Parricides follow a similar course. They are very numerous in southern and insular Italy, with the exception of the Greek portion, but very numerous also in the heart of Piedmont. Poisonings abound equally in the islands and in the heart of Calabria, but here the climate is plainly not responsible. Infanticide is likewise very frequent in Calabria and Sardinia, but it rages also in Abruzzo and Piedmont, showing itself to a certain extent independent of the climate. Highway robbery accompanied by homicide is, for the same reasons, very abundant in upper Piedmont, in Massa and Port Maurice, as upon the extreme boundaries of Italy and in the islands. Aggravated theft, common in Sardinia and Calabria and at Rome, shows another maximum at Venice, Ferrara, Rovigo, Padua, and Bologna, and is accordingly almost independent of the climate.[1] The same climatic principle holds in France, where murders and homicides are most prevalent in the south, with some exceptions that may be explained by racial influence. Parricide and infanticide, on the contrary, are most numerous in scattered districts in north, center, and south alike, not from any climatic influence, but essentially because occasional causes are at work in these places.

[1] Ferri, "Omicidio," 1895.

CHAPTER II

INFLUENCE OF MOUNTAIN FORMATION UPON CRIME — GEOLOGY — SOILS PRODUCING GOITRE, MALARIA, ETC.[1]

§ 11. Geology

MY earlier investigations showed me that geological conditions have very little influence upon political crime, and that, accordingly, in France uprisings are equally frequent upon the different formations, aside from a slight divergence in the case of the Jurassic and Cretaceous.[2]

The same remark applies to crimes against persons in France, where for a period of fifty-four years we find the following distribution of these offenses, in departments predominantly

Jurassic and Cretaceous	21%
Granite	19%
Clay	22%
Alluvial	21%

The same proportions, with almost no differences, hold for crimes against property.

§ 12. Orography

Upon investigating the relation of the general conformation of the country to frequency of crimes against persons, we find

[1] The material for the following chapter is drawn from the excellent "Criminal Statistics" of Bodio, and the remarkable topographical and statistical atlas in Ferri's "Omicidio" (Turin, 1895); also from the following: Reclus, "Geographie"; Dechassinaud, "Étude de la Statistique Criminelle de France," Lyons, 1881; De Collignon, "Contribution à l'Étude Anthropologique de Population Française," 1893; *Id.*, "Indice Cephalique suivant le Crime en France," Arch. d'Anthrop. Crim., 1890; Topinard, "La Couleur des Yeux et Cheveux," 1879. — For Italy: Livi, "Saggio di Risultati Antropometrici," Rome, 1894; *Id.*, "Sull' Indice Cefalico degli Italiani," Rome, 1890. — For the statistics of convictions: "Compte Criminelle de la Justice en France," 1882 (containing the number of convictions for the period from 1826 to 1880); Socquet, "Contribution à l'Étude Statistique de la Criminalité en France, de 1876 à 1880," Paris, 1884; Joly, "La France Criminelle," 1890.

[2] See "Délit Politique," p. 77.

that during fifty-four years the minimum, 20%, occurred in the level country; the mean, 33%, in departments that were hilly, while the maximum, 35%, occurred in mountainous departments. This is without doubt due to the fact that the mountains offer more opportunity for ambuscades, and also breed a more active race. I have no doubt that there is an actual connection between criminality and a greater activity, for I have found the same distribution to hold true in France for genius and for revolutionary tendencies, both being more frequent in the mountainous departments and less so in the plains.[1] Rape, while almost equally common in the mountains (35%) and among the hills (32%), is much more common in the level country (70%), certainly because of the greater and denser population resulting from the large cities. The same may be said about crimes against property, and for the same cause; for these crimes reverse the order of frequency given for crimes against persons, and while reaching 50% in the plains, show 47% in the hilly departments, and only 43% in the mountains. In Italy this orographic connection is less clear. We find the maximum of crimes against property (201 to 100,000 inhabitants) in the valley of the Po on the one hand, and in the mountain and coast districts of Calabria and Leghorn on the other. In Tonquin piracy is favored by the system of irrigation, which facilitates the operations of bandits on the sea coast.[2]

§ 13. Malaria

Of the districts of Italy that are most visited by malaria, where between five and eight to the thousand of the population die of it (Grosseto, Ferrara, Venice, Cremo, Vercelli, Novara, Lanciano, Vaste, San Severo, Catanzaro, Lecce, Foggia, Terracina, and Sardinia), five out of the thirteen, Grosseto, Ferrara, Sardinia, Lecce, and Terracina, show the maximum number of crimes against property. On the other hand there seems to be no connection between the occurrence of malaria and of homicide. In southern Sardinia, where malaria is most frequent, there are fewer crimes of this character, and also fewer sexual

[1] See "Crime Politique," ch. iv. [2] Corre, "Ethnol. Crim.," 43.

crimes, than in the northern part. The same is true of France, where those departments that are most scourged by malaria (Morbihan, Landes, Loire-et-Cher, Ain) show the smallest number of homicides and rapes.

§ 14. Goitrous Districts

The great districts of Italy in which goitre and cretinism are indigenous, and in which the soil has great influence on the health and intelligence of the inhabitants (like Sondrio, Aosta, Novarra, Cuneo, and Pavia), show no corresponding degree of criminality. All have less than the average number of homicides, of thefts, and (with the exception of Sondrio) of sexual offenses also. The same remark can be applied to the goitrous districts of France, of which the majority have only from 1.0 to 5.7 homicides to a million inhabitants. Only in the departments of Basses and Hautes Alpes and Pyrénées Orientales is the number of homicides greater (9.76 to the million). For theft, also, the goitrous districts show very low figures, with the exception of the departments of Doubs, Vosges, and Ardennes. It is worthy of note, however, that in almost all goitrous districts there is to be observed in the performance of crimes a greater degree of cruelty, mingled with lasciviousness.

§ 15. Influence of the Mortality Rate

Of the twenty-three French departments that show a minimum mortality rate,[1] seven (30%) have more than the average number of murders. These are: Lot-et-Garonne, Aisne, Maine, Côte d'Or, Eure, Haute Saône, and Aube, giving an average of 13.9%. Of eighteen departments with an intermediate mortality rate, six (33%) show a higher number of assassination than the average. They are Indre-et-Loire, Aube, Basses Pyrénées, Herault, Doubs, Seine-et-Oise, and Vosges. The eighteen departments have 15.4% of murders, that is to say, about as many as the first group. Of twenty-five departments having a maximum mortality rate, seven (28%) exceed the average number of murders. They are: Basses Alpes, Haute Loire,

[1] Bertillon, "Demographie de la France," 1878.

Seine, Seine Inferieure, Bouches du Rhône, Corsica, and Var, which give an average of 28%. If, however, the last two departments be omitted, as showing an abnormally high degree of criminality, the figure is only 20%, much nearer the other two. With regard to thefts, of twenty-four departments with a maximum mortality fourteen exceed 90%, and the same is true of seventeen of the eighteen departments with an intermediate mortality rate. Of twenty-five departments having a minimum mortality eight pass 90%.

To sum up, then, it may be said that there exists no relation between the mortality rate and the frequency of theft, while the frequency of murder increases as the mortality rises. In Italy this may be especially well seen in Sardinia, Sicily, and Basilicata. Revolts, likewise, are more common in districts where the mortality is greatest. Out of twenty-seven departments in France with a minimum mortality, fifteen manifested republican tendencies under the Empire; but of twenty-seven departments with the highest mortality, twenty were republican.

CHAPTER III

INFLUENCE OF RACE — VIRTUOUS SAVAGES — CRIMINAL CENTERS — SEMITIC RACE — GREEKS IN ITALY AND IN FRANCE — CEPHALIC INDEX — COLOR OF HAIR — JEWS — GYPSIES

§ 16. Influence of Race

WE have already seen — and it will become clearer as we proceed — that the notion of crime existing in the mind of the savage is so vague that we are often led to doubt its existence in the primitive man altogether.[1] However, many tribes seem to have a relative morality all their own, which they apply in their own fashion, and immediately we see crime arise among them. Among the Yuris in America the respect for property is so great that a thread is sufficient for a boundary line. The Koryaks and the Mbayas punish homicide committed within the tribe, although they do not regard it as a crime when committed against outsiders. It is plain that without some such law the tribe could not hold together, but would soon disintegrate.

There are, however, tribes to whom even this relative morality is repugnant. So in Caramansa in Africa, alongside of the honest and peaceful Bagnus, who practice rice culture, we find the Balantes, who live by hunting and robbery alone. These put to death any who steal in their own village, but nevertheless steal from other tribes themselves.[2] The one who steals best is most esteemed among them, and is even paid to teach their children to steal as well as chosen to lead their marauding expeditions. Not unlike these are the Beni-Hassan of Morocco, whose chief business is theft. These are disciplined, and live under their own chiefs with rights recognized by the government, which makes use of their services in the recovery of stolen

[1] See my "Homme Criminel."

[2] Revue d'Anthrop., 1874.

goods. They are divided into oat-thieves, horse-thieves, village-thieves, and highwaymen. There are among them mounted robbers, who flee so quickly that pursuit is futile. They often slip into houses naked and covered with oil, or hide themselves under leaves in order not to frighten the horses. They begin to steal at the age of eight.[1] In India there exists the tribe of the Zacka-Khail, who live by theft. When a boy is born to them they dedicate him to his future profession by passing him through a hole broken in a house-wall, and saying to him three times, "Be a thief."

The Kurubars, on the other hand, are noted for their honesty. They never lie, and would rather starve than steal. They are therefore set to keep watch over the harvest.[2] Spencer also notes certain peoples as inclined to honesty, such as the Todas, the Ainus, and the Bodos. These are in general peoples among whom war is held in slight esteem, and who are much engaged in trade. As a rule they do not contend among themselves, but leave their affairs to be regulated by the chiefs, and restore half of what is offered to them in their bartering if it appears to them to be too much. They do not apply the *lex talionis*, are not guilty of cruelty, honor women, and nevertheless, strange to say, are not religious. Among the Arabs (Bedouins) there are honest and industrious tribes; but there are also many others who lead a parasitic life. These are noted for their spirit of adventure, their reckless courage, their need of continual change, their idleness, and their tendency toward theft. In Central Africa Stanley found some tribes distinguished for honesty, and others, like the Zeghes, showing a tendency toward robbery and homicide. Among the Kafirs and Hottentots there are individuals who are especially savage and incapable of working, and wander about living by the labor of others. These are called Fingas by the Kafirs, and Sonquas by the Hottentots. (Mayhew.)

In our civilized world, to note the proof of the influence of race upon crime is both easier and more certain. We know that

[1] De Amicis, "Maroc," p. 205.
[2] Taylor, "Sociétés Primitives," Paris, 1874.

a large number of the thieves of London are of Irish parentage, or are natives of Lancashire. In Russia, according to Anutschin, Bessarabia and Kherson furnish all the thieves of the capital, and the number of convictions in proportion to the number of indictments in their case is unusually great. Criminality is transmitted among them from family to family.[1] In Germany, the districts in which there are colonies of gypsies are recognized as those where the women are most inclined to steal.

§ 17. Criminal Centers

In every part of Italy, almost in every province, there exists some village renowned for having furnished an unbroken series of special delinquents. Thus, in Liguria, Lerice is proverbial for swindlers, Campofreddo and Masson for homicides, Pozzolo for highway robberies. In the province of Lucca, Capannori is noted for its assassinations, and Carde in Piedmont for its field thefts. In southern Italy, Soro, Melfi, and St. Fele have always had their bandits since 1860, and the same is true of Partinico and Monreale in Sicily.

This predominance of crime in certain countries is certainly due to race, as history clearly shows in the case of some of them. Thus, Pergola near Pistoja was settled by gypsies, Masson by Portuguese outlaws, and Campofreddo by Corsican pirates. Even to-day the dialect in the latter place is half Corsican, half Ligurian. But the most famous of all is the village of Artena in the province of Rome, which Sighele describes thus:[2]

"Situated on the summit of a hill, in the middle of a green and smiling plain, under a mild sky, this village, where misery is unknown, ought to be one of the happiest and most honest. But the reverse is the case, and its inhabitants have an evil celebrity throughout all the surrounding country as thieves, brigands, and assassins. This reputation is not a recent acquisition. In the Italian chronicles one often meets the name of Artena, and its history can be summed up as one long series of crimes.

[1] "Sitz. d. Geogr. Gesellsch.," 1868, St. Petersburg.
[2] "Arch. di Psichiatria ed Antrop.," XI, Turin, 1890.

"The seriousness of the evil may be seen from the following statistical table:

ANNUAL NUMBER OF CRIMES TO 100,000 INHABITANTS

Crimes	Italy (1875–88)	Artena (1852–88)
Homicides murders, and robberies, followed by homicide	9.38	57.00
Assaults	34.17	205.00
Highway robberies	3.67	113.75
Thefts, simple and aggravated	47.36	177.00

"Artena, then, is marked by a number of assaults, homicides, and murders six times as great as that of the average of Italy, and by a number of highway robberies thirty times as great. And yet these figures give only a very imperfect idea of the boldness and ferocity of the criminals of Artena. To have this properly appreciated it would be necessary to describe all the crimes, to tell how they commit murders there in broad daylight in public places, how they strangle the witnesses who dare to tell the truth to the judges."

The cause, according to Sighele, lies in the character of the inhabitants and the influence of earlier governments, which elsewhere gave rise to brigandage and the Camorra; further, in the inability of the authorities to punish the guilty, because the witnesses are bribed or intimidated into keeping silent; but above all, in the influence of heredity. In fact, in an investigation of the proceedings instituted against inhabitants of Artena since 1852, Sighele came across the same names repeatedly, father, son, and nephew following one another at intervals as if driven by a fatal necessity. The name Montefortino, belonging to an ancient family of Artena, was already celebrated for crime as early as 1555. Paul IV in 1557 was obliged to condemn to death all the inhabitants of this town, and authorized any one to kill them and destroy their castle, "that it might no longer furnish a nest and refuge for base thieves."

It is to be noted that in Sicily brigandage is almost exclusively confined to that famous valley of the Conca d'Oro, where the robber tribes of Berbers and Semites had their first and most lasting places of refuge, and where the anatomical type, the customs, the political and moral ideals still retain the Arabian imprint, as the descriptions of Tommasi-Crudeles are sufficient to prove.[1] Moreover, here, as among the Arabs, cattle-stealing is the chief crime. With these facts we can easily be persuaded that the blood of this people, at once conquerors and robbers, hospitable and cruel, intelligent and superstitious, inconstant, restless, and impatient of restraint, must have its influence in Sicily in fomenting the sudden and implacable revolts and in perpetuating brigandage. This latter, it is to be noticed, is often mixed with politics, as it is in the case of the parent Arabian stock, and excites neither the horror nor the aversion displayed by peoples less intelligent, indeed, but richer in Aryan blood, such as those of Catania and Messina in this same island of Sicily. A very different sort of community is that of Larderello in the province of Volterra, where for sixty years no homicide or theft or even misdemeanor has been committed. That race is a factor in the great criminality of the places mentioned I am the more persuaded through having observed in the case of most of the inhabitants a taller stature than in the neighboring regions.

In France, also, a race of criminals has been discovered by Fauvel in a row of villages along the border of the forest of Tierache, a continuation of the forest of Ardennes.[2] In every place where this race predominates there are continually violent brawls, to which the authorities most often have to shut their eyes. The stranger who ventures among these people exposes himself to the insults of the women as of the men. Even among the well-to-do the same brutality often shows itself through a certain polite varnish. This half-barbarous condition is aggravated by frequent alcoholism; and the people, scorning agricultural pursuits, betake themselves to work in the forests or in

[1] "They are sober, patient, and persevering; they are open to friendly approaches; they have an inclination to gain their ends secretly and silently; they are at once hospitable and given to robbery. The lower classes are superstitious, the upper classes haughty. A man will say, 'I am a brigand,' as if it meant no more than, 'I have blood in my veins.' To inform against a homicide is to transgress the code of honor." "La Sicilia," Florence, 1874.

[2] "Bulletin de la Société d'Anthropologie," 1891.

the iron-works. Their real preference, however, is smuggling. They are a little below the average in height, but have powerful muscles, with broad, strong jaws, straight nose, pronounced eyebrows, and thick, dark hair. This last characteristic separates them at once from the blond-haired race who inhabit the villages near them, with whom they associate only rarely.

§ 18. Europe

In his "Homicide" Ferri shows clearly the influence of race upon the distribution of crime in Europe, Latin and Teuton occupying the opposite extremes of the scale, both for homicide in general, and also for aggravated homicide and infanticide. The same is true with regard to suicide and insanity, except that here the order is reversed and the Teuton shows the maximum in each case, and the Latin the minimum.

§ 19. Austria

Very often, however, it is not possible to arrive at an exact estimate of the influence of race from the figures furnished by criminal statistics, for we encounter a whole complexus of causes which prevents us from drawing a definite conclusion. For example, women show the minimum degree of criminality in Spain, Lombardy, Denmark, Slavonia, and Göritz, and the maximum in Austrian Silesia and in the Baltic provinces of Russia. But here the cultural influence is more in evidence than the racial. For where the women are educated like the men, as in Silesia and the Baltic provinces, or where they take part with the men in the struggle for existence, they approach men more nearly in the degree of criminality. The same thing may be said of the greater criminality to be observed in the Austrian empire chiefly among the youths, especially in Salzburg and Austria proper, as compared with the Slavs and Italians of Göritz, Carinthia, and the Tyrol.

§ 20. Italy

The following table presents a summary of simple homicides (including assaults followed by death) and aggravated homicides (including highway robbery with homicide) for which indictments were brought in the different provinces of Italy in the years 1880–83 inclusive:

Provinces of Italy with the population in 1881	Number of indictments for homicide to the million inhabitants	
	Simple	Aggravated
Piedmont (3,070,250)	47	34
Liguria (892,373)	40	29
Lombardy (3,680,615)	22	21
Venetia (2,814,173)	34	25
Emilia (1,706,817)	27	24
Romagna (476,874)	103	76
Umbria (572,660)	102	70
Marches (936,279)	94	53
Tuscany (2,208,869)	76	42
Latium (903,472)	178	90
Abruzzo (751,781)	174	76
Molise (365,434)	286	104
Campania (289,577)	217	81
Apulia (1,589,054)	117	46
Basilicata (524,504)	214	86
Calabria (1,257,883)	246	104
Sicily (5,927,901)	205	122
Sardinia (682,002)	122	167

It is apparent, then, that these crimes are most frequent in the provinces where the population is predominantly Semitic (Sicily, Sardinia, Calabria) or purely Latin (Latium, Abruzzo), as compared with those where the population is Teutonic, Ligurian, Celtic (Lombardy, Liguria, Piedmont), or Slavic (Venetia). Now beside the original inhabitants, the Ligurians in the north, the Umbrians and Etruscans in the center, the Oscans in the south, and the Siculi, of Ligurian origin, in Sicily, the principal social elements of the Italian population are the Teutons, Celts, and Slavs in the north, the Phenicians, Arabs, Albanians, and Greeks in the south and on the islands. It is, then, to the African and oriental elements (the Greeks excepted) that Italy owes the frequency of homicide in Calabria, Sicily, and Sardinia; while the occurrence of a smaller number, as in Lombardy, is due to the large Teutonic element in the population.

The effect of race is clearly to be seen in certain localities whose inhabitants differ ethnically from the surrounding population, and where the relative frequency or infrequency of crime coincides with the racial difference. Thus we have a striking contrast in Tuscany, where Siena shows 39 homicides to the million, Florence 43, and Pisa 60; while Massacarrara shows 83, Grosseto 102, Lucca 119, Arezzo 134, and Leghorn 140. Now it is true that in Massaçarrara the quarries, and in Grosseto the marshes, produce special living-conditions; but the ethnic influence is incontestable in the province of Lucca, which is differentiated from the rest of Tuscany by the greater stature and dolichocephaly of its inhabitants (the latter characteristic being found in Massacarrara also), and the greater tendency to emigration. One may refer also to the effect of the Ligurian blood, calling to mind how often the ancient Ligurians revolted against the Roman rule. But in Leghorn the racial influence is especially evident, and the origin of this is well known. Leghorn, in the sixteenth century, was merely a marshy village, having 749 inhabitants in 1551. Its first settlers were the Liburni, an Illyrian people, inventors of the Liburnian galley, and notorious pirates. To these were added Saracens, Jews, and Marseillais, and later adventurers and pirates invited by the Medici.[1] Leghorn, which from 1879 to 1883 showed the greatest proportion of indictments for crime, furnished likewise, in comparison with the whole of Tuscany (including Arezzo), the highest numbers for aggravated homicide, rebellion, and aggravated theft. This state of affairs cannot be accounted for by the greater density of the population, for the density at Milan is the same (919 to the square mile), and that at Naples is much greater (3976). Neither is it due to a greater preponderance of the urban population, for the urban residents in Naples constitute 94% of the total population of the municipality, in Milan 92%, and in Leghorn only 80%; while nevertheless insurrections and aggravated thefts are much more frequent there.

[1] Lombroso, "Troppo Presto," 1889.

Another very significant contrast is to be observed in the southern part of the peninsula. Here the summary of simple homicides shows certain localities in the provinces of Campobasso, Avellino, Cosenza, and Catanzaro with a relatively high criminality, and localities in the provinces of Benevento, Salerno, Bari, and Lucca, where the frequency of homicide is small in comparison with the neighboring provinces of Aquila, Caserto, Potenza, Reggio, and especially Naples. In the last the social environment would naturally be expected to be provocative of crime. Now it is difficult not to deduce a causal connection between the presence of Albanian colonies and the great number of crimes of violence in the provinces of Cosenza, Catanzaro, and Campobasso. On the other hand, the less frequent occurence of simple homicide in Reggio, Naples, and especially in Apulia (Bari and Leccc) depends in great part upon the Greek element of the population. To understand the presence and extent of this element it is only necessary to recall the ancient Magna Græcia, the later Greek colonies which arrived during and after the Byzantine supremacy, and the earlier migrations of the Iapygo-Messapians. "Even to-day," says Nicolucci, "the physiognomy of the greater part of the natives of these provinces recalls this type, through which shines pacific sweetness of character." [1] To the effect of the Greek element must be added the ethnic influence of the Norman occupation.

As regards the marked infrequency of simple homicide in Salerno and in Benevento, it is impossible not to recall the Lombard element which was dominant in the duchy of Benevento and Salerno so long and to such an extent that it has been able to resist the assimilating power of the native Italians, and to preserve to this day the tall stature and blond hair, noticeable in the midst of the types indigenous to the peninsula. (Ferri). The quite different influence of the Albanian, Greek, and Lombard elements upon the criminality in these contrasted localities is confirmed by the distribution of aggravated homicide, and highway robbery with homicide. Salerno and Reggio, indeed, form exceptions, having relatively high figures; but Naples, thanks to its Greek blood, shows, notwithstanding the

[1] "Etnografia dell' Italia," 1880.

density and poverty of its population, a small number of homicides, matching the figures for Bari and Lecce.

Sicily, also, offers a striking example of the influence of race upon homicide. The eastern provinces, Messina, Catania, and Syracuse, show a number of homicides much smaller than the provinces of Caltanisetta, Girgenti, Trapani, and Palermo. Now Sicily differs greatly in the character of its population from the neighboring part of the peninsula, partly because of the numerous northern peoples (Vandals, Normans, French) which have conquered and ruled the island. But on the eastern coast it is the Greek element that is predominant, and it is impossible not to refer to this fact the smaller number of homicides occurring there; nor, on the other hand, to see in the large admixture of Saracen and Albanian blood the reason for great frequency of homicides in the south and north. Reclus writes:

"At the time of the siege of Palermo by the Normans (1071 A. D.) there were five languages spoken in Sicily, — Arabic, Hebrew, Greek, Latin, and the popular Sicilian. Arabic remained the dominant language even under the Normans. Later the French, the Germans, the Spaniards, and the Aragonese contributed to make of the Sicilians a people different from their Italian neighbors in dress, manners, customs, and national feeling. The differences existing within the Sicilian population itself are very great, since now one race now another gets the upper hand in the mixture. Thus the people of the Etna provinces, who are without doubt of Hellenic origin — being in fact the purest of the Greeks, since they have not been mixed with the Slavs — have an excellent reputation for deportment and amiability. The inhabitants of Palermo, on the contrary, among whom the Arab element is greater than anywhere else, have in general serious faces and dissolute manners."[1]

The criminality of Sardinia is equally characteristic, whether one compares it with that of the continent, and even more with that of Sicily, or considers the almost constant contrast between the north (province of Sassari) and the south (province of Cagliari). Ethnically Sardinia is differentiated from Sicily because the Phenician domination, begun in remote antiquity and renewed in Carthaginian times, was both more extensive and

[1] Ferri.

of longer duration in Sardinia than in Sicily, so that even to-day the Sardinian skull may partly serve to illustrate the ancient Phenician dolichocephalic type. The Saracen elements in Sardinia are less significant, though there are two Saracen colonies, — Barbaricini in the province of Sassari, and Maureddi, near Iglesias, in the province of Cagliari.[1] This racial difference certainly contributes to produce the higher average of crimes against persons in Sicily (notwithstanding the relatively small number in the eastern provinces), and, on the other hand, the higher average of crimes against property in Sardinia. For example, in comparing Sardinia with Sicily one sees a striking contrast in the number of simple homicides, which comes out still more strongly in the number of assaults. In the case of aggravated homicides, indeed, the figures for Sicily are lower on account of the small number in the eastern provinces, but the total of all crimes against persons, including homicide, simple and aggravated, and highway robbery accompanied by homicide, is much greater than in Sardinia. In crimes against property, on the contrary, Sardinia, on account of the preponderance of Semitic blood, goes far beyond Sicily, especially in aggravated thefts and in forgeries; whereas in violent crimes against property, such as highway robbery, extortion, and blackmail, Sicily again takes the lead somewhat.

In Sardinia, moreover, a contrast is to be observed between the two provinces of Sassari and Cagliari in the very type of the inhabitants, and in their social and economic life. The north has agriculture and manufacturing more developed, while the south has its mines, near Cagliari, Iglesias, etc. Now it is well known that the province of Cagliari is more decidedly Phenician, whereas in the province of Sassari the Spanish element dominates, and this fact doubtless coöperates with the economic conditions to cause the greater frequency of forgery and aggravated theft in the province of Cagliari, and of homicide, and highway robbery with homicide, in the province of Sassari.

Another example of the influence of race is found in the criminality of Corsica, which notoriously gives the maximum number of homicides (infanticide and poisoning excepted) for the

[1] Nicolucci, "Etnografia dell' Italia."

whole of France, but shows a very small number of thefts. By comparing the number of persons sentenced for homicide in Corsica from 1880 to 1883 with those sentenced in those parts of Italy that give the highest figures, the following data are obtained:

PERSONS SENTENCED IN 1880–83

	Yearly average to 100,000 inhabitants				
	Corsica	Sardinia	Sicily	Calabria	Molise (Campobasso)
Simple homicides and assaults resulting in death	11.2	8.6	14.3	21.5	19.1
Murders and highway robberies with homicide	9.5	19.8	9.6	9.0	5.2

This means that although Corsica belongs to France politically, it is Italian both in race and in the character of its crimes. Reclus remarks:

"Of the two islands, Sardinia and Corsica, once united, it is Corsica, notwithstanding its political connection with France, that is by geographical position and by its historical traditions most Italian."

Thus the marked differences between the criminality of Corsica and that of Sardinia are to be explained in great measure by racial causes, and this explanation is confirmed by the great resemblance existing between the criminality of Corsica and that of Sicily. The fact is that in Sicily the Saracen element came to dominate all the others, and this same stock, more fierce than covetous, exercised a great influence in Corsica. We know that

"the ancient inhabitants (Ligurians and Iberians, or, as some think, Sicanians) were followed by the Phenicians and the Romans, but especially, up to the eleventh century, by the Saracens, and after these by the Italians and the French."[1]

[1] Nicolucci.

It is, then, to their Saracen blood that Corsica, Sicily, and, in part, Calabria owe their intense homicidal criminality, together with their lower degree of criminality, as regards property.

§ 21. Races in France

A glance at the distribution of crimes in France shows that it is to the Ligurian and Gallic races that we owe the maximum of crimes of blood. This is proved in detail by the summary of the various crimes in the departments that furnish figures above the average. From such a summary we discover that the tendency toward murder increases as we pass from the departments having a Cimbric population (1 out of the 18, or 5.5%, showing a number of murders above the average) to the Gallic departments (with 8 out of 32, or 25%, above the average), then to the Iberian (with 3 out of 8, or 37½%), and Belgian (6 out of 15, or 40%), and finally to the Ligurian departments, all of which (100%) show more than the average number of murders. The series for rape is slightly different: first, Iberian departments (2 out of 8, 25%), next Cimbric (6 out of 18, 33%), Belgian (6 out of 15, 40%), Gallic (13 out of 32, 41%), and finally, as before, the Ligurian (6 out of 9, 67%). In crimes against property, on the other hand, we see the Belgians, the most industrial of the races, lead, with 67% of their departments above the average, followed closely by the Ligurians and Iberians, with 60% and 61% respectively, while the Cimbric and Gallic elements show only 30% and 39%.

As I have shown in my "Crime Politique," the dominant influence of the Ligurian and Gallic races is determined by their greater activity. The Ligurian peoples of France furnished the maximum of insurgents (all the departments, or 100%, being above the average), and the maximum number of men of genius (60% of the departments being above the average). The Gallic departments come next, with 82% for insurgents and 19% for men of genius; the Belgians, 62% and 33%; while the Cimbric departments showed only 38% for insurgents with scarcely 5% for men of genius; and the Iberians furnish the minimum, with 14% and 5% for insurgents and men of genius respectively.

§ 22. Dolichocephaly and Brachycephaly

I have attempted to discover the relationship between criminality on the one hand, and the cephalic index and the color of the hair on the other, being convinced that more reliable indications of the influence of race might be obtained in this way. In studying crime in Italy in relation to the cephalic index, I have seen from the plates of Livi that in 21 provinces having a preponderance of dolichocephaly (index from 77 to 80 inclusive), the average of homicides and assaults is 31%, while the general average in Italy is 17%. In all the dolichocephalic provinces, with the exception of Lucca and Lecce, that is to say, in 19 out of 21, the proportion of homicides is above the average. The provinces where mesocephaly (index, 81 to 82) dominates fall below the dolichocephalic provinces in homicide, giving an average of 25%. But where brachycephaly (index, 83 to 88) is most abundant the figure is 8%, an average much below that for the country as a whole.

It must be noted, however, that the dolichocephalic provinces are in the south, with the exception of Lucca, which is also an exception to the parallelism of dolichocephaly and crime; that the brachycephalic provinces, with the exception of Abruzzo, are all in upper Italy; and that the ultrabrachycephalic are to be found in the mountainous regions, which all have a smaller number of crimes of blood. As for the mesocephalic population, it is to be met in southern Italy, or in the warmer parts of upper Italy, like Leghorn and Genoa, so it must be conceded that the influence of climate enters here with that of race. In the case of theft the difference is much smaller. Though observable, it is far less marked than in the case of homicide, as may be seen from the fact that the dolichocephalic provinces have 460 thefts to the million inhabitants, the mesocephalic 400, and the brachycephalic 360.

In France [1] the crimes against persons give an average of 18 to the 100,000 in the brachycephalic departments, and of 36 in the dolichocephalic, including Corsica (Collignon); but without Corsica it gives an average of only 24, the average for the whole

[1] See "Compte Criminelle de la Justice en France."

country ranging from 24 to 33 to the 100,000. If we follow the figures given by Ferri we find an even smaller difference. According to him the crimes of blood among the dolichocephalic part of the population (without Corsica) amount to 13 to the 100,000, and to 19 in the brachycephalic departments. From this it is evident how much greater influence climate has upon crimes of blood than has race; for in Italy, where the dolichocephalic part of the population is collected in the south, its preponderance in crime is enormous. But in France, where it is distributed everywhere, in the south, in the north (Pas-de-Calais, Nord, Aisne), and in the center (Haute Vienne, Charente), it furnishes no precise data, and sometimes even gives smaller figures than the brachycephalic population. In the case of crimes against property, however, the difference in France is remarkable. The long-heads show 44 crimes to the 100,000, and the round-heads only 23.

In general, there is everywhere a preponderance of crime in the districts dominated by dolichocephaly. In France the long-heads have furnished the greatest number of revolutionists and geniuses; and it is among the dolichocephalic Gauls and Ligurians that the princes and peoples have been found who offered most resistance to conquest. This is apparently in complete opposition to the teaching of criminal anthropology, according to which criminals are nearly always ultra-brachycephalic; but it is in reality of great value as enabling us to show the better that the exaggerated brachycephaly of criminals is a plain mark of degeneracy.

§ 23. Light and Dark Hair

In investigating the relation of the color of the hair to criminality in France, I have found that in the departments where dark hair predominates the figures for murder reach 12.6% (or 9.2% without Corsica), while the light-haired departments give only 6.3%. It is to be noted, however, that dark hair is especially abundant in hot districts, Vendée, Hèrault, Var, Gers, Landes, Corsica, Bouches-du-Rhône, Basses-Alpes, Gironde, etc. The influence of climate is perhaps, therefore, not to be excluded. Similarly blond hair (except in Vaucluse) is more frequent in the departments with a northern climate, Pas-de-Calais, Nord, Ardennes, Manche, Eure-et-Loire, which, as has been shown, have a smaller number of crimes of blood.

In Italy the proportion of blonds in the whole of southern Italy is below the average of the kingdom,[1] except in Benevento, where it reaches the average, and in Apulia, Naples, Campania, Trapani, and eastern Sicily, where it is only a little below the average. Now in all southern Italy crimes of blood are below the average, and in the province of Benevento they give a figure which, although rather high (27.1%), is nevertheless below that of the neighboring provinces. The same is true of Apulia, eastern Sicily, Syracuse, and Catania, which all show a low degree of criminality (Syracuse 15, Catania 28, Lecce 10). In these provinces the blond color of the hair is directly connected with the Lombard (Benevento) and Greek races (Sicily), and it is for this reason that they are less criminal. I have found no connection with race, however, in the blond oasis of Perugia, nor in the brunette oasis of Forli, in central Italy.

The blond population inhabiting the neighborhood of the Alps is in direct connection with that of the mountains themselves, and shows, as does the latter, only a slight criminality. But the cause here is merely orographic. On the other hand, the brunette oasis of Leghorn and Lucca coincides with a criminality greater, even in crimes of blood, than that of the neighboring parts of Tuscany, and, as here the color of the hair is accompanied by a special dolichocephaly without being explicable by any orographic cause, it seems to me that we have a new proof of the influence of race upon crimes of blood. In the case of crimes against property there is no evident correspondence. For example, the province of Treviso, where the inhabitants are very blond, gives the maximum of criminality, and Ferrara, where the population is very dark, is nearly equal to it.

§ 24. Jews

The influence of race upon criminality becomes plainly evident when we study the Jews and the gypsies, though very

[1] See Livi, "Archivio d'Antrop.," 1894.

differently manifested in the two races. The statistics of many countries show a lower degree of criminality for the Jews than for their Gentile fellow-citizens. This is the more remarkable since, because of their usual occupations, they should in fairness be compared, not with the population in general, but with the merchants and petty tradespeople, who have, as we shall see, a high record for criminality. In Bavaria one Jew is sentenced for every 315 of them in the population, and one Catholic for every 265. In Baden, Jewish criminality was 63.3% of the Christian criminality. In Lombardy, under the rule of Austria, there was during the space of seven years one Jew convicted for every 2,568 inhabitants. In Italy in 1855 there were only seven Jews in prison, five men and two women, a proportion much smaller than that prevailing among the Catholic population. Recent investigations made by Servi show that in 1869, out of a Jewish population of 17,800 there were only eight sentenced. In Prussia, Hausner has observed a slight difference to the discredit of the Jews, there being one Jew indicted to each 2600, while the Christians show one to 2800. This is in part confirmed by Kolb, according to whom the following were recorded:

In Prussia in 1859,[1]

1 Jew	indicted	for	each	2793
1 Catholic	"	"	"	2645
1 Protestant	"	"	"	2821

From 1862 to 1865, however,

1 Jew	indicted	for	each	2800
1 Protestant	"	"	"	3800

In Bavaria,

1 Jew	indicted	for	each	315
1 Catholic	"	"	"	265

In France from 1850 to 1860, on the average,

the Jews	indicted	were	.0776%	of	the	adults
" Catholics	"	"	.0584%	"	"	"
" Jews	"	"	.0111%	"	"	total population
" Catholics	"	"	.0122%	"	"	" "

In 1854 there were 166 Jewish criminals; in 1855, 118; in 1856, 163; in 1858, 142; in 1860, 123; in 1861, 118 — a slight

[1] "Handb. der Vergleich. Statistik," 1875, p. 130.

decrease in the later years.[1] In Austria, however, the number of Jews convicted was 3.74% in 1872, and 4.13% in 1873, figures higher by some fractions than those for the rest of the population.[2]

The fact of a special type of Jewish criminality is more certain than a greater or less degree of criminality. Among the Jews as among the gypsies the hereditary form of crime predominates, and in France they reckon whole generations of rogues and thieves among the Cerfbeers, Salomons, Levis, Blums, and Kleins. Those convicted of murder are rare, and, where they are found, they are captains of bands organized with rare skill, like those of Graft, Cerfbeer, Meyer, and Dechamps. These master rogues had regular traveling agents, kept ledgers, and showed such a degree of cleverness, patience, and tenacity as made it possible for them to evade for many years the attempts to bring them to justice.

Most of the Jewish criminals in France have their own special kinds of rascality, like the trick with the ring, when they pretend to have found an object of value; or the "morning call," which gives them an opportunity to rob the chambers of sleepers who have forgotten to lock their doors.[3]

The Russian Jews are principally usurers, counterfeiters, and smugglers, carrying this last pursuit to the extent of smuggling women, exporting them to Turkey. Smuggling is organized among them in semi-governmental fashion. Whole towns on the border, like Berdereff, are peopled almost entirely by Jewish smugglers. Often the government has the town surrounded by a cordon of soldiers, and upon making a search finds immense stores of smuggled goods. The smuggling is carried so far as even to be an obstacle to commercial treaties with Prussia. In Prussia there were formerly great numbers of Jews convicted for forgery and for defamation, but more frequently for bankruptcy and for receiving stolen goods, a crime which frequently eludes the clutches of the law. To the prevalence of this last crime among them is due the great number of Jewish words

[1] Servi, "Gli Israeliti in Europa," Turin, 1872.
[2] "Stat. Uebers. d. k. k. österreichischen Strafanstalten," 1875.
[3] "Vidocq," DuCamp, Paris, 1874.

incorporated into the thieves' slang in Germany and England, since the thief looks upon the receiver of stolen goods as a master and guide, and in consequence easily adopts his language. Every great enterprise of the famous band of Mainz was planned by a *kochener*, or Jewish receiver of stolen goods. There was a time in France "when nearly all the leaders of the great bands had Jewesses for concubines." Many causes formerly impelled the Jews to these crimes, as also to the unlawful gains of usury: greed for gold, discouragement, desperation, exclusion from office and from all public assistance, and the natural reaction against the persecutions of the stronger races, from which they had no other means of defense. They were often merely shuttlecocks between the armed brigands and the feudal lords, and were forced to be accomplices in order not to become victims. One need not be astonished, therefore, if their criminality appears great; and it is fair to note that from the time when the Jews have been permitted to enter political life their tendency to special crime has diminished. We have forced upon us here anew the difficulty of coming to universally valid conclusious upon the basis of statistics alone.

Even though the criminality of the Jews can be proved to be less than that of other races, a very different situation appears when we turn to the question of insanity, in which they have an unfortunate leadership.[1] Here, however, it is not so much a matter of race as of intellectual work, for among the Semitic races in general (Arabs, Bedouins) insanity is very rare.

§ 25. Gypsies

With the gypsies the case is quite different. They are the living example of a whole race of criminals, and have all the passions and all the vices of criminals. "They have a horror," says Grelmann,[2] "of anything that requires the slightest ap-

[1] In Bavaria there is one insane person to each 908 Catholics, 967 Protestants, 518 Jews; in Hanover, one insane person to each 527 Catholics, 641 Protestants, 337 Jews; in Silesia, one insane person to each 1355 Catholics, 1264 Protestants, 604 Jews. In Denmark there are 5.8 insane Jews and only 3.4 insane Christians to the 1000 of each. (Oettingen.)

[2] "Histoire des Bohemiens," Paris, 1837; Perdari, "Sugli Zingari," Milan, 1871; Pott, "Zigeuner," Halle, 1844; Colocci, "Gli Zingari," Ancona, 1889.

plication; they will endure hunger and misery rather than submit to any continuous labor whatever; they work just enough to keep from dying of hunger; they are perjurers even among themselves, ungrateful, and at once cruel and cowardly, from which fact comes the Transylvanian proverb that fifty gypsies can be put to flight with a wet clout." Enlisted in the Austrian army they cut a sorry figure. They are revengeful to excess. One of them, to revenge himself upon his master, who had beaten him, dragged him to a cave, sewed him up in a skin, and fed him upon the most loathsome food till he died. With the intention of plundering Lograno they poisoned the sources of the Drave, and when they believed the inhabitants dead invaded the district in a body and were only frustrated through the discovery of the plot by one of the citizens. Gypsies have been known in a fit of rage to throw their own children at the head of their opponent like a stone from a sling. They are vain, like all delinquents, but they have no fear of shame. Everything they earn they spend for drink and ornaments. They may be seen barefooted, but with bright-colored or lace-bedecked clothing; without stockings, but with yellow shoes. They have the improvidence of the savage and that of the criminal as well. The story is told that once when a party of them had repulsed a body of troops from a trench, they called out, "Flee, flee, for if we had any lead left we would kill you all." The enemy, thus informed how the matter stood, turned back and massacred them. Without morals, they are nevertheless superstitious (Borrow), and would believe themselves to be damned or dishonored if they were to eat eels or squirrels, although they devour half-putrefied carrion. They are given to orgies, love a noise, and make a great outcry in the markets. They murder in cold blood in order to rob, and were formerly suspected of cannibalism. The women are very clever at stealing, and teach it to their children. They poison cattle with certain powders in order to get the credit of curing them, or perhaps to get their flesh at a low price. In Turkey they also practice prostitution. They all excel in some form of rascality, such as passing counterfeit money or selling sick horses for sound. As the name "Jew" with us is synonymous with usurer so in Spain *gitano* is synonymous with rascally cattle trader. In whatever condition the gypsy finds himself he always maintains his impassivity, does not seem to concern himself with the future, but lives from day to day, despising all forethought.

"Authority, laws, rules, principles, precepts, duties, — these are notions and things insupportable to this strange race. To obey or to command is equally odious to them, it is a burden and a bore. They have no more conception of property than they have of duty; 'I have' is as foreign to them as 'I ought.'[1] Result, consequence, foresight, the connection between past and present, all are unknown to them."[2]

Colocci believes that they have special routes, used also by refugees, thieves, and smugglers, which they indicate by special marks (the *Zinken* of the Germans). Of these the most frequently used is the *patterau*, formerly a trident, but now made in the shape of a Latin cross. These signs marked along the course of the highways, or drawn with charcoal on the walls of the houses, or cut into the bark of the trees, become a conventional means of saying to later bands, "This is the gypsy route." In the first *patterau* the direction is indicated by lateral lines, in the second by the longer arm of the cross. Stopping places are marked by the mysterious *swastika*, which is without doubt derived from the ancient East Indian symbol, possibly the original of our cross. "When they wish to leave the place where they are," wrote Pechon de Ruby in the sixteenth century, "they set out in the opposite direction from that which they are to travel, and after going half a league retrace their steps."

Like criminals and the pariahs from whom they are descended, they have a popular criminal literature which glorifies crime, as in the following dialogue between father and son:

Father. "Holla, Basil, if you are to become great, by the cross of your father, you must steal."

Son. "And afterward, father, if I am discovered?"

[1] The word *ought* does not exist in the gypsy language. The verb *to have* is almost forgotten by the European gypsies, and is unknown to the gypsies of Asia.

[2] Colocci.

Father. "Then you must take to your heels, joy of your sire."
Son. "To the devil with your cross, father! You do not teach me well." [1]

It is to be noted that this race, so low morally and so incapable of cultural and intellectual development, a race that can never carry on any industry, and which in poetry has not got beyond the poorest lyrics, has created in Hungary a marvelous musical art — a new proof of the genius that, mixed with atavism, is to be found in the criminal.[2]

[1] Colocci.
[2] See Lombroso, "Atavism and Evolution," in *Contemporary Review*, July, 1895.

CHAPTER IV

CIVILIZATION — BARBARISM — AGGREGATIONS OF POPULATION — THE PRESS — NEW KINDS OF CRIME

§ 26. Civilization and Barbarism

AMONG the numerous social problems there is one especially whose certain and complete solution concerns us greatly. It is that of the influence of civilization upon crime and insanity. If we judge by statistics alone we shall conclude that the problem is already solved, for in every country of Europe, except England, we find that crime and insanity are each year increasing out of proportion to the growth of the population.[1]

[1] In France from 1826 to 1837 there was one person indicted to each one hundred of the population; in 1868 the indictments had reached one to fifty-five. (Dufau, "Traité de Statisque," 1840; Block, "L'Europe Politique," 1870.) From 1825 to 1838 the indictments (excluding political crimes and fiscal misdemeanors) rose from 57,470 to 80,920. In 1838 the indictments increased from 237 (to the 100,000) to 375; in 1847 to 480; from 1854–55 to 1866 they sank to 389, to increase again to 517 in 1874, and to 552 in 1889. There was, then, an increase of about 133% in 50 years. (Joly, "France Criminelle," p. 10.)

In Austria there were:

In 1856,	1	conviction	to	1238	inhabitants,	1	indictment	to 832
" 1857,	1	"	"	1191	"	1	"	" 813
" 1860,	1	"	"	1261	"	1	"	" 933
" 1861,	1	"	"	1178	"	1	"	" 808
" 1862,	1	"	"	1082	"	1	"	" 749

(Messedaglia.)

In England and Wales there was:

From 1811	to 1815	1	prisoner	to	each	1210	inhabitants
" 1826	" 1830	1	"	"	"	568	"
" 1826	" 1830	1	"	"	"	477	"
" 1846	" 1848	1	"	"	"	455	"

From 1805 to 1841 the population increased 49%, the crimes six times more than the population. In some counties, Monmouthshire for example,

But Messedaglia rightly observes in this connection how easy it is to make a mistake in attempting to solve, on the basis of statistics alone, complex problems into which many factors enter at the same time. The continual increase of crime and insanity can, in fact, be explained by changes in the civil and penal laws, by a greater tendency to bring accusations, by the easier access to asylums for the insane, and by the greater activity of the police.

One thing appears certain: civilization and barbarism alike possess crimes peculiar to them. Barbarism, by deadening the moral sensibilities, diminishes the horror of homicide, which is frequently admired as an heroic act. By making revenge a duty and confusing might with right, it increases crimes of blood and encourages associations of malefactors, just as among the insane it develops religious mania, demonomania, and imitative insanity. On the other hand, family ties are stronger, while sexual excitement and insane ambition are less frequent, and consequently parricide, infanticide, and theft are less frequent.

The types of civilization which man has hitherto produced, according to Guglielmo Ferrero, are two: the type characterized by violence, and that characterized by fraud. They are distinguished by the form which the struggle for existence takes. In the primitive civilization the struggle is carried on purely by force, and wealth and power are achieved by arms, at the expense either of foreigners or of weaker fellow-citizens. Commercial competition between two peoples is carried on through armies and fleets, that is to say, by the violent expulsion of competitors from coveted markets. Judicial contests are decided by the duel. In the civilization characterized by fraud, on the other hand, the struggle for existence is carried on by cunning and deceit, and the wager of battle is replaced by legal chicanery; political power is obtained, no longer at the point of

the population increased about 128%, crimes 720%. (Aberdeen, "Discorso," 1876.)

In Italy there were:

From 1850 to 1859, 16,173 indictments for serious crimes, and 7,535 convictions.

From 1860 to 1869, 23,854 indictments, and 10,701 convictions.

From 1863 to 1869 crimes increased one-tenth, the population about one-twentieth (Curcio, *op. cit.*)

the sword, but by money; money is extracted from the pockets of others by tricks and mysterious maneuvers, such as the operations of the stock-exchange. The commercial warfare is carried on through the perfection of the means of production, but still more through the perfection of the art of deceit, the skill acquired in giving the purchaser the impression that he is getting a good bargain.[1] To the first type there belong Corsica, part of Sardinia, Montenegro, the Italian cities of the Middle Ages, and in general nearly all primitive civilizations. To the second type, on the other hand, belong all the modern civilized nations, that is to say, those among whom the capitalistic régime has reached its complete development. The distinction between the two types is not, however, so absolute in reality as it is in theory, for characteristics belonging to the two different types are often found mixed together in the same society.

Now since pathology, in the social field as in the physical, follows in the pathway of physiology, we discover these same two means of contest in the criminal world. As a matter of fact, there are two forms of criminality manifesting themselves in our day side by side: atavistic criminality, which is a return on the part of certain individuals of morbid constitution to the violent means of the struggle for existence now suppressed by civilization, such as homicide, robbery, and rape; and "evolutive" criminality, which is no less perverted in intent but more civilized in the means employed, for in place of violence it uses trickery and deceit.[2] Into the first class of criminals fall only a few individuals, fatally predisposed to crime; into the second any one may come who has not a character strong enough to resist the evil influences in his environment.

Sighele rightly observes that the same division occurs in the two forms of "collective criminality," which are to be found, the one in the upper and the other in the lower ranks of society. On the one side are the rich or well-to-do, who in politics and business sell their votes and influence, and by the aid of intrigue, deceit, and speculation steal money from the public. On the other hand are the poor and ignorant, who, in anarchist plots,

[1] Ferrero, "Violenti e Frodolenti in Romagna," in "Il Mondo Criminale Italiano," Milan, 1894.

[2] Sighele, "Delinquenza Settaria," Milan, 1898.

in demonstrations, and in insurrections, attempt to revolt against the situation into which they are forced and the wickedness of those in high places. The first of these two forms is essentially modern and evolved, the second is atavistic, brutal, violent; the former is a thing of the brain, and proceeds by cunning device, like imposture, misappropriation, or forgery; the latter is a thing of the muscles, and works by violent means, like insurrection, bomb-throwing, or assassination. Italy in the last few years has offered only too frequently the sad spectacle of the simultaneous breaking out of both forms of criminality. On the one hand, we have had in Sicily brigandage and famine riots, to which a pious or interested lie has given another name and ascribed other causes, and at the same time we have seen at Rome, in connection with the bank scandals, the gross immorality of the wealthy classes.

I have given in my "Homme Criminel" examples of crimes of blood committed in the Middle Ages by special associations. But it may be asked, "Why, if in ancient times these criminal associations existed everywhere, have they persisted in certain countries only, disappearing from the others?" The answer is easy if we consider the partially civilized condition of the peoples, and especially the condition of the governments which maintain and foster this barbarism, the first and continual source of these perverted associations. "The more governments are organized as parties," says d'Azeglio very truly, "the more will parties organize themselves into governments." When the royal post-office violated the privacy of letters, and, bargaining with the thieves, allowed them full liberty for all their excesses in brothels and prisons, the very necessities of the situation contributed to protect the Camorrist, for he was the one person who could carry a letter safely, protect one from assassination, ransom a stolen object at a fair price, or even pronounce, in minor matters, judgments doubtless as just as, and certainly quicker and less costly than, those offered by the regular tribunals. The Camorra was a kind of natural adaptation to the unhappy circumstances of a people rendered barbarous by bad government.

Brigandage, in its turn, has often been a kind of wild justice against oppressors. In the period of serfdom in Russia, the moujiks, indifferent to life and embittered by constant suffering for which no one cared, were all ready to avenge themselves by homicide, as is proved to us by a song made public by Dixon. "There is no great Russian family," says the well-known author of the work on European prisons, "which does not include in its history the violent death of one of its members." The immobilization of capital and avarice drove the rich men of southern Italy to usury and unbelievable plundering of the poor peasants.

"In Fondi," writes Jorioz, "many became brigands on account of the extortions of the mayor, Amante. Coppa, Masini, and Tortora were driven to brigandage by the way their inhabitants were abused with impunity." "The peasants of southern Italy," said Govone to the investigating committee, "see in the brigand the avenger of the injustice with which society overwhelms them. The dissensions between rich and poor over the division of certain lands which formerly belonged to ancient barons but of which the title was now in doubt, or which had been promised to all, especially to the poor farmers; the hatred which divided the few representatives of the lesser nobility in the communes of southern Italy; and the acts of vengeance practiced against the clients of one or another — these were the principal causes of brigandage. Of 124 communes in Basilicata there were only 44 without a brigand, and these were the only ones where the administration was in the hands of honest mayors. Of the two communes, Bomba and Montazzoli, near Chieti, the first, where the poor were well treated, had no brigands, while the second, where they were abused, had a great number of brigands." "In the small estates of southern Italy," observes Villari very truly, "the Middle Ages still exist in the midst of modern civilization, only in place of the ancient baron we have to-day the plebeian creditor." "We have in Sicily," writes Franchetti, "a class of peasants who are almost slaves of the soil; a second class, consisting of persons who consider themselves superior to the law; and a third, and this the most numerous, who regard the law as useless and have exalted to the dignity of a principle the custom of securing justice for themselves by their own efforts. And where the majesty of the law is misunderstood and despised, its representatives cannot be respected. The public official in Sicily is flattered and fawned upon so long as the originators of the abuses and tyrannies there hope to have him for an accomplice, or at least as a silent spectator of their misdeeds; but as soon as a man is discovered who is faithful to his duty, he is detested, hunted, assailed, and opposed by every possible means."

"After the abolition of feudalism," continues Franchetti in

another place, "the external form of the social relationships had to change, even if the real nature of those relationships did not. The absolute power of the great had ceased to be a legal institution, together with the jurisdiction and police power of the nobility. The instrument which must now be employed to cover up abuses was the officer of the state or city. But bribery did not always suffice to secure his connivance; it was necessary to employ special artifice. Some device must be used to acquire or retain control over those whose economic condition did not directly reduce them to practical slavery. Brute force had to give place, in part, to trickery and cunning. . . . But for all that, violence was not done away with, at least in a large part of the island. Nothing had come to break up the ancient traditions, and the instruments for carrying them into effect had not ceased to exist. The former officers of the feudal barons, though thrust to one side, were still there, to say nothing of the men who had already committed some crime, or were ready to do so, and who could not fail to be numerous in a country where the opportunity for crime and the powerlessness of the law were traditional. But now the officers, like the criminals, plied their trade on their own account, and whoever wanted their aid had to treat with them both."[1]

"The word *malandrino* in Sicily loses its significance as a term of infamy and comes to be used among the people as a laudatory designation, proudly borne by many honorable persons. 'I am a brigand (*malandrino*)' means for them that the speaker claims to be a brave man, afraid of nothing, especially not afraid of justice, which they confuse with the government, or, rather, with the police."[2]

This false conception of morals, this lack of perception of the distance between honesty and double-dealing, explains how it is that the brigand finds accomplices among the peasants and even among the proprietors, with whom he lives and who regard crime as a new means of speculation. This state of things, according to the reports of the prefects, is the worst plague in Sicily, for while the real brigands who roam the country are few in number, at certain times they become legion, reinforced by their peasant auxiliaries. Further, the great proprietors themselves make use of the brigands for the purpose of exacting ransoms, annulling wills, and establishing their tyranny over their

[1] Franchetti, "Condizioni Politiche e Amministrative della Sicilia," Florence.

[2] Tomassi-Crudeli, *op. cit.*

fellow-citizens. From this comes also their repugnance to laying information, which seems to them more immoral than murder itself, so that a dying man may conceal the name of his murderer to the last. It is not homicide that arouses their aversion, but the law. Accordingly, in the few cases in which accusation is brought, the crime still goes generally without punishment. Thus in the province of Naples, of 150 brigands taken with arms in their hands, 107 were acquitted by the jury, and only 7 convicted.[1] The situation is the same in the Romagna, as Alfred Comandini has shown us,[2] and, according to Bourde and Bournet, in Corsica also.

"The cause of all our ills," writes Comandini, "is the abuse of wine, the wide-spread custom of carrying arms, and the political associations that have come down as a tradition from the despotic times when all classes took part in them even at the peril of their lives. Their aspirations were honorable, but very often they favored the escape of a prisoner, because, if arrested, he might betray them. These associations have no longer any political or educative aim, not even that of mutual assistance. They afford oftenest only an occasion for drinking together, generally at the expense of the richer members, and this usually degenerates into fighting and brawling, in which from their traditional duty of aiding one another large numbers are frequently involved."

But even more significant than the situation in the Romagna is the example which Corsica gives of an unconscious criminality, derived from social-historical conditions, as well as from the purely historical influences already pointed out.

"The frequency of murders committed out of revenge," writes Bournet,[3] "is known to all the world, but it is not so well known how trivial the causes often are. That a dog belonging to a Tafani was killed by a Rocchino caused the death of eleven members of the two families. In 1886 there were 135 attacks upon persons, or 1 to 200 inhabitants; that is to say, four times more than in the department of the Seine. Of these 135 attacks, 52 were made as a result of quarrels and brawls. No witness can be made to testify. In Palermo there were 60 persons present at a crime, all of whom swore that they had seen nothing."

[1] Jorioz, "Il Brigantaggio," 1875.
[2] "Le Romagne," Verona, 1881.
[3] Bournet, "Criminalité en Corse," 1887, in "Archivio di Psich.," VIII.

Bourde, following the reports of the constabulary, estimates the number of bandits at from 500 to 600.

"It all comes back to this," he says, "that the peasants in remote villages, who are enemies to the chief of the clan, are persuaded that there is no justice. The Corsicans are very proud, scorn physical labor, and till the soil only unwillingly. They are better endowed intellectually than morally, and have a way of their own of regarding good fortune and conscience. Their organization is very similar to the Roman patrician system. Fifteen or twenty families rule all the rest, some having control of only a hundred votes, others having thousands of electors to express their will. For two hundred years fifty families have been devoted to a single one. Independent life is impossible, for he who stands alone comes to nothing. The members of a family risk their lives with a sublime self-abnegation for the sake of one of their number. Two consciences struggle for supremacy in the island, the modern conscience, inspired by the principles of right and equity, and the ancient Corsican conscience, which cannot raise itself above the interests of the family association. The latter generally prevails, and the effects of it were seen in the proceedings of the jury which valued the land condemned for the railways. The jury, presided over by Casabianca, the chief of the most powerful party in the island, made itself notorious by its partiality. Benedetti, an enemy of the party, received 2000 francs for a vineyard of 17 ares, while a certain Virgitti, a follower of Casabianca's, received 13,000 francs for a vineyard of 19 ares, and so on. In Corsica even the victims thought these injustices natural, and would have practiced them themselves if they had had the power. The justices of the peace are all-powerful, but very partial and devoted to the interest of the party that has elected them. In making up the voting lists they do as they like, striking off the names of those who might injure them, and adding the names of those who may be useful; and this in spite of the courts of appeal and cassation. Serious crimes not infrequently result. The artifices employed at elections are numerous and varied, and often have a tragic ending. At Palneca the mayor, Bartoli, three times postponed the voting, waiting for a favorable moment. The fourth time (Sept. 28, 1884) he and his partisans fortified themselves early in the morning in the town hall, and when their adversaries arrived they could not enter. These, exasperated, attempted to storm the place, but were repulsed with fire-arms. All day shots were exchanged from one house to the other, with deaths and wounds resulting. Bartoli's opponents told the prefect that they 'would rather die than endure such slavery.' In 1885 in all France there were 42,523 misdemeanors in rural districts. Corsica alone had 13,405 of them, nearly a third!"[1]

The progress of civilization, by endlessly multiplying needs and desires, and by encouraging sensuality through the accumulation of wealth, brings a flood of alcoholics and general paralytics into the insane asylums, and crowds the prisons with offenders against property and against decency. Statistics show us, in fact, that most crimes of this character committed in the great cities among the cultivated classes are on the increase.[2] Sighele shows us for his part that modern collective criminality has the same characteristics.

[1] Bourde, "En Corse," 1887. Arch. di Psich., VIII.
[2]

	Crimes against persons	Suicides	Thefts	Offences against decency
Prussia, 1854	8.9 %	.43%	88.41%	2.26%
" 1859	16.65%	.52%	78.17%	4.68%

(Oettingen, *op. cit.*)

France:

From 1831 to 1835:

Indecent assaults upon		Abortions	Infanticides	Suicides	Thefts	Homicides
Adults	Children					
2.95%	3.64%	.19%	2.25%	3.83%	14.40%	14.40%

From 1856 to 1860:

6.20%	20.59%	.97%	67.45%	6.18%	11.83%	11.83%

The ratio of burglaries and highway robberies in Corsica to those in France was	as 0.38	to 1
Of rapes	" 0.50	" 1
" parricides and bankruptcies	" 0.	" 1
" extortions	" 3.	" 1
" rapes of young girls	" 23.	" 1
" homicides	" 32.	" 1

(Robiquet, "Les Crimes en Corse," 1862.)

Confronted by these two forms of collective criminality it is natural to ask ourselves, "Why does the criminality of the rich take the form of cunning, while that of the poor is based upon violence?" The answer is easy. The upper classes represent what is really modern, while the lower still belong in thought and feeling to a relatively distant past. It is, then, logical and natural that the former should show the result of modern development in their collective criminality, and that the latter should remain, on the contrary, still violent, not to say absolutely atavistic.

Bagehot has said:

"In order to be persuaded that fineness of feeling diminishes in proportion as one descends the social scale, it is not necessary to visit savage peoples; it is enough to talk with the English poor, or even with one's own servants."[1]

In the second place, if the criminality of the rich is a pathological phenomenon indicative of the defectiveness of the ancient social organization that has come down to us, that of the lower class, on the contrary, may appear to be the premature announcement of a new era about to arise. It is for this reason that the former bears all the marks of senile cunning, while the latter has the reckless audacity of youthful strength. Finally, the rich constitute the majority, if not in number, at least in power and in the strength of their position. The poor, on the other hand, represent the minority. Now it is characteristic of all minorities to be bolder and more violent than the majority. They have to conquer, while the majority have only to keep what they have gained. More energy is called out by the chance to attain something, or reach a distant goal, than by the need of guarding a present possession. Victory softens and enervates, while the desire to conquer increases the courage a hundredfold.[2] It is, in fact, with a minority as it is with a single individual who is attacked by a number of persons. Such a one shows a degree of strength which he would not at all manifest if others were at hand to aid him. Necessity increases the de-

[1] Bagehot, "Lois Scientifiques du Developpement des Nations," Paris, 1880.

[2] Sighele, *op. cit.*

fensive power of those who stand alone and feel their weakness. The instinct of self-preservation, aroused by danger, gives to the organism the courage of despair. In the field of crime this natural law cannot fail to show itself among the lower classes, who have to contend against great odds and make up for their natural weakness by the boldness and violence of the means they employ.

However painful it may be to admit that civilization has succeeded only in changing the kind of crimes, and perhaps in increasing their number, the fact itself is easy to understand, when one sees how much more advantageous the progress of education has been for attack than for defense.

§ 27. Congestion of Population

To the reasons which we have just enumerated must be added others of a different order. On account of railways, and governmental and commercial concentration, civilization tends continually to make the great centers of population still larger and to overpopulate the principal cities. And, as is well known, it is in these that are found crowded together the greatest number of habitual criminals. This unfortunate concentration of crime is to be explained by the greater profits or the greater security which the large cities offer to criminals. But this, perhaps, is not the only reason, for if in the cities vigilance is more relaxed, prosecution is more active and systematic; and if temptations and inducements to crime are more numerous, so are the opportunities for honest labor. I believe that there is another influence at work which is more powerful still. The very congestion of population by itself gives an irresistible impulse toward crime and immorality.

"There is," writes Bertillon, "a kind of violent and morbid tendency that moves us to reproduce the feelings and movements which we see around us. Many causes contribute to this: youth, femininity, and above all (as Sarcey says) the mutual contact of sentient persons, which gives added strength to the natural impressions that each one has by himself. The air is filled with the dominant opinion, and transmits it like a contagion."

It has been observed that even the crowding together of horses develops the tendency to sodomy. All these causes, together with the parallelism that always exists between the development of the sexual organs and that of the brain, and also with better nutrition, partly explain for us the great increase of crimes of sensuality, a characteristic of modern criminality harmonizing with the constant increase of prostitution so marked in the large cities. It is for this reason that women are more criminal in the more civilized countries. They are almost always drawn into crime by a false pride about their poverty, by a desire for luxury, and by masculine occupations and education, which give them the means and opportunity to commit crimes of the same character as the men, such as forgeries, crimes against the laws of the press, and swindling. Civilization increases the number of certain crimes, just as it increases certain forms of insanity[1] (paralysis, alcoholism), because it increases the use of stimulants, which, while almost unknown to savages, have become a veritable necessity to the civilized world. Thus we see to-day in England and America, that in addition to the abuse of alcohol and tobacco there is creeping in that of opium and even of ether; and that in France the consumption of brandy grew from eight liters in 1840 to thirty in 1870.

§ 28. The Press

Civilization, by favoring the creation and dissemination of newspapers, which are always a chronicle of vices and crimes, and often are nothing else, has furnished a new cause of crime by

[1] Taking, for example, the statistics of the most advanced country in the world — the United States — we see in the valuable Census of the United States (Compendium of the Tenth Census (1880) of the United States, Pt. II, p. 1659) that the insane, who numbered 15,610 in 1850, 24,042 in 1860, and 37,432 in 1870, had increased by 1880 to 91,997; while the population, which was 23,191,876 in 1850, reached 38,558,371 in 1870, and 50,155,783 in 1880. That is to say, while the population doubled itself in thirty years, the number of the insane increased six times; further, in the last ten years the population increased 30%, but the number of the insane 155%. — In England and Wales there were in 1859 18.6 insane persons to the 10,000; in 1885, 28.9; in 1893, 39. — In Italy ("Archivio Italiano per le Malattie Nervose," 1888, Verga) there were in 1874 51 of the insane to 100,000; in 1877, 54.1; in 1880, 61.25; in 1883, 67.7; in 1885, 66.0; in 1888, 74.

inciting criminals to emulation and imitation. It is sad to think that the crime of Troppmann brought the circulation of the *Petit Journal* up to 500,000 and that of the *Figaro* to 210,000, and it was doubtless for this reason that this crime was imitated almost immediately in Belgium and in Italy. Note the following strange crime. During the absence of the proprietor R. his strong box was forced. His assistant was immediately arrested and the exact sum taken was found upon him, — indeed, the assistant admitted of his own accord that he had taken the money, but without evil intent. He had, in fact, without the necessity of breaking into the safe, much larger sums under his control, and this with the consent of his employer, who had great confidence in him. He had committed the crime, he said, only in order to try a trick that he had read the day before in the newspaper. His employer, knowing him to be a constant reader of the papers, declared that he accepted this explanation, and as soon as the assistant had been acquitted reinstated him in his position. In Paris in 1873 one Grimal decided to commit a crime in order to get himself talked of, like certain great criminals of whose exploits he read in the newspapers. With this aim he committed arson, but notwithstanding his confession his guilt was not believed. He maltreated his wife with the result that she died, and avowed himself the cause of her death, but he came out of this affair also with the verdict of "not guilty." Then it was that the case of the widow Gras fell under his eye, and in order to imitate it he threw nitric acid into a friend's face, thereby killing him, and then went about telling everyone of his crime. The next day he first hastened to read the account of the murder in the *Petit Journal*, and immediately afterwards went to give himself up as a prisoner. It was perfectly obvious that reading criminal tales and various other reports in the papers suggested to him the idea of his crimes.

The same may be said of those novels which deal almost exclusively with the acts of criminals, like those at present fashionable in France. Thus in 1866 two young men, Brouiller and Serreau, strangled a tradeswoman. When arrested they declared that the crime had been suggested to them by reading a novel by Delmons. "Some," says La Place very truly, "have received from nature an organism inclined to evil, but their inclination is turned into action only by hearing or seeing the misdeeds of others." Some years ago a package of ten stolen bonds was found done up in a paper, upon which the thief had written these gloomy lines taken from a novel by Bourrasque: "Conscience is a word invented to frighten fools and to make them submissive in their misery. Thrones and millions are only to be gained by violence and fraud." In the great cities many are incited to crime in the places where cheap lodgings may be obtained for the night. "Many," says Mayhew, "are brought to the lodging-house through being thrown out of work, and from the lodging-house are drawn into theft."

The political laws and the new forms of popular government imposed by modern civilization, and in part also by a pretended liberty, favor in every way the formation of societies, under the pretext of social amusements, administrative enterprises, or mutual aid. The example of Palermo, Leghorn, Ravenna, Bologna, the history of Luciani and Pagge, and that of Crispi and Nicotera, show us how short the distance is from such generous enterprises to the most immoral violence and even to crime. In North America some societies have gone so far as to commit crime with impunity, and in two of the most flourishing cities (New York and San Francisco) even officially, and have almost succeeded in legitimizing their frauds. The political revolutions which are more frequent with these forms of government cause an increase of certain crimes, either because they bring together crowds of people or because they excite violent passions. "Spain is a prison," says an illustrious Spaniard, "where it is possible to commit any crime whatever with impunity, provided one cries in favor of this or that, or gives to his crime a political appearance." The number of criminals acquitted there rose in five years to 4065, four times what they were in France.[1] It is not astonishing, then, that in Spain crimes are proportionately more numerous than elsewhere.

Wars, like revolutions, increase the number of crimes, because of the increased massing and contact of men, — as was proved in Italy in 1866 (Curcio), and in North America during

[1] Armengol, "Estudios Penitenciarios," 1873.

and after the Civil War.[1] Sexual crimes, which before the Revolution of 1848 in France were from 100 to 200, increased first to 280 and then to 505, and with them illegitimate births increased also.

After all this it is easy to comprehend, without the necessity of citing figures, how much crime is increased when the criminals are herded together in prisons, where, according to the avowal of the criminals themselves, the greatest wickedness is a title to glory, and virtue is a badge of shame. Civilization, by multiplying great penitentiaries, gives by that same means a greater extension to crime. This is the more true since a blamable solicitude has introduced charitable and philanthropic institutions (reform schools, etc.) which suffice to undermine the character of respectable individuals, but not to soften the heart of a hardened culprit. We shall see how, after the introduction of the ticket-of-leave, there was noted in 1861–62 in England a great increase of delinquents, as had already occurred in 1834 after the inauguration of the transportation system.[2] The houses of correction, which seem inspired by a truly humanitarian feeling of charity, through the single fact of their bringing together a mass of depraved individuals exercise an influence quite other than salutary and almost always directly opposite to that for which they were instituted. It is worth noting here that the illustrious Olivecrona attributed the great number of Swedish recidivists to the vices of the penitentiary system and to the custom of submitting young offenders to the same discipline as the adults.[3]

§ 29. New Crimes

Civilization introduces every day new crimes, less atrocious perhaps than the old ones but none the less injurious. Thus in London the thief substitutes cunning for violence; in place of burglary he practices purloining by means of special apparatus;

[1] Corre, op. cit. p. 78.

[2] From 2649 in 1863–64, the criminals increased to 15,049 in 1873–74. In the colonies to which those convicted for crimes of violence were transported, these crimes increased until they were half as numerous as all others, while in England they remained only one-eighth as numerous. (Beltrano-Scalia, 1874.)

[3] "Des Causes ce la Récidivie," Stockholm, 1873.

in place of porch-climbing he uses swindling and blackmail by the aid of the press.[1] Homicide with the aim of getting the benefit of life insurance is an example of a new form of crime committed by some physicians, and favored too often by new advances in scientific knowledge. Thus the knowledge that the symptoms of arsenic poisoning are similar to those of cholera suggested to two doctors, during the cholera epidemic in Magdeburg and Monaco, the idea of first insuring and then poisoning many of their patients.[2] In Vienna a new crime has been invented which consists in appropriating goods that have been ordered for an imaginary society.[3] The anarchists have brought into fashion the use of dynamite against persons and buildings. Recently there has been introduced in Chicago the electric bludgeon, and also a small torpedo, which, being slipped into the intended victim's pocket, explodes and blows him to pieces. Civilization, by relaxing the bonds of the family, not only increases the number of foundling asylums, which are the nurseries of criminals, but also multiplies the desertions of adults, rapes, and infanticides.

Notwithstanding these unhappy consequences, we must not allow ourselves to be led into an indiscriminate condemnation of the fruitful progress of civilization, since even in the matter of crime the change has not been altogether prejudicial, for, if for the time civilization has been the cause of the increase of crime, it has certainly mitigated its character. On the other hand, where progress has reached its height it has already found means of treating the diseases it has produced, with its asylums for the criminal insane, its system of separate confinement in the penitentiaries, its industrial institutions, its savings banks, and especially its societies for the protection of children, which prevent crime almost from the cradle. (See Part III.)

[1] "Quart. Review," 1871.
[2] Pettenkoffer, "Theorie der Cholera," 1871.
[3] Rundschau, Vienna, 1876.

CHAPTER V

DENSITY OF POPULATION — IMMIGRATION AND EMIGRATION — BIRTH-RATE

§ 30. Density of Population

THE influence of civilization in reference to crime may be seen better by examining one by one its different factors, and in the first place that of density; for history teaches us that crime appears only when a certain density of population has been reached.

Prostitution, assaults, thefts (as Reclus, Westermarck, and Krapotkin have rightly remarked), show themselves but rarely in primitive society; as among the Veddahs, who assemble only at the rainy seasons, and among certain Australian aborigines, who meet only for the yam harvest. It is for the same reason that when animals are not associated together or domesticated the equivalent of crime rarely appears among them, because their brutal instincts lack the means of manifesting themselves. When circumstances change, and the formation of tribes and clans gives opportunity for it, crime, which has hitherto lain dormant, breaks out with violence. Even among the less compact barbarous societies crime is relatively rare, even if more ferocious; while in our more civilized society crime multiplies, and the five or six forms of crime prevalent among barbarians have become with us legion.

A single glance at the thefts, homicides, and political upheavals of Europe in reference to density of population shows us that (with the exception of some contradictions, the result of the effect of temperature, which increases homicides and insurrections in the south and thefts in the north) theft increases with density, while homicide diminishes. We see, in fact, in the following table, that of seven countries having a low density, only two, Spain and Hungary, have very high figures for homicide; and of eight countries having a maximum density, Italy alone shows a great number of homicides. The reverse is true with regard to thefts. With regard to revolts we can come to no immediate conclusion; for we see in countries of equal density (Poland, Austria, Switzerland) the greatest differences in the number of revolutions, while revolutions are lacking in other countries with great differences of density, like England, Russia, and Hungary. In the Middle Ages Corsica, with a very sparse population, had a great number of revolutions, forty-five in four centuries, according to Ferrari.

CRIMES AND DENSITY IN EUROPEAN COUNTRIES

Population to the square mile	Countries	Homicides [1] to 1,000,000 inhabitants	Thefts [2] to 100,000 inhabitants	Insurrections [3] to 10,000,000 inhabitants
47	Russia	14	...	...
85	Sweden and Norway	13	...	13
85	Denmark	13	...	13
85	Spain [4]	58	53	55
132	Portugal	25	80	58
158	Austria [4]	25	103	5
158	Hungary	75	103	5
171	Poland	10	...	13
179	Switzerland	16	114	80
184	France [4]	18	116	16
223	Germany [4]	5	200	5
259	Italy [4]	96	72	30
290	England [4]	7	136	7
316	Ireland	9	91	30
420	Belgium	18	134	...

The influence of density of population appears more clearly in our country, especially if one examines the various crimes in

[1] "Almanach de Gotha," 1886–87.
[2] Ferri, "Omicidio," 1895.
[3] Lombroso and Laschi, "Le Crime Politique," Turin, 1895.
[4] Bodio, "Relazione della Commissione per la Statistica Giudiziaria," 1896.

detail with reference to the different degrees of density. In Italy for example, we find: [1]

Number of Crimes to 100,000 Inhabitants

Population to the sq. kilometer	Homicides	Thefts	Resistance to police	Rapes	Swindling
From 20 to 50	11.0	199.0	23.7	18.8	52.6
" 50 " 100	6.03	144.4	25.4	16.4	45.0
" 100 " 150	6.0	148.0	23.5	14.5	58.5
" 150 " 200	5.1	153.0	24.6	12.3	54.6
" 200 upwards	3.5	158.0	29.5	18.7	50.4

We see, therefore, that homicide decreases as the density increases, especially in the great cities, so that Milan, Naples, Leghorn, and Genoa, with the most different races and climates (Greek, Celtic, Ligurian), give a like decrease in the number of homicides; and on the contrary we see the number regularly increase where the density is least, that is to say, in the hotter parts of the country, and in the islands, where society is more barbarous and criminal bands more common.

Theft, rape, and resistance to the officers of the law also diminish with the increase in density, to rise again rapidly, however, with the excessive density of the great cities (Padua, Naples, Milan, Venice). Swindling follows an irregular course, but nearly always in the direction opposite to the density, — a fact which arises from the strong participation of the islands, especially Sardinia, in this crime, and also from the strong bias in favor of old racial customs in the provinces of Forli and Bologna, where swindling is widespread. The latter place is proverbial for swindling, and Dante in his *Inferno* makes Venedico say: "I am not the only Bolognese weeping here; this whole place is full of them." [2]

So also in the recent French statistics we find the following: [3]

[1] Bodio, "Annuario Statistico Italiano," 1894, Rome.

[2] *E non pur io qui piango Bolognese:*
Anzi n'e questo luogo tanto pieno.
Canto XVIII.

[3] Ferri, "Omicidio," 1895.

Population to the square kilometer	Number of crimes to 100,000 inhabitants		
	Thefts	Homicides	Rapes
20 to 40	63	4.41	19.0
40 " 60	96	1.42	20.4
60 " 80	100	1.40	19.0
80 " 100	116	1.20	30.0
100 and over	196	1.88	34.0

We see that theft becomes more and more frequent as the density increases. Homicides and rapes, on the contrary, show the highest proportion with the minimum or the maximum of the density. This contradiction is explained by the fact that where the population is most compact occur the great industrial (Seine-Inférieure, 92) and political (Paris, 18) centers, and ports of immigration (Boûches-du-Rhône, 45), where the opportunities for conflict are more frequent; and where there is the minimum of density (Corsica, 200); Lozère, 41; Hautes-Alpes, 24) there is the maximum of barbarism, and we have seen that assaults and assassination are there often regarded more as necessities than as crimes.

The same thing is true of political insurrections, as I have proved in my " Crime Politique." A study of the revolutionary and of the ultra-conservative populations of the French departments shows that the former are always more numerous in the districts where the density is greater. In studying the relationships of the density of population and the monarchical reaction in France, we find that in the departments with the denser population popular opinion is more inclined toward republican ideas. On the other hand, Basses-Alpes, Landes, Indre, Cher, and Lozère, which have no more than forty inhabitants to the square kilometer, in the elections of 1877–81–83 gave a high percentage of votes to the monarchical party. The same is true in Vendée, Nord, Hautes-Pyrénées, Gers, Lôt, and Aveyron, which have not over sixty to the square kilometer; and a similar phenomenon has been noticed in the case of the plebiscites (Jacoby).

When, on the contrary, the population reaches a high degree of density, as in the departments of the Rhône, the Loire, Seine-et-Oise, and Seine-Inférieure, we see the revolutionary spirit take on a great development, as Jacoby has already remarked (*op. cit.*). The greatest revolutionary tendency is found in the departments with a compact population, followed by those with a moderate density; while in the departments with a minimum density the conservatives prevail.

It is easy to understand that where the urban population is densest political agitation is also most frequent. This is to be noticed especially in Paris, where, as Viollet-le-Duc writes,[1] "the whole civilized world empties its scum, making a cosmopolitan city where a mob without country, principles, or traditions presumptuously directs the elections, and takes advantage of the misfortunes of the country to overturn the government and put itself in power." Thus it was that after the Commune, out of 36,809 individuals arrested, there were 1725 foreigners and 25,648 provincials.

"It is the failing of countries too thickly populated," concludes Maxime du Camp, "that in them the provincial life can be developed only imperfectly.

"Great capitals are dangerous for the political peace. They are like a suction-pump: they draw everything in and let nothing out. France has too big a head, and like a hydrocephalous patient is subject to real outbursts of maniacal fury. Such an outburst was the Commune."

On the whole the influence of race and climate blots out that of density, but the influence of this latter is still to be detected, both in the number of thefts, which it increases, and of homicides, which it diminishes.

§ 31. Immigration and Emigration

It is an undeniable fact that there exists a striking contrast between Italy and France, a complete contradiction, which, as we shall see, applies to wealth as well as to crime. In Italy homicides decrease regularly with the increase in density of the population, while in France they increase extraordinarily when the maximum density is reached (though Paris, to be sure, in

[1] "Mémoires sur la Défense de Paris," 1871.

this regard falls below Seine-et-Oise, which surrounds it). The contradiction is, however, explicable. The situation in Italy is due to the increasing influence of civilization exercised by the great centers, which diminishes the traditional propensity to regard the taking of life in revenge as a duty or even as a right; and further it is due to the degree of what Ferri calls "criminal saturation," caused by the excessive number of crimes of blood, so great as to be incapable of further increase. The contrast offered by France, however, is due to the special condition there produced by a new element, namely, immigration, which is lacking in Italy. This increases the density of the population, it is true, but in a manner particularly fraught with consequences, since it introduces into the country more than 1,000,000 foreigners at an age and under conditions which render them especially prone to crime, and further concentrates the process at certain points only. In fact, the maximum of homicides, 45, is given by Boûches-du-Rhône, a department which is one of the great centers of immigration, having 50,000 Italian residents. If, however, we take Joly's graphic presentation of criminality by the native country of the criminal, thus eliminating the factor of immigration, we find that Boûches-du-Rhône goes down from the maximum degree, 86, to 62; Hérault from 81 to 63, Alpes Maritimes from 83 to 45; without speaking of the department of the Seine, where out of 40,000 persons arrested only 13,000 were born in the department, for if Paris imports a great many rogues, she exports a great many also. Hérault itself would have a good record, but one city (Cette) spoils everything. Of 10 persons indicted it furnishes nearly 7; it supplies by itself half of the cases tried at the court in Montpellier, a fact due especially to the great number of recidivists, who throng here and sleep in the open, and to the foreigners. In 1889 there were 21 foreigners indicted to 118 residents; that is to say, while the proportion of natives was 2 to the 1000, that of foreigners was 19 to 1000. The same thing is true in Marseilles of the laborers working at the port. "It is these foreigners," writes Joly, "who furnish the strongest contingent to the thefts, assassinations, anarchistic riots, assaults, etc."

In 1881	there	were	17	rapes	to	1,000,000	French
"	"	"	"	60	"	"	"	foreigners
In 1872	"	"	18	"	"	"	French
"	"	"	"	46	"	"	"	foreigners

It was known already that the immigrants showed a high degree of criminality.

From the recent statistics of the United States [1] it is seen that the States which receive the greatest number of immigrants, especially Irish and Italians, give the highest number of crimes. Thus:

California	0.30	criminals	to	1000	population,	33%	immigrants
Nevada	0.31	"	"	"	"	41%	"
Wyoming	0.35	"	"	"	"	28%	"
Montana	0.19	"	"	"	"	29%	"
Arizona	0.16	"	"	"	"	39%	"
New York	0.27	"	"	"	"	23%	"

On the other hand,

New Mexico	0.03	"	"	"	"	6.7%	immigrants
Pennsylvania	0.11	"	"	"	"	13.0%	"

This runs counter to the notion of the effect of density of population upon crime. Montana with 0.3 inhabitants to the square mile, Wyoming with 0.2, Nevada with 0.6, and Arizona with 0.4 have, notwithstanding their low density, an enormous contingent of crimes, on account of immigration; while New York, with 151 inhabitants to the square mile, and Pennsylvania, with 95 inhabitants to the square mile, where the density is very great, have a much lower criminality. The District of Columbia also, which contains 2960 inhabitants to the square mile, shows relatively low figures.

Of 49,000 individuals arrested in New York 32,000 were immigrants.[2]

Of 38,000 prisoners in North America, 20,000 were children of foreigners.[3]

In France it has already been observed that in 1886

of 100,000		settled residents	8	came	before	the	courts
"	"	who had changed residence	29	"	"	"	"
"	"	foreigners	41	"	"	"	"

[1] "Compendium of the Tenth Census (1880) of the United States." Pt. II, p. 1659.

[2] Brace, "The Dangerous Classes."

[3] Bertrami-Scalia, *op. cit.*

At present in France immigration has trebled; from 1851 to 1886 it increased from 380,381 to 1,126,123.

Joly [1] has rightly remarked that when the tide moving men to emigrate is weak it draws the stronger and more intelligent, but when it becomes too violent it sweeps along good and bad alike. In fact, the greater part of the criminality of the immigrants is furnished by the border provinces, where emigration is easy. Thus in 1886 there were 4 convictions to 100,000 Swiss, 18 among the same number of Spaniards, 23 Italians, and almost no English or Russians. In Paris, in the same way, in proportion to their numbers, the Belgian and Swiss colonies furnished three times as many of the persons arrested as did the English or Americans. The Italian colony, which is hardly four times as large as the Austrian, furnished 15 times as many arrests.[2] On the other hand, the less stable the immigration is the more crimes it furnishes. The Belgians, who become naturalized Frenchmen, commit fewer crimes than the Spaniards, who are nearly always merely temporary residents.

The situation is similar with reference to migrations within a country, expecially migrations of a wandering sort, like that of pedlars. For example, in a study made at St. Gaudens, from which many of the French pedlars start out (about 7000 in a population of 36,000), it was found that they furnished a very high proportion of crimes, both of fraud and of violence. From 41 in 1831–69 these had increased to 200 and 290 in 1881; and the abandoned children, adulteries, and divorces were also very numerous.

Sarthe is one of the best of the departments of France in point of criminality; but if we take account of crimes committed by natives who have emigrated it rises 34 degrees in the criminal scale. For analogous reasons the department of Creuze rises from the third to the eighteenth place, owing to its 45,000 immigrants caused by the instability of labor.

Many come to the great cities honest but with false ideas of the new situation that has enticed them, and are, in consequence, easily led astray, and little by little become criminals. The young girl, having yielded to seduction, becomes a prosti-

[1] "France Criminelle," 1890.

[2] Joly, *op. cit.*

tute; the workman, lacking work, falls into idleness, and, surrounded by companions who incite him to evil and tempted by the allurement of a thousand pleasures that he sees others enjoying, becomes a thief. There are repentant workmen who hope to make themselves forget and to redeem themselves by work, but they soon relapse, either through again running into temptation or through inability to cover up the past. Finally there are evil-doers who come to the city only to commit crime. In the small towns, as Joly very well says, it is necessary to seek opportunity for crime; in Paris the opportunity comes to you and draws you. High livers are themselves a cause of crime, especially crimes against public decency. In Paris such crimes may be committed with such clever shifts that they no longer appear to be criminal.[1]

"The full-blooded Parisian mingled in the excesses of the Commune only in a very moderate degree," writes Maxime du Camp. "The scum of the provinces fermented in Paris. The ruined men, the empty-headed, the envious, rushed to the city, puffed up with a sense of their own importance, and, because they had become excited in the village wineshops, believed themselves capable of ruling the world. Paris must realize their dream or perish; but Paris did not even know their names, and to expiate this grave offense it must fall."

The emigrant in general (as I have already pointed out in the second edition of my "Homme Criminel") is that human product of society which has the greatest tendency toward associated crime. For emigrants are the most necessitous part of society, the least closely watched, have no feeling of shame, escape justice most easily, and make a great use of thieves' slang. Thieves are almost always nomads.[2] Emigrants from Abruzzo formed the greatest contingent of the Mancini Band. (Jorioz). The small immigration of the *Garfagnini* to the quarries of Carrara produces crime even after the return of the workmen, for they come back drunkards, cynics, and members of secret societies. In centuries past these same migrations were already a cause of crime.[3] The band of Fiordispini, for example,

[1] Joly, *op. cit.* [2] *Op. cit.* Vol. I, Pt. 3, Chap. X.
[3] De Stefani, "Dell' Emigrazione di Garfagnana," 1879, Milan.

was originally composed entirely of tinkers, candle sellers, harvesters, and pedlars, who were already too much noted for sporadic crime. Even emigrants who are migrating because of religious fanaticism, and hence ought to be farthest from crime, nevertheless contribute notably to the number of cases of associated crime. The word "mariulo" seems to be derived from the custom of crying in chorus, "Vive Maria!" prevalent among the pilgrims to Loretto and Assisi — a custom which did not prevent them, however, from committing rapes and robberies, believing these expiated by their pilgrimage.[1] Pilgrimage was for them a convenient means of committing crime and a still more convenient means of doing penance for it. It was like the famous lance which first wounded, but immediately afterward healed the wounds. I have found a proof of this in a decree of the king of France, dated September, 1732 (recalling other decrees of 1671 and 1686), in which pilgrimages were prohibited as a frequent cause of grave crimes.[2]

[1] Lozzi, "Dell' Ozio in Italia," Florence, 1870.

[2] It seems worth while to give the text of it here: "His Majesty, calling to mind the declarations of the late king, his great-grandfather, dated August, 1671, and January, 1686, which prohibit (under penalty of condemnation to the galleys for life, in the case of men, and in the case of women other penalties at the discretion of the judges) to any of his subjects to go on a pilgrimage to Santiago in Galicia, to Our Lady of Loretto, and to other places outside the realm, without express permission of His Majesty, countersigned by one of his secretaries of state with the consent of the bishop of the diocese;

"His Majesty being informed that, notwithstanding these orders, many of his subjects neglect to ask permission or abuse the permission in different ways when obtained, and under a specious pretext of devotion abandon their families, their parents, their masters, their professions, their trades, in order to be free to lead a wandering life, full of idleness and licentiousness, which often leads them into crime;

"That others, leaving the realm in the hope of establishing themselves more advantageously, find in the end neither the advantages nor the help which good conduct in their native land would have brought them; and that the greater part of them die miserably upon the road, or run the risk of being enlisted, whether they will or not, in the armies of neighboring powers;

"That often it happens that soldiers in the service of His Majesty mingle with these vagabonds and on account of the great number of these have an opportunity to desert;

"His Majesty, judging it necessary for the good of the service and of the public to put an end to these disorders by suppressing the pretext that gives rise to them, expressly forbids any of his subjects, to whatever age, sex, or condition they may belong, to go on a pilgrimage to Santiago in Galicia, to Our Lady of Loretto and Monteferrato, and other places outside of our realm, for any cause or pretext whatsoever, and this under

This is doubtless the reason why places endowed with celebrated shrines have generally the worst reputations, as d'Azeglio remarks in his "Recollections."

The influence of emigration explains clearly why, in the relation of homicides to density, Italy differs from France. In the latter country in the ten years, 1880 to 1890, there was a yearly average of only 11,163 emigrants, while in Italy the number in 1892 reached 246,751, with the yearly average about 124,000.[1]

§ 32. Birth-rate and Immigration

These investigations of emigration solve in great part another problem which seems to present a complete contradiction in Italy and France. Granting the influence of density of population upon certain crimes, it would appear that these crimes ought to follow the variations of the birth-rate, and that, for example, theft, which increases with the greater density, ought also to increase with a higher birth-rate. In France, however, we see rape and assassination increase with the maximum density, but in inverse ratio to the birth-rate. Corre, and Joly after him (*op. cit.*), have observed in France the maximum criminality in the departments having the lowest birth-rate.

Birth-rate	Crimes against persons	Thefts	Rapes
19.00	64	83	17
16.47	66	99	26
14.05	89	186	29

The fact is that in France the lower birth-rate stands in direct relation with the immigration of foreigners. This is the more easily explained, as Maurel observes,[2] since where there is a lower birth-rate there is also a smaller number of men. Now

penalty of being condemned to the galleys for life in the case of men, etc., etc.

"Declaring null and void all permits previously granted."

[1] "Statistica dell' Emigrazione Italiana," Rome, 1894.

[2] "Revue Scientif.," Nov. 12, 1895.

according to Joly's observations with regard to Cette and Marseilles, the deficiency of the population resulting from the falling off of the birth-rate is made up by foreign immigrants, Genoese and Calabrians especially, who bring about an enormous increase in the number of crimes. Another contradiction is furnished by the very prolific class of workmen, in contrast with the miserly, and consequently sterile, peasant class. Thus in districts where there are great numbers of workmen, as in Seine-Inférieure, Nord, and Pas-de-Calais, one sees, in comparison with the departments of Cher and Indre, a great number of crimes, notwithstanding the higher figure for births.

But on the whole the antagonism between birth-rate and crime predominates. Thus Paris, a part of Champagne and Normandy, and all the Mediterranean departments except Gard show a sharp decline of the birth-rate, and a no less sharp increase of the number of crimes. (Joly.) In Tarn-et-Garonne, a very poor department without resources or means of communication, there is to be noted an increase in the population and a smaller number of crimes; while rich and fertile departments become stripped of their native population, and have more crimes and a larger foreign contingent. (Joly.) Brittany, on the other hand, Cher, Seine, Drôme, Vienne, and Vendée have more legitimate births, fewer crimes, and more early marriages. All this has less connection with the birth-rate than with the immigration that makes up the deficit in the native population; and also, as we shall see, with the avarice that lies at the root of the whole matter.

But the influence of immigration is demonstrated to us by the inversion of the rule regarding birth-rate and crime in Italy, where there is no immigration, but on the other hand an emigration amounting on the average to 193 to the 100,000 inhabitants yearly.[1] We find in the statistics of Coghlan that the increase in the number of immigrants to New South Wales (1884–86) was accompanied by an increase in the number of crimes, but on the other hand the increase in the number of emigrants leaving (1883–88) also corresponded with the increase in the number of crimes (1884–88). If we take advantage of

[1] Del Vecchio, "Sull' Emigrazione," Rome, 1892.

Bosco's new investigations [1] to study the influence of immigration upon homicides in the United States in 1889, we find these facts: among those held for homicide, 95 to the million were born in the United States, while 138 to the million were foreigners, distributed as follows:

Denmark, Sweden, and Norway	5.8 to the 100,000
England	10.4 " " "
Ireland	17.5 " " "
Germany	9.7 " " "
Austria	12.2 " " "
France	27.4 " " "
Italy	58.1 " " "

That is to say, there were twice as many in proportion to the population (except in the case of the French and Italians) as in the native country. This confirms the observation that here, as in France, immigration produces a disadvantageous selection, even allowing for the fact that the age of the immigrants corresponds to that which in Europe gives the largest number of homicides.

In Italy it is nearly always the case that the maximum number of births occurs in the districts which are most notorious for their criminality, as well as for their poverty. Thus from 1876 to 1888 the annual average was 40 births to the 1000 inhabitants in southern and insular Italy, and only 36 throughout the rest of the country. In the same way in Sicily, out of four provinces most given to homicide, Girgenti, Trapani, Caltanissetta, and Palermo, three have the maximum birth-rate.[2] However, another factor comes into play here, the lack of self-restraint due to the excessive heat, which causes all Malthusian precautions to be forgotten in the act of procreation.

However, the excess of births in southern Italy is neutralized by the high mortality rate and by emigration. For this reason, notwithstanding the greater birth-rate, the average family in 1881 was 4.10 in Sicily, and 4.50 in Basilicata, as against 5.17 in Venice, and 4.92 in Tuscany.

Comparing next the countries of Europe having the maximum birth-rate (1876–90):

[1] "L'Omicidio negli Stati Uniti," 1895.
[2] Bodio, "Statistica penale," 1879–83.

England	34.0	Germany	31.1
Italy	37.3	Hungary	44.0

and those having the minimum birth-rate:

France	24.6	Ireland	24.9	Switzerland	29.4

we find a coincidence with homicides only in the case of Italy and Hungary, which are in complete contrast with England and Germany, these having a high birth-rate and few homicides. Among the nations with a minimum birth-rate Ireland alone has a low figure for homicide. And if in England and Germany a greater number of thefts corresponds to the greater birth-rate, this is not true of Hungary and Switzerland. It follows then that on the whole there is here no parallelism.

§ 33. City and Country

The influence of density is further shown by the effect in France of residence in the city or in the country. It is especially to MM. Fayet, Cosquet, and Lacassagne that we owe the most diligent investigations of this subject. It is shown by their studies that from 1843 to 1856 the persons indicted in the country were more numerous, while since 1863 those in the city have been in the majority.[1]

	Homicides to 100,000	Births to 100,000
Caltanissetta	46.2	4400
Catania	26.9	3900
Girgenti	70.7	4600
Messina	19.2	3900
Palermo	42.5	3900
Syracuse	15.7	4000
Trapani	40.2	4300

The emigration from the country to the cities is such that the rural emigrants constitute a fifth part of the urban popula-

[1] See Lacassagne, in my "Archivio di Psichiatria ed Antropologia Criminale," III, p. 311. Fayet had already noted in France in 1830–46 1 rural indictment to 405 inhabitants, and 1 city indictment to 165. ("Journal des Econ.," 1847.)

tion; and it is the better and more intelligent who emigrate, thus lowering the level of the country and in return bringing back to it the vices and customs of the city.

To sum up, the indictments for crimes against property have diminished in the country about two-thirds, and in the cities one-half. Thus there were:

In 1843 73% in the country, 64% in the city
" 1878 27% " " " 36% " " "

Indictments for crimes against the person were more numerous in the rural population from 1823 to 1878, but the number decreased after 1859 much more than in the cities. For crimes against the person in France the following statistics are given:

	In the country	In the city
In 1850	1819	830
" 1851	1894	836
" 1870	1180	732
" 1871	1239	603

As regards homicide, Socquet demonstrates that at an earlier period, 1846–50, the persons indicted in the country were three times as numerous as those in the cities, in the proportion of 20 to 7.6; while at a more recent period, 1876–80, they were only twice as numerous, 63 to 31. From this it appears that criminality in the country diminished, and in the city increased nearly a third. Those indicted for murder were:

	Rural	Urban
1846–50	72%	65%
1876–80	26%	31%

That is to say, there was a diminution in the latter period in both city and country, but much greater in the country. In indecent assaults upon adults the rural districts exceed the urban, doubtless because of the lack of houses of prostitution. Thus there were in the same periods:

	Rural	Urban
1846–50	74%	24%
1876–80	67%	27%

with a decrease in the country and a slight increase in the city. The number of indictments for indecent assaults upon children declined in the country from 59% in 1846–50 to 53% in 1876–80; while in the cities during the same time it rose from 39% to 45% (Socquet), favored by idleness, the abuse of alcoholic drinks, and especially by the satiety produced by over-refinement. That in abortions the city leads is unmistakable. There are twice, and latterly even three times, as many as in the country, while in infanticide the country leads. This is doubtless due to the greater ease of securing accomplices for an abortion in the city, and the slighter fear of being discovered.

Indictments for:

Abortions in France.[1]	To the million inhabitants	
	1851–55	1876–80
Abortions in France:		
Country	9.3	4.2
City	18.6	14.5
Infanticide:		
Country	32	35
City	21	22

The curve for crimes against property shows that economic crises are more deeply felt in the country than in the city.[2] Revolutions and the vintage have a different effect upon the number of indictments in the city and in the country. In the country indictments increase in the years of the abundant vintages. Revolutions, on the other hand, make themselves but slightly felt in the country, and only in the years following political crises, while in the city they are felt at once and keenly (Lacassagne).

The urban and the rural districts have each their own specific type of criminality. The crimes in the country are more barbarous, having their origin in revenge, avarice, and brutal sensuality. In the city the criminality is characterized by laziness, a more refined sensuality, and by forgery. This phenom-

[1] Socquet, "Contribution à l'Étude de la Criminalité en France," 1826–80.

[2] Lacassagne, *op. cit.*

enon of the increase of crimes against public decency in the cities, and the relative decrease of crimes of blood, is greatly accentuated when we study the very large urban centers. In France, for example, the department of the Seine has already reached a figure for homicide (19.9) lower than that of the departments which surround it; Seine-et-Oise giving 24.3, and Oise giving 25.8 (Ferri). The figures for infanticide are relatively even lower, while for rape upon children the figures are enormous. The number of thefts is also very high (244). In Italy, in the crimes against common honesty, the chief cities, Turin, Venice, Bologna, and Rome, have the predominance over the neighboring districts. The same is true with regard to crimes against public decency (Turin, Genoa, Venice, Bologna, Naples, Rome, and Palermo). In homicides Rome alone holds the first place (for causes of which we shall speak later), followed by Turin. In all the other principal cities homicides are decreasing. Vienna has 10.6 homicides to the million inhabitants, while Austria as a whole has 25; but Vienna has 116 thefts to 113 for the country at large. In Berlin the crimes against property, theft, fraud, and vagrancy really decreased from 1818 to 1878, notwithstanding the great change of population; while, on the other hand, crimes against persons increased (except during the war of 1870).[1] The number of homicides, however, is smaller than in the provinces, being 11.6 to the million inhabitants, while in Breslau it is 18.2, in Magdeburg 12, and in Constance 16. In thefts, on the other hand, Berlin goes beyond all the provinces except one. In England the phenomenon is still plainer. There are at present to the 100,000 in London 15 suspected persons at liberty, with 50 in the other English cities, and 60 in the country districts. Just so there are in London 3 to 4 suspected houses to the 100,000 population, 3.9 in the country, and 18 in the other cities.

[1] Starke, *op. cit.*

CHAPTER VI

SUBSISTENCE (FAMINE, PRICE OF BREAD)

§ 34. Subsistence

ONE of the factors which complicate the effects of climate and density, often to the point of their becoming inextricable, is that of the difficulty or ease of obtaining subsistence.

Following Oettingen's comparisons of the number of crimes in Prussia with the price of the necessary foods, we see that the food problem plays a part equal to, or even greater than, that of civilization. For with cheap food crimes against property (except arson) decrease, while those against persons, especially rape, increase.

Year	Rapes	Cases of Arson	Crimes against property	Crimes against persons	Price of grain, potatoes, etc.
1854	2.26	0.43	88.41	8.90	217.1
1855	2.57	0.46	88.93	8.04	252.3
1856	2.62	0.43	87.60	9.32	203.3
1857	4.14	0.53	81.52	13.81	156.3
1858	4.45	0.60	77.92	17.03	149.3
1859	4.68	0.52	78.19	16.63	150.6

In Prussia in 1862, when the price of potatoes, etc., was very high, crimes against property were in the proportion of 44.38 to 15.8 for those against persons. When the price of provisions fell, the former went down to 41, while the latter rose to 18. The famine of 1847 increased the crimes against persons 24%.[1] We have still plainer proof in the statistics for Prussia from 1854 to 1878, as given by Starcke.[2]

Years in which the price of wheat per 50 kilograms was :

[1] Wappaeus, "Allgemeine Bevölkerungs Statistik," 1861.
[2] "Verbrechen und Verbrecher," 1884, Berlin.

	Inhabitants		
	More than 12 marks	Less than 10 marks	Between 10 and 12 marks
Crimes in general	1 to 172.9	190.6	179.8
Thefts	1,990	2,645	2,512
Forest thefts	50.8	48.2	49.5
Forgeries	76,283	71,787	68,600
Bankruptcies	77,600	56,300	56,200
Crimes against public order	4,282	3,587	3,055
Arson	68,328	46,960	71,666
Assaults	37,328	54,463	45,933
Homicides	109,937	118,225	95,000
Infanticides	230,700	227,000	227,000

We see here that, while the price of wheat partly influences crimes in general, it has a direct effect only upon forest thefts, of which the maximum corresponds to the maximum price of provisions. On the other hand, it is clear that the minimum price of wheat, corresponding to a maximum of well-being, coincides with a breaking out of assaults, homicides, and cases of arson. This may be explained by the fact that when the price of bread is low the abuse of alcohol is made possible. The medium price of grain corresponds with the greatest frequency of forgeries, bankruptcies, and crimes against public order. In France, in Corre's graphic tables (Fig. 1) we see that from 1843 to 1883 the line for the frequency of misdemeanors (nearly all against property), as well as that for suicides, rises continually, and keeps nearly parallel with the line for the price of bread as far as 1865. At this point, however, while the line for misdemeanors continues to rise, that for the price of bread goes down, proving that other factors enter in here, reducing the cost of subsistence to the place of second importance. The line for crime proper shows no parallelism with the price of bread. Rossi comes to the same conclusions in a study of the criminality of Rome, Cagliari, etc., with respect to heat and the price of grain for the period from 1875 to 1883.[1]

[1] "Archive de Psych. et Antrop. Crim.," 1884.

The number of crimes against property (excluding aggravated theft and highway robbery) is affected at the same time by

Fig. 1.

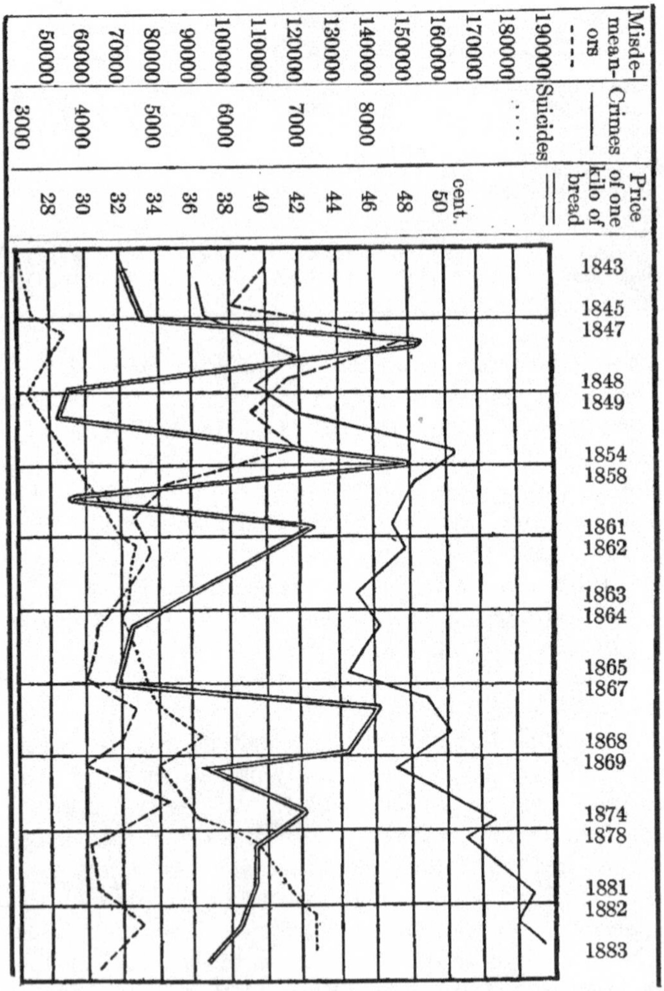

the winter temperature and the price of food. In Rome, in fact, during these nine years the highest number of crimes

(70,738) was reached in 1830, when a very high price of wheat and a rigorous winter coincided; while in 1877, when the price of wheat was high but the winter particularly mild, the number of crimes reached only 61,498. In 1881, when the price of wheat decreased noticeably, and the mean winter temperature increased, there was also a notable decrease in the crimes against property. From 70,730 the number went down to 59,815, a diminution which continued through the years 1882 and 1883, while at the same time the price of grain and the rigor of the cold decreased also. The action of the temperature upon assaults and other crimes against persons from 1875 to 1883 amounted to nothing, while for each increase in the price of food there was a corresponding decrease in the number of these crimes, and *vice versa.*

But of all studies of the influences at work in the different kinds of crime in Italy, the most conclusive is that of the hours of labor necessary to obtain the equivalent of a kilogram of wheat or bread. In this way the price of food is corrected for variations in wages.[1] We see here, in Figures 2 and 3: 1st, that all crimes against property (except where contradictory factors come too powerfully into play) run with great fidelity parallel to the curve of the hours of work necessary to procure the equivalent of a kilogram of bread or grain. Thefts increased from 137 to 153 during the period 1875–77 with the increase of the hours of work, and decreased from 184 to 111 in the period 1879–88 with the decrease in the number of hours. Commercial crimes, forgeries, etc., were not affected. 2nd. Crimes against morality increase as the necessary hours of labor diminish. Thus from 1881 to 1888, a period in which the hours of work fell from 122 to 92, these crimes increased from 3.11 to 5.25. In England, Scotland, and Ireland the statistics for 50 years, which Fornasari di Verce has examined for me, show an analogous relation between crime and the variations in the price of grain; that is to say, crimes against property without violence increase generally with the price of grain, as in 1846–47; while crimes with violence are almost wholly unaffected by food

[1] Fornasari di Verce, "La Criminalita e le Viconde Economiche in Italia," Turin, Bocca, 1895.

Fig. 2

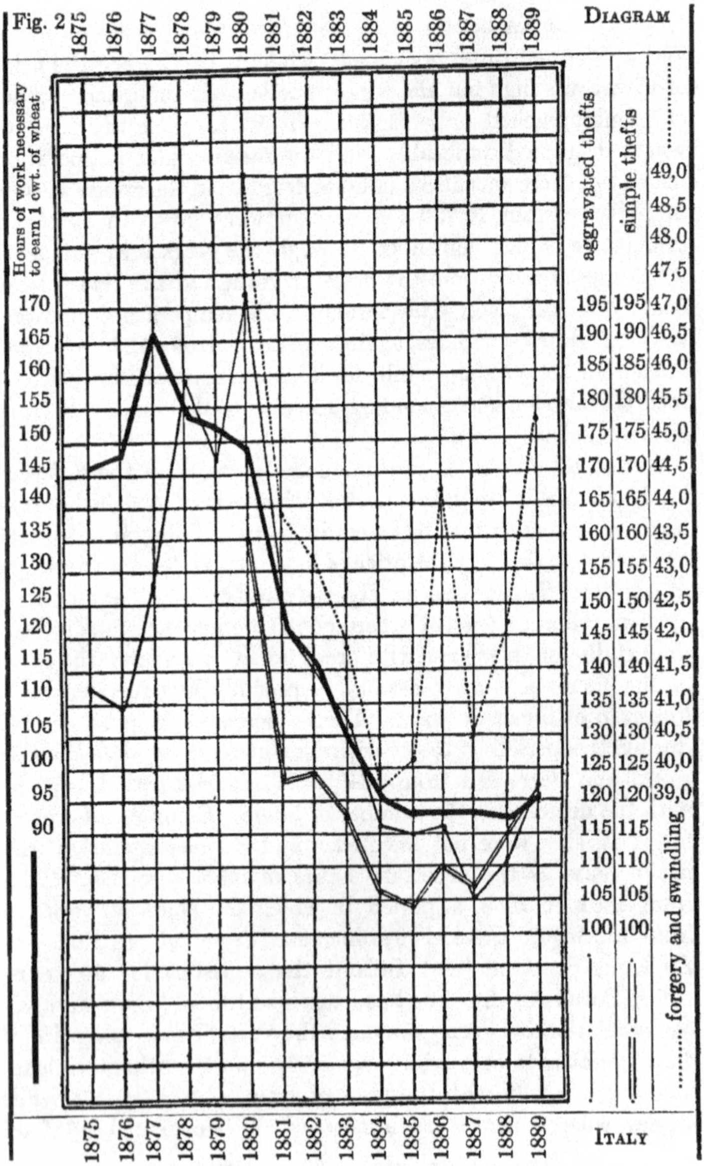
DIAGRAM
ITALY
Hours of work necessary to earn 1 cwt. of wheat
aggravated thefts
simple thefts
forgery and swindling
1875
1876
1877
1878
1879
1880
1881
1882
1883
1884
1885
1886
1887
1888
1889

prices. In 1842–45 and 1862–63 they fell with the fall of the price of grain, but rose in 1881–86 notwithstanding the cheapness of bread. Fraudulent crimes against property, forgery, counterfeiting, etc., and likewise crimes against persons, were not influenced by prices. For New South Wales similar conclusions may be drawn from the investigations of Coghlan. (Fig. 4.)

The effect of the price of provisions upon murder is uncertain or negligible, the latter being also true of assaults. The influence upon theft is very great, as is also the inverse effect upon crimes against good morals, which increase with the falling off in the price of food. Famine lessens sexual vigor, and abundance excites it; and while the need of food drives men to theft, the abundance of it leads to sexual crimes. The same observations hold good for the scarcity of work and reduction of wages. It has been remarked that women and domestic servants are more apt than others to be drawn into crime by the scarcity of food, doubtless because they feel it more. Especially is this the case with domestic servants, who, because of intermittent periods of good living, lose the power of resistance to privation. But, admitting the action of scarcity of food upon the increase of thefts and of abundance upon the increase of homicides, assaults, and debauchery, it is easy to understand its slight influence upon the variation of criminality in general, if one group of crimes increases with a given state of the market, and another group decreases under the same conditions, and *vice versa*. Even when the price of food moves in a constant direction it does not modify essentially the proportion of certain crimes. For example, in Italy the effect of the rise in price of food upon aggravated thefts is very marked; yet the greatest difference is between 184 and 105, that is to say, a variation of 79 to the 100,000. Likewise, when the sexual crimes increase on account of the low price of food, the greatest difference is 2.14 to the 100,000, — a fact easy to understand when one thinks of the greater influence of heredity, climate, and race.

At times there arises a strange contradiction in the effect of high prices on homicide. Ordinarily when bread is dear, money is lacking to buy alcoholic drinks, and homicide and highway robberies diminish. But it happens sometimes that in order to procure drink men will commit these crimes in greater number, as in New South Wales. Morbihan and Vendée, according to Joly, are the most moral departments,[1] and wages there have increased little, while the necessaries of life have doubled in

Fig. 3.

ITALY

	Number of hours of work necessary to earn		Cases before		
			Theft		Imposture and embezzlement
	One cwt. grain	One cwt. bread	Aggravated	Simple	
1875	146	...	137.48	...	...
1876	148	...	134.06	...	...
1877	166	...	153.61	...	...
1878	154	...	184.77	...	...
1879	152	...	172.10	...	...
1880	149	207	196.84	160.04	49.04
1881	122	181	146.46	123.24	43.84
1882	116	176	140.98	124.26	43.24
1883	104	167	131.07	117.30	41.85
1884	96	149	116.77	106.89	39.61
1885	93	146	115.25	104.84	40.19
1886	93	145	116.73	110.83	43.85
1887	93	147	105.91	107.98	40.56
1888	92	147	111.44	115.80	42.21
1889	95	149	122.19	121.83	45.37

price; but there is less abuse of alcoholic drinks there. In Boûches-du-Rhône, on the other hand, wages have incrcased 30% and provisions 15%; in Hérault wages have increased 60% and provisions much less; yet these departments are counted among the most immoral, just because of the greater abuse of alcohol there.

One thing is certain, however, and that is that while famines are rare and steadily decrease in number, thefts are constant and always increasing.[2] From all this it is easy to understand

[1] "France Criminelle," p. 353. [2] Joly, *op. cit.*, p. 358.

why the part which lack of food and real poverty play in crime is smaller than is generally believed. In the statistics of Guerry the thefts of provisions form hardly 1% of the total number of thefts, and even with those hunger has less to do than gluttony. Of 43 classes of objects stolen in London, sausages, fowls, and

Fig. 3.

ITALY

THE COURTS (TO 100,000 INHABITANTS)

Homicide		Assault	Sexual offences	Resistance to the government	
Aggravated	Simple				
4.00	10.71	...	...	0.24	1875
4.50	10.45	...	...	0.14	1876
3.49	9.30	...	...	0.25	1877
3.91	10.86	...	...	0.67	1878
6.54	13.79	...	3.45	0.45	1879
5.87	12.48	147.38	3.11	0.37	1880
5.35	11.08	151.48	3.95	0.34	1881
5.54	10.17	157.10	3.76	0.37	1882
4.98	10.08	165.10	3.66	0.66	1883
5.02	9.68	167.18	4.12	0.61	1884
4.72	9.27	145.41	4.29	0.45	1885
4.52	9.13	158.83	4.56	0.42	1886
4.11	8.38	180.61	4.41	0.49	1887
4.26	9.11	192.27	5.25	0.26	1888
4.19	8.17	178.78	5.62	0.26	1889

game stood 13th; sugar, meat, and wine, 30th; and bread the last of all. Joly remarks that in the French statistics from 1860 to 1890, while thefts of money and bank-notes were most numerous (396 : 100,000), thefts of meal, oats, domestic animals, etc., were only 55 to the 100,000. Maré writes:[1]

"It is seldom that hunger leads to theft. Young men steal knives and cigars, and when provisions are stolen, the grown men take liquors, the women bonbons and chocolate."

[1] "Un Joli Monde."

The same may be said of prostitution.

"If hunger and destitution," says Locatelli, "are sufficient to drive a young girl to prostitution, it would be necessary to con-

Fig. 4

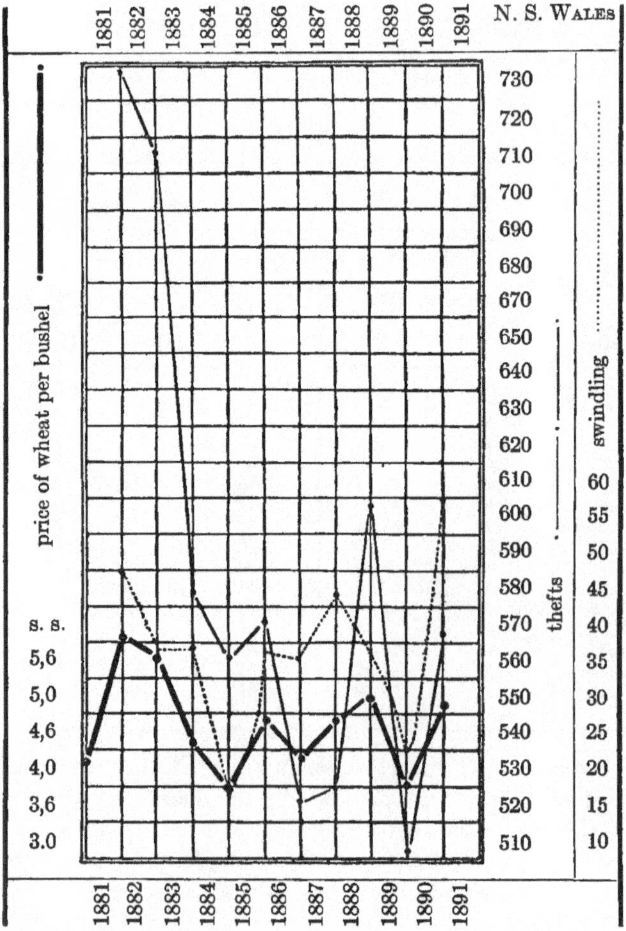

fer Montyon prizes upon the myriads of virtuous daughters of the people who, notwithstanding the greatest privations and seductions of every kind, never sell themselves, but remain pure and chaste."

It is not impossible that with time we may arrive at such a point as to be able to show how certain kinds of food favor certain crimes. We know that a vegetarian diet renders those who make use of it mild and tractable, while animal food makes men cruel and violent. This is doubtless why the Lombard peasant patiently bears the evil treatment of his masters, while the Romagnol, addicted to a pork diet, revenges himself with violence.

§ 35. Insurrections

The influence of hunger in insurrections also has been much exaggerated, as I have shown in my "Crime Politique." In Faraglia's valuable book, "Storia dei Prezzi in Napoli," which gives us the price of food year by year for nearly nine centuries, we find 46 great famines, in the years 1182, 1192, 1257, 1269, 1342, 1496–97, 1505, 1508, 1534, 1551, 1558, 1562–63, 1565, 1570, 1580, 1586–87, 1591–92, 1595, 1597, 1603, 1621–22, 1623–25, 1646, 1672, 1694–97, 1759–60, 1763, 1790–91, 1802, 1810, 1815–16, 1820–21. Now, these 46 years of famine coincide with insurrections only six times, namely, in 1508, 1580, 1587, 1595, 1621–22, 1820–21. In the celebrated insurrection of Masaniello (1647) many other causes were associated with the economic situation, such as the madness of Masaniello,[1] the hot season, and the cruelty of the Spaniards. For if in 1646 there was a famine, in 1647 there was abundance, if not of grain, at least of fruits, meat, lard, and cheese. Moreover, there was no insurrection during the terrible famine of 1182, which lasted five years, and in which men could scarcely find weeds for food. Neither was there any revolt during the famine of 1496–97, when so terrible an epidemic resulted that people of the cities had to flee to the country; nor during that of 1565, when the distress was so great that rotten cabbage leaves sold for the price that would normally have purchased fresh and good ones. Nor was there an insurrection in 1570, when "the poor left the provinces, and streamed toward Naples in crowds, famished, emaciated, sick, hoping to save their lives by flight, and filling the streets with their misery." Finally, there was no insur-

[1] C. Lombroso, "Tre Tribuni Studiati da un Alienista," 1887.

rection during the famine of 1586. It is well to recall here that if there were revolts in France in 1827, 1832, 1847, running parallel with economic crises and dearths, there was also a very high summer temperature; and that during those of 1834, 1864, and 1865 we find nothing clearly indicating either an economic or a meteorological cause. In Strasburg between the periods 1451–1500 and 1601–25 the average price of beef rose 134% and that of pork 92%, while many years the wages of the workmen sank 10%, and yet there was no insurrection.[1] In 1670, during the extreme famine in Madrid, the workmen organized themselves into bands and plundered the houses of the rich, killing the proprietors, and not a day passed that some one was not killed for the sake of bread; and yet there was no real insurrection.[2] In India it has been possible to follow the consequences of terrible famines step by step. That of 1865–66 caused the loss of 25% of the population of Orissa, and of 35% of the population of Puri, and yet there was no insurrection there in those years. The most noted famines of the last hundred years, at least in Nelhore, one of the provinces which has suffered most through lack of rain and density of population, took place in the following years: 1769–70, 1780, 1784, 1790–92, 1802, 1806–07, 1812, 1824, 1829, 1830, 1833, 1836–38, 1866, 1876–78.[3] In the famine of 1769–70 a third of the population died. In 1877–78 it is estimated that, in addition to the normal number of deaths, more than 5 millions out of a population of 197 millions died by famine.[4] Yet these famines gave rise to no insurrection. The great Indian mutiny of 1857–58 was due [5] in great part to aversion to the innovations (railroads, telegraphs, etc.) introduced by civilization, to the conspiracies of the dethroned princes, and, according to Hunter, to the belief among the Sepoys that their cartridges were to be greased with pork fat.[6] Here, then, prolonged hunger was less powerful than superstition. The other Indian rebellions which are known to us

[1] Martini, "Preussiche Jahrbücher," Nov., 1895.
[2] Buckle, IV.
[3] Hunter, "Imp. Gaz. of India," 1881.
[4] Hunter, "The Indian Empire," 1882.
[5] Hunter, *op. cit.*
[6] Kaye, "History of the Sepoys," 1865.

had no relation to the scarcity of provisions; neither the insurrection of Bohilla in 1751, nor that of the Sikhs in the Punjab in 1710, nor that of the Sepoys in 1764; neither the little semi-dynastic insurrections among the Synts in 1843, nor of the Sikhs in 1848. It is worthy of note that the province of Orissa, which is that most tried by famines, has the smallest number of insurrections.

All this is to be explained by the fact, already shown by our studies of the effect of tropical and polar climates, that when men's vitality is lowered they have not enough energy to resist. Thus, the excess of human misfortunes is rather less likely to produce revolutions than great prosperity. This is entirely in accord with what has been observed in criminal statistics, namely, that famine and great cold diminish in general all crimes against persons, especially rapes and homicides.[1]

[1] Lombroso, "Crime Politique et Criminalité," Paris, 1895; Id. "Pensiero e Meteore," Milan, 1875.

CHAPTER VII

ALCOHOLISM

§ 36. Alcoholism and Food Supply

AS we have seen in the preceding chapter, the effect of food supply cannot be separated from that of alcohol. Indeed, this latter is so powerful a factor in criminal ætiology that it absorbs the other almost completely.

§ 37. Pernicious Effect of Alcohol

It is a well-known fact that alcohol, so far from rendering extreme temperatures more tolerable, increases the danger from great heat and cold alike, so that in the polar regions and in India soldiers and sailors, thinking to acquire greater resistance to fatigue by the use of alcoholic beverages, simply aggravate their condition. It is doubtless for this reason that in the Russian campaign the northerners suffered more than the more temperate Latins. It has been proved in cholera epidemics that drunkards, and even simple "drinkers," are afflicted in greater numbers than abstemious persons.[1] Abortions are also more frequent among women who drink, and for this reason families of drinkers show a fecundity from 2 to 4 times less than that of temperate and sober couples. This fatal liquor can, then, stimulate carnal passion to the point of violence and crime without thereby increasing the birth-rate.[2] Alcohol is one of the principal causes of the rejection of recruits in the Swedish

[1] Among abstainers cholera gave a mortality of 19.9%, as against 91% among drinkers.

[2] Marriages of drinkers gave an average of 1.3 children, those of abstainers, 4.1. (Baer, "Alkoholismus," Berlin, 1878.)

army for weakness or lack of development. These rejections rose to 32% in 1867, and fell to 28% in 1868 after the promulgation of the liquor laws. In the French departments where, on account of the scarcity of wine, there is more use of spirits, as in Finistère, the exemption of conscripts from 72 rises to 155 (Lunier). Alcohol influences the stature. The tall Woljaks, after having used brandy to excess, diminished in stature until they fell below middle height; and we have seen that the beautiful women of the valley of Viu lose their beauty and stature after having taken to the use of brandy. There is no cause for surprise, then, at the diminution of the average duration of life caused by the use of alcoholic drinks. Brandy should be called not *eau de vie*, but *eau de la mort*. Neisson's calculations show that the mortality among drinkers is at least 3.25 times greater than that of abstainers.[1]

§ 38. Pauperism

All this prepares us to understand that one of the most evident and serious effects of alcoholism is pauperism, The progeny of the alcoholic are blind, paralytic, impotent. Even if they begin life with wealth, they must necessarily become poor. If they are poor, they are incapable of working.

It is true that with the increase in wages the number of drunkards grows disproportionately, and in consequence the number of misdemeanors also. When the wages of the miners in Lancashire increased from 4 shillings to 7 and 9, the mortality caused by drunkenness rose from 495 to 1304 and 2605, and crimes from 1335 to 3878 and 4402. But it is still worse when wages go down. Then alcohol is drunk to supply the place of clothing and food, that cold and hunger may be more easily borne; and alcohol in its turn makes the drinker constantly weaker and poorer, and keeps him always closely imprisoned in its fatal domain. It may be said, then, that alcoholism is the product

[1] A man of 20 addicted to drink has an expectancy of life of 16 years, an abstainer of the same age has an expectancy of 44 years. A beer drinker would have 21.7 years, a drinker of spirits, 16.7; a drinker of both beer and spirits, 16.1. Of 97 children of alcoholic parents only 14 were normal. (Baer, *op. cit.*)

both of superfluity and of poverty. This was seen in Aix-la-Chapelle, where between 1850 and 1860 wages increased a fourth, and alcoholism increased also; but it increased still more when, after the crisis in America, 80 factories closed and wages were cut down a third. The number of poor families rose from 1865 to 2255, and the wine-shops from 183 to 305; the prostitutes increased from 37 to 101, while the marriages decreased from 785 to 630. At the same time cases of theft and arson were multiplied.[1] In the famine of 1860–61 it was noted in London that not one of the 7900 members of the temperance society had applied for aid.[2] Huisch has observed that of each £100 received in alms £30 are spent for drink; and Bertrand and Lee have remarked that the most miserable municipalities are those where the use of alcohol has increased inordinately and the wine-shops have multiplied. A striking proof of the deleterious effects of alcohol is given by Upper Silesia. The misery was there so great that persons were dying of hunger, and at the same time alcoholism raged so frightfully that bridal couples reeled before the altar, and parents came intoxicated to the baptism of their new-born children. A preacher of Silesia wrote: "Where intemperance reigns, misery and crime follow the body like its shadow."[3] It has already been noted that drunkenness is one of the chief causes of separation and divorce in Germany; and furthermore it is known that the children of divorced parents and second marriages furnish a strong contingent to crime and prostitution.

§ 39. Alcoholism and Crime Statistics

From all this it is easy to see the connection between alcoholism and crime from a social as well as a pathological point of view. The first proof of this is to be found in the statistics which show a continual increase of crimes in civilized countries.

[1] Thun, "Die Industrie am Niederrhein," 1890.

[2] From 1823 to 1826 the almshouses of Philadelphia received yearly from 4000 to 5000 paupers who had been ruined by drink. Of 3000 indigent persons in Massachusetts about 2900 found themselves in the same condition. (Baer, *op. cit.*, p. 582.)

[3] Baer, *op. cit.*

This increase can be justified by the growth of the population only to the extent of from 13% to 15%, but it is all too easily explained by the abuse of alcoholic drinks, the consumption of which increases at just the rate at which crime increases.

A further clear proof is to be found in Ferri's study of criminality in France,[1] which brings into relief the parallelism of crime with the consumption of wine and spirits, at least in the years of exceptionally good vintages (1850, '58, '65, '69, '75), and of exceptionally poor ones (1851, '53, '54, '66, '67, '73). 1870, the year of the war, is an exception, as in that year military statistics crowd out judicial ones; 1876 forms another exception and one which I cannot explain, not having the statistics of the successive years before me; while in 1860–61 the vintage seems to have postponed its effect upon crime by one year. The parallelism is the stranger and more noteworthy because several authors pretend to attribute a fatal influence to spirits only and not to wine, so that, as we shall see, it is proposed to encourage the distribution of wine in the countries most inclined to crime. Now, from these statistics the relation of the consumption of alcohol to homicides and assaults is not so evident as that of wine, except in the years 1855 to 1868, and 1873 to 1876. And this is easy to understand, for brawls are more easily started in the wine-shops than in the establishments of the brandy sellers, where the stay is too short for an opportunity to be given for quarrels.

Another proof of the relationship of drink and crime is to be found in the observed fact that the days and months when crimes are most frequent are just those when alcoholic drinks are most abused. So Schroeter reports[2] that in Germany out of 2178 crimes 58% took place Saturday night, 3% Sunday, and 1% Monday; and that upon these same days sexual crimes, rebellion, and arson took the lead with a ratio of 82%. In Italy in 1870, the only year in which a record of this kind was kept, the same fact was noted.[3]

[1] Lombroso, "Homme Criminel," 1895.
[2] "Jahrbuch der Westphälischen Gefängnisse," 1871.
[3] In the official statistics of 1870 the following percentages of the various

Ferri discovered the surprising fact that in France, in the period from 1827 to 1869, while the crimes against persons in general fell off rapidly from August to December, the serious bodily assaults, on the contrary, showed a marked increase in November, when the new wine comes in. It is to be noted that it is a question of the infliction of grave injuries, such as come before the assizes, and not of the mere wine-shop brawls, such as are tried before the minor courts. Dixon has found a single place in America that has been exempt from crime for some years notwithstanding its large population of working men. This is St. Johnsbury, Vermont. But here there is absolute prohibition of the sale of fermented beverages, beer, wine, etc., which are furnished, like poisons, by the druggists upon the written demand of the consumer, with the consent of the mayor, who writes the name of the person concerned in a public register. In Belgium, it has been estimated alcoholism causes 25% to 27% of the crime. In New York, of 49,423 persons arraigned, 30,509 were habitual drunkards. In 1890, in the whole

crimes were committed on holidays (there being one holiday on the average to five working days):

	Assizes	Ordinary tribunals
Resistance to the officers	68.1	78.5
Rape	65.4	67.4
Parricide, uxoricide, infanticide	56.9	...
Murder	72.8	74.8
Homicide	78	76
Assault with fatal result	71.3	...
Malicious assault	69.6	...
Threats and vagrancy	...	72.4
Highway robbery	61.5	...
Theft	61.2	66.8
Exposure and substitution of infants	...	34.8
Receiving and buying stolen goods	63.9	...
Misappropriation of public funds	...	39.3
Forgery	47.8	49.4
Calumny and false accusation	12	...
Highway robbery with homicide	31.2	...
Bankruptcy	26.4	48.2

Accordingly all the crimes of violence and against persons take the lead on holidays, as compared with fraudulent and premeditated crimes.

United States, out of every 100 prisoners, 20 were drunkards, 60 were moderate drinkers, and 20 were abstainers.[1] In Holland, four-fifths of the crimes are attributed to the abuse of alcohol, seven-eighths of the brawls, three-fourths of the attacks upon persons, and one-fourth of the attacks upon property. Three-fourths of the crimes in Sweden are attributed to alcoholism. This applies especially to assassination and other crimes of blood, but thefts and frauds are largely due to an alcoholic heredity. In England, 10,000 out of 29,752 convicted by the assizes, and 50,000 out of 90,903 convicted by the magistrates, had been drawn into crime by frequenting public houses.[2] In France Guillemin estimates the criminals resulting from the abuse of alcohol at 50%, and Baer places those in Germany at 41%. The greatest proportion of drunkards is to be found in those departments where, on account of the small production of wine, a larger quantity of spirituous liquor is consumed. Of the criminals observed by Marro, 73% abused alcoholic drinks, and of these only 10% were normal. In my "Centuria di Criminali," Rossi found that drunkenness ran up as high as 81%, of which 23% was begun in infancy. There was a difference of only 10% in the frequency of alcoholism among youths and among adults. Of 100 criminals below 20 years, 64% were already addicted to drink; from which we may see that this vice is very precocious.

§ 40. Physiological Effects

All substances which have the power of exciting the brain in an abnormal manner drive one more easily to crime and suicide, as well as to insanity, with which last the other two are often inextricably confused. This tendency has been observed among the Medjidubs and the Aïssaonas, who, not having any narcotics, bring on intoxication by a prolonged oscillatory movement of the head. "They are dangerous people," says Berbrugger,[3] "fierce, and inclined to theft." Opium-smokers,

[1] Bosco "L'Omicidio negli Stati Uniti d'America," 1897.
[2] Baer, *op. cit.*, p. 343.
[3] "L'Algérie," 1860.

also, are often seized with homicidal fury; and under the action of hashish Moreau felt himself impelled to steal.

The effects of wine are still more pernicious, and worse still, spirits, which may be called wine with its harmful principle concentrated. But most harmful of all are such liquors as absinthe and vermouth, which, in addition to alcohol, contain drugs that poison the nervous centers.[1] Neumann in 1876 showed how alcohol alters the hemoglobin, diminishes by one-fourth the capacity of the blood corpuscles to take up oxygen, and produces congestion in the membrane and cortex of the brain. From this there results dilatation of the blood vessels, paralysis of the muscular fibers of the walls of the vessels, œdema, and finally fatty degeneration of the irritated nerve cells. Kräpelin [2] showed that from 30 to 45 grams of absolute ethyl alcohol more or less checked and paralyzed all the mental functions. The stupor, which resembles physical fatigue in its effect, increases with the dose of alcohol absorbed, lasting for small quantities 40 or 50 minutes, and for larger quantities 1 or 2 hours. In the smaller doses the paralysis of the mental functions is preceded by a period of activity or acceleration which lasts 20 to 30 minutes at most.

But this observer has further demonstrated that the effect of alcohol is not the same for all psychological functions; that while one may have a transitory acceleration of motor innervation, the intellectual functions, such as apperception, conception, association, are checked and almost arrested even by the smallest doses of alcohol. The same may be said with regard to sensation. It follows that the initial period of excitation produced by small quantities of alcohol, is only a kind of fireworks, due to several factors coming together, especially to the increase of external associations of ideas, associations of words, sensations, etc., to the detriment of internal associations, those more logical and profound. Under the influence of alcohol the over-excited motor centers give the drunkard an illusory power, impelling him to the most brutal acts. The association of ideas

[1] "Revue Scientifique," 1897.

[2] "Ueber die Beeinflussung einfacher physicher Vorgänge durch einige Arzneimittel" (Jena, Fischer, 1892).

is disturbed, and the drinker repeats without cessation the same barren platitudes, the same coarse jests. This likewise is to be explained by the initial acceleration of the psychomotor activities, by which painful mental inhibitions are intercepted. Alcohol, after it has once driven its unhappy victim into this evil path, holds him fast there, since, after a drunkard is once made, the noblest sentiments become paralyzed and the soundest brain diseased. This is a new experimental proof of the truth of the statement that crime is the effect of a morbid condition of the organism. Thus, with alcoholics, the schlerosis which affects the brain, spinal cord, and ganglia, as well as the liver and kidneys, shows its effects in one set of cases, in dementia, uremia, or jaundice, according to the part affected, and in others by crime.

But unhappily crime is the commonest and most frequent consequence, a truth of which there is superabundant evidence. I met recently in prison a very remarkable thief, who, as they all do, boasted of being a thief, and did not know how to talk in anything but thieves' slang; and yet neither his education nor the shape of his head gave any indication of what impelled him to crime. I soon learned the cause, however, when he told me that both his father and he were drunkards. "You see," he said, "since I was a boy I have had a passion for brandy, and now I drink from forty to eighty small glasses of it, and the brandy drunkenness passes away after I have drunk two or three bottles of wine." [1] Habitual drinkers are not only immoral and beget children who are defective, delinquent, or precocious debauchees,[2] as we shall show by the history of the Juke family, but intoxication itself is a direct cause of crime. Gall tells of a brigand named Petri, who felt himself impelled to homicide when he drank; and he mentions a woman in Berlin who, when intoxicated, was seized with sanguinary desires.

Alcohol, then, is a cause of crime, first, because many commit crimes in order to obtain drink; further, because men sometimes seek in drink the courage necessary to commit crime, or an excuse for their misdeeds; again, because it is by the aid of

[1] "Archivio di Psichiatria e Scienze Penali," 1890.
[2] Ann. Med. Psich., 1877.

drink that young men are drawn into crime; and because the drink-shop is the place for the meeting of accomplices, where they not only plan their crimes but also squander their gains. It has been estimated that in London in 1880 there were 4938 public-houses which were the resorts of criminals and prostitutes exclusively.

Finally, alcohol has a direct relation to crime, or rather to the prison, since after his first imprisonment the liberated criminal, having lost his reputation and all connection with his family, seeks compensation and oblivion in drink. This is why we often find alcoholism among recidivists, and it also explains the fact observed by Mayhew, that in the afternoon nearly all the thieves of London are intoxicated, and generally die of drink between the ages of thirty and forty. The same thing is found among the transported convicts of Noumea, who drink not only from settled habit, but also to forget dishonor, separation from family and country, and the cruelties of the wardens and their companions; and perhaps also to drown remorse. Wine becomes among them a regular medium of exchange. A shirt is worth one liter, a coat or pair of trousers, two. There is nothing, even to the kiss of a woman, that may not be bought with wine.[1]

§ 41. Specific Criminality

It will be useful here to observe what crimes are especially influenced by alcoholism. From Baer's statistics[2] of the penitentiaries and jails of Germany, shown on the opposite page, it appears that alcoholism occurred oftenest in the case of those charged with assaults, sexual offenses, and insurrections. Next came assassination and homicide; and in the last rank those imprisoned for arson and theft, that is to say, crimes against property. These, however, are more numerous than the others with habitual drunkards. The minimum occurs in the case of forgery and swindling, and with reason, for, as several swindlers have said to me, "it takes a clear head to carry out a shrewd scheme." According to Marambat,[3] of 3000 convicted persons

[1] Simon Meyer, "Souvenirs d'un Déporté," p. 376, Paris, 1880.
[2] "Der Alkoholismus, seine Verbreitung, etc.," Berlin, 1878.
[3] "Revue Scientifique," 1888.

investigated by him, 78% were drunkards; vagrants and mendicants lead with a figure of 79%; murderers and incendiaries showed 50% and 57% respectively; and thieves, swindlers, etc., 71%. In general, 88% of the crimes against persons were committed by alcoholics, and 77% of the crimes against property. Marro, also, found that among drunkards highway robbers held the first place, 82% being addicted to drink; of brawlers, 77% were the same; of thieves, 78%; then swindlers with 66%, murderers with 62%, and ravishers with 61%. Vétault found that of 40 alcoholic criminals, 15 were homicides, 8 thieves, 5 swindlers, 6 sexual criminals, 4 brawlers, 2 vagrants. We may say, in general, that the serious offenses, especially the infliction of bodily injuries and crimes against property (simple theft and robbery), are those in which the influence of alcoholism makes itself more decidedly felt, but that its action is less evident in the latter class of cases than in the former.

	Total	Alcoholic Criminals		
		In general	Occasional	Habitual
I. In Penitentiaries				
Assaults	773	575 (75.5%)	418 (72.7%)	157 (27.3%)
Robbery and murder	898	618 (68.8%)	353 (57.1%)	265 (42.9%)
Simple homicide	348	202 (63.2%)	129 (58.6%)	291 (41.4%)
Sexual crimes	954	575 (60.2%)	352 (61.2%)	223 (38.8%)
Theft	10,033	5212 (51.9%)	2513 (48.2%)	2699 (51.8%)
Attempted homicide	252	128 (50.8%)	78 (60.9%)	50 (39.1%)
Arson	304	383 (47.6%)	184 (48.0%)	199 (52.0%)
Premeditated homicide	514	237 (46.1%)	139 (58.6%)	98 (41.4%)
Perjury	590	157 (26.6%)	82 (52.2%)	75 (47.8%)
II. In the Common Jails				
Sexual offenses	209	158 (77.3%)	113 (73.3%)	41 (26.7%)
Resistance to officers	652	499 (76.5%)	445 (89.0%)	54 (11.0%)
Assaults	1130	716 (63.4%)	581 (81.1%)	135 (18.9%)
Arson	23	11 (48.0%)	...	...
Theft	3282	1016 (32.0%)	666 (63.5%)	382 (36.5%)
Fraud, forgery, etc.	786	194 (24.7%)	111 (57.2%)	83 (42.8%)

In studying the influence of alcohol upon the criminality of Great Britain and Ireland, there are to be found, according to Fornasari di Verce, some strange differences. (1) With the increase of the consumption of alcohol crimes against property without violence frequently decrease, though irregularly; [1] and with the falling off of the use of alcohol crimes increase. There are, however, some exceptions. Thus, in 1875–76 they increased with the increased consumption, but in 1877–78 increased also, notwithstanding a diminution in the use of alcohol. (2) Upon violent crimes against property the consumption of alcohol has no certain influence. (3) Fraudulent crimes against property mostly decrease with the greater consumption of alcohol. From 1870 to 1875, and from 1863 to 1865, as the consumption rose, these crimes descended from 276 to 260, and from 519 to 238. From 1848 to 1855, however, the two increased together. Consequently, independent of the consumption of alcohol, there is now an increase, now a diminution, of these crimes. Thus while the use of alcohol went on diminishing from 1875 to 1884, fraudulent theft sometimes increased, sometimes decreased. (4) Forgery and counterfeiting also decreased up to 1884 with the lowering of the price of wine, but after that increased notwithstanding the lower price. (5) Crimes against persons seem to follow the fluctuations of the consumption of alcoholic beverages, increasing gradually with the rise in the price of alcohol, as in the period 1848 to 1857. They do not, however, decrease with the lowering of the price in the period 1873 to 1889.[2] (6) The other crimes have no very clear relation with the consumption of alcohol; but misdemeanors and violations of police regulations decrease with the diminution in consumption.[3]

Finally, it may be remarked that although a very important factor, in England, where it makes itself felt with most intensity,

[1] That the increase or diminution of the consumption of alcohol exercises no great influence upon the crimes against property without violence may be seen, for example, from the fact that these crimes increased from 20,035 to 23,571 in 1847, and from 21,545 to 23,017 in 1854, paralleling an increase in the consumption of alcohol. But, on the other hand, they diminished in 1864 and 1871 from 14,075 to 13,202, and from 12,294 to 11,265, notwithstanding the noticeable increase in consumption, from 0.85 to 0.90, and from 1.23 to 1.27.

[2] Fornasari di Verce, *op. cit.*, p. 198.

[3] Fornasari di Verce, *op. cit.*, chaps. 62–68.

alcoholism enters as a cause into no more than 77% of the cases. In New South Wales there is no correspondence to be found between alcohol and crime, except in the case of theft and arson.[1]

§ 42. Antagonism between Alcoholism and Crime in Civilized Countries

It is a remarkable fact that in civilized countries, where alcohol is most abused, as in New South Wales and England, its influence becomes weaker and weaker, and Bosco shows that in the United States, only 20% of the homicides are addicted to drunkenness, while 70% on the contrary are sober (*op. cit.*). This fact has already been explained by Colajanni and Zerboglio.[2] It is not, according to them, that alcohol has any less terrible effect upon individuals, but that the abuse of it occurs where civilization is already very far advanced and protects the individual from great crimes by increased inhibitory power and a greater psychic activity. This is why England, Belgium, Norway, and Germany, which are the countries where the maximum quantity of alcohol is consumed but civilization is most advanced, furnish a smaller contingent of homicides than Spain and Italy, where less is consumed.[2]

Here is a recent table of alcoholism in Europe:[3]

	Consumption of pure alcohol per capita (in gallons)	Homicides to 100,000 inhabitants
Austria	2.80	25.0
Spain	2.85	74.0
Germany	3.08	5.7
Italy	3.40	96.0
United Kingdom	3.57	5.6
Belgium	4.00	18.0
Franec	5.10	18.0

This explains, as Colajanni very truly remarks,[4] why in France the serious crimes caused by alcoholism, which were from 7% to

[1] Coghlan, *op. cit.*

[2] "L'Alcoolisme," Turin, 1893.

[3] Coghlan, "The Wealth and Progress, etc.," Sydney, 1893.

[4] "Arch. di Psich.," VII.

11% in the period from 1826 to 1840, descended to 5% and 3% in the period from 1861 to 1880. Alcoholism continues and even increases, but at the same time the inhibitory power given by civilization also increases. It is for this reason that crimes diminish notwithstanding the influence of alcohol. We must add that in the north the effect of the cold plays a large part; and although, on the one hand, it induces men to drink, on the other hand it lessens their impulsiveness and hence their tendency to homicide.

§ 43. Political Disturbances

Alcohol is a powerful factor in insurrections. This fact has not escaped the attention of leaders of rebellions, who have often taken advantage of it to attain their ends. Thus in Argentina Don Juan Manuel, himself an alcoholic, found a powerful aid to his political schemes in the explosions of popular rage produced by drink. For the same reason alcohol was a political weapon in the hands of Quiroga, Franco, Artigas, and their wild followers, of whom several, like Blacito and Ortoguex, became themselves the victims of *delirium tremens* (Ramos-Mejia).[1]

The abuse of spirituous liquors in Buenos Ayres in 1834 is unbelievable. In that year there was consumed, besides hundreds of hogsheads of brandy, 3836 *frasqueras*, 263 hogsheads, and 2182 demijohns of gin, 2246 hogsheads of wine, 346 barrels of beer, as well as cognac and port. During the French Revolution it was alcohol that inflamed the bloody instincts of the crowd and the representatives of the revolutionary government. Among the latter we may recall Monastier, who, being intoxicated, had Lassalle guillotined, and the next day did not remember the order he had given. The envoys from Vendée in three months emptied 1974 bottles of wine (Taine), and included in their number Vacheron, who violated and then shot down women who resisted his alcohol-inflamed desires. It has been asserted that during the *coup d'état* of the second of December, enormous quantities of wine were distributed to the troops. Certainly alcoholism was no stranger to the disturbances of 1846, among the chiefs of which, according to Chenu,[2] there

[1] Lombroso and Laschi, "Le Crime Politique et les Revolutions."
[2] "Les Conspirateurs," 1849; Lombroso, "Le Crime Pol., etc."

were two drunkards, Caussidière and Grandmesnil. It is also certain that alcoholism played a great part in the Commune, thanks to the great quantity of wine and spirits to be found in the besieged city. Despine[1] notes in this connection that dipsomania recruited the greatest number of the soldiers of the Commune, who were drawn by the hope of gratifying their unfortunate appetite by pay and pillage, and whom alcoholism made indifferent to danger and wounds. The Communist general, Cluseret, himself in his *Mémoires* does not attempt to conceal the fact.

"Never," he says, "have the wine-sellers made so much money as at that period." [He himself often had to have heads of battalions arrested for intoxication, not only between night and morning, but also between morning and night.] "When things began to look black for the besieged insurgents, when the Versailles troops were threatening Fort d'Issy at close range, what did the defenders do? The taverns and wine-shops of the village were crowded with customers stupefied by drink. At Asnières, on the very eve of the capitulation, the National Guard, following its laudable custom, smoked, slept, ate, and drank."

§ 44. Alcoholism and Evolution

In the "Man of Genius" I have shown that a number of men of genius, and certain of their parents, were alcoholics (Beethoven, Byron, Avicenna, Alexander, Murger); but one may say that this is rather an effect and complication of genius than a cause, for these great and powerful brains need ever some new stimulant. Parallel to this is the fact that the more civilized peoples more easily fall a prey to alcoholism, as a necessary consequence of their greater cortical excitability.

§ 45. Tobacco

According to Venturi,[2] criminals show a greater number of users of snuff, not only than normal persons, but also than the insane (criminals, 45.8%; insane, 25.88%; normal persons, 14.32%); and among the criminals themselves those guilty of

[1] "De la Folie," etc., Paris, 1875.
[2] Venturi, "Archivio di Psich.," VII, 630.

crimes of blood show a higher percentage (48%) than do thieves and forgers (43%). Criminals and lunatics form this habit very early, which is not the case with the normal man; but while the habit grows upon the insane in the asylums, with criminals it is not similarly increased by detention in prison.[1] The prostitutes of Verona and Capua nearly all take snuff, and those who do not, smoke. Marambat[2] asserts that the passion of a minor for tobacco leads to idleness, drunkenness, and finally crime. Of 603 delinquent children from 8 to 15 years of age, 51% had the habit of using tobacco before their detention; of 103 young men between 16 and 20 the proportion of tobacco users was 84%; of 850 mature men 78% had contracted this habit before the age of 20. Of these, 516, or 57%, had been imprisoned for the first time before the age of 20, while of those who had never made use of tobacco the proportion of those imprisoned so young was only 17%. Of vagrants, beggars, thieves, swindlers, etc., 89% are tobacco users. Among convicts who are drunkards 74% use tobacco, among the others only 43%. The number of recidivists among those who smoke is 79%, and only 55% among those who do not. Temperate prisoners show 18% of recidivists among those who do not smoke, and 82% among those who do.

It is clearly to be seen, then, that there is a causal connection between tobacco and crime, like that which exists in the case of alcohol. But, as in the case of alcohol, it is a curious fact that the countries where the consumption of tobacco is greatest have a lower criminality.[3] This contradiction is frequently met in our researches; but it soon disappears, because the abuse of these stimulating substances, as in the case of alcohol, takes place especially among civilized people, who learn to control themselves.

[1] Venturi, *op. cit.*

[2] "Archiv. di Psich.," V, 378.

[3] Consumption of tobacco in pounds *per capita:*

Holland	6.92	Germany	3.00	Spain	1.70
Austria	3.77	France	2.05	Italy	1.34
Denmark	3.70	Switzerland	1.87	Russia	1.23
Belgium	3.15				

(Coghlan, "Wealth of New South Wales," 1895.)

§ 46. Hashish

Stanley found in Africa a kind of brigands, called Ruga-Ruga, who were the only natives who used hashish to excess. According to a tradition of Uganda, crime appeared among the sons of Kinto after they had taken up beer-drinking.

§ 47. Morphine

To the foregoing intoxicants many more may be added. The Malay running amuck is impelled to his homicidal mania by the intoxication of opium. The Chinese opium-eater is at once apathetic, impulsive, and inclined to suicide and murder. Many female swindlers have both the morphine habit and a tendency to hysteria; and those addicted to the use of morphine generally have the moral sense largely obliterated, and are in consequence the more inclined toward swindling, and sometimes toward homicide and sexual offenses.[1] The slave to morphine loses little by little the power of resisting impulsive tendencies, to such an extent that he equals or surpasses the smoker of hashish, with whom criminal tendencies are common. A Chinaman, in order to get money for opium-smoking, staked even his own fingers, which he cut off, joint by joint, as he lost. Dr. Lamson, a morphine user, poisoned his brother-in-law with morphine, without comprehending the gravity of the act. When slaves to morphine are undergoing a forced abstinence they show rage, melancholy, and a tendency to suicide and homicide, but especially toward theft for the purpose of procuring the desired drug (Guimbail). Marandon de Montijel reports the case of an advocate who, being refused morphine on board ship, broke into the ship's stores to procure it. A woman suffered so from being deprived of morphine that she ended by prostituting herself in order to obtain it. Another, addicted to the use of morphine, murdered her granddaughter, and maintained that the drug drove her to acts of violence.[2] An hysterical woman, 28 years old, committed a fraud by getting goods to the value of 120 francs under a false name, but, with a strange improvidence,

[1] Charcot, *op. cit.*
[2] Guimbail, "Annales d'Hygiene Publique," 1891.

returned to the store a few days after and returned part of the goods, saying that she was not satisfied with them. She had sold the rest to buy morphine, for she owed the druggist 1600 francs, and when he refused her further credit she committed her offense.

§ 48. Spoiled Maize

Indian corn that has become spoiled must be regarded as a cause of crime. Experimental observations have shown that hens and good-natured dogs, fed upon spoiled maize, become fierce after a time. I have already in my "Études Cliniques sur la Pellagre" (1872), and in my "Traité sur la Pellagre" (Turin, 1890), told stories of criminals, where the original factor was pellagra, that is to say, the use of spoiled Indian corn. Thus a man afflicted with pellagra out of avarice starved his children, and killed one of them for having stolen a few potatoes out of his field to appease his hunger. A woman threw her new-born child into a well almost publicly. Another stole to satisfy an insatiable appetite, and said, "I should be capable of eating a man." All three had acquired moral insanity at an advanced age through being poisoned by maize.

CHAPTER VIII

INFLUENCE OF EDUCATION UPON CRIME

§ 49. Illiteracy and Crime

THE absolute parallelism between education and crime, which many maintained several years ago, is to-day rightly regarded as an error. Marro found that of 500 criminals and 500 honest men in Turin there were:

	Criminal	Honest
Illiterate	12%	6%
Knowing how to read and write . .	75%	67%
Educated	12%	27%

with, it is true, a larger proportion of criminals among the illiterates, but also among those who could read and write.[1]

Morano proved in 1878 in Palermo that of 53 crimes committed in the school, 34 came from the pupils and 19 from the teachers, who certainly did not lack for education.[2] Curcio found one convict in Italy to 284 of the illiterate population, and one to 292 of the educated, — figures which, with a slight increase of literates among the criminals, would balance one another. These very slight differences become in certain categories of crime still less marked. Three-sevenths of the convicts had received elementary instruction; one-half of those guilty of sexual offenses, one-half of the minor offenders, and ten twenty-fifths of the criminals against persons and property had received some instruction (Curcio, *op. cit.*). And while criminals in general give an average of from 50% to 75% of illiterates, criminals who are still minors average only 42%, and in some provinces still lower. In Lombardy, for example, only 5% of the juvenile offenders are illiterate, and in Piedmont

[1] "Caratterie dei Criminali," 1886, Turin.
[2] Lombroso, "L'Incremento del Delitto," p. 80.

17%. As early as 1872 it had been estimated that to 453 illiterates there were 51 who could read, 368 who could read and write, 401 who could read, write, and count, and 5 who had received a higher education.[1] According to Joly, the department of Herault, which in 1866 gave the minimum of illiterates (1%) among the conscripts, at that time held the lowest place in the scale of criminality; whereas now that it has a great number of schools it has mounted to the highest; and a similar statement may be made of Doubs and Rhône (*op. cit.*). On the other hand, Deux Sèvres, Vendée, and Lot with 12, Vienne with 14, Indre with 17, Côtes-du-Nord with 24, and Morbihan with 35 illiterates furnish the minimum degree of criminality (*id.*). Levasseur calculates that of 100 persons indicted in France there were:

	1830–34	1840–50	1850–60	1860–70	1875	1878
Knowing how to read	38	41	48	55	60	95
Having higher education	2	3	3	5	4	4

Thus in less than 30 years criminals with more or less education doubled in number. Tocqueville shows that in Connecticut criminality has increased with the increase in instruction. In the United States the maximum figures for criminality (0.35, 0.30, and 0.37 to the 1000) were noted in Wyoming, California, and Nevada, which gave the minimum number of illiterates (3.4, 7.7, and 8.0%); and the minimum figures for criminality were found in New Mexico (0.03), South Carolina (0.06), Alabama, Mississippi, Georgia, and Louisiana, which had the highest number of illiterates. Nebraska, Iowa, Maine, and Dakota were exceptional, having a small number of criminals and illiterates both, as a result of other causes which we shall see presently. In England the counties of Surrey, Kent, Gloucester, and Middlesex, where there is a higher degree of education, gave the maximum degree of criminality, while the minimum was shown

[1] Cardon, "Statist. Carceraria," Rome, 1872.

by the more illiterate districts, North Wales, Essex, and Cornwall.[1] In Russia, where education is much less common, Oettingen (3d ed., p. 597) calculates that 25% of the convicts know how to read and write, and even 29% of the men, while of the population at large only 8% can read and write. "Examine," says Lauvergne, "the records of the courts, and you will see that the most unreformable criminals are all educated" ("Les Forçats," p. 207). But Coghlan gives us a still better proof in his "Wealth of New South Wales" (Sydney, 1895). There the percentage of illiteracy among the general population in 1880 was 12; the illiterate prisoners were 5.5% of the illiterate population,

	Persons arrested	Illiterate	Knowing how to	
			Read	Read and write
Against persons	3,355	222	39	3,094
Against property with violence	990	60	14	916
Against property without violence	4,873	331	69	4,473
Rioting, drunkenness	32,878	2,348	473	30,057
Counterfeiting	157	3	4	150

and the more or less educated prisoners 6.2% of the educated population. In 1891 the general percentage of illiteracy was 7%, the illiterates imprisoned 4.1%, and the educated persons imprisoned 4.7%. That is to say, absolutely as well as relatively, that persons who had received instruction committed

[1] Mayhew, *op. cit.*:

	Convicts to 10,000 inhab.	Percentage of illiterates
Gloucester	26	35
Middlesex	24	18
North Wales	7	35
Cornwall	8	45

more crimes than the illiterate. From 1881 to 1891 pupils in the schools increased from 197,412 to 252,940, and the persons arrested from 39,758 to 44,851. For each 10 new schools opened there were 5 more arrests; and this was true in all the different branches of crime.

§ 50. Diffusion of Education — Its Advantages

However, an impartial examination of the figures for these last years brings the comforting assurance that education is not so fatal as it appears at first to be. It favors crime only up to a certain point, after which its influence is the other way. Where education is widely diffused the list of educated criminals increases, but the list of illiterate criminals increases still more, which shows that the criminality of the class with a moderate amount of education is decreasing. Thus in New York, while the whole population showed 6.08% of illiteracy, and the immigrants who furnish the greatest proportion of criminals only 1.83%, the criminal class showed an illiteracy of 31%.[1] Of the homicides recently convicted in the United States,[2] 33% were completely illiterate, 64% could read and write, and 3% had a higher education, while the illiteracy of the population at large was only 10%. In Austria, while the young and moral population of Salzburg and the Tyrol have no illiterates, the criminal population show an illiteracy of from 16% to 20% (Messedaglia). In the recent statistics of Joly (*op. cit.*) we find that in France, to the 100,000 inhabitants:

6	departments	had	7	to	10	illiterates	to 9	indictments
13	"	"	10	"	20	"	" 9	"
3	"	"	20	"	50	"	" 9	"
11	"	"	50	"	61	"	" 9	"

Here crime increased with a moderate education, and decreased with a higher education. In France also the following percentages of illiteracy were found: [3]

[1] Brace, "The Dangerous Classes of New York," 1871.
[2] Bosco, "L'Omicidio negli Stati Uniti," 1897.
[3] Oettingen, 3d ed., p. 597.

	Among soldiers	Among criminals
1827–28	56	62
1831–32	49	59
1835–36	47	57
1836–50	47	48
1863–64	28	52
1865–66	25	36
1871–72	20	37
1874–75	18	36
1875–76	17	34
1876–77	16	31

The illiterates in each of the two categories diminish each year, then, but much more slowly among the criminals; and we may add that the criminals under 21 years of age decreased from 1828 to 1863 by 4152 individuals. The facts appear still more clearly if we study the number of pupils in Europe, following Lavasseur,[1] and the proportion of pupils in the public and private schools to the population, following Bodio,[2] together with the statistics of homicides and thefts given by Ferri, and those of revolutions given in my "Crime Politique." We shall find the following data:

	Pupils to 100 inhabitants	Homicides (1880–82) to 100,000	Thefts to 100,000	Revolutions to 10,000,000
Prussia	17.8	5.7	246	5
Switzerland	16.1	16.4	114	80
England [3]	16.4	5.6	163	7
Netherlands [3]	14.3	5.6	...	..
Sweden [3]	13.6	13.0	...	..
Austria	12.5	25.0	103	5
France	14.5	18.0	103	16
Belgium [3]	10.9	18.0	134	..
Spain	9.1	74.0	52.9	55
Italy	7.6	96.0	150	30
Russia	2.4	14.0	?	..

1 "Bulletin de la Société de Statistique," 1895.
2 "Di Alcuni Indici Misuratori de Movimento Economico," 1891.
3 Public schools only.

From this we see that the number of homicides decreases with the increase in the number of pupils, except in the case of Russia (with only 14 homicides, notwithstanding the minimum number in the schools, 2.4), and of Switzerland, which has high figures for both pupils and homicides. Thefts follow the opposite course. They rise in England, Belgium, and Prussia with the greater number of pupils in the schools, and fall in Spain with the smaller number. Revolutionary tendencies give contradictory results. This relation is maintained to a certain point everywhere if we study the nations severally. In Italy the parallelism between homicide, rape, and ignorance is complete, the minimum, mean, and maximum of ignorance corresponding with those of the two crimes mentioned, as seen in the following table:

NUMBER OF CRIMES TO THE 100,000 INHABITANTS WITH ILLITERACY

	86–80%	80–50%	50–0%
Homicides [1]	32.3	22.9	6.6
Rapes [1]	23.6	11.3	10.2
Frauds [1]	41.0	63.0	50.0
Thefts [2]	141.0	160.0	119.0

We have seen in France and England that crimes of blood are becoming more and more rare in the large cities, where they are nearly always committed by peasants and mountaineers; while crimes against property, on the other hand, are on the increase. A similar situation prevails in Italy with regard to recidivists, just because they are more educated. In Belgium great crimes have decreased each year since 1832, falling from 1 to 83,573 of the population, which was the figure for the year mentioned, down to 1 for each 90,220 in 1855. In Switzerland great crimes have decreased 40% since 1852. In France the more serious

[1] Bodio, "Relazione alla Commissione di Statistica Giudiziaria," 1896.

[2] Ferri, "Omicidio" (Atlas), 1895.

crimes, those passed upon by the assizes, had fallen from 40 to the 100,000, which was the figure in 1825, to 11 to the 100,000 in 1881; while the offenses which came before the magistrates rose from 48,000 to 205,000. There is, it is true, an augmentation of crime amounting to 133%; but crimes of blood have diminished, while sexual crimes have been on the increase. From 1826 to 1880 thefts increased 238%, frauds 323%, breach of trust 630%, and sexual crimes 700%. Vagrancy is four times greater, and offenses against officials five times. Bankruptcies have risen from 2000 up to 8000, and while the number of merchants has increased, of course, this increase has not been in the same proportion. These differences express the influence of education. But this influence has been more remarkable as well as more favorable in England,[1] where from 1868 to 1892 the number of prisoners fell from 87,000 to 50,000, and the number of adult criminals from 31,295 to 29,825. Yet the population increased in the same time 12%, and now it is calculated that there are but 21 illiterates out of every 100 indicted. This diminution occurs especially in London, where schools are more numerous and widely diffused.

§ 51. Special Criminality of the Illiterate and of the Educated

All this explains a phenomenon which appears at first completely self-contradictory, namely, that education now increases crime and now decreases it. When education is not yet diffused in a country and has not yet reached its full development, it at first increases all crimes except homicide. But when it is widely disseminated it diminishes all the violent crimes, except, as we shall see, the less serious crimes, the political crimes, or the commercial or sexual crimes, because these increase naturally with the increase of human intercourse, business, and cerebral activity. But education has an indisputable influence upon crime in changing its character and making it less savage. Fayet and Lacassagne show that in

[1] "English Judicial Statistics," 1895; Joly, "Revue de Paris," No. 21, 1895.

France: (1) Among illiterates the crimes which lead are infanticide, abortion, theft, formation of criminal bands, robbery, and arson; (2) among those who can read and write imperfectly, extortion, threatening letters, blackmail, robbery, injury to property, and assaults predominate; (3) among those who have received a moderate education, bribery, forgery, and threatening letters prevail; (4) among the well educated the predominant crimes are forgeries of commercial papers, official crimes, forgery and abstraction of public documents, and political crimes (*op. cit.*). The minimum of forgeries and the maximum of infanticides are found among the illiterate. With the convicts of a higher education the prevailing crime is forgery of public documents, breach of trust, and swindling. Infanticides and violent crimes are lacking.

Accordingly there is a type of crime for the illiterate, namely, the savage type; and one for the educated, the milder, but more cunning type. In the same way, according to the most recent studies of Socquet[1] we see that in France the illiterate criminals gradually diminished in the period 1876–80 in comparison with the period 1831–35. Homicides and murders have decreased among them by half, infanticides and abortions by a third, and sexual crimes nearly a half. The violent crimes of educated criminals are, on the whole, diminishing, while their other crimes are nearly at a standstill. As to political crimes, these increase constantly among the educated. History teaches us that it has been the highly civilized states (Athens, Genoa, Florence) which furnished the maximum number of revolutions; and it is certainly not among the illiterate that the nihilists and anarchists get their recruits, but among the more highly educated. Of this I have given abundant proof in my "Crime Politique." In Austria the crimes which prevail among the illiterate are robberies, abductions, infanticides, abortions, murders, bigamy, homicides, malicious injury to property, and assaults. In Italy, following the remarkable study of Amati,[2] we find:

[1] "Contribution à l'Étude de la Criminalité en France."
[2] "Istruzione e Delinquenza in Italia," 1886.

Crimes, 1881–83	Illiterate	Able to read and write	More highly educated
Political crimes	54%	36%	10.0 %
Frauds	38%	55%	7.0 %
Homicides	62%	37%	0.12%
Thefts	65%	34%	1.7 %
Rapes	48%	44%	8.0 %
Rebellions	49%	48%	3.1 %

Among 500 individuals who had a higher education there were in 1881–83 the following number of the crimes specified (the second figure giving the number to the 1000):

Forgeries	76–152
Homicides	44– 88
Thefts	40– 80
Frauds	57–114
Extortions	38– 76
Highway robberies	22– 44
Sexual crimes	34– 68
Bankruptcies	33– 66
Perjuries	2– 4
Assaults	13–26
Parricides	2– 4
Political crimes	14–28
Crimes against religion	1– 2
Destruction of property	4– 8
Arson	9–18
Instigation to crime	6–12
Abortions	1– 2

That is to say, the figures are higher for forgery, fraud, sexual crime, bankruptcy, theft, extortion, and homicide; and lower for assault, highway robbery, parricide, and arson. Accordingly, while the illiterate lead in homicide and theft, the fully and partly educated together show a high figure for political crimes, and an absolute majority of the rapes and frauds.

But it should be observed here that the above statistics belong to a period when thought was completely free in Italy, and when, therefore, the comparatively few political uprisings did not draw into their ranks the better part of the population; hence the relatively large number of illiterates. Now, however, those condemned for political crimes belong to the more highly educated strata of the nation. The same thing is true of Russia, where the greatest number of political offenders is furnished by the educated class. Thus from 1827 to 1846 the nobles exiled to Siberia for political causes were 120 times as numerous as the peasants. Of 100 women condemned for political crimes in Russia, 75 were well educated, 12 could read and write, and 7 were illiterate.[1]

It cannot be said, then, that education always acts as a preventive of crime, nor, on the other hand, that it always impels toward crime. When it is really diffused among all classes, it has a beneficial effect, diminishing the number of crimes among those moderately educated, and making the character of them milder.

§ 52. Education in the Prisons

However, if education is valuable for the population in general, it nevertheless ought not to be extended to the inmates of prisons, unless it is accompanied by a special training designed to correct the passions and instincts rather than to develop the intellect. Elementary education is positively harmful as applied to the ordinary criminal; it places in his hands an additional weapon for carrying on his crimes, and makes a recidivist of him. The introduction of schools into the prisons, at once bringing bad men into contact with each other and developing their intelligence and power, explains, to my mind, the great number of educated recidivists. For statistics show us that of crimes against property, made easier by education, recidivists committed over twice as many (67.4%) as non-recidivists (28.47%), while their crimes against persons were relatively much fewer. It is doubtless the elementary instruction given in the prisons of France, Saxony, and Sweden that accounts for the large number of forgeries committed by recidivists. The pickpocket and cut-throat learn in prison, at the expense of the state, to make false keys, to make counterfeit money, to engrave banknotes, and to commit burglaries.

§ 53. Dangers of Education

"Knowledge," says Seymour, "is power, not virtue. It may be the servant of good, but it may also be the servant of evil." To put the same truth in other words, the simple sensory knowledge of the form of the letters or the sound which indicates an

[1] E. N. Tarnowski, "Juridicesky Vestnik," 1889.

object, or the knowledge even of the great technical and scientific advances which have been made, does not raise the moral plane in the least degree. Indeed, it may become, on the contrary, a powerful instrument for evil, by creating new crimes that more easily escape the clutches of the law. Thus the advancement of science may enable criminals to use the railroad, as was the case with Tiebert in 1845; or dynamite, as with Thomas; or the telegraph and cipher messages, as in the case of the Venetian, Fangin, who used this means to indicate to his accomplices the courier who was to be robbed. Caruso, the bandit, was accustomed to say that if he had known the alphabet he would have conquered the world; and the murderer Delpero declared at the foot of the gallows that the cause of his ruin was the education which his parents had procured for him, since it had made him prefer idleness to poorly paid labor. Finally, all criminals learn, by reading the accounts of trials, of which they are very fond, to put into practice the arts of their predecessors. Thus, among 150 vagrants, Mayhew found 50 who had read "Jack Sheppard" and other stories of criminals, and who declared that this reading had inspired their first steps in a life of crime.

From the lowest education to the highest among us Latins, with whom crime is continually increasing, there is no teaching given that does not open the wound rather than heal it; and especially is this the case with political crimes. We live in a stirring time when the days are years and the years centuries, and we would have our young people live in an atmosphere thousands of years old. The best intelligence has not time enough to take in that part of knowledge that is necessary to all (like natural history, hygiene, modern languages, and economics), and we would have the youth spend his precious hours in learning to babble dead languages and dead sciences, and all this to make him a man of good taste. It seems ridiculous to waste ten or twelve years on flowers and musical scales. The mighty torrent of modern life, laden with facts, passes before us and we do not see it. How it will make our descendants smile to think that thousands and thousands of men have seriously believed that some reluctantly learned and quickly forgotten fragment of the classics, or, worse still, the dry rules of ancient grammar, were the best means of developing the mind and forming the character of a young man, better means than the exposition of the most important facts, better means than study of the causes of those facts. In the meanwhile we are creating generation after generation whose brains are crammed with study of the form only, and not of the substance; and, worse than this (since the form may be transmitted in some masterpiece), with an adoration of the form which amounts to fetichism, and is the more false, blind, and sterile the longer it has been profitlessly employed.

It is from this sort of education that has come the adoration of violence that has been the starting point of all our rebels, from Cola di Rienzi to Robespierre. What is the whole classical education but a continual glorification of violence in all its forms? In this matter all political parties are alike, so deep-seated is evil. The clericals cry *Hurrah!* at the dagger-thrust of Ravaillac, and the conservatives do likewise at the wholesale execution of the Communists in 1871. What wonder, then, that in a society saturated with violence, violence breaks out from time to time on all sides in storm and lightning? It is not possible to declare with impunity that violence is holy, with the proviso that it is to be used only in a certain way, for sooner or later some one will come to transfer the gospel of force from one political creed to another.

I am glad that my illustrious master Taine has preceded me in this line of thought. In his last pages he has given an almost posthumous admonition to us poor Latins, so vain-glorious, and so obstinately attached to that which is our ruin.

"The true learning, the true education," writes Taine,[1] "is acquired by contact with things, by innumerable sense-impressions which a man receives all day in the laboratory, the workshop, the court-room, or the hospital, impressions which enter by the ears, the eyes, the nose, to be consciously or unconscously assimilated by him, and which sooner or later suggest to him a new combination, a simplification, an economy, an improvement, an invention. Of these invaluable contacts, of

[1] "Revue Philosoph.," 1894–95.

all these assimilable and indispensable elements of mental life, the French youth is deprived just at the most fruitful age. For seven or eight years he is shut up in school, cut off from the personal experience that would give him a correct and vivid idea of things, of men, and of the way to equip himself for life.

"It is too much to demand of young people that upon a set day they shall present themselves in the examination-room in the possession of all knowledge. As a matter of fact two months after the examination they have forgotten everything; but in the meantime their mental vigor declines, freshness and fertility disappear. The accomplished man, or rather the man who is no longer capable of any change, becomes ticketed, resigned to a life of routine, perpetually turning the same wheel.

"On the other hand, the Anglo-Saxons [the only race in Europe, as we shall see, among whom criminality is declining] have not our innumerable special schools. Among them instruction is given not by the book, but through the object itself. The engineer, for example, is educated not in the school but in the workshop, a thing which permits each man to reach the grade suited to his intelligence: workman or builder, if he can rise no higher, engineer, if his talents permit. With us, on the other hand, with the three grades of instruction, for childhood, youth, and young manhood, with the theoretic and scholastic instruction imparted by means of benches and books, the mental tension is simply increased and prolonged by the prospect of examinations, diplomas, degrees, and commissions; while our schools do not give the indispensable equipment, namely, a sound and firm understanding, will, and nerves. So the entrance of the student into the world and his first steps in the field of practical action are oftenest but a succession of unfortunate falls, from which he emerges bruised even if not crippled. It is a rough and dangerous experiment. His mental poise is disturbed, and is in danger of not being reëstablished. The disillusioning is too rude and too violent."

Finally, education often incites to evil by creating new needs and aspirations without giving the power to gratify them. Especially is this brought about by the mingling of good and bad elements in the school, an influence the more dangerous when the teacher himself inclines to evil, particularly in sexual relations, as has been observed in Italy and Germany.[1]

In this matter I am much of Dante's opinion:

[1] Oettingen, *op. cit.*

"Chè dove l'argomento della mente
S'aggiunge al mal voler ed alla possa,
Nessun riparo vi puo far la gente."[1]

"You reckon," says Joly, "upon the school's supplying the place of the parents, who are kept occupied at their work, or who lack the knowledge or ability to do their duty by their children; and you count, on the other hand, on the family to supply the deficiency of the moral training of the school. But while each waits for the other, they unite in accomplishing nothing."

[1] "Where intelligence is united with power and wickedness, the efforts of men are vain." ("Inferno," XXXI.)

CHAPTER IX

INFLUENCE OF ECONOMIC CONDITION — WEALTH

§ 54.

THE influence of wealth is a factor much more disputed than that of education, and the most impartial examination of the facts fails to give a complete solution; for the investigator fails to secure a sufficient number of decisive proofs. Bodio himself in his classic work, "Di Alcuni Indici Numeratori del Movimento Economico in Italia" (1890), shows that it is impossible to give an answer to the question, What is the actual wealth of Italy? It is impossible to place a valuation upon all the agricultural and mineral wealth, because we have no exact statistics of mining and agriculture. A statement of all individual properties is impossible for lack of a simultaneous appraisal of all real and personal property. It is necessary, therefore, to rely upon private statements as found in deeds-of-gift and wills. The average wage must be arrived at hypothetically upon the basis of the minimum necessary for living, which itself, in turn, is based upon conjectural data. To estimate wealth on the basis of taxes alone is seen plainly to be impossible when one reflects that the errors of the assessors by themselves would be sufficient to overthrow all calculations, without considering the numbers of business men, bankers, and even professional men who escape taxation more or less completely. This is why the results in this division of the subject, however one may attack it, hardly succeed in establishing an exact relation between wealth and the more important crimes.

§ 55. Taxes

The following tables present a comparison of the number of the principal crimes compared with the sum total of all taxes paid by the inhabitants of the various provinces, including taxes upon consumption (internal revenue, tobacco, salt, etc.), direct taxes (farm property, real estate generally, personal property, etc.), and taxes upon business.

MAXIMUM WEALTH

Average tax paid per capita, in francs	Province	Sexual Crimes	Frauds	Thefts	Homicides[1]
74.9	Leghorn	26.4	76	224	21.3
71.3	Rome	22.1	65	329	27.8
55.1	Naples	20.7	48	161	26.7
54.5	Milan	11.7	47	157	3.4
45.6	Florence	12.6	48	120	9.9
42.5	Genoa	17.2	59	147	7.8
41.4	Venice	14.3	138	246	6.6
38.4	Turin	17.9	103	121	9.1
33.3	Bologna	11.3	104	216	7.6
33.0	Cremona	6.8	59	134	2.3
31.7	Ferrara	7.2	33	387	6.1
31.4	Mantua	15.6	88	254	7.8
		15.6	70.6	206	11.3

MEAN WEALTH

Taxes	Province	Sexual Crimes	Frauds	Thefts	Homicides
26.9	Port Maurice	10.1	94	135	6.2
25.4	Novara	8.1	34	100	6.3
25.1	Grosseto	22.4	50	105	15.4
24.6	Caserta	17.0	44	189	31.2
24.4	Cuneo	6.9	52	87	8.8
24.1	Ancona	11.7	128	100	19.0
23.5	Palermo	21.8	35	150	42.5
23.3	Lecce	16.7	52	126	10.3
23.0	Bergama	9.5	38	115	4.0
22.5	Forli	7.4	172	174	21.5
20.4	Cagliari	17.2	68	296	21.8
20.3	Perugia	12.7	32	140	15.9
		13.4	66	143	17.0

[1] The data are all from Bodio (1879–83), except the thefts, which are from Ferri. The taxes are taken from the "Annuario del Ministero della Finanze, Statistica Fin." (1886–87).

MINIMUM WEALTH

Taxes	Province	Sexual Crimes	Frauds	Thefts	Homicides
10.5	Belluno	6.3	25	108	5.1
13.6	Sondrio	13.0	31	120	5.4
14.0	Teramo	14.7	37	108	20.4
14.7	Cosenza	34.8	30	125	38.2
15.0	Campobasso	22.2	42	190	41.2
15.4	Aquila	18.5	44	118	31.1
15.8	Chieti	31.1	76	119	25.7
16.3	Reggio Calabria	30.5	26	214	30.5
16.4	Messina	17.9	29	148	19.2
16.5	Ascoli	13.3	40	82	11.9
16.6	Avellina	23.3	42	179	45.4
18.3	Macerata	9.8	102	273	13.0
		19.6	43	148	23.0

The next table is formed by arranging these figures in groups, and adding to them the data for the years 1890–93 furnished by Bodio, in which he includes, besides the thefts tried at the assizes, those coming before the minor courts:

	Wealth, 1885–86			Wealth, 1890–93 (Bodio)		
	Maximum	Mean	Minimum	Maximum	Mean	Minimum
Fraud	70.6	66.0	43.0	55.13	39.45	37.39
Sexual crimes .	15.6	13.4	19.4	16.15	15.28	21.49
Thefts . . .	206.0	143.0	148.0	361.28	329.51	419.05 [1]
Homicides . .	11.3	17.0	23.0	8.34	13.39	15.40

[1] Bodio includes rural thefts.

From which it appears that fraudulent crimes increase positively with the increase of wealth, and the same is true of thefts, but if we add rural thefts we get the maximum where wealth is least; and this last is always true of homicides. This shows more clearly the influence of mere poverty upon the minor crimes. We have already shown in the chapter on subsistence that, in Germany, while thefts in general became less frequent in the years when the price of grain was lowest, and increased when the price was very high, thefts from the forests, on the other hand, pursued the contrary course. But these thefts, which still recall the ancient time when land and pasture were common property, are bound up with old tradition, and only exceptionally represent the immorality of a country. The results for sexual crimes are more unexpected. They show their minimum in Italy where wealth is moderate, and their maximum where there is the minimum of wealth. Italy thus presents an exception, as the usual course of sexual crimes is to increase with the increase of wealth. An examination of the figures shows, likewise, that there are individual provinces which give figures very far from the average of their several groups.

§ 56. Inheritance Taxes

De Foville believes that it is possible to estimate private wealth upon the basis of the declarations in wills;[1] but if we study Pantaleoni's[2] very valuable statistics for Italy, we shall see with what difficulty we shall arrive at any idea of the relation of crime to wealth. In fact, in studying the table given on the following page, we draw the conclusion that the richest districts, Piedmont, Liguria, Lombardy, and Tuscany, have a proportion of crimes against property less than the average of the kingdom; the same is true of the districts which in wealth come nearest the average, Venice and Emilia. The poorest regions, Sardinia, Sicily, and Naples, have a high criminality; but Umbria and the Marches, which are also poor, show a very low figure for crime. Thefts are very rare in Tuscany, Lombardy, Emilia, Piedmont, and Liguria, which are the richest districts, and also in one of the poorest, the Marches. In Sicily they are moderately numerous, and in Venice a little more so, a fact to be explained by the

[1] De Foville, "La France Économique," 1870.

[2] Pantaleoni, "Delle Regiona d'Italia in Ordine alle loro Ricchezze ed al loro Carico Tributario" (Giornale degli Economisti, 1891); Id., "L'Entita e le Variazioni della Richezza Privata in Italia dal 1872 al 1888" (Giorn. Econ. 1890).

intense misery of the agricultural population of the latter district. The richest district, Latium, and the poorest, Sardinia, have the greatest number of thefts; so that here there is no evident parallelism with wealth. Bodio observes that in the case of Latium it is necessary to take account of the disturbing influence of the capital upon both crime and wealth. The inheritance taxes are in this case an unreliable measure of the wealth of the locality, since there is capital concentrated here which belongs to other districts. Besides this, there is at Rome, on account of special conditions of rural property and the system of cultivation in use, a very limited number of persons who have immense properties, a fact which has a disproportionate effect upon the inheritance taxes. The smallest number of frauds is found in Umbria and the Marches; then come Tuscany, Emilia, Venice, Piedmont, Liguria, and Lombardy, which are the richer districts. The district of Naples furnishes fewer frauds by a great deal than it would seem it should because of its comparative poverty.

INDICTMENTS. (AVERAGE TO 100,000 POPULATION, 1887–89)

	Average Wealth	Thefts	Frauds	Highway robberies	Homicides	Assaults
Latium . . .	3333	639	116	18	25	513
Piedmont } Liguria } .	2746	267	44	7	7	164
Lombardy . .	2400	227	44	3	3	124
Tuscany . .	2164	211	34	6	7	165
Venice . . .	1935	389	43	3	4	98
Reggio . . .	1870	320	49	7	13	287
Emilia . . .	1762	250	38	6	6	130
Sicily	1471	346	65	16	26	410
Naples . . .	1333	435	47	6	21	531
Marches } Umbria } . .	1227	222	33	3	10	239
Sardinia . .	....	670	113	14	20	277

The minimum number of highway robberies is shown by Venice and Lombardy (rich) and by Umbria and the Marches (poor); the medium number by Tuscany, Emilia, Naples,

Piedmont, and Liguria. Sardinia and Sicily, which are poor, are joined with the wealthy district of Latium in giving the maximum. The great contradictions are very apparent.

§ 57. Lack of Employment

One would be tempted to believe at once that unemployment must exercise a perceptible influence upon criminality. It is, however, of little importance. In New South Wales [1] the effect of periods of idleness upon the workmen is almost nothing. Wright [2] maintains that at the time of industrial depressions all crimes are increased, but he presents no proof. When he says that of 220 convicts in Massachusetts, 147 were without regular work, and that 68% of criminals have no occupation, he only bears witness that criminals do not like to work, a fact that is very well known. In the United States 82% of the murderers about whom the facts were ascertainable were occupied when they committed their crime, and only 18% were without work.[3] It seems, then, that unemployment is not a cause of crimes of violence.[4] The fact that the majority of criminals have almost never a settled trade does not contradict this. They never had an occupation and never wanted to have one, while the real unemployed are those who have had work and lost it through circumstances beyond their control, or practically so, allowing for strikes.

§ 58. Days of Work

A surer criterion for this question is to be found in the number of days' wages equivalent to the annual price of food for one individual. (See Table.[5]) This approaches

[1] Coghlan, *op. cit.*

[2] Wright, "The Relations of Economic Conditions to the Causes of Crime," Philadelphia, 1891.

[3] Bosco, "L'Omicidio negli Stati Uniti d'America," 1895.

[4] Compare Fornasari di Verce, *op. cit.*, chaps. 32–33, 44–48.

[5] The comparisons of criminality on the different nations set forth in this table must be received with some caution because of the different moral and legislative conditions in the different countries — a thing to be especially noted, as Bodio observes, with reference to sexual crimes. It is an important fact, however, that the figures for homicides given in the latest statistics (Bodil, "Sul Movimento della Delinquenza nel 1893," p. 51) do not change the relative position of the countries, except that England takes the first place and Scotland the second.

Days of work equivalent to a year's food 1		Number of Persons (to the 100,000 Inhabitants) convicted for: Homicide 2		Assault 3		Sexual offenses 4		Theft 5	
England and Wales, Scotland, Ireland	127	Scotland	0.51	England and Wales	2.67	Spain	1.03	Spain	59.63
Belgium	130	England and Wales	0.56	Ireland	6.24	Ireland	.85	Belgium	110.44
France	132	Ireland	1.06	Scotland	11.59	Scotland	1.41	France	110.95
Germany	148	Germany	1.11	Spain	43.17	England and Wales	1.66	Italy	165.89
Austria	152	Belgium	1.44	France	63.40	Italy	4.01	Ireland	65.81
Italy	153	France	1.53	Germany	126.40	Austria	9.33	England and Wales	165.63
Spain	154	Austria	2.43	Italy	155.35	France	10.26	Scotland	268.39
		Spain	8.25	Belgium	175.39	Belgium	13.83	Germany	226.02
		Italy	9.53	Austria	230.45	Germany	14.87		

Note.—Column 1 is taken from Mulhall's Dictionary of Statistics (quoted by Coghlan, *op. cit.*); and columns 2–5 are figured from the data published by the Director of Italian Statistics ("Movimento della Delinquenza secondo le Statistiche degli Anni 1873–83," Rome, 1886).

closely to the study which we have already made of the cost of subsistence.

We see here (1) that excess of labor in connection with a minimum wage, that is to say, with a lack of proper nourishment, has a certain correspondence with homicide. In fact, Scotland, England, and Ireland, which have the minimum number of days' work, have also the minimum of homicides, 0.51, 0.56, 1.05; and Spain and Italy, which have the maximum, have the maximum of homicides, 8.25, 9.53. (2) Further, there is a certain correspondence in the case of assaults. England, Ireland, and Scotland, which have the minimum necessary days of work, 127, have also the minimum number of assaults, 2.67, 6.24, 11.59; Austria and Italy have a maximum number of days of work, 152 and 163, with the maximum of assaults likewise, 155, 230. But there is at the same time an exception in the case of Spain, which has a small number of assaults, with a large number of days, and also in the case of Belgium, which shows a large number of assaults, 175.34, with only 136 days of work, a fact certainly to be traced to the influence of alcoholism. (3) The influence is reversed in the case of sexual offences. Of these one frequently observes the lower numbers where the number of days' work required is highest. Thus Spain, where 154 days are required, has but 1.03 sexual crimes; while Belgium, which has next to the smallest number of days of work, 130, has next to the highest number of these offenses. The United Kingdom, however, which shows the minimum number of days, has the second lowest number of sexual crimes. (4) The number of thefts is apparently in no way affected, for we see all degrees of this crime in countries with both high and low figures as to days of work, as in Spain, Belgium, France, Italy, etc.

§ 59. Savings Banks

I have thought that the number of the depositors in the savings banks would give more reliable data for the real wealth of a country, because this would give the measure of the principal source of wealth, — foresight and economy, — and hence measure how prevalent among the people are the forces that inhibit vice and crime. As a matter of fact, we have already seen that in France wealth is in direct relation to the lower birth-rate, which at bottom corresponds to greater foresight and to greater inhibitive power.

According to Coghlan (*op. cit.*) we find in Europe:

	Persons to each savings-bank book	Crimes to 100,000 inhabitants	
		Homicide	Theft
Switzerland	4.5	16	114
Denmark	5	13	114
Sweden	7	13	...
England	10	5.6	163
Prussia	10	5.7	246
France	12	18	103
Austria	14	25	103
Italy	25	96	150

These figures show how homicides decrease as the number of bank books increases, while the contrary is true of thefts. In Italy, it is true, from the very limited data that we have, we see that the greatest number of savings-bank books, while corresponding, as elsewhere, with the smallest number of homicides, corresponds also with the smallest number of thefts.[1] The average of the different crimes in the 20 Italian provinces that have the greatest number of savings-bank books (1 to from 3 to 6 inhabitants), in the 20 with the smallest number (1 to from 15 to 24), and in the 20 that have a medium number (1 to from 8 to 13), is as follows:

Average number of crimes in 20 provinces in which number of books is —

	Maximum	Intermediate	Minimum
Fraudulent crimes	57	45	45
Sexual crimes	11	12.6	20
Thefts	132	133	160
Homicides	10	12.6	27.4

[1] "Annuario Statistico Italiano," 1892.

As we have seen in the case of taxes in Italy, so it is here; where there is less foresight and saving, as evidenced by the number of savings-bank books, there are more crimes of blood, thefts, and rapes, but less swindling, while these relations are just reversed for the maximum and moderate degrees of wealth. This simply means that a country still barbarous is more inclined to violence than to cunning. But the same peculiarity with regard to Italy that we noted in connection with the taxes is again apparent here, namely, that rapes, which elsewhere increase with wealth, here are most common in the poorest provinces.

However, where race and climate already impel to evil, wealth, as I have already said, can do nothing. Thus we find a high number of homicides in the richest provinces, like Palermo with 42, Rome with 27, Naples with 26, and Leghorn with 21. These apparent exceptions are explained by the geographical position of Palermo and Naples, by race at Leghorn, and in Rome by race, abuse of alcohol, and political conditions. The contrary is true of the poorer provinces in which geographical position, climate, and race exaggerate the influence of poverty; for the highest figures are to be found in the southern and insular provinces. In the case of sexual crimes also there are analogous exceptions and explanations, since a large number are to be found in the rich provinces of Leghorn (26) and Rome (22), while among the poor provinces a very small number is shown by Reggio, Emilia, Vicenza (4), Belluno and Rovigo (5), Udine (7), etc. Here again the explanation is evidently ethnic and geographic. This proves indirectly that the high figures shown by the poorer provinces in southern Italy and the islands are connected not with economic peculiarities, but with race and climate.

§ 60. Savings in France

As regards France, by estimating the wealth in the several departments on the basis of the number of savings-bank books to 1000 inhabitants, we find that crimes invariably increase directly as wealth increases. Thus:

Departments where the degree of wealth is —

	Average number of		
	Homicides	Thefts	Rapes
Minimum	64	83	17 [1]
Medium	86	99	26
Maximum	89	186	29 [2]

[1] Minimum wealth, 0 to 100 books to the 1000 inhabitants (Corsica 20, Ardèche, 97).
Medium wealth, 100 to 200 books (Lot 101, Loire-et-Cher, 190).
Maximum wealth, 200 to 406 books (Seine 201, Sarthe 406).
[2] "Annuaire d'Economie Politique," Paris, 1886.

The striking difference of the influence of savings in France and in Italy is explained, up to a certain point, in the same way that we have explained the difference that we found between the two countries in the influence of density (see Chapter V); namely, that it is to the richest districts of France, where manufacturing is most developed, that the emigrants flow; and these commit, in general, four times as many crimes as the French. Now from 1851 to 1886 the number of immigrants into France tripled, and the quality of the immigrants deteriorated as their numbers increased; for in the beginning it is the better elements that come in, but later, when the current that carries men from one country to another becomes too strong it carries the worst elements with it (Joly). The department of Nord has four times more foreigners than Boûches-du-Rhône, and 19 times more than Hérault; but it has 9 times more naturalizations than the former, and 75 times more than the latter. That is to say, the foreign element in Nord is much more stable and assimilable, being largely Belgian, while Hérault is much frequented by Spaniards. Immigrants are also drawn into France by the low birth-rate and by the frequency of strikes, which give them hope of finding work.[1]

In southern Italy climatic and ethnic factors come into col-

[1] Joly, "France Criminelle."

lision with the economic factor. We have already seen that in consequence of the joint effect of the Semitic element in the population, and the hot climate, all crimes against persons, and in part those against property, are abnormally increased. But it would be a great mistake to suppose that these explanations are sufficient. We have still to look for a graver cause. If we compare certain districts of Italy, like Piedmont and Lombardy, with parts of France that are similar in race and climate, we shall see that under nearly identical conditions opposite phenomena occur. In Italy the greater savings correspond with the smaller number of crimes, while in France the contrary happens. Here we must see the cause in the fact that in France the maximum wealth is enormously greater than in Italy, at least four times as great, in fact. This is the more important since in many places in France this wealth, being too quickly acquired, drives its possessors to the greatest debauchery, so that, as Joly well puts it, to amuse oneself and to debauch oneself become synonymous. We find a direct proof of this in the fact that in Italy moderate and maximum wealth both lead to the same results, just because there is so much resemblance between them; while in France, on the contrary, the maximum degree of wealth differs enormously from moderate means, and in consequence produces contrary results. In Italy the increase of savings is an effect of economy rather than of positive wealth, while in France, at least in the manufacturing districts, especially in Hérault and Boûches-du-Rhône, savings accounts are an indication of a wealth so great that it too often degenerates into an occasion for wild speculation. Hence it is that we find all the advantages of wealth in one country, and all the disadvantages in the other. Moderate wealth, slowly accumulated, restrains from crime; inordinate wealth is no longer a rein, but a spur and an incentive to crime.

§ 61. Agriculture and Manufacturing

In fact, where manufacturing crowds agriculture hard, and still more where it displaces it entirely, we see the number of crimes increase immediately. Indeed, if we divide France (as in the study "Sur la Criminalité pendant 50 Ans" above) into agricultural, mixed, and manufacturing districts, we see that crime nearly always increases as we pass from the first named to the last. Of 42 agricultural departments only 11, or 26%, go beyond the average number of assassinations in France; while the average is exceeded by 10 out of the 26 departments of mixed industry, or 38%, and by 7 out of 17 manufacturing departments, or 41%. Rapes upon adults and crimes against persons show similar results.

Percentage of departments exceeding the average of all France in:

	Rapes	Crimes against persons
Agricultural Departments (42) . . .	33%	48%
Mixed (26)	39%	39%
Manufacturing (17)	52%	59%

These figures are certainly to be explained by aggregations of population and the coming in of immigrants.

"In the department of Hérault," writes Joly, "fraud came in permanently with wealth. Never were there more attempts at bribery, whether of the local officials or of the highest representatives of the central administration. . . . A case has been cited to me in which the entire municipal council fraudulently evaded the payment of their own taxes. This evil was the greater for going unpunished, the jury having brought in an acquittal. . . .

"Was not this general demoralization produced, or hastened and aggravated in any case, by the crisis in wine-growing, which has permitted these people since 1874 to make enormous gains with their wines? As a matter of fact, it was in 1874 that Hérault passed from the 5th place as regards criminality, up to the 61st, and in 1884 it went on to the 81st."[1]

"From the day," writes Joly again, "when the peasants, hitherto poor, could change their uncultivated land into vineyards, from the day when, thanks to the railroads, their products increased enormously in value before their eyes . . . from that day they became greedy. . . . The man who has gambled aud won in the stock exchange dreams only of stocks and bonds, and of cornering the market. Now all wealth gained without

[1] Joly, "La France Criminelle," p. 112.

effort resembles a little money won by gambling, and has the same effect upon the mind. 'It is good fortune,' said the commissioner of Cette, 'that has ruined this country.'"

When Bocage was poor it was honest. "Now those who steal have possessions themselves, and the well-to-do peasants commit more crimes than the vagrants" (Joly). In the east in the department of Eure, and in the west in Calvados, manufacturing and agriculture are backward, and there is little criminality. In Vire the inhabitants live by working the ground and crime is almost unknown.

§ 62. Wealth as a Cause of Crime

Those, consequently, who affirm that criminality is always an effect of poverty, have not considered the other side of the question, and observed the cases where crime is the effect of wealth. Rapidly acquired wealth, which is not balanced by a high character or by a lofty religious or political idealism, is harmful rather than helpful. Spencer also has said of wealth, that according as the fundamental character of a people is good or bad, it leads to virtue or vice; and especially is the latter the effect of excessive wealth, which, like excessive power or excessive education, is a natural instrument of despotism, of all sorts of sexual and alcoholic abuses and, in consequence, of crime. Accordingly, wealth is now a check, now a spur to crime, just as we have seen is the case with education, civilization, and density of population, and as we shall see to be true of religion.

Here is the criterion which must especially be kept in mind in the ætiology of crime. For according to our character and stage of development the same cause now destroys and now saves us. Thus we shall see apparent contradictions disappear and even contribute toward a full explanation. Thus in the United States, those states which have the highest criminality have now the maximum and now the minimum of wealth (as shown by the data obtained directly from individuals in taking the census).[1] We see there that the richest states have a low criminality. Rhode Island, for example ($183 per capita), has a criminal figure of 0.11; Massachusetts, with nearly the same

[1] Scribner's "Statistical Atlas of the United States," 1880.

degree of wealth ($178), has nearly twice the criminality, 0.20, almost the same as the District of Columbia, 0.21, which has a moderate degree of wealth ($112), as has also Wyoming, which, however, shows nearly twice the criminality, 0.35. Some poor states like Dakota ($30 per capita), Alabama ($19), and New Mexico ($19), give the lowest criminal statistics, from 0.04 to 0.03; but here we encounter a contradiction, for Delaware, with a criminality figure of only 0.05, has a moderate amount of wealth ($82). We have seen above how in France and Italy criminality in general increases, only changing its character; we have seen that Artena furnishes the maximum of crime for Italy, and yet that there no one, according to Sighele, is really poor, all being small land-holders, etc. This does not prevent the fact that, when a state of barbarism prevails, as in Corsica, crimes against persons increase, as simple thefts do, in the years and in the districts in which there is extreme poverty.

§ 63. Explanation

The cause of all this is only too clear. On the one side poverty and the lack of absolute necessities impel toward the theft of indispensable things for the satisfaction of the individual's own needs.[1] This is the first cord binding poverty and assaults upon property. On the other hand, poverty makes men impulsive through the cortical irritation following the abuse of wine and alcohol, that terrible poison to which so many of the poor resort to still the pangs of hunger. Account must be taken also of the degeneration produced by scurvy, scrofula, anemia, and alcoholism in the parents, which often transforms itself into epilepsy and moral insanity. Poverty also drives men to commit brutal eliminations of individuals who are an unwelcome burden upon the family, recalling the parricides and infanticides committed by savages under similar circumstances. Poverty is indirectly a cause of sexual crimes, on account of the difficulty which the poor have of obtaining satisfaction through prostitution; on account of precocious promiscuity in factories and mines; and also because of the frequency of infantilism or

[1] Mayr, "Die Gesetzmässigkeit in Gesellschaftleben," München, 1877; Fornasari, *op. cit.*

feminism among the boys.[1] On the other hand, when a slight temptation toward evil is presented to an individual in comfortable circumstances, he is rendered physically and morally stronger by sufficient nutrition and a sounder moral training, and is less pressed by need, so that while he feels the impulsion to do evil, he can more easily resist it.

But wealth, in its turn, is a source of degeneration from other causes, such as syphilis, exhaustion, etc. It drives men to crime through vanity, in order to surpass others, and from a fatal ambition to cut a figure in the world, which, as we have seen, is one of the greatest causes of crimes against property. Also, as Fornasari has very truly remarked, where wealth is absolutely the greatest it is always accumulated in the hands of a few, so that at the same time there is always great poverty, more keenly felt because of the contrast. This favors the tendency toward crime on the one hand, and on the other furnishes better opportunities for it. Besides, it should be noted[2] that where wealth is least, the crowding in of population is least, especially of dangerous individuals, who gather in the richer districts to carry on their criminal practices more easily, as, for example, in France, at Cette.

If it is true, on the other hand, that urgent need drives the poor to wrongdoing, it is only to a very limited number of crimes, although these are the more violent ones; while the artificial wants of the rich, although less urgent, are more numerous, and the kinds of crime among them are infinitely more numerous also, as well as the means of escaping punishment, encouraged by the example of persons high in politics. Thus we see, in Italy, ministers guilty of crimes against the public who remain in power, in spite of the discovery of their crime, and even use it as a means of fortifying their position. It is only in France and England that the people refuse to be governed by criminals.

As for sexual and alcoholic crimes, the first satisfaction made possible by wealth never sufficiently appeases the blasé, but

[1] See my "Homme Criminel," Vol. I.

[2] See Ferri, "Dei Sostitutivi Penali," in Arch. di Psich., I, p. 88; "Studi sulla Criminalita in Francia," in "Annali di Stati," s. 2a, v. XXI, p. 183; Fornasari, *op. cit.*

drives them on to seek new excitements, such as rapes upon children,[1] sodomy, the misuse of morphine, cocaine, etc. Too great wealth, then, instead of being a preventive, is often a spur to new crimes.

"There are many," says Joly, "who have nothing and want nothing, and many who have too much and are always ambitious to possess more; and besides, just as in war killing *en masse* and at long range seems remote from the idea of homicide, so, in great cities, to ruin at a distance by fraud or bankruptcy an enormous number of people, does not seem really a crime, even to many timid people."

The born criminal finds, on the whole, more opportunities for crime in wealth than in poverty, but the case is still worse with the occasional criminal.[2] It is only necessary to study the physiognomy of Baihaut, De Z——, Tanlongo, etc., to be convinced that these were not congenital criminals, and, without politics, would never have become criminals.

§ 64. The Preponderance of Poor Criminals

But why, some one may object, are those convicted almost always poor? We see, for example, in the "Statistica Penale" for 1889, that 100 Italians indicted, of whom it was possible to know the economic condition, were divided as follows in the years given:

	1887	1888	1889
Indigent	56.34	57.45	56.00
Having only the necessaries of life	29.99	30.77	32.15
Fairly comfortable	11.54	9.98	10.13
Well-to-do or rich	2.13	1.80	1.72

[1] See above. While educated persons furnish 5% to 6% of all criminals, they furnish 12% of those guilty of rapes upon children; that is to say, while there is one criminal in twenty belonging to the liberal professions, in these crimes there is one in eight (Starkenburg, "Das Sexuelle Elend der Gebildeten," 1895).

[2] *Criminel par occasion* (elsewhere *d'occasion*). Lombroso uses this expression usually to indicate one who is a criminal by force of external circumstances, as distinct from the born criminal; but he sometimes employs it for the man of one crime as distinguished from the habitual criminal. — TRANSL.

These figures agree with those published by Guillaume, Stevens, and Marro,[1] in showing us an enormous disproportion of crimes among the poor.

But before we let ourselves be led away by these figures, which appear to be flatly contrary to our conclusions as to the evil effect of wealth, it is necessary to remember that the conviction of rich men is very rare, and that, when they violate the laws, as Marro very truly says, they are not put into prison so easily as the poor. The rich man has in his favor the influence of his fortune, his family, his social relations, and his intelligence. This is often enough to save him from prison, and always gives him able defenders. In the private asylums, which are used only by the rich, the morally insane are very numerous, though there are but few in the public asylums and the prisons; which means that wealth helps to clear up the pathology of the born criminal, while poverty obscures it. Further, in the contest between classes, the courts are used as a means of dominating the poor, who are already, *a priori*, convicted as such. The upper classes are accustomed to say, "Poor as a thief," and, alas! what is worse, to turn the proverb around.

> "If," as Colajanni says, "some of the delinquencies of the poor remain concealed, whether because the moral sense is deficient among them and for this reason no information is laid, as in the case of sexual crimes, or because the offenses take place under such conditions that they are not discovered, as in the case of field thefts, does it always happen that all the crimes of the rich come to light? Is there an army corps set aside to discover the crimes of the rich, as there is for the offences committed in the fields and forests?"

And have there not been cases of parliamentary and political immunity, flagrant or secret, — a kind of right of asylum, enormously extended to take in all delinquents having political power, ministers, deputies, great electors, journalists? A great

[1] Guillaume, "État de la Question des Prisons en Suède"; Stevens, "Les Prisons Cellulaire en Belgique"; Marro, "I Caratteri dei Delinquenti," Turin, 1887.

poet has told us that rags allow crime to be seen at once through their rents, while gold conceals and defends it.[1]

To sum up: the economic factor has a great influence upon crime, not, however, that poverty is the principal cause of it, for excessive wealth, or money too quickly acquired, plays a large part as well; and poverty and wealth are frequently neutralized by the effect of race and climate.

[1] "Through tatter'd clothes small vices do appear;
Robes and furred gowns hide all. Plate sin with gold,
And the strong lance of justice hurtless breaks;
Arm it in rags, a pigmy's straw does pierce it."
(SHAKESPEARE, "King Lear," Act iv, Sc. vi.)

CHAPTER X

RELIGION

§ 65.

THE influence of religion also is complex, even more so than that of civilization or wealth. We have seen that there are criminals who are very religious (especially in the country, and in relatively uncivilized localities), and also criminals who are irreligious, even atheistic.[1] We have seen that among church-goers, criminals and honest men are almost equally numerous,[2] and often the criminals are in the majority.[3] Of 700 criminals examined by Ferri 1 alone was an atheist, 1 was indifferent, and 7 were devout and even found in religion an excuse for their crime. One of these said, "It is God who gives us the instinct to steal"; another, "Crimes are not sins, for the priests also commit them"; and still another, "I have sinned, it is true, but the priest pardoned me at confession." The greater number were as careless of punishment in the hereafter as they were of human punishment. Thus a murderer, when Ferri asked him whether he did not fear the wrath of God, answered, "But God has never punished me yet." "But you will go to hell." "Oh, I may go, and I may not." And a third: "We shall see whether we shall be punished, when we are dead."

If we rely upon the somewhat limited statistics available in this matter, we shall find that there are fewer criminals where atheists abound, than where, under equal conditions, either Catholics or Protestants dominate. This fact may proceed from their greater degree of education, the more so as in Europe

[1] See my "Homme Criminel," Vol. I.

[2] Maxime Du Camp, while examining 33 convicts during mass noted that 3 were reading the mass, 1 sat with head covered and eyes fixed upon the altar, 1 knelt, 1 pretended to be reading the mass but really read the "Magasin Pittoresque," 1 was weeping, while 26 sat at table reading or working.

[3] See my "Homme Criminel," Vol. I.

atheists are especially numerous among the more highly educated. A certain amount of energy is necessary to separate oneself in religious feeling from the general and conventional modes of thought. The same power of inhibition which enables one to resist the imitative instinct makes it possible also to resist the impulse toward crime.

Joly, who nevertheless insists upon the ennobling influence of the external practices of religion, cites Normandy as an example of a district where the respect for ritual religion is very great, and yet at the same time there is a high degree of criminality. This is expressed in a proverb which he quotes as being in use among the inhabitants of Lozère: "Lozerian, rosary in one hand and knife in the other." He further illustrates his point by the following occurrence, which happened in Ardèche: Two groups of men had fallen into a quarrel at the market, and they had already raised their great iron-shod sticks when suddenly the Angelus sounded. The two hostile parties immediately lowered their clubs, uncovered, made the sign of the cross, and recited the Angelus. . . . But the prayer finished, they seized their weapons again, and the fight began anew. Joly observes that although in France the girls are more carefully instructed in religion than the boys, nevertheless the number of female juvenile offenders has not diminished; and if, on the whole, there is a decrease in juvenile crime, this is among the boys. Reclus [1] writes that there is a chapel at Treynier where they go to invoke the "Madonna of Hatred" to procure the death of some detested person. In speaking of Sicily the advocate Locatelli says:

"It is impossible to conceive the corrupting influence which must have been exercised upon the poorer classes by these thousands of priests, possessed of wealth and influence, idle, but endowed with the spirit and sensuality of all southern people. For them seduction, adultery, and incest itself were pardonable sins. The murderer who revealed his crime and excused himself on the ground that he had been provoked or injured, or even merely that he was in great poverty, was not only absolved, but also released from the necessity of satisfying

[1] "Geographie Universelle," II, 618.

the secular court, even where an innocent man had been arrested in his place. The witness who hid the truth from the judge in order to escape danger, or to avoid compromising a neighbor, was equally certain of reconciliation with God through the mediation of the confessor. The rich man, who secluded his own women with a truly Turkish jealousy, was treated with consideration if he attempted the honor of a daughter of the people. From smaller transgressions, such as forgery, a man could purge his conscience by paying the Church 32 francs and 80 centimes."

It is still only a few centuries since the great vicars-general of the richest cities granted permission to commit adultery for a whole year. In other cities the right to commit fornication with impunity for a lifetime could be obtained by the payment of a quarter cask of wine to the bishop's officer, who drew this privilege from the canon *De Dilectissimis*, in the decretals of the pope. One man even had the audacity to present to Pope Sixtus IV a petition for permission to commit this sin during the dog-days. In our own time there was a papal bull in force in Palermo until annulled in 1868, by which there was granted dispensation from the necessity of repaying unlawfully acquired money, by whatever crime obtained, upon payment of certain sums to the Church.[1] Dupin de Saint-André republished in 1879 "Les Taxes de la Penitencerie Apostolique,"[2] in which crimes are taxed according to tariffs established by Pope John XII and Pope Leo X. Thus, a layman who had killed a priest was absolved upon payment of 7 gros, and only 5 if he had killed another layman.

"If an ecclesiastic committed fornication with a nun, whether in or out of the monastery, or with one of his cousins or god-daughters, he was absolved only upon payment of 67 francs, 11 sous. If the act was against nature, 219 francs and 14 sous. A nun who had committed fornication with a number of men, whether in or out of the convent, 131 francs, 14 sous. Adultery was absolved for 87 francs and 3 sous. A layman might be absolved for adultery, however, for only 4 francs; but for adul-

[1] Quoted in full in the second edition of my "Incremento del Delitto in Italia," 1879, Turin.

[2] Published by Toussain Denis in 1520 and in Rome in 1741.

tery and incest, for 10 francs. Under John XII incest with sisters or mother cost 40 sous."[1]

Who does not know the maxims of the Jesuits of the last century? Lacroix, for example, says: "Although the natural law forbids lying and murder, under certain circumstances they are permitted." So Buzenbraun declares: "An extremely poor man may take what he needs, and may even kill anyone who tries to prevent him from taking what is necessary." In the same way Maiorca authorized regicide; and Père Longuet says: "A man does not sin against justice, and is not obliged to return the money that has been given him for killing or wounding" (*op. cit.*).

However, one thing seems clear to me, namely, that the younger religions are, the greater is their moral power, because the letter has not yet encroached upon the spirit, because the enthusiasm for new ideas occupies the mind and draws it away from crime, and, finally, because, whatever be its origin, the organism is then more free from symbols and formulas that clog its activity. This fact has been observed with us with regard to Savonarola and the Vaudois, and may still be noticed among the negroes in the United States, who, when they are converted to Methodism, renounce their idleness and practice of infanticide, so that in the districts where conversions abound the population increases noticeably. And it is a curious phenomenon that even the new religious sects created by pure paranoiacs, like the Lazarettists in Italy and the Quakers in England, brought about an immediate diminution in crime. Even the Skopzi, who castrate one another as a part of their religion, are renowned for their honesty. In northern Russia the Bialoriztzi[2] do not drink alcohol nor smoke: they wear white clothing woven by their own hands, and lead a virtuous life. The same is true of the Soutasevtzy, who reject priests, images, and military service, and as a consequence often suffer martyrdom. The "Sons of God" believe that each one is his own god, and that it is sufficient to address prayers to any neighbor. They unite

[1] Virginio Polidoro, "Della Invenzione delle Cose"; Bianchi-Giovini, "Storia dei Papi," Vol. XXI, 1864.

[2] "Revue des Revues," Oct. 15, 1895.

in wild dances in honor of God, continuing until they fall exhausted to the floor. And with all this they are very honest. The Veriginski or Tolstoïans drink only tea, and allow themselves to be maltreated without resistance, saying nothing more than "God help me," until their persecutor falls down in admiration at their feet. These new sects are veritable epidemics of virtue and saintliness.

It is a strange fact that the South-Russian sects, which are known for their sanguinary character (doubtless the effect of the hot climate, which, as we know, produces an inclination to homicide), nevertheless inspire a high morality. Thus the Doukobors kill all the children abnormal in body or mind, out of respect for the divine spirit that ought to dwell in them. One of their chiefs, Kapoustine, had all traitors to the dogmas of the sect buried alive, and in an action that was brought against him it was found that he had committed twenty-one religious homicides. All this appears to us more than criminal. Yet this sect is opposed to war, and preaches that the Czar reigns only over rogues and criminals, while honest men, the true Doukobors, have nothing to do with his laws or his authority. It is from this sect that the Molokani arose, drinkers of milk, enemies of priests, ornaments, and useless ceremonies. All educated and very honest, these people help one another, have no poor, and, to whatever place they are deported, turn the most inhospitable locality into a garden. The Mormons of America, also, were famous for their industry and probity.

On the whole, the contradiction of the influence of religion, now great and now totally lacking, disappears when one grasps the significance of the facts. Religion is useful when it is based absolutely upon morals and abandons all rites and formularies. This is a condition that can be realized only in the new religions; because while all in the beginning are moral, afterwards, little by little, they become crystallized, and ritual practices submerge the moral principle, which is less easily conceived and retained by the crowd. All members of new sects are men of one idea, which protects them, like a vaccine, against ignoble passions. It is for similar reasons that certain Protestant cities which have a more ardent religious fervor, like Geneva and London, are the only ones where crime is decreasing, notwithstanding the progress of civilization and the dense population (London alone having more people than an entire Italian province). Here it is not inhibition that comes into play, but a great religious passion, which neutralizes ignoble instincts, and combats vices and immoral tendencies with such vigor that it ends by conquering them.

"In England religion recruits thousands of fanatics, who, under the most diverse names and theories, work themselves into a fever over saving men's souls. They extend their activity over an immense field, organizing services, preachings, processions, pious works, etc.

"In the Latin countries, on the other hand, where the Catholic Church extends its domination, religion can only rarely be a preservative from vice; and this not so much because of the irreligion or scepticism of the people (a smaller factor than is generally believed, even in the country of Voltaire), but because of the very organization of the Church itself. The Catholic Church is a great disciplinary institution; it is almost an army, founded on obedience and subordination, in which each man has his place and prescribed course of action, laid down by immutable laws. Active, fanatical natures, like Dr. Barnardo, who are naturally independent and inclined to revolt, find themselves ill at ease in the Church, except in missions, which is the only department that grants individual autonomy. On the other hand they find themselves much at home in the Protestant sects, which are as free and autonomous as little clans or barbarous tribes, as is the case with the Baptists, for example, or the Salvation Army.[1]

"Further, fanaticism finds in the Germanic nations, and especially in England, a great field for its development in philanthropy, something which is almost always lacking in Latin countries.

"London is the principal city of these fanatics of philanthropy. Here are men and women of all classes and social positions, rich and poor, educated or ignorant, sane or mad, who have taken it into their heads to cure the diseases of society or to extirpate some special form of misfortune or sorrow. One has taken to heart the cruelties practiced upon children by their parents; another is concerned for blind old men; a third is concerned for the insane maltreated in the asylums; a fourth is interested in liberated convicts. And all work without ceasing, publish

[1] Ferrero, in the "Riforma Sociale," 1895.

journals, organize societies, make speeches, and sometimes succeed in bringing about great social epidemics and movements of popular opinion intense enough to result in some important humanitarian reform. This kind of activity may be an excellent substitute for political fanaticism, which results in dynamite outrages.

"But in the Latin countries such agitations would come to nothing. The tradition of the administration of charity by the public authorities or by the church is so deeply rooted that no one wants to concern himself personally with social miseries. If children are often maltreated in the great cities and the papers protest vigorously and stir up public opinion a little, public opinion will simply demand the enactment of a law by the state and then rest content, though the law will never be enforced. No one would think of founding private societies, such as they have in England, which watch cruel parents and at times come and snatch their little victims out of their hands."

This is natural. In the religions which have survived for many centuries the moral element disappears, because it conforms less to the sentiment of the masses, while only the ceremonial remains and superabounds. Of seventy-three principal articles of the Order of St. Benedict, only nine pertain to morals. In the Order of St. Columbanus one year of penance is decreed for anyone who loses a piece of the host (sacred bread), and six months for one who lets two pieces be eaten at once.

The only religions, then, which can prevent crime are those that are fanatical, passionately moral, or just arising. The others are no more effective than atheism, and perhaps less so.

CHAPTER XI

EDUCATION — ILLEGITIMATE CHILDREN — ORPHANS

§ 66. Illegitimate Children

THE influence of education upon crime is shown indirectly by the continually increasing proportion of criminals of illegitimate birth in the most civilized countries. In Prussia the illegitimate delinquents, who constitute 3% of the whole in 1859, rose by 1873 to 6%, and the women from 5% to 8%. In France, of the 800 minors arrested in 1864, 60% were orphaned or illegitimate, and 38% were the sons of prostitutes or delinquents. In Austria in 1873 10% of all the male criminals were illegitimate, and 21% of all the female.[1] In Hamburg 30% of the prostitutes were illegitimate (Hugel), and in Paris a fifth of the Parisian born prostitutes and an eighth of the country women.[2] In the prisons of Würtemberg in 1884–85 14.3% of the inmates were illegitimate; in 1885–86, 16.7%; in 1886–87, 15.3%; while the illegitimate individuals in the non-criminal population rose to 8.76%. Sichert[3] found among 3181 whom he examined in these same prisons, 27% of illegitimate criminals, or nearly double the other figures. These were divided as follows:

	Percentage of illegitimacy
Thieves	32.4
Pickpockets	32.1
Sexual criminals	21.0
Perjurers	13.0
Incendiaries	12.9

Of the habitual criminals he found 30.6% illegitimate, and 17.5%, a little more than half as many, of the accidental criminals. He found also the following:

[1] Oettingen, *op. cit.*
[2] "Parent-du-Châtelet," *op. cit.*
[3] Liszt, "Archiv. f. Strafrecht," 1890.

	Averse to work	Beggars	Vagrants
Of 1248 legitimate thieves there were	52.0%	32%	42%
Of 600 illegitimate thieves there were	52.3%	39%	49%

In Italy the statistics of the prisons show 3% to 5% among the male minors, and 7% to 9% among the females.[1] We may add that 36% of the recidivists in Italy are either natural children or foundlings. To comprehend the greater importance of these figures it is necessary to recall that a great proportion of all illegitimate children — at least 60%, and often 80% [2] — die in the first eighteen months or two years. Marbeau can then say without exaggeration that of four foundlings three die before they are twelve years old, and the fourth is doomed to a life of crime. To get at the significance of these figures more exactly I have made researches with regard to 3787 entries, nearly all adults, in the asylums of Imola (Dr. Lolli), of Padua (Prof. Tebaldi), and of Pavia, and also with regard to 1059 entries in the city hospital of Pavia in 1871, and I found that there were 1.5% of foundlings in the asylums and 2.7% in the city hospital; and nevertheless the mortality is less among the illegitimate in Pavia than in many other places.[3] Age and conditions being equal, foundlings furnish 20 times more delinquents than insane persons. We may affirm, then, with the greatest certainty, that the greater part of the foundlings that escape death abandon themselves to crime. Doubtless heredity enters largely into this result. Most of these children are the fruit of sin; they have no name to uphold, no rein to stop them when spurred by passion, no mother who, by her assiduous care, affection, and sacrifices, aids in developing noble instincts and suppressing tendencies to evil; they find an honest living hard to get and are inevitably drawn toward evil. If they have no perverse tendencies they acquire them by imitation. On the other hand, philan-

[1] "Statistica delle Carceri," Rome, 1873, CXXVIII.

[2] Of 1000 foundlings in Bordeaux in the course of 10 years 729 died. In 94 years 367,988 infants entered the foundling asylum, of whom 288,554 died in infancy, that is to say, 79%. (Angel, "Vortrag. üb. Mortal der Kinder," 1865.)

[3] 25% in the year after entrance.

thropic institutions, like orphan and foundling asylums, have also an evil influence, for, as we have seen, a multiplicity of contacts always fosters criminality.

§ 67. Orphans

That abandonment and the lack of education play a great part in producing criminality is demonstrated by the great number of orphans and step-children found in the prisons. In Italy among the juvenile delinquents in 1871–72 there were from 8% to 13% of step-children. Brace tells that in New York 1542 orphans and 504 step-children were arrested for various offenses. He adds that 55% of the criminals in the penitentiaries were without father and mother; and 60% of the children arrested had lost one parent, or their parents were separated. According to Marbeau, of 100 juvenile prisoners 15 had been abandoned by their mothers. In Italy during ten years we had an average of 33% to 35% of orphans among the delinquents; out of 580 insane adults in my clinic orphans furnished 47%, and the number of orphans reached 78% among the 1059 entering the hospital of Pavia. But it is certainly a still more important fact that we find an average of 18% to 20% of orphans among the juvenile criminals, for the proportion of orphans in the general population is lower than this. The same is true of half-orphans, who furnish 18% of the general juvenile population, but 23% to 30% of the juvenile delinquents. The Italian statistics show 26% of the delinquents to be fatherless and 23% to be motherless, while among the insane 51% have lost their fathers and 10% their mothers.

It is certain, on the other hand, that the female sex predominates among orphans who are criminals, and even more so in the case of foundlings. This is true even leaving out of account prostitution, which is a sort of minor criminality. So Oettingen arrives at the strange result, that while for each five male delinquents there is one female, in the case of foundlings there are three females to one male. This is, however, quite natural, for a woman being weaker and more passionate than a man, has more need of the support and restraint of the family to keep her in the right way, from which she is more easily turned than a man, on account of the slippery path of prostitution that is always open to her. Here the hereditary influence is very powerful, and women who have sprung from a sexual transgression are easily led into the same error, and from this to graver offenses.

The great number of foundlings among delinquents explains also the predominance of juvenile delinquents in the urban population (Cardon), and gives us the measure of the harm done by defective education and by abandonment.

§ 68. Vicious Parentage — Education

It is entirely natural that evil education should have a still more deplorably criminal effect than even abandonment. We may recall here the large proportion of criminals who are sprung from unsound parents. Sichart finds the proportion of pathological inheritance to be 36%, while Marro makes it 90%. 6.7% have epileptic parents, 4.3% are descended from suicides, 6.7% from insane persons; while in the case of those guilty of grave crimes, Penta finds an alcoholic heredity of 37%, and Marro of 41%. How can an unfortunate child protect himself from evil when it is presented to him in the most attractive colors, or, worse still, when it is imposed upon him by the authority and example of his parents, or those who are charged with his education? We shall comprehend the situation best from actual examples: V., a sister of thieves, was brought up by her parents as a boy. Clothed as a boy, she took on a masculine air, and wielded her knife vigorously. One day while on a journey she stole a cloak, and, being arrested, accused her parents of the theft. The Cornu family was composed of thieves and murderers, habituated to crime from their tenderest infancy. Of five brothers and sisters only one, the youngest, had shown a strong aversion to crime. Her parents found a means of overcoming her repugnance, making her carry the head of one of their victims in her apron for two leagues. In a little while she was so stripped of all remorse that she became the fiercest of the band and wanted to practice the most horrible cruelties upon their victims. The murderer Crocco, who at the age of three used to hit his comrades with stones and pluck birds alive, had often been left by his father entirely alone in the forest as late as his nineteenth year. Frégier tells of the son of a thief who was his father's pride because he was able at the age of three to take an impression of a key in wax. The wives of assassins, according to Vidocq, are more dangerous than their husbands, for they accustom their children to crime, and give them a present for every murder they commit.

We have seen, and shall see still more clearly in the next chapter, how numerous the criminals are who have immoral parents or families, in which case vicious education and vicious heredity work together. Here also, as in the case of abandonment, and for the same reasons, namely, prostitution and the greater persistency of the woman in crime, the number of women subject to these influences is greater than the number of men. To many readers the influence of education, as shown by these figures, will appear of little importance. But aside from the fact that we must add the figures for foundlings already cited, we must also recall the fact that many crimes have an autochthonous origin, and that many individuals are born perverse and remain perverse, notwithstanding the desperate efforts of their parents to correct them. Among the juvenile delinquents of the year 1871–72 [1] 84% of the boys and 60% of the girls belonged to moral families. This is to be explained by weakness shown by the parents early in the child's training, which later renders unavailing their most strenuous efforts to obtain obedience. Noël, Vidocq, Donon, Demarsilly, Lacenaire, Abbado, Hessel, Fra Diavolo, Cartouche, Trossarello, Troppmann, Anzalone, and Demme all belonged to honest families. Rosati told me that after his first thefts he had many times been beaten by his father and seen his mother weeping bitter tears over him, and he had promised them each time to restore the things stolen, naturally without keeping his promise. On

[1] Beltrami-Scalia, *op. cit.*

the other hand it has often been observed, and the investigations of Parent du Châtelet and Mayhew confirm the observation, that thieves and prostitutes who have become rich do their best to bring up their children to lead virtuous lives.

CHAPTER XII

HEREDITY

§ 69. Statistics of Hereditary Influence

AMONG 104 criminals whose heredity I have examined I have found the following facts:

71	showed some hereditary influence,	
20	had alcoholic fathers,	
11	"	alcoholic mothers,
8	"	criminal fathers,
2	"	criminal mothers,
5	"	fathers who were insane or had had meningitis,
5	"	insane or epileptic mothers,
3	"	mothers who were prostitutes,
6	"	insane brothers and sisters,
14	"	criminal brothers and sisters,
4	"	epileptic brothers and sisters,
2	"	brothers and sisters who were suicides,
10	"	sisters who were prostitutes.

Dr. Virgilio, who pursued his investigations under more favorable conditions, found crime among the parents of criminals in 26.80% of the cases, almost always, as with alcoholism (present in the heredity of 21.77% of the cases), on the father's side. Aside from this, with 6% of the criminals crime appeared in collateral lines.[1]

Penta,[2] also, found among 184 born criminals at St. Stefano the following:

Advanced age of parents	in 29 cases, or	16.0%
Drunkenness " "	" 50 " "	27.0%
Phthisis " "	" 17 " "	9.2%
Cerebral apoplexy of parents	" 20 " "	11.0%
Pellagra " "	" 3 " "	1.6%
Insanity " "	" 12 " "	6.5%
Insanity in ancestors or collateral lines	in 27 cases, or	14.5%
Hysteria " " " "	" " 25 " "	13.5%
Epilepsy " " " "	" " 17 " "	9.2%
Headache " " " "	" " 17 " "	9.2%

[1] Virgilio, "Saggio di Ricerche sulla Natura Morbosa del Delitto."
[2] "Archivio di Psichiatria," XII, 1891.

In 4% to 5% only were the parents perfectly sound. Later he has given us a new table of statistics of morbid heredity, embracing 447 cases arranged in two series:

	First series, 232 cases	Second series, 215 cases
Criminality of parents	30	58
Hysteria	17	38
Epilepsy	11	22
Other nerve diseases	20	65
Alcoholism	40	95
Insanity	35	50
Pulmonary tuberculosis	25	80
Advanced age of parents	23	55
Cerebral apoplexy	10	20
Predisposition to grave disease	12	20
Chronic malaria	5	20

Marro investigated the causes of death of 230 parents of criminals and of 100 parents of honest men, and found the following:

	In the case of the			
	Father		Mother	
	Criminal	Honest	Criminal	Honest
Alcoholism	7.2	2.4	2.1	...
Suicide	1.4	...	...	3.7
Insanity	6.5	2.4	5.3	...
Cerebro-spinal disease	21.1	14.6	18.2	7.4
Heart disease	6.5	14.6	3.2	18.5
Dropsy	4.3	2.4	6.4	3.7
Phthisis	5.1	2.4	10.7	...
Nervous shock, worry, etc.	2.1	2.4	4.3	...

If, in place of examining each group separately, we add together the deaths caused by alcoholism, suicide, insanity, and cerebral diseases, we find that among the 230 parents of criminals these causes constitute 32.1%, while in the case of the parents of normal persons they are only 16.1%, almost exactly half. The number who have delinquent brothers is especially great. Out of 500 criminals Marro found 68 who had one or more delinquent brothers, and the following parentage:

Insane	17
Epileptic	4
Delinquent	6
Alcoholic	34 (in 4 cases mother as well as father)
Already old	33 (in 4 cases both parents were old)

In studying the still living parents of 500 criminals, Marro found in 40% of the cases alcoholism of the father, and in 5% alcoholism of the mother, while with 500 normal persons there was alcoholism in only 16% of the cases, on the father's side. Insanity of progenitors or in collateral lines occurred in 42.6% of the criminals (16% of the normal cases); epilepsy in 5.3% (2% of the normal cases); and immoral and violent character in 33.6%. In looking into the question of parents who were insane, apoplectic, alcoholic, epileptic, hysterical, and delinquent, including also cases where there were anomalies of age and character, he found a morbid heredity in the case of from 77% to 90% of the prisoners (*op. cit.*). Sichart studied 3881 subjects imprisoned in Würtemberg for theft, rape, and fraud. In comparison with the general population he found that anomalies or crimes in the case of parents of the various classes in the following proportions:

Thieves	32.0%
Incendiaries	36.8%
Sexual offenders	38.7%
Perjurers	20.5%
Swindlers	23.6%

with the higher numbers then, in the case of thieves and incendiaries.[1] Taking account simply of alcoholism, epilepsy, and suicide in the direct line, he found a morbid heredity in 71% of the incendiaries, in 55% of the thieves, in 43% of the ravishers, and in 37% of the swindlers.

With regard to suicide of the parents Sichart and Marro found:

[1] Both the French and the German versions give the figure for sexual offenders as above; but I suspect it should be 28.7%.—TRANSL.

Suicide of parents of:	Sichart	Marro
Thieves	5.0%	...
Incendiaries	8.2%	...
Sexual offenders	3.9%	5.1%
Perjurers	2.1%	...
Swindlers	1.5%	...
Homicides	...	...

Total, 4.3%

Comparing the proportion of vicious parents of the 3000 criminals given by Sichart with those reported by Marro, we find them so divided:

	Vicious parents	
	Sichart	Marro
Thieves	20.9%	45.0%
Incendiaries	11.0%	14.2%
Swindlers	10.8%	32.4%
Sexual offenders	9.4%	28.2%
Perjurers	6.0%	...
Libelers	12.0%	...

We have here very high figures for thieves, not so high for swindlers, and lowest for incendiaries and perjurers. Of 3580 juvenile criminals of Mettray, 707 were children of convicts and 308 of parents living in concubinage.[1] Of the inmates of the Elmira reformatory, there were 13.7% whose parents were insane or epileptic; 38% whose parents were drunkards. Thompson, out of 109 convicts, found 50 who were related to one another, 3 of them being members of one family and descended from a recidivist. He noted also 2 sisters and 3 brothers, all thieves, whose father, uncles, aunts, and cousins were murderers. In one family of 15 members, of whom 14 were counterfeiters, the fifteenth appeared honest, till one day he set fire to his house, after having insured it four times over.

[1] Brace, *op. cit.*

The influence of heredity may be observed among the female offenders and prostitutes studied by Mme. Tarnowski, Marro,[1] etc., and by Parent-du-Châtelet. Of 5583 prostitutes Parent-du-Châtelet found 252 who were sisters, 13 mothers and daughters, 32 cousins, 4 aunts and nieces. One cannot read without a feeling of repugnance the speech that was made to Lacour by one of these unfortunates: "My father is in prison, and my mother is living with the man who seduced me. She has had a child by him, whom I and my brother are bringing up."

§ 70. Clinical Proofs

I have studied a child in the prison at Pavia who had very exaggerated prognathism, tufted hair, feminine physiognomy, and strabismus. He had been guilty of murder at 12 years of age, and had been besides convicted of theft 6 times; 2 of his brothers were thieves, 2 sisters prostitutes, and his mother was a receiver of stolen goods. Five brothers and a brother-in-law of the Fossay family were convicted for participation in a robbery. Their grandfather and their father had both been hanged; two uncles and a nephew were in prison. A more noteworthy proof of hereditary influence is offered by Dr. Harris, who, noticing in a certain county on the upper Hudson the great number of crimes committed by persons of the same name, consulted the registers and discovered that a great part of the inhabitants were descended from a certain Margaret, a woman of evil life, who had lived there two centuries before, among whose descendants there were

[1]

	Female criminals	Female criminals	Prostitutes	Thieves	Prostitutes
	(Salsotto)	(Marro)	(Grimaldi)	(Tarnowski)	
Father alcoholic	6.6%	40.0%	4.23%	49%	82%
Father insane	6.6%	7.6%	....	...	3%
Parents old	17.0%	26.0%	....	...	8%
Parents epileptic	2.6%	....	....	...	6%
Parents tuberculous	....	....	....	19%	44%
Parents delinquent	?	19.7%	....	...	...

200 delinquents and 200 more who were either insane or vagrants.[1]

Despine has given us another proof in the genealogy of the Lemaitre and Cretien families, which I have here arranged in tabular form that it may be taken in at a glance.

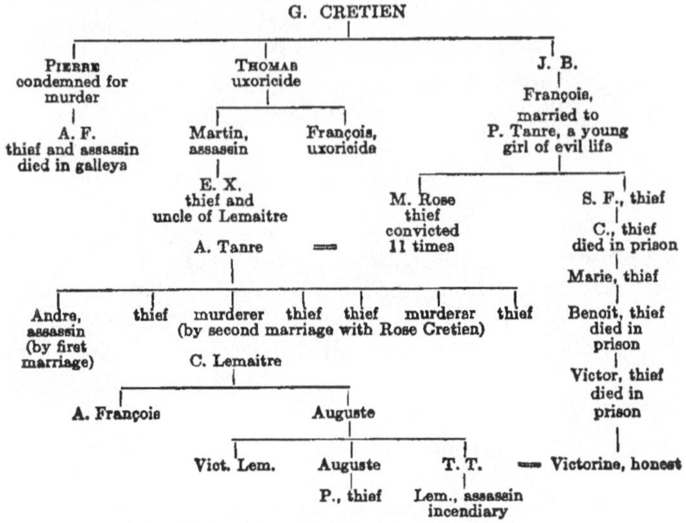

The Fieschi also were hereditary assassins.

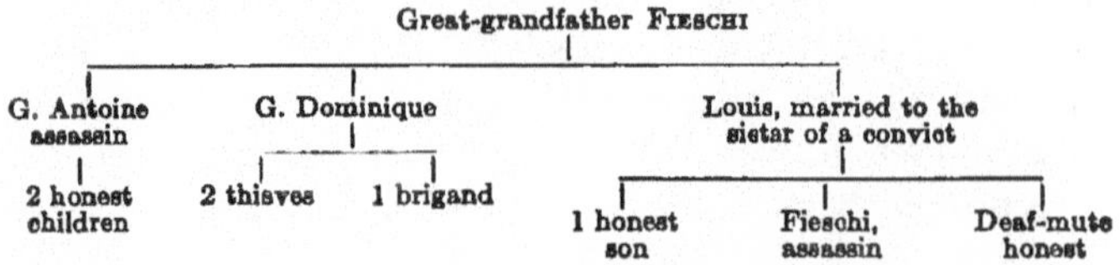

Strahan[2] gives us yet another proof of hereditary criminality in the history of a family whose descendants numbered 834 individuals, of 709 of whom it was possible to trace the history with sufficient accuracy. Among the 709 there were 106 illegitimate children, 164 prostitutes, 17 procurers, 142 beggars, 63 in hospitals for chronic diseases, and 76 criminals, who all to-

[1] "Atlantic Monthly," 1875. [This is the Juke family, described later, which was investigated by Dugdale at Harris's suggestion. — TRANSL.]
[2] "Instinctive Criminality," London, 1892.

gether spent 166 years in prison. The Y. family[1] occupied a high place in society in past times, but at the beginning of the 19th century had fallen completely into decay and consisted only of the sons of two brothers, Lu—— and René. René had passed all his life in contact with criminals without having been convicted himself. He was an original, passionately fond of cock-fights, and addicted to lechery. He had innumerable mistresses and children, so that all the children of the quarter called him "papa." One of his mistresses was the mother of a great number of criminals. The family of his brother presented nothing abnormal, except that one of his sons, learning that his uncle René had disinherited him, killed himself the day after the latter's death, and left behind him this writing:

"Let no one be accused of my death; I have killed myself to escape from insupportable enemies whom my stupidity has gained for me, and because I have not been sufficiently on my guard against the rascality of certain people."

The two mistresses of René who gave him a progeny of degenerates were Z., wife of an executioner, from whom was born a tuberculous daughter that died at 24, and F., who was also married, and accused by public opinion of having poisoned her husband. F. had 5 children, of whom 2 were by her husband and 3 by her paramour. The children of the husband were: 1st, Z., who lived separated from her husband, was a mattoid and quarrelsome. Everything furnished her with an opportunity for a lawsuit, which, however, she regularly lost. She had many paramours, among others an orator of great talent, by whom she had several children, including a celebrated poet, painter, etc. 2d, Fl., proprietress of a house of ill fame; she had two children, of whom one was blind and the other had Parkinson's paralysis. Among the children whom F. had by her paramour René, were the following: 1st, Em., who, while watching by the body of her father, became drunk with her sister-in-law. She had a daughter of evil life; also a niece who was a prostitute at 15 and a thief. 2d, Em., a peasant, who tried to hang himself. He married Fl., a woman of dissolute morals, notorious for her incestuous relations with her oldest son and

[1] Aubry, "La Contagion du Meutre," Paris, 1889.

associated in theft with her daughter, who was a drunkard. She was strongly suspected of having killed her son-in-law, and her daughter called her "The old woman loaded with crimes."

From this sad marriage were born two children: 1st, Marie, who, during a menstrual period, killed her husband, with the aid of her mother. They were both acquitted. 2d Am., who had sexual intercourse with his mother, and killed the husband of his mistress. In a collateral branch of the family of Fl., the daughter of F., there are many bankrupt merchants; a mother who, notwithstanding her numerous children, eloped with her last lover, carrying off the money-box; a husband who, after having gone off and squandered the family fortune, returned to live at his wife's expense; and a brother of Marie's second husband, who killed first his adulterous wife and then himself. In this family nearly all the members have committed one or more crimes, and those who are not criminals are suicides. But there is a collateral branch, that of Z., which is composed of persons who occupy a high place in art. This family confirms, then, the close connection that exists between genius and crime.

Laurent [1] tells us the story of a whole family of criminals, who support wonderfully the data of Marro and Aubry. In this family the paternal grandfather died of an affection of the heart. He was of weak character and completely dominated by his wife. She, nervous and eccentric, struck her husband on all occasions, and was so irascible that she even took pleasure in striking her sister when she was sick. The father was very nervous and violent, but a coward, and although he had knowledge of the dissolute conduct of his wife, he had not courage to intervene. He died of aortic insufficiency. A paternal uncle, who was very vicious and violent, struck his parents to get money from them. He took advantage of their absence to sell a part of the furniture, and tried to kill his son on account of jealousy. A cousin german of the two preceding was addicted to pederasty. The maternal grandfather was intelligent, but a drunkard, and served two years in prison for theft. He was a captain under the Commune, but was punished for misconduct. He

[1] "Les Habitués des Prisons."

was unbalanced, brutal, and coarse. By his first marriage he had four daughters, whose mental state we shall describe later. The maternal grandmother abandoned her children, and dissipated the week's wages in company with her husband. She died of cancer of the uterus. The mother, very vicious, idle, and violent, married at the age of 20 and had two children by her marriage. At 23 she abandoned her husband to live with a young man, by whom she had a son. She later returned to her husband and by him had a fourth child, yet during this time was the mistress of a wine merchant. To this paramour succeeded another, and at the age of 35 she brought into the world a fifth child. Abandoning her family and children without concern, she spent her time playing cards in dives and quarrelling with drunkards. She tried several times, while in a state of drunkenness, to kill her husband. At 37 she had, by one of her lovers, a sixth infant, who died of meningitis. She became pregnant once more, and abandoned definitely the conjugal roof, taking her daughters with her but giving them up to the first comer, to surrender herself to drink. At the age of 39 she became pregnant once more, and had her paramour produce an abortion. This woman had three sisters. The first was vicious from infancy and abandoned herself to a life of prostitution at the age of 16. So irascible was she that in a fit of jealousy she tore off another woman's ear. The second sister, dull, lascivious, and given to drink, had three children, one of whom at the age of 9 she threw out of the window for some trifling reason; and another time, without apparent cause, she threw it in front of the wheels of a carriage. It suffered from meningitis, but recovered. The third sister was weak-minded and dissipated, and used to get drunk in company with her husband.

Let us pass on now to the examination of the third generation, which includes 8 children: 1st, A young girl of 19 years, very blond, not very intelligent, very hairy, with a high-arched palate, and frontal protuberances strongly developed. Malicious and jealous, she put pins in her brothers' broth. When ten years old she was found in a dive with some young men, giving herself up to a precocious debauch. 2d, A young man of 18 years, a workman, economical and honest but nervous and stubborn and of weak character like his father. 3d, An adulterous daughter of 15, vicious, a drinker, and a gourmand. She frequented the wine-shops, was often drunk, and stole from the show-cases of the grocers. 4th, A daughter of 14, lazy, deceitful, thievish, irascible, egoistic, coquettish, and lascivious. Her figure is constantly contracted by a nervous twitching, her physiognomy is one continual grimace. Having no family feeling she takes advantage, when her grandmother is asleep, to pinch her legs, in revenge for punishments that she herself has received. 5th, An eight-year-old boy, rickety, scrofulous, very nervous, irascible, and despotic. He has paroxysms, when he breaks anything that comes into his hands. 6th, An adulterous daughter, who died at 16 of meningitis.

The famous thief Sans Refus was the daughter of a thief named Comtois, who died upon the wheel in 1788, and of a female thief named Lempave. Marianne, the most skilful member of the Thiebert band, was the child of two thieves, her father being a recidivist five times over. She first saw light on the highroad, in a stolen cart.[1] Sighele has studied all the proceedings instituted against the inhabitants of Artena since 1852 and has continually met the same name; father, son, and nephew follow one another at intervals, as if impelled by a fatal law. In the last trial there were two families concerned who were already known in criminal annals. One was composed of seven members, the other of six, father, mother, and four sons, not one lacking.

"It is appropriate in this connection," says Sighele,[2] "to quote the words of Vidocq: 'There are families in which crime is transmitted from generation to generation, and which appear to exist only to prove the truth of the old proverb, *Like father, like son.*'"[3]

§ 71. Elective Affinities

We see that this heredity, rendered so active by the union of two criminal families, from which organized bands naturally

[1] Lucas, "De l'Hérédité Naturelle, p. 487.
[2] "Archivio di Psichiatria," 1894.
[3] "Bon chien chasse de race."

arise, has its source in a kind of elective affinity impelling the delinquent woman to choose a lover or husband from among those most inclined to crime. We may recall the elective affinity which, in the Y. family, drove René to choose his mistresses among the prostitutes and delinquents; as well as the marriages of the Cretien and Lemaitre families. We find another striking example of this affinity in the fatal sympathy of the Marquise de Brinvilliers for Sainte-Croix; and in that of Louise Poch—— and Marie Catel——, thieves, swindlers, and prostitutes, for Rossignol. The former of these felt herself drawn to him when her rival told her in prison of his exploits. Marie Catel——, born of a noble family, was already ruined at the age of 14, and at 15 she had committed highway robbery as Rossignol's accomplice. In Turin there was a certain girl named Camburzano who became the mistress of a thief while not yet nubile. When sent to a reformatory she escaped, and the same day joined herself with an assassin named Tomo, whose accomplice she became, and the instigator of his most atrocious murders.

§ 72. Atavistic Heredity in the Juke Family

But the most striking proof of the heredity of crime and of its relation to prostitution and mental diseases is furnished us by the fine study which Dugdale has made of the Juke family.[1] The originator of this deplorable family was a certain hunter, fisher, and libertine, called by Dugdale "Max Juke," who was born some time between 1720 and 1740. He became blind in his old age. He had numerous descendants, 540 legitimate, and 169 illegitimate. All the ramifications of his posterity cannot be traced down to the present; but we have the lines of descent from 5 daughters (3 of whom were prostitutes before they married) as well as that of some collateral branches, for 7 generations. We give the tabular summary of the family:

[1] Dugdale, "The Jukes" (Putnam, 4th ed., 1911), reprinted from the "Thirtieth Annual Report of the Executive Committee of the Prison Association of New York for 1874."

		Total number in generation	Parentage by Sex		
			Total of each sex	Legitimate	Illegitimate
Second generation	Juke women	5	5	1	..
	X men	5	5	2	..
Third generation	Juke women	34	16	15	1
	X women	16	7	3	..
	Juke men	...	18	12	6
	X men	...	9	...	2
Fourth generation	Juke women	117	46	38	..
	X women	...	25	6	1
	Juke men	...	57	46	3
	X men	59	34	5	1
Fifth generation	Juke women	224	119	94	17
	X women	...	33	4	2
	Juke men	...	102	70	20
	X men	84	51	11	3
Sixth generation	Juke women	152	63	33	13
	X women	...	2	...	..
	Juke men	...	48	27	20
	X men	5	3	...	..
Seventh generation	Juke women	8	3	1	2
	Juke men	...	...	...	..
Total generation	Juke women	...	252	182	33
	X women	...	67	13	3
	Juke men	...	225	155	49
	X men	...	102	18	6
Juke blood		540	477	377	82
X blood		169	169	31	9
Grand total		709	645	368	91

NOTE. — X indicates persons not of Juke blood

We see from this table the singular connection existing between prostitution, crime, and sickness; for from the same hereditary causes we find:

"Max"

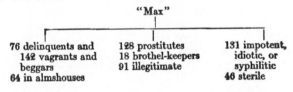

76 delinquents and 142 vagrants and beggars 64 in almshouses	128 prostitutes 18 brothel-keepers 91 illegitimate	131 impotent, idiotic, or syphilitic 46 sterile

Marriage Relations				Barren persons	Kept brothels	Syphilis	Pauperism				Crime		
Married	Had bastards before marriage	Had bastards after marriage	Prostitutes				Out-door relief No. persons	No. of years	Almshouse, No. of persons	No. of years	No. of persons	Years in prison	No. of offenses
5	3	..	..	..	..	..	..	..	..	..	..	..	..
5	..	..	..	..	..	..	..	..	..	..	..	..	..
13	1	1	3	5	..	..	3	20	2	2	..	..	..
4	..	..	3	..	..	..	1	23	..	..	..	..	..
11	..	..	4	4	..	1	6	54	3	6	1	..	1
5	..	..	4	..	..	1	2	14	3	5	2	3	2
26	6	8	12	3	5	12	18	122	7	7	5	1	7
15	3	..	4	4	1	7	8	53	3	3	2	½	2
22	..	..	4	7	1	6	19	129	8	12	12	11	15
19	..	..	15	1	3	2	11	50	3	3	10	13	11
37	6	3	36	5	5	25	24	100	12	18	9	¼	15
15	2	1	14	4	..	2	11	49	2	4	1	¼	1
21	..	..	12	7	..	7	25	87	11	21	18	72	41
26	..	..	14	6	2	4	14	33	..	..	2	8	16
2	2	..	2	..	1	..	..	..	3	8	2	½	2
1	1	..	..	..	..	..	..	..	..	..	..	..	..
1	..	..	..	..	..	..	..	..	7	7	2	6½	2
2	..	..	1	..	..	..	..	..	..	..	..	..	..
..	..	..	..	..	..	..	..	..	..	..	..	..	..
..	..	..	..	..	..	..	..	..	..	..	..	..	..
83	18	12	53	13	11	37	45	242	24	35	16	1¾	24
35	6	1	21	8	1	9	20	125	5	7	3	¾	3
55	..	..	20	18	1	14	50	270	29	46	33	89½	59
57	..	..	34	7	5	7	27	97	6	7	24	24	29
138	18	12	73	31	12	57	95	512	53	81	49	91¼	83
92	6	1	55	15	6	16	47	222	11	15	27	24¾	32
230	24	13	128	46	18	67	142	734	64	96	76	116	115

but connected with them by marriage or cohabitation.

We see the delinquents scantily represented in the second generation, but multiplying with extraordinary rapidity, and rising from 29 in the fourth generation to 40 in the fifth: just as the number of prostitutes rises from 14 to 35 and 76; and of beggars, which increases from 11 to 56 and 74. They diminish in the sixth and seventh generations, only because Nature herself makes an end of the matter through the sterility of the women, which affected 9 individuals in the third generation and 22 in the fifth, and also by the early deaths of the children, which rose as high as 300 in the last years. The members of this family passed altogether 116 years in prison, and received poor-relief for a total of 830 years. In the fifth generation half the women were unchaste, and a correspondingly high number of the men criminals. Of the seventh generation the oldest individual had reached the age of only 7 years, yet 6 members of it were in almshouses. In 75 years the maintenance of this family and the damage done by them cost the state $1,300,000.

It has been shown that in all or nearly all the branches of this family the tendency to crime, unlike the tendency to pauperism, was strongest with the eldest son, always following the male line in preference to the female. This tendency was accompanied by excess of vitality, fecundity, and vigor, and was more developed in the illegitimate lines than in the legitimate, a statement which is also true of the other forms of immorality. Thus, by comparing the 38 illegitimate members of the fifth generation with the 85 legitimate members we get the following:

- 38 illegitimate
  - 4 drunkards
  - 11 beggars, idiots, or prostitutes
  - 16 convicts, 6 of whom were convicted for serious crimes
- 85 legitimate
  - 5 convicts
  - 13 beggars or prostitutes

The figures here given for prostitution represent only a small part of the sexual immorality, as is proved by the large number of bastards (21% of the males and 13% of the females), of syphilitics, and "harlots,"[1] of whom there were 60% in the second generation (3 daughters out of the 5), 37% in the third, 69% in the fourth, 48% in the fifth, and 38% in the sixth, an average of 52.40%. In addition there were 42% of harlots among the women who married into the family. The data with regard to exaggerated fecundity and to prostitution tend to prove that sexual excesses are one of the most serious causes of pauperism, which, in its turn, appears to be hereditary in its character, especially with the women, and to gain recruits

[1] Dugdale uses this word for women who have been guilty of any unchastity, reserving the term "prostitute" for professionals. — TRANSL.

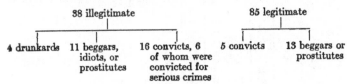

by preference among the young. Pauperism, again, is bound up with crime and disease, on account of the great number of individuals who become tainted with syphilis, or have bodily deformities, or inherit a tendency to crime or vagrancy. On the other hand, it is noted that in the families where the brothers are criminals, the sisters give themselves up to prostitution, and are indicted only for sexual offenses. So Dugdale says (p. 26), "Prostitution in the woman is the analogue of crime and pauperism in the man." It may be seen here how prostitution arises by heredity, without being explainable by destitution or other causes, and is checked only by the intervention of an early marriage. The distribution of the bastards as to sex (21% of the males, 13% of the females) shows a curious predominance of the male sex, while the opposite is true among the legitimate offspring. Among the first born, also, where legitimate, daughters predominate; and where illegitimate, sons. The following table shows us the connection between crime and prostitution on one side, and disease and deformity on the other:

Diseases, Malformations, and Injuries

	Deformed	Blind	Deaf and dumb	Insane	Idiotic	Tuberculosis of lungs	Syphilitic	Constitutional Syphilis	Epileptic	Total number diseased, etc.	Number of diseased persons receiving relief	Percentage
Juke blood . .	1	10	..	1	1	1	29	22	..	65	33	50.77
X blood . . .	..	1	1	..	..	1	13	3	1	20	15	56.47
Total . . .	1	11	1	1	1	2	42	25	1	85	..	...

Altogether Dugdale found 200 thieves and other criminals, 280 beggars or invalids, 90 prostitutes or women afflicted with syphilis, all descended from one drunkard; to which should be added, as additional consequences, 300 children dying prematurely, 400 men infected with syphilis, and 7 assassinated.

This is not a unique case. The savage Galetto of Marseilles was a nephew of Ortolano, ravisher and cannibal; Dumollard was the son of a murderer; Patetot had assassins for grandfather and great-grandfather; Papa, Crocco, and Serravalle had grandfathers who had been in prison, and Cavalante's father and grandfather both were convicts. The Cornu family were assassins from father to son, as were the Verdures, the Cerfbeers, and Nathans. Of this last family 14 members were incarcerated at one time in the same prison. Mocc——, a brazen adulteress, who poisoned her husband, was the issue of an incest; and prostitutes are nearly always daughters of delinquents or drunkards. Mme. de Pompadour was the daughter of a drunken thief who had been pardoned.

§ 73. Insanity of Parents

As all these dismal genealogies prove to us, a certain number of the parents of criminals are afflicted with insanity. I have found in the case of 314 criminals whose descent was known to me, 7 whose fathers were insane, 2 who had fathers that were epileptic, while in the case of 4 the mother, in 2 cases the father, in 3 a brother, in 4 an uncle, and in 1 a cousin, were afflicted with cretinism. Of 100 other criminals 5 had insane mothers, 3 insane fathers, 6 insane brothers, and 4 had epileptic brothers. I had under my care in Pavia a family whose genealogy alternated between criminals and prostitutes, as seen by the following outline:

Fe . . . ri, insane at 80, with hallucinations

- L., insane, committed incest
  - Thief at 9
  - Thief committed incest
  - Suicide
  - Prostitute
  - Prostitute
- Insane, guilty of assault
  - Thief
    - Prostitute

Another family that I have investigated was as follows:

Ala . . . poisoned his wife == Wife, epileptic

- G Murderer
- D Suicide
- A Killed in brawl
- P Maniac
- A Drunkard at 15
- F Prostitute

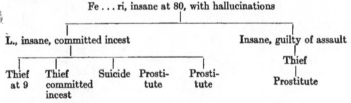

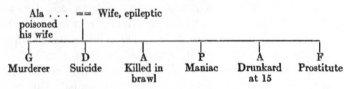

In the cases of 67 insane criminals Moeli found in 61%, insanity or epilepsy of parents; 15%, suicide or criminality of parents; 21%, insanity of brothers or sisters.[1] Kock,[2] leaving aside all doubtful cases, found that 46% of criminals were of morbid descent. Virgilio studied 266 convicts, all, however, with chronic diseases, 10 of them being insane and 13 epileptic. He found insanity of 1 parent, generally the father. Epilepsy was present with still greater frequency, being found in 14.1% of the cases. In 6 cases the father was eccentric, in 1 the mother; in 1 case the father was a semi-imbecile. One ravisher had a deaf-mute father. Penta found insanity among the parents of 16% of the criminals investigated by him. At Elmira, N. Y., in 1890, 127 of the prisoners had insane or epileptic parents. Marro and Sichart found:

Insanity of Parents

	Sichart	Marro
Incendiaries	11.0%	28.5%
Sexual criminals	3.5%	10.2%
Thieves	6.4%	14.5%
Swindlers	5.5%	10.3%
Perjurers	3.1%	...
Homicides	...	17.0%
Guilty of assault	...	14.0%

Gottin, who set fire to the house of his benefactor, had an insane grandfather; Mio had his father and grandfather both insane; Jean de Agordo, a parricide, had insane brothers; Martinati's sister was a cretin; Vizzocaro, at once parricide and fratricide, and Palmerini, an assassin, both had insane brothers and uncles; Bussi, insane father and mother; Alberti, an insane father and grandfather; Faella, an insane father; Guiteau had an insane father, uncles, and cousins; Perussi, a forger and murderer, who was born in an insane asylum, had an insane mother, who committed suicide, and a father with megalomania; Verger had a mother and sisters who were suicides; Goudfroy, who

[1] "Ueber irre Verbrecher," 1888.

[2] "Zur Statistik der Geisteskrankheiten in Würtemberg," p. 161, Stuttgart, 1877.

killed his wife, mother, and sisters, after insuring their lives in his favor, had an insane grandmother and uncles; Didier, a parricide, had an insane father; Louise Brienz, who killed her husband, had an epileptic mother and an insane sister; and Ceresa, Abbado, and Kulmann all had insane parents.

In this connection we find the same thing true of the insane as of criminals. Golgi, Stewart, and Tigges have proved that insane men are more apt to have insanity on the paternal side than on the maternal,[1] as is also the case with criminals. However, it is important for the purposes of medical jurisprudence to note that insanity of the parents is less frequent with criminals than with the insane. Among 3115 insane persons Tigges found that 28% had insane parents, while Stewart's figure is 49%, and that of Golgi 53%. If we take in also the hereditary influence of epilepsy and other nervous diseases, Golgi gives us a figure of 78%.

§ 74. Epilepsy of Parents

Knecht found epilepsy among the parents of 15% of the criminals examined by him; Ribaudo, investigating 559 military prisoners, found 10.1%; Penta found 9.2% among the parents of 184 born criminals. Clark showed that 46% of the parents of epileptic criminals had epilepsy, and only 21% of the parents of non-criminal epileptics. Dejerine, however, gives the figures as 74.6% and 34.6%, but, though higher, the ratio between criminal and non-criminal remains the same. Marro and Sichart found the following percentages of epileptics among various classes of criminals:

	Sichart	Marro
Thieves	2.1%	3.3%
Swindlers	2.0%	1.3%
Incendiaries	1.8%	...
Sexual criminals	1.2%	...
Perjurers	...	...
Homicides	...	7.0%

[1] Stewart, "On Hereditary Insanity," London, 1874.

§ 75. Alcoholic Heredity

Penta found alcoholism in 33% of the parents of criminals, and I myself have met it in 20%. At Elmira, of 6300 criminals under age, 38% had drunken parents. Legrain [1] found that 157 individuals, belonging to 50 different families of alcoholics, showed the following: Insane, 54%; alcoholics, 62%; epileptics, 61%; having convulsions, 29%; morally insane, 14%; having meningitis, 6.5%. According to Baer the following percentages of the parents of criminals were drunken: In Saxony, 10.5%; Baden, 19.5%; Würtemberg, 19.8%; Alsace, 22.0%; Prussia, 22.1%; Bavaria, 34.6%. Sichart and Marro found the parents of criminals alcoholic in the following proportions:

	Sichart	Marro
Thieves	14.3%	46.6%
Swindlers	13.3%	32.4%
Incendiaries	13.3%	42.8%
Perjurers	11.1%	...
Sexual Criminals	14.2%	43.5%

Marro found also 49% in the case of parents of homicides, and 50% of the parents of those guilty of assault. Thus those guilty of crimes of blood show the highest figures, followed closely by thieves.

In Italy alcoholism of the parents is much less frequently a cause of insanity than of crime, being found in the case of 17% of the insane but in 22% of those imprisoned at Aversa for long terms. Legrain observed that precocity is the first characteristic of alcoholic heredity. He found children who were alcoholics even at four years. Another characteristic is the impossibility of withstanding the effects of alcohol. Thus a father had been a drinker for seven years without having his brain affected, while his son was thrown into a delirium by two days' orgy. Further, alcoholic heredity manifests itself by an imperious need of larger and larger doses of alcohol. All these characteristics are frequently met in criminals.

[1] "Dégénérescence Sociale et Alcoolisme," Paris, 1875.

§ 76. Age of Parents

Marro, in investigating this subject, has come to the following conclusions:

"Among criminals against property the children of young parents abound, except in the case of swindlers, among whom they are rare. Swindling demands, in fact, dissimulation and artfulness, rather than physical quickness and force, which are the gifts of youth, as the former qualities are the properties of a maturer age."

He found descent from elderly parents very numerous in the case of those committing crimes against persons, appearing in the case of 52.9% of the homicides, while the percentage for the general population is only 17. On the other hand, only 3% of this class of criminals were found to have youthful parents. Among those punished for assaults, old and also very young parents were much more numerous than in the general population (40% and 13.5% respectively). This is easy to comprehend when we remember that callousness is as much a preparation for brawling and insurrection as excess of vivacity. Among ravishers, on the other hand, the proportion of elderly fathers falls to 30%; but there is also a higher number of elderly mothers than normal. Marro, taking 21 as the beginning of maturity for women and 37 as the beginning of decadence, arrives at the following table of percentages of criminal, normal, and insane persons, according to the mother's age at their birth:

Age of Mother

	Immature	Mature	Decadent
Murderers	6.4%	54.8%	38.7%
Guilty of assault	21.2%	57.5%	15.1%
Ravishers	15.6%	59.3%	25.0%
Highway robbers	27.2%	63.6%	9.0%
Burglars	19.4%	61.1%	19.4%
Pickpockets	22.5%	64.5%	12.9%
House thieves	20.0%	62.5%	17.5%
Thieves	17.9%	64.1%	17.9%
Swindlers	12.1%	14.2%	13.6%
General average of criminals	18.5%	63.7%	17.9%
Normal	12.8%	76.4%	10.7%
Insane	20.0%	58.8%	21.1%

The law observed for the fathers in the different classes of delinquents holds good for the mothers also. The percentage of elderly mothers, as of elderly fathers, is especially high with murderers and ravishers, though in the case of the latter, to a more limited extent for both parents. Both fathers and mothers are frequently young in the case of those guilty of assault and theft, and especially is this true with highway robbers. Marro has studied the conduct in school of 917 pupils, with reference to the age of their parents, with the following results:

Conduct of Children in School

Age of parents	Good	Medium	Bad
Under 26 (father)	44%	31%	23%
From 26 to 41 (father)	47%	34%	17%
Over 41 (father)	51%	31%	16%
Under 22 (mother)	53.9%	28.3%	17.7%
From 22 to 37 (mother)	48.3%	32.2%	18.4%
Over 37 (mother)	41.3%	41.3%	17.2%

The maximum of bad and the minimum of good children are to be found where the father is young, but on account of the mildness and docility of character belonging to women, especially in youth, the greatest proportion of good children are to be found among those born of young mothers.

With regard to pupils whose parents both belong to the same age period the following results are reached:

Conduct of Pupils

Age of parents	Good	Medium	Bad
Immature	39%	39%	21%
Mature	40%	35%	15%
Decadent	41%	41%	16%

Marro found that fewer delinquents than normal persons had parents belonging to the same age period, there being 63% of the former to 70% of the latter. In the case of pupils the maximum of intelligence and the minimum of good conduct were found where both parents were very young.

The age of complete development of the parents gives the maximum of good conduct and the same proportion of intelligent children as when the mother is of full age. In the period of decadence of the two parents, both good conduct and intelligence are less often found than in the preceding period.

§ 77. Synthesis

Of all nervous anomalies the most typical as a sign of degeneracy, aside from cretinism, is the neurosis of the criminal. This recalls the phenomenon that was so striking in the history of the Juke family, the excess of vigor and fecundity in the earlier generations, neutralized in later generations by child-mortality, and finally giving place to complete sterility, such as occurs in the case of "freaks" and too violent crosses. Penta counts among the signs of degeneracy found in the born criminal a great fecundity rendered futile through the speedy dying out of the offspring. Of 104 brothers of criminals whom he studied, 70 died at an early age. Of 100 parents of criminals, 53 showed an exaggerated fecundity and 23 a partial sterility. Of 46 criminals, 10 showed exaggerated and 31 restricted fecundity. In studying the figures of Marro and Sichart we find that epilepsy is more common with the parents of thieves; suicide with those of incendiaries; alcoholism with those of thieves and ravishers; and insanity with the parents of incendiaries. We have seen from the Juke family that males, especially the eldest, are more often affected by a criminal heredity than females, and illegitimate than legitimate children, the relations being inverted in the case of pauperism, in which organic weakness plays a greater part. We have seen that in heredity, for normal as well as for criminal men, the influence of the father exceeds that of the mother. Thus Marro found the diseases given below to have their hereditary influence from the paternal or maternal side in the following ratios:

	From father	From mother
Alcoholism	7.0%	3.1%
Insanity	6.5%	5.0%
Diseases of spinal cord	21.0%	18.0%
" " heart	6.5%	3.2%
Phthisis	5.0%	10.0%

Here the mothers lead only in the last.

In the parents of homicides vicious tendencies are found with 23% of the fathers and only 7% of the mothers; of those guilty of assault, 20% of the fathers are of evil character and 16% of the mothers. We may say that the mother has the power of transmitting her emotional characteristics to her children more than her intellectual characteristics. These conclusions agree with the general laws of heredity set forth by Orchanski.[1] He shows that heredity being a function of the organism of the parents, it corresponds at any given moment to the energy of their other functions and to their general physical condition. Each of the parents shows a tendency to transmit his own sex, and the one that prevails is the one nearest the period of maturity.

Resemblance to the father prevails, but more in the case of boys than girls. The same principle holds true for structure, although the boys show more variability, the girls more stability. If one of the parents is diseased there is a tendency, stronger in the case of the father, to transmit the disease to children of the same sex as the parent affected. This phenomenon shows itself especially in the case of neuropathic parents, phthisical parents reversing the relationship. Transmission of disease, consequently, is progressive with the father, regressive with the mother; the pathological condition of the father tends to repeat itself in the children. Morbid heredity depends, then, upon two factors, — the sex of the parent and the intensity of the morbid condition. Males inherit diseases from both parents and in greater intensity, having a tendency to transform functional

[1] Orchanski, "L'Eredità delle Famiglie Malate," Turin, 1896.

disorders into organic ones; while females show the opposite tendency.

To sum up: the organic type is constantly being fixed by heredity. The children themselves have a large part in the manifestation of heredity, by the fact that they can assimilate more or less actively the hereditary characteristics. Hereditary influences are not all manifested at any given moment, or once for all. They are latent in the organism and manifest themselves gradually throughout the whole period of development. Everything organic is subject to the general laws of heredity; the characteristics inherited by any part of the organism follow the general course of the development of that organ, and reaches its highest point at the period of the organ's greatest development. The antagonism between the influence of the father, which favors variability and individuality, and that of the mother, which tends to preserve the type, has already been observed in the determination of the sex of the offspring. The same contest goes on in the matter of transmitting disease, which the mother diminishes by transmitting her own diseases in milder form and combating the morbid tendencies of the father. There is the same difference between the parts that the male and female children play in inheriting, as there is in that which the father and mother play in transmitting hereditary characteristics.

CHAPTER XIII

AGE — PRECOCITY

§ 78. Age—Precocity

ONE of the few striking differences between crime and insanity is found in the part played by age. A glance at the following tabular comparison between nearly equal numbers of insane, delinquent, and normal persons shows that criminals are most numerous at the ages between 20 and 30, at which ages the number of normal persons and of insane is much lower, while the latter are most numerous between 30 and 40.

Age	Italians			English	Austrians
	Normal	Insane	Criminals	Criminals	Criminals
	20,011	20,011	26,590	23,768	12,786
Under 20 . . .	43.55%	6.18%	12.9%	25.10%	10.4 %
20 to 30	17.01%	2.34%	45.7%	42.40%	42.6 %
30 " 40	14.32%	26.21%	28.8%	16.80%	27.67%
40 " 50	10.67%	22.19%	11.6%	8.40%	12.1 %
50 " 60	7.89%	14.02%	3.8%	4.20%	5.9 %
Over 60	6.56% [1]	9.34% [1]	0.8% [2]	2.0% [3]	12.4 % [4]

[1] Lolli, "Statistica del Manicomio di Imola," 1874.
[2] Cardon, "Statistica delle Carceri," Rome, 1871.
[3] Mayhew, *op. cit.*
[4] "Die Oesterreichen Strafanstalten," Vienna, 1874.

It will be noted that from the age of 40 on, the percentage of the insane is twice that of normal individuals and criminals; while these latter after the age of 50 are less than half as numerous relatively as normal persons of that age.

A more detailed analysis shows that the maximum of criminality is found at ages ranging from 15 to 25 years. In England the proportion of juvenile crime is declining, and the percentage of criminals under 21 will be seen to be less than the percentage of the normal population falling within this age group, while from 22 to 30 the criminal percentage is double the normal.[1]

In Austria one-sixth of the convicts are between 14 and 20 years of age, and four-sixths between 21 and 40.

Of 1477 criminals condemned to death in France:

107 were between 16 and 30
534 " " 30 " 40
180 " " 40 " 60
69 " 60 or over

Of 46 criminals studied by me, 35 had commenced their criminal career at the following ages:

1 at 4 years	5 at 10 years	3 at 13 years
2 " 7 "	4 " 11 "	3 " 14 "
6 " 8 "	3 " 12 "	7 " 15 "
1 " 9 "		

Twelve others confessed that they had run away from home to escape either punishment or work. Ten per cent of the inmates of the reform school at Turin admitted freely that they had learned to steal before 12, not from necessity, but led by the encouragement and instructions of their companions. In the hundred criminals investigated by Rossi and myself we found 35 who had begun to drink between the ages of 2 and 10, and of these 25 drank only brandy; 6 had become addicted to the practice of masturbation before the age of 6, and 13 had had sexual

1

	In England	
	Criminals	General population
12 and under	1.1%	13.5%
13 to 16	3.2%	22.5%
17 to 21	18.1%	9.59%
22 to 30	32.4%	16.6%
31 to 40	21.0%	12.8%
41 to 50	13.1%	10.0%
51 to 60	3.3%	7.48%

(L. Levy, "Journal of the Statistical Society," 1882.)

intercourse before the age of 14,[1] — all of which shows great precocity in vice.

Marro found that of his 462 criminals 18% had become delinquents before the age of 13. Manzoni has very well hit off the principal source of this early leaning toward crime, namely, the mania to pass as full-grown; in his famous novel he says: "Gervais, on account of having had a hand in something that savored of crime, thought he had become a man like the others." Marro, in his studies of the conduct of pupils in the schools, found that there were two periods especially marked by bad conduct, — the first between 11 and 13 years of age, and the second between 16 and 17.

Precocity in crime points to the fact that criminality, much more than insanity, is an inherited characteristic. This reminds us that precocity is one of the distinguishing features of savage peoples, — a new proof of the atavistic origin of crime. In this connection certain customs of the nature-peoples are interesting. Thus the young men in certain African tribes, upon attaining their majority, strip themselves and withdraw to the woods, where they remain until they have killed some one.

We may also certainly ascribe to atavistic influence an institution like that of the *scuonero* in Naples, which, for the fifteen-year-old boys, means to play the tyrant, to carry clubs or revolvers, to have love affairs, and to put parents and policemen in their proper places. It is thus a sort of juvenile "Camorra," in which the highest honor belongs to him who has wounded or killed some one. Another proof of the same influence is found in the Sicilian word "*omerta*," which means either manliness or brigandage.

§ 79. Supposed Scale of Crime

In one case I have found a true gradation in the character of the thefts of a young criminal, who began as a boy by stealing 4 sous to buy a top. He then stole 8 sous, then 1 franc, and finally 3 francs. But, in general, the ascending scale of crime is

[1] Rossi, "Una Centuria di Criminali," 1885.

imaginary, for many enter the criminal course by the great door of homicide and rape, while the most atrocious crimes are often the most precocious. There was found one day in Milan an old man riddled with 82 wounds, who was believed at first to have been the victim of an atrocious act of revenge. It was discovered that his murderers were five youths of from 15 to 19 years, who had committed this horrible crime for the purpose of getting money for a visit to a brothel, and that all had wanted to have a part in stabbing the victim.

All great criminals have given proof of perversity in their youth, especially at the age of puberty and sometimes even before. This was true of Bonsegni at 18 years of age, of Boulot at 17, and of the Marquise de Brinvilliers at 18. At 7½ Dombey was already a thief, and added sacrilege to his theft at 12. At 3 Crocco tore out the feathers of living birds; Lasagne cut out the tongues of cattle at 11; at the same age Cartouche stole from his schoolmates; while Mme. Lafargue, as a child of 10, strangled fowls. Feuerbach tells of a parricide who had taken great delight as a child in making hens jump about after he had put out their eyes.

"The tendency to theft," says Locatelli, "shows itself in extreme youth, beginning with little pilferings at home and increasing gradually. Murderers, on the contrary, become such all at once, frequently at a tender age. It is for this reason that children below the age of puberty who have already committed homicide are less rare than second-story thieves of the same age."

In the prisons of Paris there are no less than 2000 youths from 16 to 21 years of age, 996 of whom are incarcerated for murder or theft, and the assassinations committed by these young criminals are marked by the most horrible ferocity. Maillot and Gille killed their benefactress with the aid of their comrades, and bit off her fingers to get her rings. The youngest of this band was 15 and the oldest 18. Each of the Parisian bands of young assassins included a girl who had scarcely reached nubility.[1]

[1] D'Haussonvile, "L'Enfance à Paris," 1876.

Pipino, Bagnis, Quartery, Verzeni, Moro, and Prevost began with assassination. Prevost later was an irreproachable agent of police for 21 years. Martin killed his own wife, having previously been perfectly reputable. Charles IX was cruel from childhood.

§ 80. Criminality at Different Periods of Life

Each period of life has its own form of criminality, as Quetelet, Guerry, and Messedaglia have very well shown. Youth and old age are found in Austria to furnish the greatest number of sexual crimes, 33%. Guerry also finds the two highest points for these crimes to be between 16 and 25, and between 65 and 70 years. In England the greatest number of crimes contrary to nature are committed by persons between 50 and 60; but doubtless what is taken for crime at this age may often be the result of creeping paralysis and senile dementia. Another tendency which is observable in youth is that toward arson (30.8% in Austria); and in this case also it is to be noted that mania before the age of puberty is apt to take the form of pyromania. A similar observation may be made with regard to theft; but Quetelet observes that if the tendency toward theft is one of the first to show itself, it also makes itself felt throughout the whole life, and is common to every age-period.[1]

In the period of manhood the predominant crimes are murders, homicides, infanticides, abortions, and rape, amounting in Austria to about 80%. At a riper age there is an increasing number of libels, frauds, breaches of trust, crimes contrary to nature, instances of blackmail, and of aid given to criminals. In old age there are to be observed crimes contrary to nature, aid to criminals, breach of trust, swindling, and, what furnishes a new analogy with the crimes of youth, arson. We may get a more exact notion of the distribution of crime according to age from the following table, in which is given the number of persons out of 1000 of the same age who were indicted in France between 1826 and 1840:[2]

[1] Quételet, "Physique Sociale," p. 325.
[2] After Guerry, "Statistique Morale de la France," p. 84.

Age	Theft	Rape	Assault	Murder	Homicide	Poisoning	Fraud	Libel	Total
Under 16	0.4	0.1	0.1	0.2	0.1	0.3	0.1	0.1	0.3
16–21	16.0	14.1	10.9	7.3	6.0	3.4	3.8	4.6	12.2
21–25	18.4	14.3	13.5	15.3	14.2	9.5	10.1	9.1	15.8
25–30	14.7	12.6	20.1	16.6	14.1	13.9	11.8	8.8	14.6
30–35	13.7	11.1	18.7	14.0	15.3	12.2	13.4	11.0	13.3
35–40	10.7	8.8	11.8	11.1	10.8	11.3	12.8	11.7	10.8
40–45	6.6	7.5	6.8	8.3	9.7	13.0	11.5	11.0	8.9
45–50	6.4	6.4	6.8	7.3	8.2	9.4	9.7	10.0	7.0
50–55	4.5	4.1	4.7	5.8	6.3	6.5	7.6	9.3	5.1
55–60	3.1	4.4	3.3	4.5	5.2	4.8	5.5	8.3	3.9
60–65	2.6	4.8	2.9	4.0	4.3	4.8	5.4	6.9	3.4
65–70	1.8	5.2	1.6	3.0	3.2	5.1	3.9	5.4	2.5
70–80	1.2	4.5	0.8	1.7	1.7	3.0	3.0	3.8	1.6
Over 80	0.4	2.1	0.5	0.9	0.6	2.8	1.4	...	0.6

CHAPTER XIV

SEX — PROSTITUTION

§ 81. Sex

ALL statistics show that women are much less criminal than men, and this will be even more striking if we regard those guilty of infanticide as outside of the regular criminal class. In Austria female criminals do not reach 14% of the total; in Spain they are under 11%, while in Italy they are only 8.2%. Bringing together the different data [1] we get the following table, showing the part played by women in crime in different countries of Europe:

	Men	Women	Number of men to 1 woman
Italy (1885–89)	84.1	15.9	5.2
Great Britain (1858–64)	79.0	21.0	3.8
Denmark and Norway	80.0	20.0	4.0
Holland	81.0	19.0	4.5
Belgium	82.0	18.0	4.5
France	83.0	17.0	4.8
Austria	83.0	17.0	4.8
Baden	84.0	16.0	5.8
Prussia	85.0	15.0	5.7
Russia	91.0	9.0	10.1
Buenos-Ayres (1892)	96.4	3.6	27.1
Algeria (1876–80)	96.2	3.8	25.0
Victoria (1890)	91.7	8.3	11.0
New South Wales	85.5	14.5	5.8

Bringing together the figures for all classes of delinquents convicted in Italy during the years 1885–89, we get the following yearly averages:

[1] A complete bibliography will be found in Lombroso and Ferrero's "Female Offender."

For the men	For the women
186,825	54,837

If, however, we take account of the fact that the cases passed upon by the justices of the peace are the least serious, those which come before the Assizes are the most serious, and those which come before the Tribunals are of a degree between the two, we shall see that the female offenders are distributed in an inverse ratio to the gravity of the crime. Thus for each 100 men the following number of women were convicted in the three classes of courts:

Justice courts	21.8 women
Tribunals	9.2 "
Assizes	6.0 "

Almost all the statistics show that women take up a life of crime later than men. Oettingen places the climax of female criminality between the 25th and 30th years, while Quetelet calls it about the 30th year. With men the maximum of criminality is reached at 24. In Italy in the years from 1885 to 1889, for each 100 crimes committed by male delinquents of the various age periods, the following were committed by female delinquents:[1]

	Justices of the peace	Tribunals	Assizes
Under 14	22.5	10.1	0.0
14–21	22.2	9.0	3.3
21–50	21.6	8.4	5.5
Over 50	23.1	10.5	11.1

We see, accordingly, that for all classes of crimes female criminality reaches its highest point, as compared with that of men, at the most advanced age; that is to say, when the special characteristics of sex have been effaced by age, and when prostitution no longer offers a career. The second highest period of female criminality is to be found in the age below 14, when the

[1] Rencoroni, "La Criminalità Femminile" (Arch. di Psichiatria, 1893).

sex characteristics are not yet fully developed.[1] This is not true, however, of the gravest offenses; for among the girls below 14 there was not one convicted at the Assizes, while of the boys of that age there were 4650 convicted out of 10,000,000.

In Germany 3.8% of the female offenders and 2.6% of the male are over 60 years old. For every 100 criminal men over 60 there were 25.4 criminal women of the same age, while between the ages of 21 and 40 there were only 19.6 criminal women to 100 men. During the years 1876–80 among the juvenile delinquents there were 16.3 girls under 16 to 100 boys, and 17.7 girls under 21 to 100 boys of like age. Female delinquency has, then, one of its high points during youth, a fact to be explained by prostitution among girls not yet of age. According to Parent-du-Châtelet 15% of the French prostitutes were over 17 and under 21 years of age, while according to Guerry 24% of the London prostitutes were under 20.

§ 82. Specific Criminality

Women as criminals are naturally active in other spheres than those which men occupy. In Austria women are most

[1] In Italy in the years 1871–72 juvenile criminals of the two sexes were divided into age groups as follows:

	Of 100 girls	Of 100 boys
Under 10	25.5	18
11 to 14	43.5	57
15 to 18	27	23
Over 18	4	2

In Austria out of 100 criminals of either sex there were:

Age	Women	Men
10 to 20	12.7	10.6
20 to 30	42.1	39.6
30 to 50	24.5	27.8
50 to 60	14.0	12.5
60 to 70	7.3	5.7
Over 70	2.9	1.6

often guilty of abortion, bigamy, libel, participation in crimes, arson, and theft; they are more rarely guilty of homicide and forgery. In France their principal crimes are infanticide, abortion, poisoning, parricide, maltreating of children, domestic thefts, and arson. In England they are beginning to be more often guilty of passing counterfeit money, perjury, and libel; and homicide also is slowly increasing there. In studying the situation in Italy, Rencoroni (*op. cit.*) arrived at the following results:

Crimes (assizes)	Average of three years		To 1,000,000		Women to 100 men
	Men	Women	Men	Women	
Crimes against the State .	9.2	0.6	5.472	0.036	0.5
Forgery and commercial crimes	345.8	24.0	22.822	1.440	6.9
Vagrancy, etc.	114.6	1.0	6.876	0.066	0.8
Sexual crimes	251.0	15.6	17.6	1.16	5.16
Abortion, infanticide . . .	10.8	51.6	0.618	3.086	476.8
Homicide, murder	144.0	49.2	75.504	2.952	3.4
Poisoning	4.4	5.4	0.264	0.324	122.7
Assault	899.2	34.2	59.346	2.052	3.8
Highway robbery . .	473.2	5.8	35.630	0.348	1.2
Theft	910.8	60.8	60.060	4.012	6.6
Fraud	22.8	1.4	1.368	0.084	6.3
Receipt of stolen goods . .	92.2	18.6	5.520	1.116	20.2
Arson	42.2	3.8	2.652	0.228	8.6

We saw above that on an average 6 women are condemned at the Assizes for each 100 men. The figures are higher for the following crimes:

	Number of women to 100 men
Receiving stolen goods	20.2
Poisoning	122.7
Abortion, infanticide	476.8
Arson	8.6

These four crimes, then, seem to have a closer connection with the feminine nature.

That women less often are engaged in highway robbery, murder, homicide, and assault is due to the very nature of the feminine constitution. To conceive an assassination, to make ready for it, to put it into execution demands, in a great number of cases at least, not only physical force, but a certain energy and a certain combination of intellectual functions. In this sort of development women almost always fall short of men. It seems on the other hand that the crimes that are habitual to them are those which require a smaller degree of physical and intellectual force, and such especially are receipt of stolen goods, poisoning, abortion, and infanticide. I specify intellectual force and not education, for it is well known that poisoners are often well educated persons. Quételet has already remarked that these differences proceed not so much from slighter perversity of character as from a more retired way of life, which gives less opportunity for such crimes as highway robbery; and from a smaller degree of strength and intelligence, on account of which women commit fewer murders and crimes requiring the use of the newspapers. But in domestic crimes they equal, and sometimes even exceed, the men. In poisoning they reach 91% and in house-theft 60%, to say nothing of abortion and infanticide. If we add that the great number of sexual offenses committed by men are not only equalled but surpassed, at least in the eyes of the psychologist, by prostitution on the part of the women, and that in the more civilized countries and periods the criminality of women continually increases until it approaches that of men, we find that the analogy between the two is greater than would have been believed possible at first sight.

§ 83. Prostitution

The comparative infrequency of the arrest of women for vagrancy [1] is due in part to the fact that women are less given to drink, in part to the fact that they are less employed in trade, and finally to the fact that in youth prostitution completely takes the place of crime.[2] With this unhappy profession idle-

[1] The American reader will have to remember that in the United States as Dugdale points out, "vagrancy" as applied to a woman is frequently only an "official euphonism for prostitution." — TRANSL.

[2] For the complete demonstration of this see the work of Lombroso and Ferrero cited above.

ness and vagabondage are inseparably bound up. If cases of prostitution are included in the criminal statistics the two sexes are at once placed on an equality, or the preponderance may even be thrown on the side of women. According to Ryan and Talbot there is 1 prostitute to each 7 women in London, and in Hamburg 1 to each 9. In Italy, in the great centers, they form 18% to 33% of the female population of like age.[1] In some countries the proportion has doubled and in some increased even tenfold. In Berlin the number of prostitutes increased from 600 in 1845 to 9653 in 1893. In 1876 Du Camp placed the number of secret prostitutes in Paris at 20,000.

We have seen, and shall see more and more, how the physical and moral characteristics of the delinquent belong equally to the prostitute, and how great the sympathy is between the two classes. Both phenomena spring from idleness, misery, and especially from alcoholism. Both are connected, likewise, with certain organic and hereditary tendencies, as Dugdale has demonstrated in connection with the Juke family.

"When I compare the data brought together in technical writings," says Locatelli, "with the results of my own experience, I am convinced that those authors have fallen into error who allege that the principal cause of prostitution is abandonment, or the misery into which many of the young girls of the proletariat are plunged. Prostitution, in my opinion, like theft, springs from vicious natural tendencies of certain individuals. Lack of education, abandonment, poverty, and bad example can be considered at most as secondary causes; just as family care and instruction may serve as salutary checks upon evil tendencies. The tendency to prostitution proceeds from a fundamental lack of the sense of modesty, which often manifests itself at the same time as the absence of all sexual feeling, for many of these unfortunates are of an apathetic temperament. They are automatons, who concern themselves with nothing and have almost no feeling; in their many and fleeting relationships they show no preference. If they ever show favor to some particular lover, they do it, not from sympathy, but because it is the custom of their associates; they show themselves as indifferent to homage as to the most brutal abuse."

This apathy, it is true, is interrupted from time to time by violent and fugitive fits of passion;[2] but here also there is a striking

[1] Castiglioni, "Sulla Prostituzione," Rome, 1871.
[2] Lombroso and Ferrero, *op. cit.*

resemblance to the criminal, with whom apathy, insensibility, violent and transitory passion, and idleness are dominant characteristics.[1] But even if we hold strictly to legal definition and official statistics, it is plain that a part of the army of prostitutes must be enrolled as criminals also. Guerry observed that in London 80% of the female criminals under 30 years of age came from among the prostitutes, and 7% of those over that age. Furthermore, prostitution, like female criminality, tends to increase with increasing civilization and approach to male criminality in amount. In London in 1834 the female criminals were 18.8% as numerous as the male, and in 1853 25.7%; while in Spain the figure was as low as 11%, in France 20%, in Prussia 22%, in Scotland 23%. In Austria in general the female criminality is 14% of the male, but in Vienna it is 25%.

But aside from these facts many other grave reasons make us suspect that the criminality of women is greater than the statistics show. The crimes mentioned above to which women are particularly addicted are just those which are most easily concealed and most rarely lead to trial. To this may be added the well known fact of the greater obstinacy and intensity of criminality when it appears in a woman. Thus in America delinquent girls have shown themselves more incorrigible than boys. However, it must be remembered in this connection that female criminals show fewer marks of degeneracy than criminal men.

§ 84. Civilization

In both sexes, but especially in the case of women, we see that the more serious crimes regularly increase as civilization decreases. On the other hand, the relation of the degree of civilization with vagrancy and similar offenses and with sexual crimes is not so definite. The following table gives the ratio which the frequency of the various crimes in southern and central Italy bears to that of the more civilized part of the kingdom:

[1] Lombroso, "Homme Criminel," Vol. I.

NUMBER OF CRIMES TO 1 COMMITTED IN NORTHERN ITALY

	Central Italy		Southern Italy	
	By men	By women	By men	By women
Murder and homicide	5	4	12	24
Assault	3	2	6	11
Highway robbery	1/3	5	4	5
Theft	1/4	2/3	1/3	3/5
Arson	1/3	2	6	6

Abortion and infanticide are more frequent at an early age the more civilized a country is, but more frequent at an advanced age the less civilized it is. This appears to be due to the fact that the more civilized a country is, the more will fear of public dishonor induce a young girl who becomes pregnant to take criminal means to save her reputation. But where these crimes are most frequent between 21 and 40, it is not a clinging to reputation so much as an unfortunate custom that is the cause. It may be remarked in this connection that abortion is a widespread practice among savages.

The number of persons sentenced by the "correctional tribunals" in France increased from 1831 to 1880 by 180% for the men and 110% for the women. The increase of school instruction in France, then, left the female criminality even lower than before in proportion to that of the men. While in 1888 among the recidivists 1% of the men had a higher education and 9% an elementary education, none of the women had a higher education and only 5% an elementary one; of the men 30% were absolutely illiterate, and 47% of the women. Of 244 criminals transported in 1887–88, 30% of the men and 39% of the women were illiterate, 53% of the men and 51% of the women could read and write, 15% of the men and 10% of the women had an elementary education, and 2% of the men but none of the women had a higher education. The same phenomenon is equally to be found in Germany. In 1854 23% of the crimes were committed by women, in 1878 only 16%;

so that in this period there was a constant diminution in female delinquency. In the country the infanticides are more frequent, and in the cities the abortions. Thus in Germany in 1888 out of 172 infanticides only 1 took place in Berlin, while of 216 abortions 23 occurred in Berlin. In France 75% of the infanticides take place in the country, and 60% of the abortions in the cities.

In many of the more highly civilized countries, such as England and Austria, female delinquency appears for a moment to be approaching that of men; but this is due to the influence of petty offenses, drunkenness, vagrancy, etc., while as regards crimes proper, the criminality of women is much less than that of men and tends to diminish rather than increase. In countries still barbarous, female delinquency is infinitely less, so that in Bulgaria Laveleye found almost no women in the prisons. If we look at the effect of great cities upon each crime in particular we see that assaults, highway robberies, and thefts are more numerous in the great cities than in the small towns or in the country. In Berlin, for example, the increased density of the population is a manifest cause of the increase of crimes committed by women; in fact, 21% of the crimes in the capital are committed by women, as against 16% for the Empire at large. In England during the years 1859 to 1863 for every 100 men convicted at the Assizes there were respectively 35, 36, 38, 33, 31, and 32 women; but among the arrests made by the London police during about the same period (1854–62) there were 57 women to 100 men, while in Liverpool the number was 69, and in Dublin 84.

Fewer crimes against property are committed by married women (and men) than by unmarried; but of crimes in general the married woman above 30 years of age commits more than the unmarried, though a similar statement cannot be made with regard to married men until they have passed the age of 70, — a fact which may be attributed to crimes against the person, against the state, etc.

§ 85. Recidivists

In France the number of recidivists has increased as follows:

PERCENTAGE OF CRIMINALS WHO ARE RECIDIVISTS

Year	Men	Women
1851–55	36	16
1856–60	30	16
1861–65	42	17
1866–70	45	17
1871–76	51	19
1877–80	53	21

Male criminals are, then, much more apt to become recidivists than women, and this tendency increases with advancing civilization, as the figures show; and this may fairly be maintained, notwithstanding the allowance that must be made for error because of the fact that nowadays recidivists are much more easily recognized than formerly. It is well known that prisoners in penitentiaries relapse into crime almost immediately upon their release, or at least within a short period of years, as shown in the following table:

RELEASED CONVICTS BECOMING RECIDIVISTS

Year	Men	Women
1851–55	37%	26%
1856–60	34%	23%
1861–65	37%	24%
1866–70	40%	25%
1871–75	39%	22%
1876	40%	26%
1877	39%	23%
1878	45%	24%

In Germany the results are a little different (Starke). Although in 1869 there was a somewhat smaller proportion of recidivists among the female criminals, the number rose gradually, and by 1882 had reached the percentage shown by the men.

RECIDIVISTS IN GERMANY

Year	Men	Women	Total
1869	71.44%	64.98%	...
1870	74.00%	74.22%	...
1871	80.38%	78.35%	...
1872	77.29%	74.16%	76.74%
1873	80.66%	77.46%	80.13%
1874	77.98%	77.16%	77.84%
1875	79.03%	84.26%	79.85%
1876	79.66%	78.17%	79.42%
1877–78	78.47%	76.76%	78.25%
1878–79	79.13%	75.80%	78.61%
1879–80	77.13%	75.19%	76.84%
1880–81	76.42%	77.77%	76.47%
1881–82	78.76%	78.86%	78.87%

Messedaglia has shown that repeated relapses into crime are more frequent with Austrian women than single relapses, while in the case of male criminals the two are about equal. The same thing is observed in Prussia, where 16% of the female cases are of women arrested for the first time, 17% are women arrested after the first relapse, 24% after the 6th, and 30% after 7 or more relapses.

In conclusion we may affirm:

1st, Female delinquency is only a fourth or a fifth that of men, and only one-sixteenth if we consider simply serious crimes.

2d, Female criminality reaches its highest point, as compared with male criminality, in advanced age, the period of youth coming second, and middle life last. Taking the criminality of women absolutely, without reference to that of men, we find the maximum in old age good only for the more serious crimes.[1] In both sexes the proportion of crimes committed in youth is very high.

3d, In comparing the criminality of the two sexes we find women participating more often in crimes which require less bodily strength, less culture, and less intellectual energy.

[1] According to Mayr the maximum of criminality is found in men between 18 and 21, and in women between 30 and 40.

4th, In both sexes youth leads in crimes resulting from sudden anger, and maturity in crimes that require premeditation. With women, however, the period of maturity leads in murder, homicide, and arson. Middle life (from 21 to 50 years) exceeds the two others in the total number of crimes.

5th, The figures for crime in general, as well as for each class of crime, for each sex, and in each country, are in general very consistent. In Italy, however, among the men serious crimes are decreasing, minor offenses increasing among both sexes, but in the case of the women serious offenses are on the increase also.

6th, Abortion and infanticide appear to be committed by women more from feelings of shame and less from ancient custom, the more civilized the country. Thus in northern Italy these crimes are more common in youth, in southern Italy they are committed by the mature.

7th, The effect of great cities upon the increase of crime is more marked in the case of women, and shows itself especially in the multiplication of assaults, highway robberies, and thefts.

8th, Prostitution largely takes the place of crime for women, thus explaining why women seem less criminal than men, and also giving a probable reason why female criminality is greatest in old age, when prostitution no longer offers a profession.

CHAPTER XV

CIVIL STATUS — PROFESSION — UNEMPLOYMENT

§ 86. Civil Status

WE know that the age of maximum criminality is between 15 and 25, and that the majority of female delinquents are prostitutes or minors; it is hardly necessary to add, then, that it is the unmarried who show the greatest criminality. Taking out those who have not yet reached marriageable age, we get from the statistics for Italy for the years 1890 to 1894, the following number of persons sentenced out of 1000 in the same condition in life: unmarried, 48.9; married, 29.7; widowers and widows, 14.3. In Austria the proportion of the unmarried among the criminals is 35% greater than among the rest of the population, while the proportion of married criminals is 13% less than that of married persons in general. Widowers sentenced for crime are a smaller part of the criminal class by 56% than are widowers in the normal population. Similar relations obtain among the insane, and for similar reasons. According to Verga there is 1 insane person to 474 unmarried persons between the ages of 20 and 60, and 1 to 1418 married persons. Upon the basis of the statistics for 1841–57 Girard found:

1 insane person to 2169 unmarried
1 " " " 7094 married
1 " " " 4572 widowers

With regard to sex Lunier found for the years 1856–62:

1 insane person to 2629 men, 2931 women, unmarried
1 " " " 4754 " 5454 " married
1 " " " 3421 widowers, 3259 widows

It is, however, to be noted that among criminals, as well as among the insane, widows are much more numerous than widowers, a fact that Messedaglia in Austria and Lolli in Italy explain by the greater number of widows to be found in the population. It has been noted in Austria, Italy, and France that married men and widowers who have children commit offenses much less frequently than the childless. The contrary is true according to Guislain and Castiglioni, however, with regard to the frequency of insanity, a fact explainable by the anxiety occasioned by the needs of a large family.[1]

§ 87. Professions

It is rather difficult to determine the influence of occupation, on account of the system of classification and nomenclature commonly employed in statistics, — a system which, however useful for economists, is hardly suited to the purposes of the anthropologist; as, for example, when there are grouped together innkeepers and merchants, soldiers and agricultural laborers, metal-workers and cabinet-makers, or artists and professional men. The comparison becomes additionally difficult when the statistics of recruits and the census statistics each have their own mode of grouping. According to the latest Italian statistics the following numbers of convictions (to the 1000) occurred in the various classes of occupation:

Agriculture	8.9
Manufacturing	7.4
Commerce	12.8
Public service and the liberal professions	3.5
Domestic service	3.6

The greater criminality among merchants may be explained by the greater activity of business life, as well as to the increase of this class since the last census in 1881. They furnish not only the large number of commercial frauds that would naturally be expected, but also a considerable number of libels and other similar crimes. The offenses most common among the agricultural population are theft (26%) and assault (22%). This class furnishes only a very small number of the other forms of crime. Among factory-workers also there are a large number of convictions for theft and assault, but in comparison with the agricultural population they show more of a tendency toward

[1] Verga, "Se il Matrimonio," Milan, 1870.

resistance to the officers of the state (11%), and toward libels and frauds.

If we go on now to take up certain occupations in detail, we shall see that the highest proportion of persons convicted is found among pedlars (44 to the 1000), and of these relatively large numbers are for theft (30%), resistance to officers (20%), and sexual offenses. Butchers also show a large number of convictions (37 to the 1000), being guilty principally of resistance to the authorities and frauds in business. Then come draymen and cab-drivers (26 to the 1000), who are arraigned most frequently for resistance to the authorities, and for crimes against property and persons. The learned professions and domestic service contribute only a small quota of criminals (2.94 and 3.93 to the 1000). In the first class forgery is the most common crime, and house-theft in the second. Marro found in Turin the smallest number of delinquents (2 to the 1000) among the huntsmen, priests, students, school-teachers, fishermen, and umbrella-makers. A fairly small number (8 to the 1000) he found among the lithographers, marble-workers, carriage-makers, gardeners, masons, and tanners; and a somewhat higher one (14 to the 1000) among the brokers, writers, weavers, and hairdressers, the last being guilty of sexual crimes almost exclusively.

The following table gives the percentages of certain professions among criminals compared with the percentages of the same professions in the normal population:

	Among criminals	In normal population
Masons	11.0 %	2.5%
Bakers	6.9 %	1.6%
Locksmiths	8.3 %	2.3%
Shoemakers	7.3 %	3.2%
Students	0.33%	3.1%

Bakers and masons have a strong representation, because they are paid daily and have no need of a long apprenticeship. The occupations carried on in the city which involve most exposure to alcoholism (cooks, shoemakers, innkeepers), which bring the poor into contact with the rich (domestic servants), or which furnish the means of committing crime (masons and locksmiths), furnish a large contingent of criminals, and an even higher proportion of recidivists. A philological confirmation of part of the above is found in the derivation of *coquin* (rascal), from the Latin *coquus* (cook). The occupations which bring men less into contact with their fellows, such as those of peasants and boatmen, furnish the smallest proportion of criminals, and also of recidivists. In France the greatest tendency to sexual crimes is found among the shoemakers, — a fact to be referred to their alcoholism, and to the effect upon the genital organs of their position when at work. The same attitude toward crime in the case of the various occupations is found in the other civilized countries. The following table gives the number of persons (to the million) convicted in Austria, classified according to occupation:

Persons engaged in agriculture		
Proprietors and tenants	46.8	49.3
Stewards	53.2	
Workmen	51.6	
Persons engaged in manufacturing and commerce		
Entrepreneurs	23.8	37.7
Agents	13.0	
Workmen	45.5	
Other occupations		
Property owners and stockholders		15.9
Learned professions		6.1
Domestic servants		133.6
Other occupations		26.0
Persons without occupation (including women and children)		4.8
General population of Austria, excluding those without occupation		49.9

Leaving out of account the persons without profession, as including the women and children, the smallest contingent of crime is furnished by the property-owners and members of the learned professions.

If we divide crimes of violence into those which are premeditated and those which are not, we get the following numbers (to the million inhabitants) for the various occupations:

	Premeditated	Not premeditated	Infanticide
Landed proprietors	17.3	25.3	4.2
Agricultural laborers	14.4	26.2	11.0
Manufacturers	8.9	12.7	2.2
Workmen in factories	18.2	24.3	3.0
Property owners and stockholders	8.2	6.2	1.4
Liberal professions	3.3	1.4	1.4
Domestic servants	24.7	11.2	97.7

In France the various occupations are grouped in a manner different from that employed in Austria, and they are also given less in detail. In the group of liberal professions are included army officers, capitalists, and stockholders (a very numerous class in France). The industrial and commercial classes are not distinguished, nor are country proprietors distinguished from farm-laborers. During the years 1876–80 there were the following numbers of convictions (to the million inhabitants) for crimes of violence:

Persons without occupation, beggars, vagrants, prostitutes, inmates of almshouses	59.2
Domestic servants	25.9
Agricultural class	24.3
Industrial and commercial class	18.1
Liberal professions	10.6

In all the groups, aside from those without occupation, we find a complete analogy with the Austrian statistics, and may draw the conclusion that analogous social conditions produce analogous results in different countries.

In France, according to Yvernés there were in 1882 the following indictments for each 100,000 males of the same occupation:

Property owners and stockholders	6
Public officers	12
Farmers	16
Farm servants and laborers	24
Industrial workers	25
Liberal professions	28
Transportation and merchant marine	35
Commercial class	38
Personal servants	49
Occupations not classified or unknown	54

According to Tarde's last researches,[1] the number of persons convicted in France, to 10,000 of each class of occupation, is as follows:

Agriculture	0.84
Manufacturing	1.32
Commerce	1.00

In France, as in Italy, the agricultural class furnishes a smaller contingent of criminals than the manufacturing or commercial classes. We note here the enormous difference between the number of persons indicted in the country and of those indicted in the city, a fact certainly due to the harmful environment in which the latter live. According to earlier researches of Fayet, the agricultural population, which was 53% of the whole, in 1847 furnished only 32% of the crime. It is well to note in this connection that agricultural servants, though exposed to great poverty, furnish only from 4% to 5% of the crime, while servants in the city furnish 7%. This latter class, with the innkeepers, furnish one-third of the infanticides, one-sixth of the thefts, one-ninth of the poisonings, doubtless because of the loss of the sense of personal dignity that the state of dependence always brings in its train. I emphasize this especially because alcoholism is rare among domestic servants, and hence they are less exposed to one of the principal causes of crime. Fayet observes, however, that the majority of parricides, 108 out of 164, spring from the country population. Fayet further finds a considerable number of offenses against modesty among masons and painters, of rapes among cab-drivers, and of infanticides among hat-makers and laundry-workers (these last doubtless because of the large number of women so employed). Among merchants crimes against property are especially abundant, as they also are among professional and moneyed men; among the latter, unfortunately, these crimes are increasing, especially with the notaries and attorneys, and in a less degree with property owners. In France in the years 1833–39 there occurred the following numbers of crimes for each 10,000 men over 26 years of age in the specified classes:

[1] "Actes du Congrès d'Antropologie Criminelle de Genève," 1897.

Priests	10
Solicitors	52
Advocates	74
Notaries	145
Bailiffs	162

Joly rightly remarks that their knowledge of the law, their privileges, education, and well-being, ought to ensure that the professional classes would manifest few criminal tendencies. Yet on the contrary they are corrupted by success or by the parasitic character of their work, which tempts them to make the most gain out of their profession, instead of firing them with noble ambition. He notes that up to the year 1881 the number of notaries annually removed from office was from 18 to 25, but that in 1882 it was 40, in 1883 41, and in 1884 58. After a slight decrease in the next two years the number in 1887 leaped up to 75. According to the French criminal statistics the number of notaries indicted is 43 to the 10,000, while there is about 1 indictment to the 10,000 in the general population. The criminality of notaries is accordingly 43 times greater than that of the population as a whole. Notaries and bailiffs furnish more criminals than individuals of the same sex and age in the other higher professions. A tenth of the murders, a seventh of the homicides, an eighth of the parricides, an eighth of the rapes upon girls under 15, and an eighteenth of all other crimes, have been committed by professional men or men of wealth, while these classes constitute but an eighteenth part of the total population.[1] This proves clearly the corrupting influence of higher education, and at the same time shows how little influence intimidation has in overcoming temptation, since advocates and bailiffs know better than anyone else the penalties which the law threatens.

In Prussia the liberal professions furnish 2.2% of the population and 4% of the criminals; domestic servants furnished 2% of the population and 12% of the criminals.[2]

The data with regard to Russia that are accessible to me have reference to 9229 crimes of violence committed in the years 1875 to 1879. Below is given a comparison of these, as regards

[1] Fayet, "Journal des Economistes," 1847.
[2] Oettingen, "Moralstatistik," p. 37.

distribution by occupation, with the statistics for Austria and France:

	Russia		Austria		France	
	Per cent		Per cent		Per cent	
Agriculture { Proprietors . . .	47.5	60.3	18.4	50.0	. . .	50.7
Agriculture { Workmen	12.8		31.6		. . .	
Manufactures and commerce { Proprietors .	7.5	16.8	3.3	16.9	. . .	30.0
Manufactures and commerce { Workmen . .	9.3		13.6		. . .	
Day-laborers	7.7		. . .		. . .	
Liberal professions	1.8		0.2		5.0	
Domestic servants	4.9		19.6		8.1	
Occupation not determined . .	6.7		8.8		. . .	
Prostitutes and persons without occupation	2.0		4.9		6.0	

Thus, while in Austria in the space of three years there were condemned for crimes of violence 4 persons belonging to the liberal professions, in Russia in a period of five years there were condemned for the same crimes 165 persons, of whom 88 were in the employ of the government, 59 were ecclesiastics, lawyers, doctors, or technicians, and 19 were men of learning, students, or painters. The explanation of this excessive number of crimes of violence among the liberal professions in Russia is to be found in the political persecution and sectarian fanaticism which on the one hand provoke crime, and on the other are its natural consequence.

As regards the criminality of women, we find that the highest figures are to be found among those engaged in commerce, and that the most numerous crimes here are swindling, fraud, libel, and assault. The women engaged in factories and workshops are less given to theft than the women in the country, plainly because of the opportunity for field theft which the latter have. As regards the specific criminality of women in the different occupations, it may be noted that the midwives show the greatest number convicted of abortion (3 out of 100); and that those employed in domestic service come next to country women in the number of thefts (55 to the 100).[1] However, the figures

[1] Bosco, "La Delinquenza Femminile," Rome, 1897.

are too limited for us to draw any very definite and general conclusions, and in addition the great number of prostitutes confuses all our investigations, for it is certain that a large part of the country women arrive at criminal practices by the road of prostitution, carried on either openly or under the guise of service in the city. "Frequenting large cities," writes Parent-du-Châtelet, "is harmful to women from the country, who appear from the statistics to give themselves up to prostitution in direct proportion to their nearness to great centers." Half of the prostitutes of Paris come from among the seamstresses and ironers; a third from the milliners, saleswomen, and hairdressers; a twentieth from the laundresses and factory-workers; and a few from among the actresses.

§ 88. Soldiers

It is important to make a separate study of the very high criminality of the soldier class, which, according to Hausner,[1] is 25 times as great as that of the population as a whole. But there is certainly an error here, for the investigator has not excluded from the civil population the old men, women, and children. At any rate we find very different figures for Italy. If we study the crimes of the soldiers in Italy in the year 1872, we shall find that most of the charges brought are for actions which are not criminal outside of the army, such as insubordination and malingering. We find, then, one person convicted to 112 soldiers. Now if we compare this figure with the proportion of persons of the same age (between 21 and 31 years old) who were found guilty in the general population (1 to 172), we

1

	Number in population to each person convicted	
	Civilians	Soldiers
In Austria	856	78
" Holland	4330	173
" France	7460	139

shall see that while the figures for the military are worse, the difference is not so very great; and even this difference becomes less when we leave out of account the women in the civil population, since their criminality is 80% less than that of the men.

But even if we must admit that there is a real difference (as seems to be the case in Germany), it is explained by the fact that the soldier continually has arms ready at hand, is at the age most inclined to crime, is unmarried, largely idle, and forced into close contact with many individuals and in a narrow space (from which come the high figures for rape, pederasty, and criminal associations); to this may be added in time of war the habituation to deeds of blood. Holtzendorff tells that a murderer, who had been a soldier, excused himself by saying that in the Austrian war in 1866 he had seen so many men killed that one more or less seemed a small matter to him. Lucian has said, "Men who follow war have neither faith nor piety." A curious and significant fact in connection with this is furnished us by philology, namely, that many military functions were formerly exercised in such a criminal manner that they have become synonymous with crime. Thus *latrones* were officers *ad latus*, aides-de-camp of the king, but instead of playing the courtier in the fashion of the present, they committed so many depredations that their name has become confounded with "robber." In our day we can hardly believe that "pirate" was a name originally used for marines, or that "brigand" formerly meant simply a kind of sharpshooter used in attacking a town.

That warlike peoples are characterized by a high degree of cruelty is a fact that can still be seen in our own day, as Hammond has very well shown in his study of military psychology. The cruelty peculiar to the soldier is inspired partly by his contempt for the civilian class, a contempt that has come down from ancient times, and partly by having his excesses go unpunished. There are innumerable examples of such impunity in Germany, Russia, and Italy. In Coblenz a lieutenant killed with his saber a merchant who was passing, and was sentenced to one year's imprisonment, a sentence made even shorter by pardon; but when the mother of his victim complained of this in a violent letter she was fined (1894). In Berlin a soldier, named Laerke, while on guard duty, seriously wounded two workmen; his superior officers praised him highly for this proceeding and promoted him (1893). In Bologna, Monteleone, and Aquila armed officers have attacked peaceful citizens; and these examples could be prolonged indefinitely. The pretended chivalrous magnanimity, which is attributed to soldiers, is as foreign to them as it is to the Middle Ages, in which it existed only in the imagination of the romantic school. There are, it is true, exceptions, but their case is no less deplorable. These are the individuals whom the "service" has succeeded in making thoroughly servile, so that they are no longer capable of directing their own lives, are without individuality or originality, and must always lean upon someone else, while the nation from which they were drawn sorely needs powerful arms and free, strong hearts.

But what has most effect on the disproportion between the criminality of soldiers and that of civilians, is the smaller difference in the former case between the apparent criminality, as Messedaglia calls it, and the real criminality. In the army any crime is quickly brought to light and promptly punished, while in civil life, as is well known, not half the crimes committed are discovered and punished.[1]

§ 89. The Insane

The influence of occupation upon insanity is less clearly demonstrated than in the case of crime; for it is not easy to find statistics which concern themselves with both rich and poor, since these two classes are generally received into different asylums. However, from the French statistics, the completest we have, we get glimpses of interesting analogies with

[1] Of 233,181 cases brought before the examining justices in France, 70,276 had to do with offenses of which the authors were unknown. In 1862–66 in Bavaria 68% of the crimes and 54% of the misdemeanors remained unpunished because either the offenders were unknown or their guilt insufficiently proved (Mayhew).

crime.[1] The insane are more than twice as numerous in the city as they are in the country (223 to 100), and men are more often affected than women (132 to 100). Agriculturists furnish the minimum of insanity, and the liberal professions the maximum; and among these latter, artists and jurists show higher figures than officials and ecclesiastics. The investigations of Girard show the great frequency of insanity among domestics, metal workers, and miners. According to Bini and Golgi it is very common among shoemakers (1.2% to 8%), inmates of almshouses, and cooks (2% to 5%), with a very large number in the liberal professions (5%). According to the investigations of Girard and Baroffio, the military class gave the highest figures for insanity, 1.4 to the thousand. The researches of Lolly, which are the only ones for Italy that I am acquainted with, are very inclusive, and show insanity to be more common among the landed proprietors, the well-to-do classes, and the merchants than among the agricultural classes. With this latter class it is less common also than among artisans.[2]

[1] Lunier, "Nouveau Dictionnaire de Médecine," Paris, 1872; Girard de Cailloux, "Études Pratiques sur les Aliénés," Paris, 1863.

	Girard (Seine, 1852)	Lunier (France, 1856–61)
	1 insane person to each	
Artists	3292	104
Jurists	544	119
Literati	1035	280
Ecclesiastics	706	253
Physicians and pharmacists	1602	259
Officials	1621	727
Bankers	2571	5487
Domestic servants	609	...
Shoemakers and tailors	1807	...
Landed proprietors	5547	3609
Agriculturists	11,403	18,819
Soldiers	553	1711
Miners	132	...
Metal-workers	732	...
Innkeepers, etc.	1700	...

[2] According to Lolly the various classes furnish the following percentages to the total population and to the number of the insane:

	Population	Insane
Agricultural class	49.0 %	34.00%
Artisan "	12.3 %	12.90%
Domestic "	2.64%	2.17%
Landholding "	2.78%	6.23%
Commercial "	2.70%	1.66%
Ecclesiastical "	0.60%	1.37%

I must add that the occupations which accustom men to the sight of blood or to the use of dangerous weapons, such as the trade of the butcher, soldier, etc., or to a life of social or sexual isolation, like that of the shepherd, field guard, or priest, especially when the exasperation of a forced chastity is added, — such occupations, I say, call forth both in the insane and in criminals a savage cruelty in their deeds, which is often accompanied by abnormal lubricity. We may note also that poisonings are more frequently committed by physicians and pharmacists than by any other class.

§ 90. Aversion to Work

In connection with such investigations as the foregoing, it is necessary to call attention to the fact that the occupation claimed by the criminal is frequently only nominal, and his real occupation is idleness. I have discovered in Turin a strange pursuit peculiar to criminals, that of counterfeiting a trade. These men pose as joiners, locksmiths, or what not, and provide themselves with the necessary tools. But these are simply to convince the police. Their work is either all a pretense, or just sufficient in amount to prevent their apprehension for vagrancy. They lack neither the means nor the opportunity of working, but only the willingness to work. Sichart[1] found that out of 3181 prisoners 1347, or 42.3%, had an aversion to work. Grouped according to the various crimes committed, the numbers were as follows:

Total number of prisoners	Those having aversion to work
1848 thieves	961, or 52 %
381 swindlers	172, " 45 %
155 incendiaries	48, " 31 %
542 sexual criminals	145, " 26.7%
255 perjurers	21, " 8.2%

The importance of these figures is still clearer when we take into account the way they are divided between what Sichart calls "occasional criminals"[2] and habitual criminals. Of the

[1] "Ueber individuelle Faktoren des Verbrechens," in the "Zeitschrift für die gesammte Strafwissenschaft," 1891.

[2] "Criminels par occasion."

former 170, or 19.2%, showed an aversion to work, but of the latter 1170, or 51.7% — over two and a half times as many. According to the recent statistics for Massachusetts,[1] we see that out of 4340 convicts, 2991, or 68%, had no occupation. According to the Pennsylvania statistics, almost 88% of the convicts in the penitentiaries had never followed a trade, and the same was true of 68½% of the inmates of the county jails. As regards homicides in particular, Frederick Wines has shown that in 1890, out of 6958 convicts guilty of this crime, 5175, or more than 74%, had never received any instruction in a trade.[2]

The aversion to work shows itself also in the occupations which criminals adopt. Marro, having noticed that masons furnish 11% of the criminals, although they form but 3.56% of the population, got an explanation from the masons themselves. Many of them told him that they had given up other trades and taken up this, for the reason that masons receive their wages daily, without waiting for the end of the week or fortnight; which proves that they follow this trade only by caprice. I have already shown that the thieves in France are often called *pègre* or *paresseux* (idler), and that the worst criminals, such as Lacenaire, Lemaire, and Cretien, hated work more than they loved life. One may study this state of mind in the psychological tables given in the anthropological-statistical "Atlas" of Ferri's "Omicidio," where the psychology of idleness is often pointed out. Thus a recidivist, on being asked if he was willing to work, replied, "No, work shortens life." Another said quite frankly, "I have worked, but only a little, because work tires you." Another, when asked why he did not work, excused himself by saying, "I am not capable of it." Still another said, "I have no desire to work, so I have to steal if I want money."

The frequency with which criminals change their trades is noteworthy. Of 100 normal persons 86 were found to have followed always the same occupation, 13 had changed once, and 1 had had three different trades. Among the criminals however, the following had changed their occupation two or more times:

[1] Wright, *op. cit.* [2] Bosco, *op. cit.*

27	out of	40 murderers
30	" "	40 pickpockets
60	" "	77 swindlers
22	" "	39 highway robbers
28	" "	51 persons guilty of assault
60	" "	97 thieves
30	" "	39 ravishers
23	" "	41 other sexual criminals

The reports of the Elmira Reformatory give the following with regard to the occupation of 6635 prisoners:

Domestic servants	1694,	or 25.5%
Common laborers	3651,	" 55.0%
Skilled laborers	974,	" 14.7%
Without occupation	320,	" 4.8%

The figure for those without occupation would be very low, but the report goes on to add:

"It must be noted that those who declare they have a trade are almost never regularly employed.[1] Consequently the number of men entering the reformatory, who are incapable of adapting themselves to steady work, is very great; and so likewise is the number of those who remain still incapable of working, notwithstanding the system of moral stimulation applied to them, because," so Superintendent Brockway affirms, "upon 34% of the prisoners any moral incentive to work is wasted; it does not even arouse their attention."

For this reason Brockway advocates the use of the lash and corporal punishment in general, methodically and carefully but rigorously applied. He thus confirms, without being conscious of it, the analogy between the incorrigible criminal and the savage, for the latter will not work unless compelled to do so by violence, and will sometimes die under the blows inflicted upon him before he can make up his mind to it. The tendency of criminals to change their trades, and their preference for those in which the wages are paid daily and in which, consequently, liberty is less trammeled, prove to us that the aversion of the criminal for work does not proceed so much from an absolute incapacity for every form of activity, as from a distaste for every form of occupation that is regular, methodical, and strictly fixed as to hours.

[1] "Nineteenth Year Book, New York State Reformatory at Elmira," 1894, p. 38.

Marro's figures here are full of meaning and help us to understand the nature of the criminal's incapacity for work. This is not incapacity for every kind of activity, not absolute inertia. The criminal has to employ at certain times a very great degree of activity. Certain crimes, like fraud and theft, very often demand energetic action. What is repugnant to the criminal is the regularity of the mechanism of modern society, that gigantic system of cog-wheels by which each human being, assigned to his place in the clock-work, must execute at any given instant the prescribed movement. Criminals, being incapable of resisting the intermittent caprices of a character at once inert and impulsive, declare war upon a society which is not in harmony with their inclinations. In the army of labor the criminal is a guerrilla. He is capricious about undergoing fatigue, and pretends that he submits to it only when he pleases, alternating intense effort with long periods of idleness, and always refractory under the will of another. In this his character is entirely like that of the savage, who, though habitually inert, bestirs himself from time to time and gives himself up to the most fatiguing labors of hunting and war. This is the character which Robertson gives to the American Indians. He says,

"When they undertake a hunting expedition they leave their habitual indolence and put into use intellectual faculties which apparently commonly remain dormant; they become active, persevering, indefatigable."

Marro observes very truly,

"Among uncivilized peoples we find an almost total incapacity for any continued effort. Steady, uninterrupted labor is the characteristic of civilized man. The more he is liable to husband his physical strength, the more profitable his intelligence makes it, and the more he is able to use it for his own benefit and that of society."

CHAPTER XVI

PRISONS — NEWSPAPERS — IMITATION — LEADERS — OTHER CAUSES

§ 91. Prisons

ONE of the greatest factors in crime is the prison. We think that we are protecting and avenging society by imprisoning criminals, while, on the contrary, we are not only furnishing them with the means of associating with one another and giving mutual instruction, but we are giving them real enjoyment besides. "I should like to tear to pieces the man who speaks evil of the prison," sang a prisoner at Palermo. "The prison is a piece of good fortune that has befallen us, because it teaches us hiding-places, and how to steal." [1] These facts explain why we so often find in our statistics individuals who are sentenced 50 or 60 times, persons who steal simply in order to be incarcerated again. A certain man named Zucchi stole during the Assizes in order to be arrested. "Since 1852," he said, "I have passed 20 years in prison. The amnesty set me free; but I cannot live on a franc a day, and I thought I would get myself put in prison, so as to be able to eat, drink, and sleep. Your Honor, increase the sentence, for, after all, one is not so badly off in prison." [2] In Rome, in 1879, an old man of 80, who had spent 47 years in prison, begged the judge to send him back. "I do not ask for a position," he said, "but for some prison where I can live in peace. I am already 80 years old, and I shall not live long enough to ruin the government." Olivecrona tells of a convict who, on leaving the prison, thanked the director, and declared that he had never before had such good food as he had had since his incarceration.

"While the convict," says Olivecrona, "gets his 52 kilos of meat a year, the peasant ordinarily has but 25 kilos of salted

[1] Lombroso, "Homme Criminel," Vol. I.
[2] "Rivista di Discipline Carcerarie," 1878.

beef and half a hog salted for himself and his whole family. We must, therefore, place the mildness of the prison regimen as one of the causes of recidivism." [1]

§ 92. Sensation

There is another very powerful cause of crime, which, however, it is hard to estimate exactly, except, perhaps, by the increase of certain crimes in some professions. I refer to the direct influence of sense impressions. Thus, for example, there are thieves who cannot see gold without taking it. A rich banker, named Downer, entered the establishment of his barber in a state of intoxication. An apprentice of the latter, 16 years old, who up to that time had been entirely honest, hearing the jingling of the money in the banker's pocket, was immediately seized with the idea of killing him, and strangled him with a cord. Terrified at his crime he fled and confessed, declaring that if he had not heard the sound of the coin he would never have thought of committing the horrible deed. Marie Frank, 38 years old, an inveterate drinker, who had already had a period of insanity and was continually beaten by her husband, one day saw a great fire, and immediately went and set fire to twelve houses. Adele Strohm, while witnessing the execution of two convicts, conceived the idea of killing her best friend in order to die in the grace of God.[2]

§ 93. Imitation

The cases cited are doubtless to be explained in part by insanity; but still more there enters the effect of imitation, which is one of the most active causes of crime as well as insanity. In 1863 and in 1872 hardly had the newspapers begun to speak of the abandonment of children, than this crime was repeated in Marseilles 8 times in a single day (Despine). The news of the assassination of Archbishop Sibour impelled a priest to attack the bishop of Matera, although he had no grudge against him whatever. Dufresne hated a certain Delauchx, but without thinking of harming him. He read the account of the trial of

[1] "De la Recidive," 1812. [2] Despine, *op. cit.*

Verger, and getting up, he cried, "I too will do as Verger did," and killed his enemy. At Bergamo, a short time after the trial of Verzeni, two other cases of the strangling of women took place; and similar phenomena occurred in Paris after the trials of Philippe, Billoir, and Moyaux, and in Florence after that of Martinati. At the time of the trial of Roux two servants pretended that they had been garrotted by their master, after having stolen from him themselves. The poisoning of La Pommerais was followed by that of Pritchard.

This morbid stimulation is increased a hundred-fold by the prodigious increase of really criminal newspapers, which spread abroad the virus of the most loathsome social plagues, simply for sordid gain, and excite the morbid appetite and still more morbid curiosity of the lower social classes. They may be likened to those maggots which, sprung from putrefaction, increase it by their presence. These newspapers, unfortunately, have in a single Italian city as many as 28,000 readers. In New York in 1851 a woman murdered her husband; a few days afterward three other women did the same thing. Corridori killed the director of his school, who had administered a deserved reproof to him, saying before he struck him, "I will repeat the case of the director of Catanzaro," who had also been killed for a similar cause. The attempted assassination of D. James upon the railway was followed by another upon the same line (Montel).[1]

[1] Holtzendorff gives us many other examples in his magnificent work "Das Verbrechen des Mordes und die Todestrafe," Berlin, 1875.

CHAPTER XVII

ASSOCIATIONS OF CRIMINALS, AND THEIR CAUSES

§ 94.

THE ætiology of associated crime, which is the most important and the most harmful, deserves to be studied by itself.

The first cause that may be assigned to this phenomenon is tradition. The long persistence and obstinacy of such associations as the Mafia, the Camorra, and brigandage, seem to proceed in the first place from the antiquity of their existence, for the long repetition of the same acts transforms them into a habit, and consequently into a law. History teaches us that ethnic phenomena of long duration are not to be eradicated easily at a stroke. The Camorra was already in existence in Naples in 1568. We know from the edicts of the Spanish viceroys, Count Miranda, the Duke of Alcala, *et al.*, that gamblers, gambling-house keepers, and those who levied tribute on these houses on their own account, were threatened with the galleys, and also those prisoners who, under pretext of an offering for certain holy images, levied a tax upon the other prisoners.[1] Monnier remarks very truly that the etymology of *camorra* shows its Spanish origin. The word in Spanish means a quarrel, brawl, or dispute, and *camorrista* signifies a bad character. The Arabic word *kumar* means a gambling game. We learn from a novel of Cervantes that at about the time we have been speaking of there was an association in Seville exactly corresponding to the Camorra. This society, likewise, levied tribute upon every thief for an image which was held in special reverence, gave the police a part of its gains, and undertook to execute private acts of revenge, including the *sfregio*, or face-slashing. To this association were attached novices, called "minor brothers,"

[1] Mordini, "Relazione al R. Ministero," Rome, 1874; Monnier, "Sulla Camorra," 1861.

who had to hand over the entire proceeds of their thefts for the first half-year, carry messages to the "major brothers" in prison, and perform subordinate offices generally. The major brothers had a common surname, and shared equitably the sums which the associates turned into the common treasury. The thieves of Morocco also levy a tax upon the prostitutes.

Societies entirely similar to the Camorra have existed in all imperfectly civilized periods. Thus Scalia has found mentioned in the Middle Ages, in the rules of the Stinche prison and the prisons of Parma, abuses like those of the Camorra, especially in connection with gambling. We read that each roomful of prisoners had its chief, called "capitaneo" or "podestà," precisely as the modern Camorrists have their "priore"; and this mediæval Camorra used to tax the new comers, just as is the custom to-day.[1] In Don Quixote we are told how certain idle folk exacted a share of the gains of lucky gamblers in return for a prediction of the lucky or unlucky plays. This is the ordinary mission of the modern Camorrist.

Brigandage, which persists with obstinacy in southern Italy and in Sardinia, probably has its origin in historic tradition, for it already existed in the most ancient times in central and southern Italy, and Strabo mentions it in connection with Sardinia.

"In the kingdom of Naples," writes Giannone (IV, 10), "there were always bandits in the train of the invaders, Greek, Lombard, Saracen, Angevin, or Albanian, all alike thievish, cruel, and greedy."

§ 95. Religion — Morals — Politics

In countries where civilization is not yet firmly established, there exists no clear notion of morals and justice, and religion is often but the accomplice or instigator of crime. In Bari there was said daily the "Mass of the brigands," at the expense of the brigand Pasquale. "We are blessed by God," he said to a friend — "the gospels say so." The state of morality naturally falls in with these notions of religion.

[1] Beltrani-Scalia, "Storia della Riforma delle Carceri in Italia," 1868, p. 288.

"In Naples in 1877 an *Esposito*, after having assassinated an ex-camorrist by order of his chief, went to give himself up to justice in order to protect his superior from arrest. An applauding crowd accompanied him to the prison, and covered him with flowers like a hero" (Onofrio).

Where justice is quite powerless the injured person must necessarily have recourse to his own strength or that of his friends. If honor is at stake, he will seek a private revenge; or if it is a question of stolen property, he will come to a friendly understanding with the thieves. In Sicily, as was seen in the Lombard trial, one pays a certain sum to recover a stolen horse or sheep; or the thief may pay a certain sum to the person robbed, in order to avoid prosecution or the recovery of the stolen property. This proceeding recalls at every point the customs of primitive justice.[1]

There is another and very potent cause that favors the formation of associations of criminals in civilized countries. This is the admiration inspired in the weak by brute strength. Any one who has seen, in the midst of an effeminate population with their soft flesh, soft speech, and weak character, a real Camorrist, with martial brows, iron muscles, and rolling *r*'s, comprehends at once that if the Camorra had not been brought in, it would have arisen of its own accord, as the inevitable result of the contrast between these energetic individuals and the sheep-like multitude. Even the Camorrist bows to this law; a strong and violent man himself, he bows to one stronger and more violent. Monnier cites a very curious proof of this influence. A Calabrian priest, imprisoned as the result of an affair of gallantry, upon entering the prison was asked to pay the usual tax to the Camorra. He refused, and, being threatened, replied that if he had been armed no one would have dared to use threats with him. "If that is all!" said the Camorrist, and in the twinkling of an eye offered him two knives, only to drop dead the next moment. The same evening the homicidal priest, who feared the vengeance of the Camorra more than he did the justice of the Bourbon government, to his great astonishment found himself offered the office of "barattolo" in the society.

[1] See Du Boys, "Histoire du Droit Criminel."

He had been admitted as a Camorrist without his own wish. The same adventure happened to another Calabrian, who refused to pay the tax and threatened with his knife the man who tried to collect it. Onofrio writes, "In Sicily they call any one who has courage 'Mafioso.'" The Camorra is thus the expression of the natural self-confidence of the strong, when they see themselves surrounded only by weaklings.

But it is not only the strength of the few that maintains this state of things, but also the fear felt by the many. The brigand Lombardo declared that the warmest partisans of his enterprises were the respectable land-owners, who, from fear of making him their enemy, told him of the houses of their neighbors that he might rob. "They did not realize," he added, "that they in their turn would be pointed out by others, so that in the end they lost much more than if they had combined against me." "A single, unarmed Camorrist," writes Monnier, "shows himself in the midst of a crowd of thousands of people, and demands his tribute. He is submissively obeyed, much more so than if he were the regular tax-collector." "The spirit of the Camorra," writes Mordini, "persists in Naples, that is to say, intimidation persists as the result of arrogance and presumption." Monnier explains the long persistence of the Camorra and brigandage in southern Italy by the dominance of fear. The religion taught by the priests was nothing but the fear of the devil; the prevailing politics consisted of nothing but fear of the king, who held the middle class in subjection through their fear of the proletariat; while both classes were kept in order through the fear of a brutal military and police force. Fear took the place of conscience and devotion to duty. Order was kept not by elevating man, but by degrading him. And what happened? Fear became a ready weapon in the hands of the most violent.

96. Barbarism

Aside from what has been stated above, many other circumstances belonging to a state of semi-civilization may have an influence upon the prevalence of brigandage. Such a state of society offers more opportunity for successful ambuscades and safe places of refuge. Thus the forests of Sora, Pizzuto, S. Elia, Faiola, and Sila were always the resort of brigands, and the same is true in France of the forests of Osgier, Rouvray, etc. For similar reasons localities largely uninhabited and not connected with others by frequent roads are favorable for bandits. In Italy we see brigandage disappearing before the railroads, and it is never known to persist in countries crossed by numerous good highways, with many towns. The province of Syracuse, which is better provided with roads than any other in Sicily, has no brigands; while Basilicata, in which in 1870 91 out of 124 comumnes had no roads, was the province most infested with brigands.

§ 97. Bad Government

In Mexico not so very many years ago the sons of noble families thought it entirely proper to commit highway robbery, just as was the case in Paris in 1400 and in Venice in 1600. In the last years of the pontificate of Clement XIV there were recorded 12,000 homicides, of which 4000 were in Rome itself. In Venice up to the time of Napoleon there still existed the so-called *Buli*, who domineered over the people at pleasure, entirely by means of the terror they had managed to inspire. To comprehend the unhappy condition to which society was reduced at that period, it is enough to recall that the most famous men of the Republic were publicly banished for ignominious crimes. It is enough to cite Morosini, Comaro, Falieri, and Mocenigo.

Says Molmenti:[1]

"In a memorial addressed to the emperor by the communes of Castiglione, Medole, and Solferino, against Ferdinand II Gonzaga, it was proved that the assassins of the prince had murdered poor peasants, cut off their heads, and exposed them in an iron cage under the walls of Castiglione; that his men-at-arms burned farm-houses and barns, plundered the dwellings, stole money, cattle, and furniture, and cut down or rooted up the vineyards. Even in the Republic of San Marco, which, although fallen into decay, still preserved a reputation for

[1] P. Molmenti, "I Banditti della Repubblica di Venezia," Florence, 1896.

strictness, the depredations of bandits were frequent, especially in the last two centuries. All precautions, laws, threats, and punishments often remained ineffectual. If a Venetian nobleman committed a crime, the government immediately sent a band of men into the city whose peace he had disturbed. But the populace, in whom the criminal inspired the greatest respect, protected him, and the noble delinquent found a safe retreat in his own castle. The magistrates, themselves almost all nobles, after publishing decrees and sentences against the offender and making loud threats, suffered the matter to fall into oblivion. The ambassador of the Venetian Republic in Milan, sword in hand, claimed that he possessed the right of asylum. So, when one morning the chief of the Milan city-guard and his men passed before his residence, the ambassador, to punish such audacity, had a volley fired at them, and killed or wounded several."

Finally, in the times of Cartouche there existed in Paris something which resembled, if not the Camorra, at least the Sicilian Mafia. The thieves at that time were organized into bands, and had accomplices even in the ranks of the police; they had pseudo-bailiffs and spies, and enrolled a whole population in their number, innkeepers, porters, watchmakers, tailors, armorers, and even physicians. In France in 1500 the "Burgundians" and "Bohemians" were veritable bands of brigands, composed of vagrants and soldiers of fortune, who, as society became more and more civilized, withdrew into the forests of Rouvray and Estrellère, where fugitives from the civil wars went to increase their number.[1]

§ 98. Weapons

Another matter which has great influence in promoting brigandage is the carrying of weapons and familiarity with their use. The gladiators, in old Roman times, were the most terrible leaders of bands of brigands and transformed their companies into veritable armies. Tommasi Crudeli says quite rightly:

"In the whole of southern Italy, beginning with the Campagna, the knife is not to be regarded as an implement of treach-

[1] Lombroso, "Homme Criminel," Vol. II, p. 474.

ery, but rather as the sword of the people. Almost always, in fact, its use is preceded by a formal challenge. The custom of holding these duels is so deeply rooted that during the disarming of the Sicilian populace, there were established in all the districts of Palermo hiding-places in the walls, known to all the inhabitants in the districts, where they hid their knives, and from which they got them in case of a dispute."

§ 99. Idleness

The prevalence of the Mafia in Palmero is due to the absence of any manufacturing industry and to the influence of the monasteries, which is favorable to idleness. Certainly priests and monks have always been among the causes of brigandage. The province of Naples in the 18th century, out of 4 million inhabitants, had 115,000 ecclesiastics, of whom half were monks; each village of 3000 inhabitants had at least 50 priests. The priests made begging not only a trade — they made it a work of merit.

"One of the principal causes of brigandage and the Camorra," says Monnier, "was the custom, widespread among the Neapolitans, of letting their children, from the age of three on, grow up on the street. There they learned to beg, and to swear by all the saints that they were orphans and dying of hunger. The beggar soon became a rogue; and, being cast into prison, became a member of the Camorra, if he was brave, or its victim, if he was a coward."

The mild and fertile climate of Naples, as well as that of Palermo, is a help to idleness and tempts the inhabitants to lounge in the streets; it furnishes the means of life at little expense, and does not let the need and duty of working be felt. This is why associations of malefactors are more frequent in the principal cities, especially in the south, where the violent passions are more likely to provoke certain classes of crime.[1]

[1] "In my opinion," so Vincent Maggiorani writes to me, "the Mafia represents the acute period of a disease which has invaded more or less all the countries near the Orient, or deriving their population from it. I believe that the occurrences which take place from time to time in Spain are only a different form of the same malady. You will find nothing like it in northern Europe. An isothermal line marks the limits of this temperament, etc."

The formation of societies of criminals plainly depends upon the character and conditions of the country. Thus we see the Mafia and Camorra spring up again after they have been broken up and all their members deported. In 1860–61 a great number of Camorrists were deported from Naples; yet, after a short period of depression, the Camorra was more active than ever, and now dares to threaten the electoral councils, the Palladium of Italy. The Mafia, destroyed in Palermo in 1860, rose again in 1866, armed and powerful. The Camorra, annihilated in 1874 by Mordini, was resuscitated in 1877 under the régime of Nicotera; and if it has not installed its members in the highest places in the city government, it certainly has a tremendous influence in the elections. In Messina in 1866 the Camorra was destroyed, literally, by the execution of its 29 leaders. But the men who accomplished this feat, having the reputation of being brave men, made use of it to carry on the Camorra themselves as actively as their predecessors, or even more so.

§ 100. Poverty

Much has been said with regard to the effect of poverty. The pictures which Villari has drawn of the condition of our people in the south are so horrible as to make us shudder.

"In Sicily," he writes, "there is no other relation between peasant and landlord than that of oppressor and oppressed. If there comes a bad year, the peasant returns home from his labors empty-handed. If the year is a good one, then usurers take the place of hail, grasshoppers, storms, and hurricanes. The peasants are a troop of barbarians in the heart of the island, and it is not so much against the government that they rise up, as against the usury and oppression of which they are the victims. If they execrate every form of government, it is because they believe that all governments sustain their oppressors."

That poverty, however, has not all the importance that Villari would like to attribute to it (though it certainly has a great deal) is evident when one considers the facts more critically. Thus the district of Montreale, which is certainly one of the least poor in Sicily, is just that in which the Mafia recruits its worst members from among the well-to-do classes. Naples, too, where the Camorra rules, is certainly not in a worse condition than Calabria. Artena, whose criminality has been described above, is one of the richest districts in the province of Rome. Moreover, the Camorra draws more victims than true accomplices from among the poor of Naples.

§ 101. Hybrid Civilization

Still worse than the lack of civilization, as regards the encouragement of criminal societies, is the mixture of civilization and barbarism, such as is found in certain parts of Italy and in a large portion of America, where we see peoples, still half-barbarous, subjected to a system borrowed from more civilized nations. While the advantages of both stages of society are lacking, the harmful features of both are present. Thus, great cities, the increase of wealth, and food too delicate, increase vagrancy, rape, and theft, and make the discovery of crime less easy; while the jury system, the respect for personal liberty, and the ease of getting pardons are frequently causes of impunity in crime. The system of elective offices, especially when, as in some states in America, it is extended even to the judiciary, offers the criminal class a new instrument of power and illicit gain. We see associated crime extend its power to the press, to the election of legislators, and, in America, to the election of judges, thus gaining a double advantage, — immediate gain and future immunity.

§ 102. Wars and Insurrections

Political disturbances again, wars and uprisings, are factors to be taken into account in this connection. The gathering of crowds, great excitement, the ease of obtaining arms, and the relaxed vigilance of the government are all natural causes of the association of criminals. Bands so formed may become bold enough to make themselves real political factors. This is the explanation of the atrocities of Alcolea and of the Paris Commune, and of the more recent events of similar nature in Mexico and New Orleans, These occurrences, which have become unusual in our day, in former times were very frequent. In the Middle Ages the tyranny of the barons gave to brigandage the appearance of a kind of social institution, defending the vassals or avenging them upon their lords, who, in their turn, regarded robbery as a noble trade. So also in ancient times the ten years which followed the restoration of Sulla were a golden age for the robbers and pirates of Italy.[1] In 1793 in Paris, at the time of the free distribution of bread, so many vagabonds and criminals crowded in that strangers were warned not to go out at night, if they did not wish to be robbed. The thieves carried their boldness so far that they closed the highways with ropes. Charles de Rouge was chief of a band which plundered the large farms, presenting himself as a commissary of the Republic. During the Napoleonic wars there appeared in the invaded countries a band of robbers called the "army of the moon." This sham army had its sham soldiers and sham officers, and plundered conquerors and conquered alike. In earlier times there were similar bands who followed the Goths and Vandals into Italy. In modern Italy, when the Bourbons withdrew from Naples to Rome, brigandage raged in Abruzzo; and when, under Murat, the trade of brigand became dangerous, the Bourbons landed the convicts of Sicily in Calabria. He who stole the most was best received by the king. "Criminal acts," writes Colletta, "lost, in consequence, their criminal character, and crime became a kind of trade carried on all over the kingdom." To the eyes of one who recognizes the essentially immoral character of war, this breaking out of criminality is not surprising. Spencer, in his splendid study of ethics, has showed that the warlike peoples are always the most vicious.

§ 103. Leaders

If at any given moment, in a country where criminal elements are plentiful, there arises a criminal who is a genius, or has great audacity or an influential social position, we see criminal associations rise and multiply. Thus it was to the

[1] Mommsen, "History of Rome," Vol. III.

great intelligence of their leaders that the bands of Lacenaire, Lombardo, Strattmatter, Hessel, Maino, Mottino, La Gala, and Tweed owed their origin and long impunity. Cavalcanti was a robber-chief of such genius that almost all his followers, more fortunate than those of Alexander, became themselves leaders of terrible bands, like Canosa, Egidione, etc. The band of assassins and incendiaries of Longpierre escaped all inquiry, because they were organized and protected by Gallemand, the mayor of the place, who, by incendiary fires, revenged himself upon his political opponents, or depreciated goods that he wanted to purchase.

§ 104. Prisons

But the principal cause of associated crime has been, and still is, the gathering together of criminals in prisons not constructed on the cellular system. Almost all the criminal chiefs, Maino, Lombardo, La Gala, Lacenaire, Souffard, Harduin, and others, have been men who have escaped from the galleys and have chosen their accomplices from among their companions who had there given proofs of boldness and ferocity. It is in prison that the Camorra arose, and it is there alone that it first held sway; but when, under King Ferdinand in 1830, many convicts were set at liberty by the royal clemency, they carried over into free life the illicit gains and dissolute manners to which they had become accustomed.[1] Only a few years ago the Camorra chose its chiefs from among the prisoners in the "Vicaria," and the free Camorrists made no important decision without first consulting these chiefs. In Palermo[2] the criminal got his professional education in prison, and novices without prison experience were admitted only into such enterprises as required a large number of persons.

This will appear natural enough if we recall the words of the criminal of Palermo quoted in the preceding chapter: "Prison is a piece of good fortune that heaven sends us, because it teaches us fit places and companions for stealing."[3]

[1] Moniner, *op. cit.*, p. 58. [2] Locatelli, *op. cit.*
The French differs in the two places.—TRANSL.

§ 105. Influence of Race

We have already spoken of the influence of race upon crime. The same thing is naturally true of associations of criminals.[1]

The gypsies, like the Bedouins, may be called a race of associated malefactors. According to Maury, the negro in the United States, and in southern Italy the Albanians, Greeks, and at times even the native population, show the same tendency to associated crime. Saint-Jorioz said, in speaking of Sora: "This beautiful country swarms with thieves; there are as many of them as there are inhabitants." This fact explains how brigands succeed in getting themselves elected as communal counselors. The inhabitants of Castelforte and of Spigno protect the thieves on condition that they practice their calling outside the district. The people in the neighborhood of Palermo, among whom the "Mafiosi" swarm, are descended from the bravoes of the ancient barons; or, to trace their lineage still farther back, from rapacious Arab conquerors, blood-brothers of the Bedouins. "I have noticed," writes d'Azeglio, speaking of the Romans, "that in the ancient fiefs of the Middle Ages (Colonna, Orsini, Savello) there has remained in the population the imprint of that life of hatred, war, and division which was the normal yearly round in those unhappy centuries. Nearly all the young men exemplify the true type of the bravo." [2]

§ 106. Heredity

These questions of race resolve themselves finally, as a matter of course, into the question of heredity. Among the modern brigands of southern Italy there have been some who descended from the terrible Fra Diavolo. Many among the famous Camorrists are brothers, and we know of the seven Mazzardi brothers, the Manzi brothers, the Vadarelli, and the La Galas. In the United States the Younger brothers, who robbed banks in Minnesota in broad daylight, are equally

[1] Lombroso, "Homme Criminel," Vol. II.
[2] "Bozzetti della Vita Italiana," p. 187.

notorious. The band of Cuccito and that of Nathan were composed of parents, brothers, and brothers-in-law. Here, to the influence of heredity, tradition, and education, is added the power of numbers. A family of criminals is a band already formed, which, from the fact of parentage, has the means of increasing and perpetuating itself in the children.

In 1821 the communes of Vrely and Rosières were afflicted with thefts and homicides, showing on the part of the authors a great knowledge of the locality, and uncommon boldness. Terror prevented the laying of information, but the criminals were finally discovered, and were found all to belong to one family. In 1832 the thefts were renewed, and the guilty persons were no other than the nephews of the first lot of criminals. In 1852 and the years immediately following assassinations occurred again in the same communes. The murderers prove to be great-nephews of the earlier offenders, who had been active thirty years before. These facts explain to us why we see a constant recrudescence of crime in a given village. It is enough that a single one of these perverted families should survive, in order to corrupt the whole district, through the elective affinity there is between criminals. This justifies to a certain extent the barbarity of the ancients and of savages in punishing with the guilty their innocent relatives.

§ 107. Other Causes

Criminals combine very often from necessity also, in order to be able to resist an armed force, or to escape the search of the police by removing themselves from the scene of their crimes; though there is a tendency on the part of nearly all criminal bands to commit their misdeeds just around the circle of their own district.

Again, the necessity of supplying the lack of certain qualities may lead to association. Thus Lacenaire, who was a coward, joined himself to Avril, who was fierce and bloody; while Maino and La Gala, who were courageous but ignorant, associated with them Ferraris and Davanzo, who were educated. Most criminals seek in others a courage they lack themselves.

It may be added that for many of these people a crime is a sort of pleasure expedition, which is not so enjoyable unless carried on in company.

At times an association has an entirely accidental origin. Thus Tepas, just out of prison, started to rob a drunken man, when he heard himself called by Faurier, who wanted to share the booty. From this chance meeting sprung the Tepas band. "The most accidental circumstances," says Mayhew, "such as the fact of living in the same neighborhood, or street, or bearing the same name, or meeting when coming out of prison, etc., gives rise to the bands of petty thieves of London." Spagliardi tells us that the meeting places of the gamins are where bands of thieves have their origin in Lombardy.

CHAPTER XVIII

CAUSES OF POLITICAL CRIMES

§ 108.

WE have seen that political crime is a kind of crime of passion, punishable only because it involves an offense against the conservative sentiments of the human race, particularly in the fields of religion and politics.[1] We have seen [2] that it is especially frequent among the young, and in the most intelligent and cultivated nations.

§ 109. Orography

The influence which a lighter atmospheric pressure has upon this kind of crime is incontestably very great. It can be said that the most revolutionary peoples have always been found among the mountains. Witness the struggles of the Samnites, the Marsi, the Ligures, the Cantabri, and the Bruttii against the Romans; those of the Asturians against the Goths and Saracens; and those of the Albanians, Druses, Maronites, and Mainnottes [3] against the Turks. Just so it was in the Cevennes in France, and in the Valtelline and at Pinerolo in Italy, that the first efforts in favor of religious liberty were made, notwithstanding the dragonnades and the punishments of the Inquisition. According to Plutarch, the inhabitants of Attica, after the insurrection of Cimon, were divided into three parties, corresponding to the differences in the geographical configuration of the country. Those who lived in the mountains wanted

[1] For a full presentation of this subject see my "Crime Politique et les Revolutions," Pt. I., 1890.
[2] Lombroso, "Homme Criminel," Vol. II.
[3] It was the Mainnottes of Mount Taigete that first proclaimed independence of Turkey. (Gervinus, "Geschichte der Erhebung Griechenlands," 1864.)

a popular government at any price; those who lived in the plains demanded an oligarchical government; while the dwellers along the seacoast preferred a mixed form of government.

§ 110. Points of Convergence

In the places where valleys converge and where the people come most into contact with others, they are most inclined to innovation and revolution. Poland undoubtedly owes its early civilization and its revolts, as well as later its misfortunes, to the position which it occupies at the meeting point of Slav, Teuton, and Byzantine. Those departments of France that are situated upon the courses of the great rivers, the Seine, Rhône, and Loire, or which include great ports, furnish, aside from other causes, the largest number of revolutionary votes.[1]

§ 111. Density

The same thing is true of places with great density of population and great industrial activity; here, too, the revolutionary spirit shows itself in a high state of development, just as the conservative spirit predominates in agricultural and thinly populated regions.

§ 112. Healthfulness — Genius

Both the salubrity and fertility of a country exercise an influence in the development of the revolutionary spirit, as I have shown in the case of Italy by long series of figures.[2]

Genius, too, plays its part, and it is for this reason that Florence, Athens, and Geneva, cities noted for their men of genius, have also been noted for insurrections. Geniuses and revolts have likewise been numerous in the Romagna and in Liguria, which are among the most healthful parts of Italy. In France the parallelism is still clearer, for in 75 departments out of 86, genius, tall stature, and anti-monarchical parties go together.

[1] Lombroso and Laschi, "Crime Politique."
[2] Lombroso and Laschi, *op. cit.*

§ 113. Races

The ethnic influence in its turn is incontestable. By a study of the votes and the revolts in France, I have shown that the departments in which the Ligurian and Gallic races predominate have furnished the greatest number of rebels, and that the Iberians and Cimbrians have furnished the minimum. Many small districts and single cities, like Arluno and Leghorn, are known for their constant tendency to revolt.[1]

The history of the Apuanian Ligurians explains to us why to-day anarchy and insurrection often break out among them; the Ligures were continually in revolt against the Romans.

§ 114. Crossing of Races

The ethnic influence comes out very plainly in the crossing of races, which is able to make them all more revolutionary and progressive. This is a phenomenon connected with that discovered in the vegetable world by Darwin, that even bisexual plants ought to be cross-fertilized; and also with the law of Romanes, according to which independent variation is the primary cause of evolution. The Ionians give us an excellent example. They were revolutionary, and produced the greatest geniuses of Greece, certainly as a consequence of the fact that they were early crossed with the Lydians and Persians in Asia Minor and the islands, and in addition were subjected to the influence of a change of climate. The crossing of the Poles with the Teutonic race, all the more potent because the latter was in the nascent state, explains why Poland rose in so short a time to great intellectual heights, in the midst of other Slavs still barbarous, and this at a time when these very Germans who brought to the Poles the first seeds of their civilization had themselves but a low degree of culture. We have here, then, a partial explanation of Poland's continual insurrections.[2]

[1] Leghorn was settled by the Illyrian Liburni, who were notorious as pirates, and first visited the Tuscan waters simply for the purposes of plunder.

[2] The crossing with the Germans seems to have been going on even in

The climatic and racial crossing of the South American natives with the European colonists in the Spanish republics has produced a race active both commercially and intellectually, but above all things given to revolution. Modern Spain cannot boast of a Ramos-Mejas, a Roca, a Mitri, or a Pinero.

§ 115. Bad Government

A government under which the public welfare is neglected and respectable persons persecuted is always provocative of insurrections and revolutions. Persecutions make great changes in men's ideas and feelings. Benjamin Franklin, on the eve of the American Revolution, in a pamphlet entitled "Rules by which a great empire may be reduced to a small one," sums up as follows the characteristics of the bad government which, as a matter of fact, in a short time drove his country to revolt:

> "Do you wish," he writes, addressing the mother country, "to irritate your colonies and drive them into rebellion? Here is an infallible method: Always suppose them ready to revolt, and treat them accordingly. Place in their midst soldiers who by their insolence may provoke an insurrection, and then put it down with bullets and bayonets."

In a country where political reforms keep pace with the aspirations of the people, insurrections seldom or never occur. The reign of Louis Philippe in France, favorable to the wealthy classes but without any sympathy with the mass of the people, multiplied insurrections and political crimes, which disappeared in the first years of the Cæsarian-democratic government of Napoleon III, who impressed the people by his magnificence and his attempts at social reform. It is a fact demonstrated by the statistics of persons indicted for political causes from 1826 to 1880 (including offenses of the press), that the Napoleonic period (1851–70) corresponds with the minimum number of political trials.

prehistoric times. It is certain that in the prehistoric graves of Poland and of Prussia, dolichocephalic, orthognathous skulls are found, — skulls, that is to say, of Teutonic type.

	Cases "en contradictoire"	Cases of contumacy
1826–30	13	284
1831–35	90	406
1836–40	13	63
1841–45	4	41
1846–50	9	271
1851–55	4	...
1856–60	1	...
1861–65	1	...
1866–70	1	...
1871–75	10	64
1876–80	..	6
	146	1135

The struggle for supremacy between different social classes is an effect of that inequality which Aristotle calls "the source of all the revolutions."[1]

"On the one side," he writes, "are those who desire equality, and who rise in revolt if they believe they have less than others, even though they really have as much as the most favored. On the other side there are those who aspire to power, and who, although equality exists, rise in insurrection if they think that this equality has no sound reason for being."

Abuse of power by the dominant class is enough to produce a reaction; and Aristotle says again ("Politics"): "To whatever side a government inclines, it always degenerates through an exaggeration of the principles upon which it is based." In France the Revolution of 1789, which appeared to have choked the monarchical principle with the blood of the king, degenerating into anarchy, prepared the way for the Empire; and the whole process was repeated by the Republic of 1849 and the Second Empire.

1 "Politics." It is a curious fact that all the authors who have studied or written about revolutions have simply followed Aristotle. This is because he was both an observer and a genius, and living in the midst of a great number of little revolutions, saw and understood much more than his successors.

§ 116. Exclusive Predominance of One Class — Priests

Whatever the form of government, the dominance of one class or caste over another has always been a source of danger, through hindering the organic development of a country and predisposing it first to atrophy and then to anarchy. It is thus that the dominance of the clergy in Spain and Scotland, and in Italy in the Papal States and the kingdom of Naples, for a long time retarded the progress of these countries and drove them to revolt. It was for analogous reasons that the tyranny of the Roman patricians, notwithstanding their defeat, led to the conspiracies of Saturninus and of Catiline, and then to the dictatorship of Cæsar. This last, in its turn, led to the conspiracy of Brutus, which finally failed because the rise of the Empire represented a justifiable reaction of the lower classes against the oligarchy. Not infrequently members of an oligarchy, struggling with one another for power, as at Cnidos, leave the way open for the people to overthrow them. In Florence in the Middle Ages the tyranny of the nobles prepared the way for the triumph of petty tradesmen; and the abuses of this class brought about, in turn, the election of the Duke of Athens, who, although he sought to repress the abuse of power, ended by alienating the people from him and being himself driven out. When, on the contrary, the social classes and the powers pertaining to them are in a state of equilibrium, liberty is preserved and revolutions become very rare. In this way, according to Aristotle, the long duration of the Spartan government is to be explained. Power was evenly distributed between the higher classes, represented by the Senate, and the mass of the people, who chose the Ephors by public vote. Further the power of the kings was much circumscribed, and, since there were two of them, they could not easily come to an agreement, and consequently only rarely became tyrants.

§ 117. Parties and Divisions

Parties, though at times useful in the struggle of the weak against the strong, are often what Coco calls them, a means of corrupting the individual, and, through the individual, the nation. This is seen in the spectacle offered by the situation in the mediæval Italian cities, especially in Florence, where an exaggerated and intolerant party spirit led to complete political and intellectual exhaustion. Another example of this is to be found in the Argentine Republic, where the Unitaires of Buenos Ayres brought about the reaction under Rosas. They were a party of typical Utopians, revolutionary idealists, who wanted to march straight on, with head high, not deviating a hair's breadth from their course. Even on the eve of a battle they were taken up with a regulation, a formula, or a pompous phrase. It would be impossible to find men with better logic, more enterprise, or less common sense.[1]

Since parties are favorable to political liberty, the more ground they gain in the political life, the less important do secret political societies become. These latter are the fruit of oppression, since oppression turns ideas into feelings, and these in their turn produce sects and societies. Yet it is certainly to this origin that modern civilization is indebted for many reforms and other services in the political field. It is enough to recall the Carbonari in Italy, the Chartists in England, the Hetæria in Greece, and the Nihilists in Russia. The ideal of these last, it is true, has little correspondence with the feelings of the Russian people, since what Stepniak said of an earlier period is still true, that in the popular mind the Czar and God are welded together.[2]

In Italy the "Fraternal Hand," discovered at Girgenti in 1883, was originally a society for mutual aid in case of sickness or death. But soon it degenerated: certain duties occasioned certain crimes. Everyone was bound to make himself respected for the honor of the organization, to protect the women, to revenge the injuries of his comrades, and to help save them if they were accused. They ended by ordering assassinations, and executing them in the same way that a hunter chases a hare. They intimidated juries, and prevented outsiders from bidding at the public auctions. The result was that respectable persons had to affiliate with them, or buy protection against them from

[1] Sarmiento, "Civilisacion y Barbaria" Buenos Ayres, 1869.
[2] "La Russie sous les Czars," Paris, 1880.

other criminals.[1] In Ireland, side by side with the Land League, which served the country with loyalty and patriotism, there rose up the society of the "Invincibles," which numbered not more than 200 members but speedily distinguished itself by all sorts of agrarian crimes.

§ 118. Imitation

We have seen that through imitation, criminality, insanity, and hallucination become epidemic in a mob. Hence imitation becomes a powerful factor in producing an insurrection. This may occur on a large scale, one nation imitating another and producing a veritable epidemic of revolutions. This is what happened, according to Ferrari,[2] in the period from 1378 to 1494, during which the European peoples imitated the great number of Italian uprisings against the ancient lords — at Rome under Rienzi, at Genoa under Adorno, at Florence under the Ciompi, at Palermo under the Alessi, and at Naples under the Lazzari. In this period took place the insurrection of the Hussites in Bohemia, the revolts of the working-people in the free cities of Germany (Worms, Hall, Lübeck, Aix), the refusal of the burghers of Ghent to pay taxes, the Swiss war of independence, the uprisings of the Swedish peasants under Inglebert and the Croatian peasants under Harvat, and in England the religious movement initiated by Wyclif. The men of 1793 imitated, or, rather, aped, the heroes of Plutarch (Buckle), as the Napoleons imitated the Cæsars. In 1789 in France almost all the departments imitated the September massacres of Paris, and later those of the White Terror. Aristotle names as one of the causes of revolts the neighborhood of countries with other forms of government. The nearness of the oligarchical Spartan government often caused the overthrow of the democracy in Athens, and *vice versa*.

§ 119. Epidemic Ideals

Many ideals spread themselves almost like epidemics. So was it formerly with the monarchical ideal, the glory of one's

[1] Lestingi, "L'Associazione della Fratellanza" (Arch. di Psich., Vol. V, p. 462).
[2] "Storia delle Rivoluzioni d'Italia," Milan, 1870.

own king; so with the ideal of popular sovereignty; then of nationality; and so is it now with the ideal of the amelioration of economic conditions. It is not that to-day conditions are worse than they were in the days of our fathers. On the contrary, the famines, which used to mow down their millions, now gather in only a few hundreds of victims; and our workmen to-day own more shirts than many a proud noble of antiquity. But men's needs and their repugnance to the labor necessary to satisfy them have increased in proportion to the economic betterment that has been going on.

§ 120. Historic Traditions

"Every revolution," wrote Machiavelli, "lays a stepping-stone for another one." We see revolutions, as a matter of fact, repeat the form of revolutions which happened even at remote periods. Thus the Roman tribunate lived again in Rome with Rienzi and Baroncelli, and later with Ciceruacchio and Coccapieller, notwithstanding many differences in the institutions and individuals. The revolutionary tendencies of the Romagna were well known even in the Middle Ages, and Dante refers to them in the words: "The heart of the Romagna is, and ever will be, at war with tyrants." The Paris Commune imitated the revolution of 1789, as '89 had imitated the Jacquerie, while the National Assembly of Paris copied the old Provincial Assemblies. We may say that in Paris barricades have become a decennial habit, like military revolutions in Spain, attempts upon the life of the Czar in Russia, and brigandage in Greece and Macedonia.

A last proof of this influence of traditions is that those revolutionary governments perish which do not know how to hold them in honor. The greater the difference between the old form of government and the new, the more unstable is the adherence of the people. For this cause those revolutions have been most fortunate that have held the past in honor. Thus the elder Brutus kept for the people their king, under the name of "rex sacrificulus." The Cæsars, likewise, retained the Tribunate, the Senate, and other forms of the republican government, even to the extent of limiting themselves to the military title, "Imperator" (General). Just so the English in the Magna Charta professed to confirm ancient rights; and in Italy the Guelfs, following the Ghibellines in Italy, chose the captain of the people from among the nobles, as the Ghibellines had chosen their *podesta*. This did not escape the keen intellect of Machiavelli, who wrote: "Whoever would reform a free state must preserve the shadow of the old forms; in changing old institutions the human mind must be at pains to make the transformation preserve as much as possible of that which is ancient."

§ 121. Inappropriate Political Reforms

Only men ignorant of human nature, or excessively despotic, would make decrees not necessitated by the conditions of the moment, and destroy old institutions to replace them with new, not because they were demanded, but because they were in use in other social organisms. By such means a discontent with every kind of reform is awakened, and since the new is not based upon the old there results an active antipathy which produces a constant succession of revolutions. This is what happened to the reforms of Arnaldo and Savonarola. This is what came to pass when Rienzi tried to bring about a political reform which even Cavour could not carry out completely. The same situation, again, was repeated in France in the attempt of Marcel, at a time when even a constitution was not possible, to bring about a republican federation, with proportional taxation, social and administrative unity, general political rights, national authority substituted for royal, and Paris as the head of France.[1] "To reform everything, is to destroy everything," wrote Coco with regard to the Neapolitan revolution of 1799. In Spain Charles III. was able, through the power of his personality and authority, to curb the power of the clergy, and to ameliorate the condition of the country. But no sooner had he fallen from power than all his reforms ceased without leaving a regret, be-

[1] "Le Vieux Neuf," 1877.

cause they were premature. In 1812, in 1820, and in 1836, there was no lack of ardent reformers in the Spanish government, but they failed because they were not in touch with the feeling of the people. In 1814 and in 1823 the popular indignation drove out the Cortes, and Quin tells that everywhere the king passed, the crowd hurled insults at the liberals, the constitution, and the Cortes.[1]

§ 122. Religion

Religion, in Asiatic and African countries, not only mixed with politics, but was itself the only politics, sometimes revolutionary but more often reactionary, according to the character of the religion. In India, Nanak (1469) by performing miracles founded the religion of the Sikhs, which was based upon monotheism, the abrogation of caste, and the blessedness of Nirvana. The founder himself made few proselytes, but under Havogind, one of his successors, the Sikhs took up arms against the Mussulman fanaticism, won new power during the Mahratta uprising, founded a sort of republic, and to-day number nearly two millions. Mahomet put an end to fetichism, conquered Arabia, and notwithstanding his ignorance (hardly one of the *suras* of his Koran has any sense in it), he produced a revolution even in the field of science. For from 750 to 1250 A. D., with the ostensible purpose of explaining the Koran, the Arabs translated the Greek authors and made gigantic encyclopædic compilations, which were disseminated through Europe. As if to establish once for all the parallelism of religion and politics, the Convention decreed the worship of the Supreme Being, and organized the love-feast; and the populace put at its head the mad Catherine Theot, who preached the immortality of the body, and at 70 declared that she was about to become young again. The Jacobins favored the society of the *Theophilantropes*, who celebrated their festivals in Notre Dame, the new Temple of Reason, and in Saint Roch, the Temple of Genius, where, before the altars, sentimental verses from the classics were sung and feasts were celebrated for Socrates, St. Vincent, Rousseau, and

[1] "Memoirs of Ferdinand," 1824.

Washington. In ancient Israel the reaction under Jeroboam followed the reign of Solomon, because the latter, a revolutionary, at least in art and industry, had anticipated the popular mind by several centuries.[1]

Thus a reaction is sure to result whenever an attempt is made to set aside dominant customs and superstitions. One of the causes of the uprising of the Annamese against the French was the lack of reverence manifested by the Europeans for the ancient documents which were held in such honor by the natives (probably because they thought them endowed with magic power) that they had societies for the express purpose of collecting and caring for them. All the insurrections against the English in India have been caused by violations of the customs or religion of the people. Thus the Sepoy rebellion of 1857 was caused not by the violent occupation of the ancient kingdom of Oude on the part of the East India Company so much as by the preaching of Protestant missionaries, and their over-zealous attempts at proselytism, arousing the opposition of Brahmin and Mussulman alike; and further by the fact that the Sepoys were required to use cartridges smeared with pork-fat.

§ 123. Economic Influences

The influence of economic causes in many of the greatest revolutionary movements of recent centuries has been demonstrated by Loria [2] with incontestable proofs.

The strife of classes in England flared up when the nobility began to make laws that were to the interest of the land-owners, and prejudicial to manufacturing. Such was the situation when the middle classes gathered about Elizabeth and triumphed with her over Mary Stuart and her nobles. The same phenomenon was repeated with Cromwell, and with William of Orange. The same antagonism manifested itself in Germany in the sixteenth century, when the nobility, represented by the electoral princes, having exclusive political power, passed laws hostile to capital

[1] Rénan, "Études d'Histoire Israélite" ("Revue des Deux Mondes," Aug., 1888).

[2] "La Teoria Economica della Costituzione Politica," 1885.

and commerce, levying imposts on imports and exports. In Italy the contests of the Guelfs and Ghibellines masked the strife between the manufacturers and the feudal nobility.[1] In France it was the middle classes, long powerless against king and nobles, and, furthermore, excluded from the National Assembly, who stirred up the people to revolt, and put to flight both court and aristocracy. Even modern Nihilism, according to Roscher, springs from the contest between the moneyed and the landed classes. It came especially from the favor shown by the commercial classes and small proprietors to the ransom of the peasants, to the detriment of the nobility, who responded by allying themselves with disinherited men of family and all the other enemies of the middle classes. (Loria.) Tschen remarks that the prosperity of China springs from the system of canals which fertilizes it, and that every emperor who neglects the canals speedily falls.[2]

§ 124. Taxes and Changes in the Currency

Very often it is the government itself that, through ignorance of economic laws, aggravates the disorder already existing, and provokes insurrection. Thus it was in France, where one of the causes of the revolution of 1360 was that under the Valois the value of gold was changed 26 times in a single year. Similarly, in Sicily, according to Amari, the discontent occasioned by the alteration of the value of the money was not without influence in causing the Sicilian Vespers. (Loria.) In 1382 in Paris, the tax upon vegetables called forth the uprising of the Maillotins. In 1640 Mazarin doubled the taxes on food-supplies in Paris, and the people built the barricades of the 26th of August. The court, becoming terrified, treated with them and granted a diminution in the taxes of more than 12,000,000 francs. In 1639 the people of Rouen rose in insurrection with

[1] This hypothesis is certainly a bold one, but does not lack proof. For example, Bonaccorsi, the Podesta of Reggio, who had shown himself friendly to the working people, was deposed after eight months, by the Ghibellines.

[2] "Revue Scientifique," 1889.

the cry of "Death to the *gabeleurs!*" but the uprising was extinguished in the blood of the rioters themselves. The popular hatred of the tax-agents continued to be actively in evidence, however, until the government finally prohibited the use of the epithets, "publican," "extortioner," and "monopolist," against the tax-collectors. Even when a tax is just, that it should affect one class more directly than another is sufficient to stir up an insurrection. Thus the tax on grain at Pavia and the land-tax at Florence produced revolts which were inspired by the middle classes.

§ 125. Economic Crises

Industrial and commercial crises had in ancient times no very great influence in revolutions, being responsible for local uprisings merely.[1] This was the case in Rome, where, according to Carle,[2] the great agitations had for their moving cause the debts to which the people were liable, rather than the agrarian laws. During the fierce contests between the consulate and the tribunate, when economic prosperity was in no way lacking, Spurius Cassius, who proposed an agrarian law by which the common property was to be divided in part among the poor citizens, not only was not supported by the people, but was put to death, simply because he wished that the Latin allies should share in the division.[3]

§ 126. Pauperism. Strikes

It is our own time alone that has seen the great political and social revolutions, caused by the disproportion between the rewards of labor and those of speculative capital, and, further, by new needs, which make the people feel more keenly than ever before the reality of their sad condition. The Darwinian theory, it is true, concedes the difference between individuals and, in

[1] Rossi, "Il Fattore Economico nei Moti Rivoluzionari" ("Archivio Psichiatria," IX, 1).

[2] "Genesi e Sviluppo delle Varie Forme di Convivenza Civile e Politica," Turin, 1878.

[3] Mommsen, "Roman History," I.

consequence, a necessary inequality in wealth. But the sentiment of humanity, which received its first breath from Christ and which time has not been able to weaken, is not willing to permit, whatever the theory of Darwin may be, that a man who is working should die of hunger, or that a man who is willing and able to be of service should look for work in vain. When one sees that thousands of peasants in Italy, whose interests not a single representative has taken up in Parliament, are compelled to live upon spoiled maize, for which no one has thought out a remedy; when one sees that whole districts in the Alps are decimated by goiture and cretinism, simply because a hundredth part of the money wasted on useless monuments is not spent in supplying these people with wholesome water; when one thinks that in the plains of Italy, at the gates of the two largest cities, malaria rages and decimates the population;[1] one is compelled to conclude that if the peasants protest by uprisings and strikes, the responsibility falls upon those who have not found a way to remedy the evil. In France the strikes of 1882 in Roanne, Bességе, Molière, and other industrial centers in the south, and the more serious troubles in Montceau-les-Mines and Lyons, were the result of a socialistic agitation having a pronounced political character. In the United States the revolutionary Socialist party, which has its center in Chicago, seems to grow in importance constantly, partly from economic crises, occasioned especially by railroad speculation, and partly from the disregard of the proletariat on the part of both the leading political parties. Now it is to this organization that we must attribute a great part of the strikes which occur with such frequency (160 in 2 years).

In comparison with the past, our own age shows many more uprisings from economic than from military causes. Disturbances proceeding from economic conditions are most abundant in the countries that best represent modern life, like France, England, and Belgium; while it is the military rebellions that

[1] Out of 5258 communes in Italy, 2813, with a population of eleven and a half millions, are scourged with malaria, and in 2025 other communes, with a population of eight millions, there are a certain number of cases. (Bodio, "Bulletin de l'Institut International de Statistique," 1887.)

take place in countries like Spain and Turkey, which represent a bygone age. From the statistics of insurrections during the first half of the nineteenth century we get the following:

Country	Total Insurrections	Number having military causes	Number having economic causes
Spain	19	5	3
Turkey	24	9	1
Belgium	16	0	8
England	15	0	8

§ 127. Change of Environment

We find in this connection many singular contradictions. The very hot climate of Egypt makes antirevolutionists of the Semites, the Fellahs, and even of the Berbers, who, in the mountains of Algeria, are in a continual state of revolution, so that in Algiers they show the graves of seven beys, all named and killed in a single day. In new surroundings the Dutch agriculturists became the nomadic Boers of South Africa; the Norman hunters became bold sea-rovers; the pastoral Jews became merchants; and the strictly conservative Anglo-Saxons became the free innovators and revolutionaries of North America. A good government can succeed in preventing the disorders that spring from difference of race, especially when there enters the factor of the attraction which large bodies of people have for smaller bodies of a different kind. This latter is one of the most powerful factors in the fusion of the Semitic Sards with the Celtic Piedmontese, and of the thoroughly Italian Corsicans with the French. When peoples have lived in a state of isolation, the first crossings (Dorians, Romans) provoke violent disturbances; but later, as evolution proceeds, economic and political interests become more important than questions of race. Thus it is that the Poles execrate the Russians because of their despotism, notwithstanding their common Slavic blood. On the other hand, the people of the Rhine valley, although German in the main, incline more toward the French than toward the nation of their own blood, because habit and commercial interest count for more with them than race.

The dominance of different factors at certain periods, as, for example, the economic factor in our own day, is explained by the fact that, in sociology as well as in chemistry, certain agents are most active in the "nascent state." Physiology, also, teaches us that of a series of similar stimuli the first is most strongly felt. Hence it is that the influence of climate is still effective even after being hidden or weakened by the influence of race. For this reason in certain countries, as in Florence, for example, the configuration of the land has much less effect upon the occurrence of uprisings and acts of violence than it formerly had. Holland is a cold, level country, and for this reason is naturally antirevolutionary, but the battle with the sea and with foreign oppressors has had a modifying influence.

Religion has upon the whole very little influence upon the course of cultural evolution, but in the nascent state it is exceedingly favorable to revolt and revolution. New religions are almost always accompanied by a real revolution in morals and character, genuine reforms which win them adherents from among respectable people. History gives us examples of this in the rise of Buddhism, Christianity, and Lutheranism, and we see the influence still to-day in the Lazzarettists and in certain Russian sects.

§ 128. Occasional Causes

Aristotle affirms that oligarchies commonly go to pieces through the too great preponderance of certain of their members, and that when they are in difficulties they try to extricate themselves by raising insurrections. In Syracuse, he tells us, the constitution was changed because of a love-affair which drove two young noblemen and their followers to revolt. Speaking of tyrannicides he finds that they are most frequently caused by personal injuries. Bacon remarks that some too lively expressions of certain princes have sometimes been the spark that kindled a revolt. Thus Galba destroyed himself when he said,

"Legi a se militem, non emi,"[1] the soldiers no longer having any hope that he would pay them for their votes. Probus was equally lost when he uttered the words, "Si vixero, non opus erit amplius Romano Imperio militibus,"[2] for the soldiers immediately revolted against him. Even in our own century riots have originated from comparatively trifling causes. Thus in 1821 a revolt broke out in Madrid because the king either could not or would not take part in a certain procession. In 1867 Bucharest rose in revolt against the monopoly of tobacco, and the same year there was a riot in Manchester because of the arrest of two Fenians. In 1876 an insurrection took place in Amsterdam because of the abolition of one of the annual fairs.

§ 129. War

Wars are often the cause of domestic disturbances. Greek history, especially the history of the oligarchies, abundantly illustrates this. According to Soltyk, the victorious wars which the Poles waged in the 17th and 18th centuries formed one of the causes of the downfall of Poland, because they bore heavily upon the poor without any corresponding advantages, and increased the activity of the conquered peoples. The Franco-Prussian war overcame the disinclination felt in many circles toward the idea of the Empire in Germany. This is shown in the statistics of the cases of leze majesty. While the sentences for this offense from 1846 to 1848 ran as high as 342, and in 1849 reached 369, they fell to 132 and 193 in 1879 and 1880.[3] According to Renan, the two great products of the Hebrew race, the Jewish religion and the Christian, are to be attributed not solely to the prophets, but also to the perturbations produced by the Assyrian and Roman victories.

It must be added that such occasional causes of insurrections are plainly only a pretext, affording an opportunity for the outbreak of a people already predisposed to revolt. The brutality of a soldier and the lasciviousness of a prince gave occasion

[1] That he chose his soldiers, he did not buy them.
[2] "If I live, the Roman Empire will have no further need of soldiers."
[3] "Verbrecher und Verbrechen in Preussen," Berlin, 1884.

for the Sicilian Vespers and for the expulsion of the Tarquins. But to see that these things were only the occasion and not the whole cause it is only necessary to recall how many infamous crimes on the part of conquering kings and peoples Italy has suffered to go unpunished.

Part Two

PROPHYLAXIS AND THERAPEUSIS OF CRIME

CHAPTER I

PENAL SUBSTITUTES — CLIMATE — CIVILIZATION — DENSITY — SCIENTIFIC POLICE — PHOTOGRAPHY — IDENTIFICATION

§ 130.

IF crime is often really a fatal consequence of certain constitutions which are naturally predisposed to it, it is then almost irremediable; and we can no longer hope that education or imprisonment will be remedies sufficient to combat it. But we see in these cases the causes of the constant recidivism under every penal system; and, what is more important, we get a hint of the proper course for a new system of criminal therapeutics to follow.

It is no longer enough to repress crime: we must try to prevent it. If we cannot suppress it, we can at least seek for means to decrease the influence of the causes we have been studying, upon occasional, juvenile, and partial criminals.

For this purpose we must use what Ferri has so happily called [1] "penal substitutes." The idea is that the legislator, recognizing and studying the causes of crime, shall seek by preventive means to neutralize them or at least decrease their effect.

Thus in the *economic* sphere freedom of exchange prevents local scarcity, and hence removes a fertile cause of theft and riot. The lowering of customs duties, or, better still, their abolition, prevents smuggling. A more equitable distribution of taxation prevents frauds against the state. The substitution of metallic currency for the more easily imitated banknotes reduces

[1] "Sociologie Criminelle," Paris, 1890.

the amount of counterfeiting; better salaries for public officers diminish the chance of bribery and corruption; while the distribution of wood to the poor stops thefts in the forests better than a crowd of gendarmes. Broad, electric-lighted streets are better than policemen to prevent theft and rape.

In the *political* sphere, a really liberal government, like that of England, prevents anarchistic insurrections and acts of revenge, just as entire liberty of the press prevents corruption of the government and insurrections of the governed.

In the *scientific* sphere, autopsies tend to prevent poisoning in general, as Marsh's test has checked arsenic poisoning in particular. So, likewise, steamships have abolished piracy, and railroads have cut down highway robbery.

In the *legislative* sphere, proper laws for the acknowledgment of illegitimate children, for investigating their parentage, and for indemnification in cases of the breach of a promise of marriage, will diminish abortions, infanticides, and many homicides committed for revenge. In the same way civil justice at a low price will prevent offenses against the public order, juries of honor will prevent duels, and foundling hospitals will prevent infanticides.

In the *religious* system, the marriage of the clergy and the abolition of pilgrimages would cause the disappearance of many sexual crimes.

In the field of *education*, the abolition of atrocious spectacles and of gambling would be a means of preventing brawls and crimes of violence.

§ 131. Climate and Race

Let us now attempt a systematic application of substitutes for punishment, following the classification of the more serious causes of crime.

We certainly cannot prevent the effect of a hot climate upon crime, but we ought to try to introduce those institutions most fitted to temper its effects. For example, prostitution should be regulated in such a way as to diminish sexual excesses; baths of salt or fresh water should be made accessible to the whole population, as was the case in ancient Rome and is now in Calabria, for nothing diminishes the exciting effect of the heat more than cold water. Then we ought to make judicial punishments more swift and hence better adapted to affect impressionable minds; avoiding, however, a pedantic uniformity that would extend the same laws to northern districts, which need different treatment, especially as to crimes against persons and, above all, sexual crimes.

The promoter of the new Italian code [1] deplores as a very great inconvenience the disparity which exists in the judicial treatment of citizens of different parts of the kingdom, but he does not reflect that if this difference did not exist in the law, it would certainly exist in something much more substantial, namely, in public opinion, which interprets a homicide at Mazzara quite differently from the way in which it is interpreted at Aosta, a fact that is sure to make itself felt at the trial. An attempted rape upon a twelve-year-old girl is a different thing in the south, where sexual maturity comes early, from what it is in the north, and the question of the age of consent must be differently decided for different climates; but here there is necessary a careful investigation as to whether, and how far, sexual maturity is accompanied by mental maturity. We have now, in this regard, a unified law; yet it certainly has not served to diminish the number of the crimes, but only to make the law itself powerless and an object of derision. To unify the law in reality, and not upon paper simply, it would be necessary to unify the morals, birth-rate, and sexual characteristics, and more than that, to unify the climate, soil, and system of agriculture; otherwise the law would remain like the ukase which commanded the Poles to change their language. It is possible to exterminate a people, but not to take away their language, unless it is possible to change at a stroke their entire physical constitution.

It proves nothing that certain countries with populations ethnically different have a uniform law. In Corsica, thanks to the juries, the French law remains a dead letter. In Switzerland, on the other hand, each canton has its own penal laws,

[1] Zanardelli, "Progetto del Nuovo Codice Penale," Rome, 1886.

and no inconvenience has resulted from it. The United Kingdom of Great Britain and Ireland, too, has no general penal code, but a series of special laws which vary for the three kingdoms. The same situation exists in the United States. And these are the freest countries, and in England, at least, crime is on the decrease.

It is not to be desired that the specialization be extended in detail to provinces and communes, for the matter is one that affects large ethnic and climatic groups. But where gypsies, for example, are numerous, it would be absurd to treat them as citizens of Paris or London would be treated, and try them before gypsy juries.

§ 132. Barbarism

It is impossible to extirpate barbarism all at once; but its harmful effects can be lessened by clearing the forests, those natural fortresses of malefactors, by opening new roads, and by founding towns and villages in the wilder places. This last was the course taken by Liutprando in 734 to put an end to the brigandage that flourished in the uninhabited parts of Modena. To these measures should be coupled an energetic repression of the arrogance of the powerful and the revenge of the weak, those two fertile sources of brigandage. By a rational education, superstition and prejudice should be removed or made to serve against crime, as Garibaldi and Napoleon attempted to have them serve. Certain institutions, without utility for civilized countries, should be abolished; such are the jury system, the national guard, popular election of judges, and all secret societies, especially monastic societies, so favorable to hatred and wrongdoing. Emigration should be watched and regulated, and associations of criminals prevented or destroyed as soon as formed, through rewards offered to their individual members for information. Receivers of stolen goods and their accomplices, those natural propagators of crime, should be severely handled by the aid of an able police force. Finally, honest but weak citizens should be encouraged, or, if that is not possible, terrified, until, placed between fear of the criminals and fear of the law, they shall be more in awe of the latter than of the former. This is the method to which Manhes owes the destruction of 4000 brigands in four months.

When crime, not of an economic, political, or religious character, but purely ethnic, flourishes under the protection of certain free institutions, such as the inviolability of domicile, the prohibition of preventive arrest, the freedom of association, jury trial, etc., it becomes indispensable to suspend these privileges until the epidemic of crime is suppressed, as is done in the freest countries, England, America, and Portugal. It is in the interest of civilization not to allow so precious a possession as liberty to be destroyed by misuse. On this account, where brigandage, the Camorra, or the Mafia takes on a political aspect, it is necessary to pass the most severe laws to prevent the possibility of their influencing the elections. The elector who is even merely suspected of participation in these associations ought to lose all political rights; and persons arrested for such participation should be sent to distant localities exempt from endemic criminality, or, better, transported to the islands. The political tribunate, of which we shall speak later, should give particular attention to the carrying out of these measures. Finally, a restriction of the pardoning power, especially with reference to organized criminals, would be useful; and in any case it ought not to be possible for them to return to the district which is their natural field of action.

§ 133. Civilization

The harmful effects of great aggregations of population, which are those of civilization pushed to the limit, can be prevented by bringing into play new preventives to counteract the new weapons placed in the hands of crime.

The attempt may be made to prevent the evil effects of the great centers by transporting to the smaller cities institutions that draw numbers of persons to places already overcrowded, such as universities, academies, scientific laboratories, military colleges, etc. These great masses of people cannot be suddenly dispersed, but they can be clarified and the emigration of the unemployed encouraged, by furnishing free transportation if necessary. If the population increases more than its food-supply, the practice of Neo-Malthusianism must be energetically disseminated.

A certain Englishman[1] (a citizen, that is to say, of the country which is the most scrupulous about personal liberty) proposes that those houses which criminals make their habitual resort should be closely watched and, if necessary, suppressed, so that these elements of the population shall not be able to meet, and hence may become harmless, He proposes, further, to visit with severe penalties what he calls the "capitalists of crime," — the receivers of stolen goods, who almost always go unpunished.

In order to prevent the increase of crime through immigration, a sort of selection should be practiced, as is, to some extent, done in the United States. Only those should be accepted as immigrants who are sound and respectable, and have some means and manual skill. It is by virtue of such a selection as this, together with judicial investigations, that France has been able in recent years to purify the stream of immigration and obtain a decrease in crime.[2]

§ 134. Modern Police System

We have hitherto carried on our police system very much as war was made in the heroic ages, when the cleverness or muscular strength of single individuals alone decided the victory. We have very able police officers, — able as Ulysses and Achilles were in their battles; but we have no Moltke, no one corresponding to a general-staff officer, to make use in his campaigns against crime of the resources offered him by study of statistics, criminal anthropology, etc., which would multiply his personal talent by the enormous forces placed at his disposal by science. The telegraph, for example, applied to railroad trains, the railroad itself, the telephone, — these are instruments placed in our hands to be used against the new tools that civilization has furnished to crime. We may add to these a well-arranged collection of photographs of criminals.

[1] Hill, "Criminal Capitalist," 1872.

[2] Joly, *op. cit.*

In America the companies that insure against burglary have introduced electric burglar-alarms. In various American cities, likewise, the police are furnished with signal boxes, so that in case of necessity a policeman can summon assistance without leaving his beat. Guillar proposes the association of all nations for the arrest of criminals, with uniform extradition treaties and a sort of international police, who shall exchange photographs of criminals and give notice of those who are going to foreign countries, whether voluntarily or because deported — with the exception of those rare cases where the criminal has learned to support himself by a trade. For this purpose an international criminal register and an international bureau of information would be necessary.[1]

In England there has been introduced the corps of detectives, and in Austria the corresponding organization of "Vertraute," who form the aggressive force in the fight against crime. These take up the search for the criminal and push it to the end, making use of all the means at their disposal — railroad, telegraph, press — but especially a knowledge of the features, and, what is not so easily changed, the look of criminals, and of the collections of photographs of which I have spoken.[2]

§ 135. Methods of Identification

If a good police commissary in Italy wants to put his hand upon the unknown author of some crime, he has recourse to his memory, to photographs, and also to the clumsy criminal register instituted a few years ago. But in a kingdom as large as Italy, with such rapid means of communication, thousands of individuals escape observation. The best memory would not be much help. Delinquents easily succeed in eluding the police by changing their names, or, if arrested, give them a false idea of their antecedents by taking the name of some respectable person. From this one sees how necessary it is to have means of identifying accused persons with scientific accu-

[1] "Rev. de Disc. Carcer.," Bulletin Internat., 1876.

[2] In Vienna in nine months of the year 1872, 150 "Vertraute" arrested 4950 delinquents, among whom were 1426 thieves and 472 swindlers.

racy; and of all the systems proposed for this purpose that of Bertillon is undoubtedly the best.[1] At the prefecture of the Paris police, to which he was attached, there were preserved several thousand photographs of delinquents, but it became increasingly difficult to make use of these as the number of delinquents increased. For this reason Bertillon proposed to classify criminals according to the measurements of certain parts of the body which could be taken as invariable. These are: the height, the length and breadth of the head, the length of the middle finger of the left hand, the length of the left foot, and the length and circumference of the left forearm. Supposing the records to be divided up into series on the basis of these measurements, it is evident that it would be necessary in identifying a criminal, only to examine the photographs of a single series, or at most to add the series on each side, as the error in measurement could only be very small.

This system of Bertillon's is based upon the fact that when the human body has reached its complete development, it remains almost invariable, and that it is impossible to find two individuals completely alike. By the use of this method Bertillon obtained 3017 identifications between 1883 and 1890. This was the first trial of "Bertillonage." After a time it was perceived that it was possible to make the identifications by the measurements alone, without the aid of photographs. Thus far the identification had an essentially judicial character: it served to guarantee to the magistrate the identity and the antecedents of the individual undergoing trial. But a new advance allowed the utilization of this method by the police, in furnishing them with the data necessary to recognize a delinquent still at liberty and concealed under a false name. This Bertillon obtained with "speaking photographs," that is, photographs accompanied by a minute description of the individual and his particular physical characteristics.

[1] Bonomi, "Project of an Instrument for Identifying the Person," 1892; Compagnone, "Il Casellario Giudiziario," Rome, 1895; A. Bertillon, "Identification Anthropometrique, Instructions Signaletiques," Melun, 1893; Id., "La Photographie Judiciare, etc.," 1890; Lombroso, "Les Applications de l'Anthropologie Criminelle," Paris, 1892. [But see Ottolenghi, "Polizia Scientifica," Turin, 1910, who describes the latest improvements on Bertillon's system. — TRANSL.]

With this same object the author has constructed an improved "Tachy-Anthropometer," a contrivance by which the necessary measurements of the body and skull may be quickly made, and which also permits the lateral, transverse, and horizontal curves of the skull to be taken and recorded automatically by means of an electric pen. This latter system has the great advantage that the procedure is purely mechanical, and that the sources of error are much less numerous than in the regular Bertillon system; and while in the millimetric measurements the only means of verifying their accuracy is to repeat them, where the cranial outlines are taken, their precision can be tested by their direct superposition upon the head of the subject. It should not be forgotten that in the ordinary system the points of difference between individuals are very limited, while in the new system they are very numerous.

§ 136. The Press

The police force must also avail itself systematically of the services of the press. For the press is an instrument of civilization as well as of crime, and can be neither suppressed nor restricted without injury to true freedom. The thing to be done, obviously, is to utilize it for the protection of society. In Switzerland the governmental authority has a sort of handbook containing the photographs and biographies of the principal Swiss criminals. In Germany it is the custom to insert in the more popular newspapers the description of the criminals most sought for, their photographs, and the amount of the reward promised for their apprehension. At Mainz there is a newspaper published in three languages, French, German, and English ("Moniteur International de Police Criminelle," "Internationales Kriminalpolizeiblatt," "International Criminal Police Times"), which is published weekly by the police counselor, and contains the portraits and marks of the criminals sought. At Cairo in Egypt there is published every Thursday a newspaper in Arabic, "Vagai 'u 'bubulis," or Police News, edited by the bureau of police, which contains the portraits of the homicides and counterfeiters arrested, with notes of their crimes and minute descriptions. Thus the press, through that very publicity which has been heretofore a source of blackmail, fraud, and libel, may become a means of social defense.

§ 137. Plethysmography

But there is something better in prospect. We have abolished torture, and we may congratulate ourselves upon it. But though this brutal means of investigation more often deceived than gave light, it is still an evil that nothing better has arisen to take the place left empty by its abolition.

Now the knowledge of biological anomalies (anesthesia, analgesia, left-handedness, abnormal field of vision), and of psychological anomalies (the cruelty, vanity, and improvidence of criminals), may help to fill up the gap; so also, other data, like obscene and vindictive tattooing, etc. Despine has already suggested the arrest of habitual criminals when they boast that they are going to commit a crime, knowing that in these cases the act follows close upon the word. We have already (in the first volume of my "Homme Criminel") seen how the plethysmograph of Mosso is able, without affecting the health and without any pain, to penetrate into the most secret recesses of the mind of the criminal.[1] I have myself made use of this instrument in a complicated case, proving that a certain well-known criminal was not guilty of the crime with which he was accused, but was guilty of a theft, at first connected with him by this test alone, but later brought home to him by judicial investigation.

[1] The plethysmograph is a device for testing variations in the circulation of the blood, and rests for its usefulness upon the way the circulation responds to what is passing in the mind. — TRANSL.

CHAPTER II

PREVENTION OF SEXUAL CRIMES AND OF FRAUD

§ 138.

SEXUAL crimes [1] and crimes of fraud are the specific crimes of advanced civilization. How shall they be remedied?

§ 139. The Prevention of Sexual Excesses

Divorce is a powerful means of preventing a great many cases of adultery and many of those other sexual crimes that are among the saddest phenomena of modern criminality. By the statistics of Ferri [2] we see the convictions for adultery in France increased from 1864 to 1867, while in the same period in Saxony, where divorce existed, they decreased; in the German districts where the French law was in force, there were many more trials and separations than in the other districts, and the sexual crimes were more numerous. In France in the period when divorce did not exist, from 1818 to 1874, poisonings among married people were more frequent than among the unmarried (45 : 30), but in following years, on the other hand, they became fewer. In Italy it is reckoned that no fewer than 46 homicides a year occur, perpetrated with the sole object of putting an end to a union that has become insupportable. I have told in my "Homme Criminel" (Vol. II) the case of the Kleinroth family, where the sons and their mother killed the father because of his continual brutal ill-treatment. In France Mme. Godefroy, 43 years of age, had won the respect and affection of the whole district for the courage with which she had brought up nine children, and had borne for 15 years the ill-treatment of her drunken husband; but one day, when he threatened her

[1] Penta, "I Pervertimenti Sessuali," etc., 1893; Viazzi, "Reati Sessuali," 1896; Krafft-Ebing, "Psyschopatia Sexualis," 1899.
[2] "Archivio di Psichiatria," II, 500; XII, 550.

with a knife, at the end of her patience, she killed him with an iron spade; she gave herself up and was acquitted.

As regards sexual crimes in general, a considerable number are to be attributed to individual congenital tendencies, but another part, and this the greater, comes under the category of occasional crimes due to the influence of the comparative barbarism of the country districts, and to passions which have no other outlet, on account of the absence of prostitution and the difficulty of marriage; for these crimes are especially to be observed in certain mountainous countries where prostitution does not exist, and among soldiers and priests.

But the majority of these crimes are due to the effect of civilization. We have a proof of this in the fact of their increase in the western provinces of Prussia, where the civilization is highest, and in the fact that the sexual assaults upon children have increased fivefold in 50 years, while those upon adults have decreased. In France these crimes numbered 305 in 1826, and by 1882 had reached 932. The rapes upon children increased from 138 to 791, an increase of 500%. In England they numbered 167 in 1830–34; 972 in 1835–39; and 1395 in 1851–55. In Prussia, according to Oettingen, sexual misdemeanors increased between 1855 and 1869 from 225 to 925; while crimes of the same nature rose from 1477 to 2945. Modern civilization exercises a still more direct influence. By diffusing education it increases the irritation of the nervous system, which, in its turn, demands stimulations and pleasure that must always be new and more and more keen. It seems that the more a man's pyschic activity increases, the more the number of his needs and his taste for pleasures grow, especially when his mind is not occupied with great scientific and humanitarian ideas, and when his wealth permits an over-abundant diet. Of all these, the sexual need is certainly that which is most keenly felt, and this is that which, throughout the whole animal world, is in the closest connection with the cerebral system. This relationship is sometimes one of antagonism, as seen in the great fecundity of fish and the lower insects, the lesser fecundity of the higher animals, and the sterility of the worker ants and bees, and of great men; and sometimes one of parallelism, as is proved by the greater psychic force at the period of virility and by the exuberance of health, life, and intelligence to be observed among chaste men.

This insatiability with regard to pleasure in the cases of individuals of high culture, together with the abundance of opportunity, explains to us why the crimes against children increase in inverse ratio to the crimes against adults; and it further explains, together with the lack of divorce and the fact that marriages between old people are constantly becoming more numerous, the apparently strange fact that this crime, unlike all others, is most common in the case of married people. In France the unmarried furnish 41.5 of the rapes of children, and the married men 45.9: while in other offenses against persons the figures are 48.1 for the unmarried, and 40.4 for the married.

We may add that because of the continued development of foresight,[1] the more intelligent people are always seeking to engender the fewest children possible, and hence incline toward pederasty. Thus it is that I have observed among the more intelligent mountaineers, at Ceresole, for example, marriage postponed until the age of 40, in order to have fewer children; while in the mountains where cretinism is most abundant, in the Valley of Aosta, the marriages produce, at Donnaz, for example, 6.5 children, and at Chatillon, 5.1, nearly double the average.[2]

It is not too bold a hypothesis to say that marriage, where wealth and influence are preferred to beauty and health, is a transaction in which the choice is made directly contrary to the laws of natural selection; and that it consequently becomes hateful and leads not only to desertion of the marriage bed, but also to hatred and disgust at the entire sex, and in consequence to a search for sexual gratification contrary to nature. This latter certainly would not be so common if sexual needs could be freely satisfied with a beloved person of the opposite sex. Civilization, in its turn, materially influences rapes upon the immature, by multiplying workshops, mines, schools, and

[1] Ferri, "Socialismo e Criminalità," 1883.
[2] "Inchiesta Agraria," VIII, p. 160.

colleges; and thus furnishes numerous occasions for contact between adults, often unmarried, and the immature, among whom it is enough that one should be immoral, in order to corrupt hundreds. This all explains why the workmen, who furnish, according to Fayet, 30% of the general criminality, furnish 35% of the rapes upon children.

§ 140. Legislative and Administrative Measures

It is very easy to follow the old military method and say: If crimes increase, let us also increase the penalties, and we shall put a stop to them. This is an exaggeration. It is, however, true that Ferri also exaggerates when, by a series of statistics for France, covering 53 years, he tries to prove the ineffectiveness of punishment, because the continual condemnations coincide with a continual increase in the number of crimes. But if we examine these tables we shall see that if there has been an increase in the reformatory penalties visited upon those guilty of rapes upon adults, at the expense of severer punishments (56. 4: 32.2 = 1.75), on the other hand, the excess of sentences to prison over those to hard labor has diminished much more $\left(\frac{56.7}{10.2} : \frac{30.6}{12.9} = 2.34\right)$, a result which proves an increase in the severity of the penalty on the whole. Now, crimes against adults having diminished, it is clear that this severity has had a certain influence. We find another proof in the table of rapes upon children. Here it seems that the lighter penalties have increased at the expense of those that are more severe. Here, then, the severity has decreased; and we find that at the same time the number of these crimes in France has increased. The penalty, then, is not without its influence.

Yet it is incontestable that in this case we must look to preventive measures much more than to punitive ones. For this reason the schools, and the workshops where children are employed, should be supervised. An excellent substitute for penal measures in the case of pederasty, for example, is to put directoresses or married women as supervisors in the workshops where children work at night; and this measure would be the more easily put in practice, since it would be economically advantageous. It would also be necessary to prohibit child-labor in the mines, as is done by the French law of 1874 with regard to the labor of children — a law which has been in force since 1875 and coincides with a diminution in the number of rapes upon children since 1876. Another remedy would certainly be the diffusion of prostitution in the agricultural districts, and especially in localities where there are a large number of sailors, soldiers, and laborers. It is especially necessary to make sexual intercourse accessible to all dissolute-minded young men.

No law can be devised to prevent mercenary marriages, which, because of their origin, easily become repugnant. But at least a greater facility of divorce can be granted, that the antipathy may not reach the point of leading to hatred and crime. It is evident that divorce is destined to diminish the number of crimes of adultery. In the first place, it permits a legitimate sexual satisfaction to husbands, who if young and merely separated from their wives would certainly procure illegitimate satisfaction; and, in the second place, it threatens the unmarried adulterer, who now runs, at most, the risk of a duel, with the far greater danger of a forced marriage with an unchaste woman. In the present state of things the injured husband, if he has recourse to the courts, runs much more risk and is subjected to more annoyances, than the true culprit, on account of the publicity and ridicule to which he is subjected, to say nothing of the chance of the eventual acquittal of the offender. Further, divorce is a preventive against crimes of vengeance on the part of the injured husband (crimes frequent on the stage, though rare in real life), and against the new French remedy of acid-throwing it would be much better and more effective than all the efforts of the courts. Even when the author of the crime is acquitted by the court and absolved by public opinion, he remains none the less a criminal; and the killing of an adulterer, however culpable he may be, is always a kind of wild justice, left in the hands of the injured person by a custom still entirely savage. Now it is to be noted that, according to Dumas, who ought to know something about it, these murders occur oftener in legitimate marriages than in cases of concubinage, because it is in the former that the need of avenging the violation of one's own legitimate property is most keenly felt.

I have shown in a previous chapter that there are certain perverse natures which are irresistibly drawn toward one another. The marriage of such is happy for the participants, however harmful for society. But what of those cases where one of these depraved beings is united with a respectable person, when a satyr like the Frenchman Ferlin, who, by 7 servants besides his wife, had 54 children and ended by ravishing one of his own daughters, is married to a chaste and sober woman? From such cases we see new causes and forms of crime arise. The ancient jurists, who were anything but considerate to women, admitted that a woman who was beaten by her husband could not be accused if afterward she committed adultery.[1] Plainly, the ancients saw in adultery a preventive against marital cruelty. Now, divorce would be a better preventive.

But divorce alone is not sufficient. It is necessary to insist upon investigation into the question of paternity, and, above all, reparation for the woman seduced. If we cast a glance at our society we see there, as regards the sexual instinct, two opposite currents. On the one side sexual desires increase as intelligence and civilization increase — hence the great number of educated offenders; and on the other side, the means of satisfying this need becomes more and more difficult. It is from this fatal situation that sexual crimes arise. But the situation is aggravated by that prejudice which makes us regard that as a grave offense for one sex, which for the other is not even a misdemeanor; but which makes the sexual act enough of a fault in a young man to drive him to satisfy this imperious need, in his more erotic moments, by acts contrary to nature. Hence we see, added to the congenital perverts who are the inevitable effect of degeneracy, numbers of accidental perverts who need not have been made such.

[1] "Si vir uxorem atrocius verberaverit atque uxor aufugiat et adulterium committat, non poterit eam maritus accusare" (Tiraqueau, "In Leg. Connub.").

When, then, a true balance comes to be struck between the demands of nature and those of morality and duty, we shall see crimes of this character rapidly diminish. For this purpose it is necessary to make marriage less mercenary, to make legitimate sexual relations easier, to make maternity always respected, and especially to make obligatory that reparation to the woman which the law now not only does not provide, but actually prevents, by forbidding inquiry into the question of paternity. These are the true preventives, not only of sexual crimes, but also of infanticide and of many suicides and homicides, crimes which in general arise from sexual relationships; and these criminals are just those most worthy of human pity, the more so as the guilty are most often those who are otherwise respectable people.

§ 141. Fraud

Fraud and breach of trust are the most modern crimes and show the result of evolution and civilization upon crime, — a process in which it has lost all the cruelty which characterized it in primitive ages, substituting greed and that habit of lying which unfortunately threatens to become general among us. Thus if we pass from the more retired valleys into the small towns, and from the towns to the great cities, we shall see, as we pass from small to great, the commercial lie, swindling on a small scale, take on larger and larger proportions; and in the highest society, under the form of financial corporations, we shall see the true, the gigantic system of swindling flourishing permanently, sheltered behind the most high-sounding and honored, if not the most honorable, names. It is, then, natural that the common swindler, or the corrupt politician, should not be a born criminal, but a criminaloid possessing all the qualities of the normal man; so that without a propitious opportunity, such an opportunity, we may even say, as would be almost enough to corrupt an honest man, he would not have stumbled.[1]

Now, here we see a means of prevention by the dissemination of the modern economic truth that a bank which gives itself up merely to speculating in the product of money can only be a

[1] Lombroso, "Homme Criminel," Vol. II.

swindling scheme, since money cannot of its own power multiply itself. Further, we must demand, in every case, that the directors of corporate banks, having agricultural or industrial objects, shall offer effective guarantees that losses will be made good, even when a disastrous operation has been sanctioned by the stockholders. This last provision is the more necessary, since stockholders are often only convenient instruments in the hands of rogues, and are made their involuntary and unconscious accomplices.

The bankers and jewelers of London and Paris have found an ingenious method of discovering swindlers who approach them under the disguise of men of high station. They employ for this purpose dogs trained to recognize the odor of these pretended rich persons, who bathe but rarely. They make use, also, of the telephone, of instantaneous photography, and of the new telephotography, which transmits the image of the suspected client, as the telephone does the voice. Hence the swindler is in danger of being arrested before ever leaving the place where he attempts his fraud.

But it becomes much more difficult to prevent swindling when it is protected by political or governmental power. Swindling by taking advantage of political office seems to many persons to-day no more a crime, than the use of poison did in the Middle Ages, when not only the Borgias, but also the Ten in Venice, made use of it as a common political weapon. Now, from assisting a newspaper with the public money ("the public's money is no one's money") to helping a friend, and then finally one's self, is but a short step, especially for those who seek to supply the lack of genius with lack of honesty.

But here the institution of parliamentary government has its effect, especially through increasing the lack of responsibility. When we lived under a despotic government the royal concubines pocketed the public money. To-day it is the deputies who have taken their places. For these, considering themselves, like the kings, inviolable, and being even more irresponsible than the kings, naturally deny themselves nothing, unless restrained by moral sense. Find the means of putting immense treasures into the hands of men who are irresponsible and inviolable, or nearly so, and then try to tell them that they must not touch those treasures! To-day the evil is so much the greater, as the deputies and senators are more numerous, and hence more dangerous, than kings. It is easy to understand why they are more dangerous. In the electoral contest it is not intellectual qualities, and still less moral qualities, that decide the victory. Far from it! The man who has new ideas simply dashes himself against the stone wall of the people's conservative prejudices. He, who with a free conscience points out an evil and proposes the remedy, injures the interests of some powerful voters. The respectable man who does not combat abuses openly injures no one, but he also accomplishes nothing; and all run the risk of being submerged by the mediocrity, which satisfies the world with an insignificant program, or by the brazen and corrupt, who buy the needed votes.

It is necessary, then, to restrict the number of these representatives of the nation, to limit their power, and to remove their special privileges. In ordinary offenses it is just that they should be held to a greater responsibility than others, as in England, where merely the suspicion of adultery, which for most persons would not have been considered a crime, was enough to cause the fall of Parnell.

For this reason the largest liberty must be given to the press. In the present state of things the guilty not only cannot be accused, but, if they are accused, find a new resource in their own crimes; and they can, at the expense of honest men and with the aid of the law itself, indemnify themselves for the efforts which honorable men make to expose their misdeeds. This happened in France when B—— some years ago got a young journalist convicted and heavily sentenced for revealing only a small part of the truth about Panama.

Here is the place to say that in such cases to lay bare the sores is not, as some weak persons believe, to increase the evil, but on the contrary to begin the work of healing. A country which, like France, seeks to cast the light of day upon the foul places in order to purify itself, regains its rank in the estimation of the world and in popular opinion, however high may be the station of the guilty.

One of the reforms that would serve best to check political corruption would be an extensive decentralization. When a government, centralized like the Italian or the French, has the right to administer enormous sums and manage affairs involving billions, as in many of our public works, corruption inevitably arises, because the control of the public is no longer actively or directly exercised, and a wider door of impunity is left open. But if, on the other hand, the public business has to be transacted in broad daylight, under the eyes of all, the control will be more efficacious, and those weak persons whom money might corrupt will find in the publicity of their acts a means of resisting evil. Panama scandals occur always in the great central administrations, and never, or in much smaller proportions, in municipal administration.

The abuse of public office is thus a crime of the most advanced civilization, which can be prevented only by limiting the number and power of the deputies and senators, who are the natural protectors of corrupt officials; by a decentralization which will permit a more active surveillance and decrease the number of monopolies; but especially by cutting down the number of officials. Russia and Italy are really governments of officials, who absorb and stifle everything that has vital force in the country, and, under pretext of sustaining life, destroy it. Now it is possible, in the courts, for example, to replace the collective functionaries by a single judge, and thus increase the sense of responsibility and at the same time discover cases of corruption more easily. By a diminution in the number of employees it would be made possible to choose the best ones. I have proposed, for example, to choose the judges in the first place by examinations; then, for the next higher grade, by the number of decisions not revoked by the higher courts; and finally, for the higher judges, by the number of cases treated by direct citation and by their issue on appeal. This would be the most exact criterion, and at the same time a great encouragement to well-doing.

CHAPTER III

THE PREVENTION OF ALCOHOLISM[1]

§ 142.

IN combating alcoholism we should be inspired by the extraordinary efforts that the Anglo-Saxons have made. Their temperance societies have become very powerful, and by 1867 already included 3,000,000 members and published three weekly and three monthly papers. In Glasgow they spent £2000 to open coffee houses in districts where workmen most frequented the whiskey-shops. In London on holidays they opened tea-rooms and theaters able to hold more than 4500 persons. At the Congress in Baltimore in 1873 they were represented by more than 750,000 members; and in five years they boasted that they had caused the closing of 4000 distilleries and 8000 liquor saloons. In America the women were powerful allies of these inexorable enemies of alcoholism. To save their brothers and husbands they forced the liquor dealers, by their prayers and their importunate exhortations, to close their shops. Some resisted and threatened to strike them, or turned the hose on them; others had recourse to the courts, or set bears at them. But they were protected by their own weakness, by their perseverance, and by the righteousness of their cause; and even when a jury found them guilty the judge was not willing to pronounce sentence. Put to flight one day, they returned to the attack the next, so that many had to yield to their indomitable energy. In Germany and Switzerland there arose under the auspices of Forel newspapers and libraries

[1] Wilh. Bode, "Die Heilung der Trunksucht," Bremerhaven, 1890; G. Bunge, "Die Alkoholfrage," Zürich, 1890; A. Forel, "Die Errichtung von Trinker-Asylen und ihrer Einfügung in die Gesetzgebung," 1890; Id., "Die Reform der Gesellschaft durch die völlige Enthaltung von alkoholischen Getränken," 1891; Zerboglio, "Soll' Alcoolismo," 1895; Korsakoff, "Lois et Mesures Prophylactiques," Turin, 1894; Claude, "Rapport au Sénat sur la Consommation de l'alcool en France," 1897; Jacquet, "L'Alcoolisme," 1897; Legrain, "Dégénerescence Sociale et Alcoolisme," 1877.

whose sole aim was to combat the abuse of alcohol. Through the combined effect of such efforts great changes were made in institutions in this regard. In 1832 the custom was commenced of giving additional pay to every sailor who would give up his ration of grog; in the rations of the land troops spirits were suppressed (the sutlers were forbidden to sell them), and replaced by coffee and sugar, a measure which was later adopted by the great industrial companies.

In 1845 the State of New York declared against the unrestricted sale of liquor; Maine followed its example; but nevertheless the sale continued in secret. Then it was that the famous Maine law was passed, which prohibited expressly the manufacture and sale of spirituous liquors, except for medicinal purposes; the difficulty of transporting such liquors became extreme; it was forbidden to have more than one gallon in the house, and the law permitted domiciliary visits for the purpose of discovering hidden supplies. This law was adopted in some of the other states, but was largely ineffective because of the presence of foreigners and the attitude of the central government. In all the states of the Union (and later in Switzerland and Prussia) laws were passed which prohibited the sale of alcoholic drinks to students, minors, insane persons, and Indians. The dealer was made responsible for damage and injuries caused by drunkenness, responsibility for which, in Illinois, might go as high as $5000. In some States the dealer was also liable for damage to the drinker's family, caused by idleness and by diseases due to drink.

In England since 1856 the sale of liquor on holidays has been prohibited. Later in 1864 and 1870 the sale was restricted to certain hours. A fine of from 7 to 40 shillings, or a day in prison, was imposed by law upon every one found publicly in a state of intoxication. In 1871, under Gladstone (who suffered from the unpopularity of the measure), the number of public houses was limited as follows:

In the towns	In the country
1 to 1500 inhabitants	1 to 900 inhabitants
2 " 3000 "	2 " 1200 "
3 " 4000 "	3 " 1800 "

Special inspectors are appointed to control the illegal sale of liquor, and adulteration is punished by progressive fines and loss of license. By the law of 1873 it was ordered that no new licenses should be granted as long as existing licenses continued in force, and out of the money received from licenses certain sums were set aside to buy up the licenses of public houses that it was desirable to close. To these things must be added the exhortations of preachers, especially those of Father Mathew, who in 1838–40 succeeded by his eloquence alone in diminishing the consumption of alcohol in Ireland by half and cutting down the crimes from 6400 to 4100. Finally, there is the tax upon alcoholic drinks. In the United States this tax is very high; in France it pays the state more than 500,000,000 francs, and there is talk of increasing it. In Belgium it brings in more than 13,000,000.

According to the penal code of Holland, passed in 1881, drunkenness upon the public streets is punished by a maximum fine of 15 florins; upon a second offense the punishment is imprisonment for three days, and upon a third offense within a year of the first the imprisonment may be extended to two weeks. In succeeding years it may reach three weeks or more, and if the offender is capable of working he may be sent to a public workhouse for a year or more. The retailer who furnishes drinks to a child below 16 years of age is punished by imprisonment for not more than three weeks, and by a fine of not more than 100 florins. The law of 1881 forbids the sale of alcohol in quantities of less than 2 liters without the authorization of the government of the commune. This is refused when the number of shops reaches

1 to 500	inhabitants	in the large cities
1 " 300	"	" cities of from 20,000 to 50,000 population
1 " 250	"	" the villages

As a result of the promulgation of this law the number of shops, which was 40,000 in 1881, fell to 25,000 by 1891.[1]

In Switzerland the privilege of exporting alcohol, of making it, and of selling it wholesale, belongs to the government. Two-thirds of the quantity consumed must be imported; of the re-

[1] Jacquet, *op. cit.*

maining third, half is manufactured by the state, which has taken over the larger distilleries for this purpose; and the rest is sold by the 200 small distilleries. The price of sale is fixed by the Federal Council. Pure alcohol and the stronger spirits are subject to a federal tax of 80 francs to the metric quintal, and is measured by special federal officers. After the passage of this law the consumption of alcoholic drinks fell 20%. The Canton of Saint-Gall, by a law promulgated in May, 1891, gave the public authorities, communal or municipal, the power of assuming the guardianship of an habitual drinker, at the expense either of the patient or the poor-fund.

In Sweden, where alcoholism rages to the extent of being an endemic disease, the taxes on the distillation of brandy were raised in 1855–56–64, successively from 2 francs to the hectoliter to 27 and 32. The use of steam in the distilleries was forbidden, the production limited to 2610 liters a day, and distillation permitted only two months in the year (later seven months, but only in the large distilleries), in order to suppress the small ones, recognized as most harmful to the people. As a consequence the production of alcohol fell two-thirds in ten years, and the price rose from .50 to 1.30 Kr. a liter. In Sweden a corporation collected enough money to buy up the drink-shops of a district, and allowed the retailers, now become their employees, to make a profit merely upon the tea, coffee, and food that they sold. This association has found imitators in 147 Swedish cities. It sold only pure liquors, and refused to sell to drunkards or minors. Since 1813 there has existed, moreover, a law which fined a person found drunk upon the streets three dollars for the first offense, twice that for the second offense, and for the third and fourth took away his right of vote and representation. At the fifth offense he was condemned to prison or to the house of correction at hard labor for six months, and upon the sixth offense, for one year. Further (at least in Norway), the sale of spirits is prohibited upon holidays and the day before, and before 8 o'clock in the morning.[1]

Which of all these remedies has given the best result?

Many of the most energetic measures, especially the repres-

[1] "Ann. de Stat.," 1880.

sive measures, have come far from realizing the end for which they were designed, except in Switzerland, England, and Sweden. We know that from 1851 to 1857 serious crimes decreased 40% in Sweden, and lesser crimes 30%, and that this diminution constantly makes itself felt. There were 40,621 crimes in 1865, and only 25,277 in 1868.[1] In the period from 1830 to 1834, with an average consumption of 46 liters of brandy, there were 59 murders and 2281 thefts, and in 1875–78, the consumption of brandy having fallen to 11 liters, the number of murders had fallen to 18 and that of thefts to 1871 (Jaquet). At the same time the average stature and length of life had increased (Baer); and the figure for suicides of alcoholics, which was 46 in 1861, had fallen to 11 by 1869. The number of drunkards has also decreased, but not so much and in an irregular manner. At Gothenburg, for example, there was:

In 1851	1	drunkard	to	19	inhabitants
" 1855	1	"	"	9	"
" 1860	1	"	"	12	"
" 1865	1	"	"	22	"
" 1866	1	"	"	33	"
" 1870	1	"	"	38	"
" 1872	1	"	"	35	"
" 1873	1	"	"	31	"
" 1874	1	"	"	28	"

It is nevertheless true that when my colleague, Dr. Brusa, arrived in Gothenburg on a holiday, though he himself could not get a drop of wine, he met a number of persons drunk on the streets. On the other hand, it is certain that all these Draconian laws have not prevented alcoholism from increasing in France and America. It has even been affirmed that the Maine law is rather a political weapon than a hygienic measure; and that the illicit sale of alcoholic drinks, of which the very legislators who prohibit it are often guilty, furthers alcoholism by making all drinking disreputable. In France, the tax upon alcohol, which rose from 37.40 francs to 60 in 1855, to 90 in 1860, and to 150 in 1871, now actually amounts to 156.25 francs to the hectoliter of pure alcohol. Notwithstanding this, the average per capita consumption rose from 11.45 liters in 1850, to the enormous amount of 41.56 in 1892 (Claude). The same thing

[1] Bertrand, "Essai sur l'Intempérance," 1875.

in effect may be said with regard to England, where, notwithstanding the exorbitant tax of 489.20 francs to the hectoliter of pure alcohol, the consumption in the United Kingdom between 1860 and 1880 has wavered between 4.1 and 5.7 liters per capita, and from 1880 to 1893, with some slight changes, has maintained the figure of 4.5 liters. The trifling diminution is certainly less to be attributed to the tax than to the total abstainers, whose number is estimated at 5,000,000.

There is small reason for astonishment at the comparative inefficacy of these fiscal measures, if we take into account the fact that they only slightly and indirectly affect the consumer. This may easily be seen by following Dupuy's calculations:

"Suppose that a liter of alcohol costs, tax and all, about 4 francs. We know that from a liter of alcohol it is possible to make two and a half liters of brandy. Now, a liter holds 30 to 40 small glasses — let us say 33 — at 3 centiliters to a glass. From a liter of alcohol we should then get two and a half liters of brandy, or 82 small glasses. At 10 centimes a glass the retailer gets 8.20 francs. This is 4.20 francs more than the cost price. The margin is large, and leaves ample profit for retailer and wholesaler both" (Claude).

But the lack of success is due especially to the fact that no repressive law can accomplish its purpose when it runs counter to our instincts. Now among these instincts is that desire for psychic stimulation, such as one may get from wine, a need which increases with the progress of civilization. For this reason the poor miners in Scotland, who have not enough money to buy whiskey, have recourse to laudanum; and the poor of London allay the pangs of hunger in the same way.[1] In Ireland, when the preaching of Father Mathew had turned the people away from alcoholic drinks, they unexpectedly became addicted to the use of ether,[2] of which the good pastor had never thought.

[1] Colkins calculates that in 1867 there were 78,000 pounds of opium used in the United States for narcotic purposes ("Opium and Opium Eaters, Philadelphia, 1871). In Kentucky the legislature passed a law by which anyone who, through the use of opium, arsenic, or other drugs, became incapable of controlling himself, might be placed in care of a guardian, or shut up in an asylum (Fazio, "Dell' Ubbriachezza," 1875). In London 118,915 pounds of opium were imported in 1857, and in 1862, 280,750; and still more in the manufacturing centers of Lancashire (Fazio, *op. cit.*).

[2] They used a mixture of ethyl- and methyl-ether.

"This," said they, "is not wine, it is not gin, which Father Mathew has forbidden us to use; and it makes us merry for a few pence, so we drink it." They made use of it even to the point of drunkenness, frequently taking 7 to 14 grams, while inveterate users went as high as 90 grams.

The true ideal of a wise and philanthropic legislator, in the combat with alcoholism, would be to provide the people with some form of mental stimulant that would injure neither mind nor body, and would not have the danger of alcohol. Subsidies to the large theaters have been discussed in this connection. Why should not popular theaters and shows be subsidized? It would be quite fair to refuse to subsidize great theaters, since they are only for the rich, and to provide, instead, a means of mental distraction to the poor, which would be of use in preventing alcoholism. At a mass meeting in Turin in the interest of temperance, a workman asked that the theaters should be kept in operation all day on Sunday at a low price, so that the workmen might have something to keep them out of the wine-shops. This was the only rational suggestion made at the meeting, and it was indignantly rejected. Forni tells us that in a small district in the south of Italy the wine-shop keeper had the leader of a troupe of comedians thrashed, because since he had arrived there with his cheap performances (the admission price was 15 centimes) the retailer had sold only half as much wine as usual.[1] In Italy, as we shall see later, the clergy alone have organized recreations on a large scale for the feast-days, by means of which the poor can agreeably pass their time between one prayer and the next without resorting to the wine-shop. No other class has done as much.

It is necessary also to extend the use of tea and coffee, which stimulate the brain without paralyzing the inhibitory faculties as alcohol does. To do this it is not enough to increase the taxes upon alcohol: it is necessary also, as Fioretti and Magnan have suggested, to lower the taxes upon imports, especially upon tea, coffee, and particularly upon sugar, which, since it serves to make other drinks agreeable, prevents the need of alcoholic beverages. Since the dark and unsanitary dwellings, hidden in

[1] Lombroso, "Incremento al Delitio," p. 81.

narrow and dirty streets, in which workmen are obliged to live, drive them irresistibly to the wine-shop, we should widen the streets, and build for the workingman buildings with better air, and of a sort to make the domestic hearth an agreeable and respectable resting-place, to be preferred to the wine-shop.

After these measures have been adopted it will be time to come down upon the retailers of alcoholic beverages, by restricting the hours of sale at night and on holidays, by restricting the licenses, and by forcing the sale of food and coffee, particularly in the neighborhood of factories. It will be necessary to be even more strict with the proprietors of factories and mines, when they themselves sell alcoholic drinks, for by their authority they help corrupt the most sober workman. Finally, spirituous liquors should have very heavy taxes laid upon them, a measure much more moral and salutary than taxing salt and flour; and the consumption of amyl-alcohol should be prohibited, and also the use of all alcohols not rectified, including bitters, vermouth, etc., since these are the most harmful to health.

It has also been proposed to forbid the sale of alcoholic drinks on credit, and to declare contracts made in the wine-cellars not binding. A measure that seems especially practical is to have the workman's wages paid to his family in the morning instead of at night, and never on a holiday or the day before.[1] Let no one interpose the usual protest about personal liberty. For when we see the Anglo-Saxons, the most democratic people in the world, carrying their restrictions even to the hours when liquor may be sold and the amount that each person may have in his house; when we see a Gladstone the promoter and apostle of similar measures, while in Italy the hours of sale are increased, and no one raises a voice for the substitution of taxes on the wine-shops for the baneful taxes upon salt and flour, — one is driven to ask himself whether this pretended devotion to liberty is not simply the result of the avarice of trade.

§ 143. Cure

With regard to direct cure, use has been made of strychnine, bromides, tincture of nux vomica, cold baths (Kowalewsky),

[1] See "Archivio di Psichiatria e Scienze Penali," I and II, 1880; Ferri, "Sostitutivi Penali."

baths of hot air impregnated with vapor of turpentine, and sulphur baths, according to the nature of the case and its complications. Massage and gymnastics have also been made use of; and Forel, Ladame, and Bucknill have obtained good results with hypnotism where the patient was susceptible to it. Forel, Kowalewsky, Ladame, Legrain, and Magnan have introduced the rational cure of drunkenness by isolation and absolute deprivation of all alcoholic drinks for a period which Masson, Crother, and Hirsch think should be a year, Drysdale and Kraepelin nine months, and Forel from four months to a year. Magnan advises, further, a light, strengthening diet; meat, vegetables, fruits, and sweet foods, and for drinks, bitter infusions (hops, quassia), bouillon, tea, and coffee.[1] To this we may add muscular labor, especially agricultural, even for those who are not accustomed to it. But, as Magnan says,[2] what is especially necessary is a moral reëducation, by means of discussions and lectures, which shall show to these patients the danger and harm of alcohol, and awaken their affections and moral sense. For this purpose Forel has established in the country the asylum of Elletton, a kind of farm-colony, under the paternal rule of a superintendent who is at once administrator and the educator of his charges. These form one family, living in common a simple and healthful life, encouraging one another, busy with regular work, and all subjected to total abstinence. This experiment is a success in 65% of the cases. Similar methods in the United States, from the statistics of 3000 cases, show about the same percentage of success.

Magnan proposes the committal to special asylums of habitual drunkards and of all who have alcoholic delirium, even after the delirium has ceased, for 17 or 18 months — or in the case of incurables, for an indeterminate period, as is already prescribed

[1] In the "Revue d'Hygiène," 1895, Ludwig proposes an agreeable drink, the color and taste of which recalls sparkling white wine. It is made as follows: White sugar 1 kilogram, red sugar 1 kilogr., ground barley 500 gr., hops 30 gr., coriander 30 gr., elderberries 25 gr., violets 25 gr., vinegar 1 liter, water 50 liters. Take a perfectly clean cask, cut out a hole 4 or 5 inches square in place of the bunghole, and put in first the sugar and then the other ingredients; mix all carefully, and leave to steep for eight days; draw off, filter, and bottle, corking carefully. This costs about 7 centimes a liter, and resembles wine very closely.

[2] "La Médecine Moderne," Nov., 1893.

in the canton of Saint Gall, in Switzerland. Hospitals for alcoholics have a double object: first, that of protecting society by withdrawing drunkards from it; and second, that of putting the drunkards in the best condition for cure and correction. Such hospitals should receive: first, the person who has committed an offense in a drunken fit; secondly, anyone who has dissipated his own property and that of his family by his intemperance; and thirdly, any person found drunk on the street a number of times, etc. In the first class of cases the hospital is a substitute for the prison or insane asylum. In the others it is a temporary refuge. Anyone who has committed a crime in a state of intoxication, if after an investigation by experts he is proved to be dangerous, should be shut up in an inebriate hospital for an indeterminate period. In the case where a crime has been committed by an intoxicated person who is not an habitual drunkard, and he is found to be perfectly sound, he should be examined for anthropological and psychical marks of degeneracy as signs of a criminal tendency. If these are found he should not be released until a cure is assured, which means, in most cases, his permanent detention.

CHAPTER IV

PREVENTIVE MEASURES AGAINST THE INFLUENCE OF POVERTY AND WEALTH

§ 144.

IF, as we have seen, wealth that is excessive or too rapidly acquired has almost as fatal an influence as poverty, it follows that preventive measures will be efficacious only when they combat the excess of the one as well as of the other.

The first thing of importance here is to secure reforms that shall assure greater equality in the distribution of the returns of labor and make work accessible for every able-bodied person; for example, the limitation of the hours of labor according to the age of the worker and the nature of the work, especially in mines and in unhealthful trades, and the exclusion of women, also, from work at night, thus protecting their virtue and health, and at the same time bringing larger returns to a greater number of workers. For the attainment of this object it is not enough to authorize strikes theoretically. It is also necessary to permit their organization practically and not to suppress trades unions and boycotts, without which the liberty of striking is no more than a legal hypocrisy. On the other hand, the abolition of lotteries and of many holidays, the facilitation of civil actions, the turning over to the communes of lighting, road-making, schools, and water-supply, would prevent much corruption and extend to a greater number of laborers the advantages of hygiene and the cheapest market in things most necessary to life. This would make it possible to mitigate the distress of the poor, without producing any disorder or injuring the rich.

The excess of wealth, on the other hand, may be counteracted by making the rich share their profits with the laborers, and by establishing progressive taxes, especially upon legacies, taxes which shall weigh heavily upon or even annul legacies received from distant relatives, and turn these, as well as the gains of speculation and gambling, to the profit of the state and the helpless. We have already made a great step toward the expropriation and subdivision of property by abolishing ecclesiastical benefices and entailed estates, and by means of these taxes we could, without too much disturbance, bring about a still greater subdivision. Why do we allow a peasant in upper Italy to eat poisoned bread, which gives him pellagra, when we could prevent it with the law which we apply effectively in the cities? Why do we allow the dwellers in the malaria districts to die, when the sale of quinine at a low price would save them? Finally, if the want of coal prevents the expansion of certain industries, the government could extend the use of the water power at our disposal, at the expense of a small part of the enormous sums which it wastes without thought upon military and official pomp.

On the other hand, since the great country estates, by perpetuating the wealth of the few, perpetuate also the illness and poverty of the many, why should they not be expropriated to the state? and why should not more prejudicial agrarian contracts be modified, and the peasants receive a larger share in the profits? Henry George shows that if the state confiscated the land and let it directly to capable laborers, it would not only bring about a higher productivity, but also fix a minimum wage, higher than present wages, and thus encourage workmen insufficiently paid to devote themselves by preference to the cultivation of the soil.[1]

On the other hand, the poverty of the workmen, due in great part to the excess of production over consumption, inevitably draws after it a lowering of wages, a phenomenon which can only be aggravated by the competition of the markets of Japan, China, and America. We ought then to help relieve the market by encouraging consumption on the part of a greater number of individuals, by lightening imposts, duties, and especially indirect taxes that can be replaced by others not detrimental to health and morals, such as taxes on alcohol and tobacco,

[1] "Progress and Poverty," 1892.

which would affect only the rich and the vicious. England had no need of a socialistic creed in order to realize these reforms. This government, the only sensible one that Europe has, knew how to prevent the excesses of the lower classes, first in regard to the Irish question and then in the labor question (as in the case of the miners and dock-laborers), by conceding complete liberty of striking, by granting of its own accord the eight-hour day in all government shops, and by giving an equal voice to employers and to workmen in the arbitration of labor difficulties.

The excess of population being in its turn a grave cause of poverty and crime, we must direct emigration from the over-populated countries toward those which are less thickly settled. Lord Derby has said: "I have always been persuaded that if our country has escaped the greatest evils that afflict society, it is because we have always had, beyond the sea, outlets for our population and our manufactures." England, in fact, having the ocean and the means of utilizing it, has the whole world for safety-valve.

The state ought also to establish working colonies at a distance from the great centers, especially in the heart of the less advanced districts where the need of clearing and cultivation is most felt. To these colonies persons found guilty of laziness and vagrancy should be sent for a definite time, and the cost of their lodging, food, and transportation should be set aside out of their earnings.[1] Laziness can be overcome only by obligatory work, just as the muscular inertia of a limb that has remained for a long time in enforced idleness can be corrected only by continued movement, violent and often even painful. After the pastor of Badelschwing, as a measure to prevent begging and vagrancy, had introduced in Westphalia a colony of free workers, who cultivated barren strips of territory, 12 other provinces followed this example, and by this measure there were 15,000 more laborers at work in the country. Since then the number of convictions for vagrancy and begging has diminished a third. An institution of this kind brought down the convictions for vagrancy in the canton of Vaud by a half. In Holland

[1] Hello, "Des Colonies Agricole Pénitentiares," 1865.

1800 persons with their families cultivating the frontiers of Drenta cost 24 francs per annum for each person, while eliminating mendicancy at the same time. The great distress in Baden in 1850, after the failure of the great building contractors, was relieved from 1851 to 1858 by the emigration of more than 12,000 artisans.[1]

§ 145. Coöperation

In Italy and in France the first help must always be furnished by the government and the ruling classes, because our people are not used to getting themselves out of difficulties by their own efforts alone. We must however attempt to bring it about that the more needy classes shall aid one another by coöperation and mutual assistance. The immense benefit which the financial contributions of these classes bring to the state should be turned to their profit by the substitution of collective for private capital.

§ 146. Charity. Benevolence

There is to-day, however, a degree of distress which cannot be relieved by the slow methods of coöperation, collectivism, and the insufficient and tardy measures of the state. An investigation carried on by my daughter Gina [2] upon the spot proved that of a hundred families of workmen in Turin, all of whom were employed, 50% were always in debt and 25% were beneficiaries of parochial charity, without which they would have been in danger of dying of hunger. These works of charity, once the sole help in time of distress, although insufficient, are still a necessary auxiliary, and will be so until advancing civilization replaces them with preventive measures.

We must endeavor, then, to have philanthropy cast off the old monkish habit and, inspired by the new spirit, march along the road of popular economic reform. In modernizing philanthropic methods the Anglo-Saxon and Germanic nations excel, among whom the Protestant religions have popularized charity

[1] Carpi, "Delle Colonie."
[2] "Inchiesta di Gina Lombroso su 100 Famiglie Operaie," Turin, 1897.

by freeing it from ecclesiastical bonds and putting it directly in touch with the heart of the people — the best method of discovering and relieving secret distress. In England and Switzerland charity ingeniously makes use of the aid of the poor in helping the poor. Unemployed mothers, for example, are set to care for the children of those that are at work. Lodging houses are established as temporary homes for domestic servants and employment bureaus are set up for those who need work. The whole machinery works so perfectly that only small charitable contributions are necessary to maintain the institutions, while at the same time the self-respect of the beneficiary is maintained.

Geneva,[1] for example, which is one of the few cities of Europe where crime is decreasing, has 400 philanthropic institutions, including the following: 35 for children, of which 7 are for taking them to the baths, 5 for protection at home, 1 recreational, 2 schools of apprenticeship, 1 industrial, and 1 musical; 16 for old people, of which 5 are asylums, 1 for pensions at home, 10 for insurance; 48 for women, of which 4 are asylums for young girls, 1 for fallen women, 4 for unemployed domestics, 8 hospitals (5 for domestics and 3 for young girls), 1 recreational, 1 against prostitution, 1 protective, 4 employment agencies, 7 for procuring work at home, 8 for the protection of teachers, children, etc.; 46 for men, of which 11 are for industrial accidents, 8 of various nationalities to facilitate the employment of emigrants, 3 for the unemployed, 4 for recreation and lecture halls, 4 for lectures, 1 against gambling, 1 to buy tools, 1 for placing apprentices, 9 temperance, 9 people's kitchens, etc., etc. The more special institutions are: societies for the improvement of lodgings, and for sanitary lodgings at a cheap price; special savings banks which receive money in small sums and repay it in merchandise bought at wholesale; family hotels for poor foreigners, workmen in search of employment, etc. One of the most characteristic of their institutions is the Old Paper Society. This society distributes sacks to a great many families, who return them at a certain time filled with old papers. With the proceeds of the sale of these the

[1] Lombard, "Annuaire Philanthropique Genevois," Geneva, 1893.

society maintains an office and an agency which receives old clothes and other articles from the rich, has them cleaned and repaired by the destitute, and then sells them at a moderate price, or gives them away to the needy. Other agencies procure work for poor women and take charge of the business of selling the proceeds of their labor.

It is a characteristic mark that these societies conduct themselves without need of patrons. The asylums, lodgings, etc., are never gratuitous. Those who take advantage of them pay a little — as little as possible and at intervals — but on the whole societies and asylums alike are maintained by those who enjoy the benefits of them. It is a sort of evolution of charity that takes away everything humiliating about it, and makes it a strong and efficacious assistant.

§ 147. London — Asylums, Refuges, Helps for the Poor

Similar institutions, or even better ones, exist in London, the only capital in the world where crime is decreasing. London has about 120 institutions, which in 1894 assisted more than 18,000 individuals, at an expense of £173,000. The aged have naturally the greatest number of retreats (20), and after them the widows. There are establishments of all sorts, for those belonging to different trades, nationalities, and religions, for old married couples, for the support of the poor in their own homes, night-refuges, employment agencies for sailors; there are societies for the care of alcoholics, for the care of the children of prisoners, and for poor prisoners themselves. All these institutions are connected with one another and directed by central committees.[1]

§ 148. (1) *Emigration Societies*

Several societies make it their business to put a check to the increase of crime by encouraging emigration, particularly to Canada. They furnish information and aid, and organize expeditions of adults or of infants. In 1894 they directed the emigration of 7565 persons.

[1] Low, "Handbook to the Charity of London," 1895–96.

§ 149. (2) *Employment Societies*

There are 21 societies whose sole object is the procuring of employment, while others find places for boys as bootblacks and cabin-boys.

§ 150. (3) *Orphanages*

The concern felt for children is shown especially by the 60 asylums, which cared for 20,199 orphans, at an expense of 172,340 francs; homes are found for others with respectable parents, who are recompensed in this way for their sobriety; and, finally, children with sick fathers and mothers are considered, with a breadth of view quite exceptional, as being orphans and are treated as such.

§ 151. (4) *Institutions for Neglected Children*

Institutions more directly prophylactic are unquestionably those which have for their object the care, protection, and instruction of deserted children, as well as for giving temporary care to children whose parents while at work would otherwise have to leave them uncared for. There are about sixty such societies, which in 1894 saved 32,300 children from the dangers of the street, at an expense of 119,246 francs.

§ 152. (5) *Schools*

These institutions are subdivided into free schools, night schools, and vacation schools. Certain of them furnish food and clothing, and they are often designed for different classes of the population. There are about 40 of them, and in 1894 they gave instruction to more than 16,000 children.

§ 153. (6) *Care for Prisoners, Convicts, etc.*

The institutions directly applied to the diminution of criminality (societies to aid released prisoners, for protecting women in peril, temperance societies, refuges for alcoholics, societies for moral propaganda, etc.), numbered 84 in 1894, and assisted more than 67,000 individuals. Among these 36 are designed especially for women released from prison, whether fallen or criminal, or simply in danger of becoming so. Such are those societies whose object is to protect domestic servants against the perils of their position.

§ 154. (7) *Mutual Aid Societies*

Finally, the mutual aid societies also specialize as to trades, nationalities, religions, etc. There are 68, which in 1894 aided 33,340 individuals with a total of 218,796 francs.

The following is a résumé for the year 1894 of those charitable institutions of London which may have some effect upon criminality:

	Number of Beneficiaries	Amount expended
		Francs
Societies for the care and assistance of prisoners	67,577	176,030
Emigration societies	7,565	30,627
Employment agencies	4,840	26,290
Orphan asylums	20,199	172,341
Institutions for poor and neglected children	32,354	119,246
Educational institutions	16,019	108,261
Asylums, refuges, etc.	18,057	172,999
Mutual aid societies	33,340	218,796
Total	199,951	1,024,590

But the societies which deserve the greatest consideration are those which have for their object the protection of children. The English National Society for the Prevention of Cruelty to Children (imitated upon an even larger scale in New York), did not limit itself, as would have been the case in France or Italy, to securing the passage of a law. It wanted to introduce the idea and practice of justice toward children in all ranks of society, and its efforts have been crowned with success; 25,437 children, abused in every sort of way, have been rescued from those who were torturing them; 62,887 victims of negligence, suffering from hunger and cold, have received the necessities of life; while at least 603 children have been kept from mendicancy. This society, in 10 years, has been able to rescue from vice, hunger, and crime 109,304 children. While protecting these children it received more than 47,220 complaints against those who were maltreating them. Of these, 5313 remained unknown; in the case of 38,895 the society limited itself to a reprimand; 5792 it prosecuted, always with increasing success, for from the first to the second period of its existence the percentage of acquittals fell from 10.2% to 5.5%. According to the investigations of the society, the parents most cruel to their children are always those with some means. This is to be explained by the effect of the abuse of alcohol, and by a new form of criminality, for the practice of which the parents must have money on hand. This criminal device is the insuring of the life of the child whose death is awaited, hoped for, and even hastened by the beneficiaries. According to the horrible confession of one of the persons accused, certain children are worth more dead than alive. In five years the society has taken up the cases af about 19,000 maltreated children, representing for their parents a value of £95,000.

But, in order to reach such a result, and to penetrate so deeply into the most secret recesses of the criminal world, recesses almost always hidden even from the eye of the regular police, it was necessary for the society to avail itself of every assistance, even that of the administrators of the poor funds and Parliament itself. The society obtained the aid of the magistrates and judges, who, after having seen its work, recognized its competence, and have ended by giving its inspectors an almost official dignity. Better even than this, the society has obtained the coöperation of the masses. In the 10 years of its existence it has received proof of the sympathy and approval of 100,000 citizens who have facilitated the work of justice by bearing testimony. All these efforts together have brought about singularly happy results, and rarely has a second trial been necessary. Of 7398 persons against whom sentence was given, 6700 are living to-day with their children, and only 100 have had to appear in court a second time.

To what is one to attribute so marvelous a change in the parent? In great part to the punishment, the efficacy being in proportion to its duration; for the degree of improvement in the conduct of the parents toward their children corresponds in general with the number of months that they have had to spend in prison. We may add that during the imprisonment of the parent the society does not abandon the children, but, instead of the pale, miserable creatures that they were, has them flourishing and robust to turn over to their parents. When these see their children looking so well they are proud of them, and a certain natural parental love is awakened, which helps in the process of reformation. Strange contradiction of human egoism! The father formerly held his victim responsible for diseases of which he himself was the cause, and now takes pride in a show of health to which he himself has contributed nothing.

§ 155. Charity in Latin Countries

In comparison with what is done in the places just described, how limited appears the charity of Latin countries! Turin, a city three times the size of Geneva, has but 159 workingmen's societies, for mutual aid, etc., and 147 charitable institutions, of which 21 are hospitals; 43 institutions are designed for children, of which two are for delinquents, 23 are asylums for infants, 6 orphanages, 3 recreational, and 6 industrial schools. There are also 22 institutions for women, of which 11 are for those in danger, 2 are hospitals, and 9 professional schools. Among the most modern of the institutions are: a society for workmen meeting with misfortune while at work, a people's bureau, pensions for men without families (in return for payment), and a mountain and a seaside resort maintained for outings for poor children. Finally, there is the Cottolengo Institute, which receives all the sick, weak, and infirm who present themselves, up to 2000 or 3000. In southern Italy, Bartolo Longa, for the honor of the Virgin and the sanctuary at Pompeii, took 136 orphans, and 70 children of convicts, whom he instructed in agriculture and in various trades. Here the cult of the Virgin came into partnership with modern journalism,[1] by means of which the philanthropist succeeded in placing the orphans in benevolent and respectable families.

What is lacking here is: institutions to receive small savings; societies to improve the lodgings of the poor; employment bureaus and servants' lodging-houses, which need cost the philanthropist nothing, as they are self-supporting; and institutions preventive of theft. Aside from the orphan asylums, none of the institutions receive children below 10 or 12 years, and we have, moreover, neither boarding schools nor "ragged schools." Furthermore, these institutions show such excessive modesty, such a shrinking from all publicity, that I have gathered the data with great difficulty, and of a great many of them it is impossible to know anything.

§ 156. Don Bosco

Among the charitable institutions of Turin, that of Don Bosco holds the first place; for, with us charity is only truly marvelous when it appears in the person of some saint, great both in heart and intelligence, like the very justly celebrated Don Bosco.[2]

Don Bosco was 26 years old in 1841, when, while visiting the prisons of Turin, he became interested in the lot of the young delinquents, thinking that if care had been taken of them in time many of them might have been saved. From then on he received into his community the young workmen who were most exposed to temptation, getting work for them when they did not have it and visiting them at their labors. In 1850 he founded the Mutual Aid Society, the object of which was to furnish aid to the members who fell sick, or were destitute because of the lack of work. Each one pays five centesimi every Sunday, and cannot take advantage of the benefits of the society until he has been a member for six months, except where

[1] "Valle di Pompei," Anno VI, 1896.

[2] G. Bonetti, "Cinque Lustri di Storia dell' Oratorio Salesiano," Turin, 1892; Dr. D'Espinay, "Don Bosco," 1890; D. Giordani, "La Gioventù di Don Bosco," 1886; Id., "La Carità nell' Educazione," 1890; F. Cerruti, "Le Idée di Don Bosco," 1886.

he has paid down his six months' fees upon entrance, not being sick nor out of work at the time. Each sick member receives eighty centesimi a day. In Don Bosco's institutions young people of all classes of society are received, including deserted children. Don Bosco himself maintains that one-fifteenth of the youths are natural perverts.

The Salesians (or brethren of St. Francis of Sales) believe that the system of their institution exercises a beneficent influence even upon perverts, though they are not able to furnish any direct proof. Moreover, they refuse to receive incorrigibles, those who have reached the age of 14 or 15, convicts, and epileptics. There are about 200 Salesian institutions for young people in the two hemispheres. Each contains 150 inmates, or a total of about 30,000, to which must be added an average of 100 day scholars, etc., or 20,000 more. The inmates are admitted into the schools at 9 years of age and into the workshops at 12. After their admission these young people are kept under observation in separate rooms during the time set apart for food and rest, but not during working hours. They are not compelled to take part in religious exercises, though advised to do so; and no special favor is shown to those who are especially zealous in this regard. Each workshop has a clerical and a lay director. The tools and the designs are the work of the Salesians themselves. There are, besides, 50 institutions for young girls, with an average of 100 inmates and 280 day pupils. These are exclusively for instruction and for household work. But even the Salesian institutions follow the fatal tendency of the Latin nations, by admitting an excessive number of young people to classical studies (more than 500 in the institution at Turin alone), as if the country had not greater need of energetic workmen than of decipherers of musty tomes.

§ 157. Dr. Barnardo

Let us now look at the miracles of a Protestant saint.[1] One cold evening in the winter of 1866, Dr. Barnardo, who was

[1] Paolo Lombroso, "Le Case di Barnardo a Londra," 1896; "The Barnardo Homes," "Night and Day," London.

then studying medicine, and directing a "ragged school" on his free evenings, when just on the point of leaving the school, saw that one child remained in the room, standing next to the stove, without any apparent intention of leaving. Barnardo, by dint of many questions, succeeded in learning that the boy had neither father, mother, friends, nor lodging, that he slept here and there wherever he could, in the places least frequented by the police, and that many other children did the same. Moved by such excessive misery, Barnardo wanted to be sure of the truth and begged the child to guide him to the retreat of his companions in misfortune.

At one o'clock in the morning he went out with his guide, and after having passed through one of the worst quarters of London, they penetrated into a narrow court, traversed a long shed, and found themselves before a very high wall. Up this wall the boy climbed, followed by the doctor. Here a strange spectacle presented itself to their eyes: upon a very steep roof, with their heads toward the ridgepole and their feet in the gutter, lay 10 or 12 boys of from 12 to 18 years. It was there, in the midst of these pale figures of distress, that Barnardo made his vow to devote himself body and soul to that rescue work which became from that night the sole object of his life. A poor student and unknown, he yet succeeded in getting from charitable persons the sum necessary to rent a small house, capable of holding 20 children. When his refuge was ready he spent two nights in gathering in his boys from the streets. "I could not possibly," he says, "imagine or depict a more touching scene than that first night in the little old house, when, before going to sleep, my first family of 25 children knelt with me to thank our common Father for His goodness and to pray that He, who feeds even the sparrows, would not fail them in their need."

This house, opened with 25 children, prospered, and was speedily duplicated. In less than 30 years the number of houses increased to 87, which have received more than 50,000 children, from a few weeks old up to 18 or 20 years. In addition there have been founded a great variety of complementary institutions: free dispensaries, schools for the poor, Sunday schools, free kitchens, night-lodging houses, children's colonies in the country, employment agencies, temperance societies, soup-kitchens, agencies for immigrants and emigrants. It is strange to see from what a peculiar mixture of idealism, practical understanding, quick comprehension, and blind trust in God this colossal work has arisen. In each of the numerous cases which Barnardo reports, he notes as a moral conclusion what the saving of that individual cost. "With £10 sterling and the help of God," the doctor concludes, mathematically and ingenuously, "a life has been saved." In his paper, "Night and Day," published in the interest of his houses, we find notices like this: "We need a good farm under cultivation, about 50 miles from London, etc."; and to this notice, given with such simple confidence, is added a list of the needs of his great family of 8000 children: stockings, night-gowns, bed-clothes, sewing-machines, a harmonium, old linen for new-born children, and finally a magic lantern.

The same bold grasp with which Barnardo began his work of child-saving he applied to the art of finding the means of subsistence for his institutions. For this army, which grew to a total of 100,000, he took the public alone for collaborator, but he organized the work so that he had something for every one to do. Those who have money give it, and those who have none give their work, if not every day, then one day in the week. We may say of Barnardo that he knew how to transform sympathy into money, and then to recast it as charity.

In this matter how far the Anglo-Saxons have gone beyond the Latins!

§ 158. The Ineffectiveness of Charity

However useful it may be, charity is, after all, but an ineffective palliative against an immense amount of need and distress. Unavoidably subject to human passions, charity depends not only upon economic conditions, but also upon the sentimental condition of men. The effect of an intermittent pity or of the caprice of the moment, it never completely attains its end, and, considering the vastness of the abyss, is not capable of filling it up by the strenuous efforts of individuals adapted to the need. Even if the rich wish to restore in this way a part or even the whole of what has been acquired, for the most part, by means quite other than honest, it is not possible. It is as if, after shearing a lamb, one should try to fasten the wool once more upon its back. The intention might be good, but the wool would not grow again.

Three-fourths of the cases of distress, in fact, escape this remedy, and those who are helped by it are helped insufficiently and badly, entirely apart from the fact that a third of the money spent for charity goes for administration, and so comes again into the coffers of the well-to-do. Many institutions, charitable in name, merely serve to keep the poor in subjection to the church. Thus I have seen aid refused to a family simply because one of its members read a newspaper which was not even irreligious, and many times in order to get bread the unfortunate are obliged to be present at religious services as often as three times in a day, losing thereby more time than would have been needed to gain by working the means of satisfying their hunger.

Then, however disguised it may be, public charity does not usually give its help to the person who, though most needy, is also most sensitive and feels most keenly the shame of receiving alms. It debases man instead of relieving him, since it extinguishes in his heart all sense of personal dignity, and takes away every spontaneous impulse to struggle and win his own place in life.

For eighteen hundred years the saying of the gospel, "Quod superest, date pauperibus," has been preached, and yet social evil and misery have become greater and greater. If this maxim was little heeded when the religious sentiment was still very quick and general, why should it be heeded to-day, in conditions so little favorable, in a society like ours, where each one is obliged to look out for his own interests? Earlier, when small land-holdings were the rule, when communication was little developed, the landed proprietor or the master-workman could always, or nearly always, give work to the few people who asked for it. But if nowadays you were to ask the manager of a large factory to give work to all the unemployed who knock at his door, he would tell you — and rightly — that if he followed your advice he would fail at the end of a week. Now, supposing the sentiment of charity were to prevail, what could alms to individuals do against the tide of unemployment and distress which, in modern society, affects a great and continually increasing multitude of persons? Thus, the best of our institutions, mountain resorts, hospitals, etc., for the cure of poor children, only lower the morbidity and mortality from 50% to 47%. Now, by preventing night work for the young, by giving lunches to school-children, you will see this morbidity and mortality diminish in much greater proportion than with all those other institutions.

Charity and want are related to each other as two parallel lines, which can never come together, while, by having recourse to the human interests, with egoism for ally, it is possible to fill up the gap between them. Thus, the adoption of the eight-hour working day, while economizing the powers of the workman, would permit the employment of a greater number, and at the same time allow better work. The workman, now absorbed by the hard labor of the shop, which is killing him, would be able to busy himself with his family, experience the sweetness of family life instead of the mere burden of it, and be able to acquire a greater degree of culture, which would be a new weapon against crime. It is by work equitably distributed among all the unemployed, more than by charity, that the condition of the poor may be improved economically and morally. The collective control of the necessities of life, which is now limited to schools, lighting, baths, and sometimes to hospitals and tramways, if extended in the same way to food, housing, and clothing, would be a complete substitute for the charity of former times, and the true preventive of all occasional crimes. Further, by preventing the excesses and dangers of poverty and of riches, it would be useful to all classes; for the insect and the microbe which convey the diseases of the poor to the mansions of the rich are truly the Eumenides punishing the rich for forgetting the poor, just as the famine, that originates in the speculation of the rich, multiplies diseases among the poor, and these in turn come back upon those who caused them. One may say the same of many of the occasional crimes caused by the neglect of the poor on the part of the rich. Theft, anarchy, murder, and revolt are simply evil consequences coming back upon the heads of those who set the cause in motion.

CHAPTER V

RELIGION

§ 159.

IT is time to free ourselves from the atavistic tendency, which has survived unnoticed even in the most scientific observer, to regard religion as a universal panacea for crime. Let us recall how slowly we have been freed from the religious shell, from which have come the first attempts not only at morals, but also at art and science, so that once no one could be painter, sculptor, poet, architect, or physician, without first being priest (Spencer). But at length art and science, those noble plants that grew up modestly in the shadow of the temple, are completely freed from its influence, and there remains to the priest, who once dominated every department of knowledge, a monopoly not even of morals and charity; for many profess a charity and an ethics apart from religion, and on all sides there are rising ethical societies, free from all rites.

We cannot, then, find in religion, at least as it is understood in Latin countries, a remedy against crime.

"The true morality," we may say with Sergi,[1] "is instinctive; the moral sense is like the feeling of pity; if it does not already exist, neither religious nor educative influence, nor any precept, will be able to create it.

"Religion is a system of instruction by precepts, which have, like all other moral rules, an exterior sanction remote from reality and the daily life; and not only is it not able to fortify the character, but, on the contrary, it can only enfeeble it, by minimizing the personality by asceticism even to the point of annihilation.

"It is from religion that springs the monstrous phenomenon of men externally religious and respected for ecclesiastical and divine authority, and yet at the same time immoral in their social relations."

1 "Tribuna Giudiziaria," 1896.

But how is it, some one will ask, that religion shows itself at times as a useful moral force against crime? We reply, that religion can have a beneficent influence only when, being in a nascent state, it can transform itself into a violent passion. "Delia" furnishes us with a magnificent example of such a transformation.[1]

Delia lost her mother at an early age, and was carefully brought up in a convent. Seduced in the first place by a young lawyer, and then ravished by a priest while under the influence of a narcotic, she abandoned herself to a life of prostitution and drunkenness. She was three times sent to correctional institutions, and finally released because she refused all food while imprisoned. She joined a band of thieves, of which she soon became the head because of her energy and muscular agility. She fought with the police and with her own companions, so that she was arrested seven times. She aided thieves in their exploits; but she would not permit the weak to be struck in her presence, and would defend them at the risk of her own life. She was devoted to the sick, took care of them, and defended them against those who wanted to rob them. The police called her the "Wonder," but her companions called her the "Bluebird," doubtless from the color she preferred. A missionary, Mrs. Whittemore, on the 25th of May, 1891, went into the dives of Mulberry Bend, where she gathered these thieves together and tried to hold a religious service; but being excited by the arrest of two men of their band, they would not even let her sing. They would certainly have revenged themselves upon the missionaries if these had not been protected by Delia, who afterward accompanied them into the opium dens of Mott Street, where the worst criminals in New York assemble. Upon leaving her Mrs. Whittemore gave her a rose, which she made a half-mystical omen, begging her to be converted and to come to her with the flower. But the Bluebird answered, that as for money, she found it quite natural to take it from any one who had it; as for the rest, she added, "I have committed already all the sins that it is possible for me to commit, and I should

[1] Whittemore, "Delia."

not be able to live in any other way" (she was then twenty-three years old). She promised, however, to come to one of the mission halls, and kept her word. In the evening she went to return her enchanted rose, and confessed that she had passed a very troubled day, trying to drown her doubts in drink; but the more she drank the more she became the mistress of herself. In the evening, perceiving that the flower was withering, she became thoughtful, and recalled the days when she too was pure, like the rose. She saw the years falling away one by one like the petals of the flower; and immediately her resolution was taken, and she told her companions that she was quitting them. The same evening, with tears in her eyes, she presented herself at the mission, where Mrs. Whittemore embraced her tenderly, and asked her to pray with her.

From that day she gave up drink, opium, and tobacco, and asked to be allowed to go to see one of her old boon companions in prison, in order to convert him. She was sent to the hospital very ill with consumption and syphilis. When, on coming out, she was invited to drink, she resisted the inclination. When she was cured she set herself to work to convert her old companions of Mulberry Bend. She also addressed 1500 convicts at Auburn. "What have we gained," she said, "by serving the devil? Prison, misery, contempt, and disease. When I was at my worst and delighted in making others afraid of me, I was myself often afraid, and would not go to bed without a bright light burning beside me. In the morning I used to ask myself whether I would not lie in prison that night. I remember that when a lady once said to me, 'Have you found Jesus?' I replied, 'No, is he lost!' for I hated the Protestants. My religion was purely one of form. If you ask me how much time it took me to give up my life of sin forever, I will answer you: about three minutes, the time it took to ask God to do it." In 11 months she converted more than 100. She died of consumption within the year, but the stir that she made was so great that after her death 80 of her companions became, or appeared to become, honest.

I do not guarantee the conversion of these last, but that of

Delia is certain. This is proved by the change in her face as shown by her photographs. But it must be remembered that she was led to a life of prostitution and crime, not by precocious criminality but by a rape committed while she was drugged. Further, even in her criminal career, she was always the protectress of the weak. It is plain, then, that she was rather a criminaloid than a born criminal. However that may be, the promptitude of her conversion (it was, she said, an affair of three minutes) under the influence of a suggestive impression, and, further, the ardor that she brought to it, both go to prove that in this case the religious passion, in the nascent state, stifles all the other passions.

Similar cases may be adduced, like that related to me by the Baptists, of a drunken thief who was converted at a stroke by the sermons and example of the missionaries, and persevered in the right way. But these are absolutely individual, and cannot be cited in favor of religion. They furnish no proof that religion as organized with us, among whom these fruitful fanaticisms do not flourish, has any efficacy in the cure of criminality. It is to be noted, moreover, that these miracles occur especially among the Anglo-Saxons and Swiss. We are forced to conclude that what is commonly attributed to the influence of religion is really due to race and to advanced civilization, which carries these people towards great ideals and noble fanaticisms, while with the development of culture the religious sentiment each day grows weaker. It is thus that we find proofs of a noble zeal in the societies for ethical culture,[1] and among the Good Templars, which are ethical and anti-alcoholic rather than religious.

"In the Calvinistic countries," writes Ferrero, "religion enrolls thousands of fanatics, who, under the most diverse names and theories, are feverishly active, not in honor of a rite but in order to save the souls of men. In Italy, as in France, no one ever succeeds in bringing about a great flood of moral protest against the most serious social evils; and enthusiastic and active spirits must seek elsewhere for a field in which to employ their energy."[2]

[1] Pfungst, "Ueber die Gesellschaft für Ethische Kultur," 1896.
[2] "Vita Moderna," 1893.

Take the Salvation Army, for example.[1] This institution was founded by Booth, under the most eccentric exterior forms, with a military hierarchy and bizarre uniforms, but with the holiest and soberest intentions. It is a sort of a sect that has for its aim the prevention and combatting of vice and crime, even with the strangest weapons. It contends against alcoholism with meetings, cheap temperance hotels, "elevators," and people's kitchens (which last in 1895 distributed 3,396,078 meals). It fights vagrancy with dormitories, which give lodgings every night to more than 4100 persons, where many persons are converted by evangelistic meetings. The Salvation Army puts within reach of the unfortunate everything that may be able to draw them from evil ways; it enrolls them in employment agencies, which in the year 1895 alone found work for 19,372 persons; or receives them into its "elevators," special establishments, where they are employed at paid work or taught a trade if they have none, until situations can be found for them. Or they may be placed in the farm-villages of the Army, with which they may remain in relation for four years. For convicts the Salvation Army has addresses in the prisons. It enrolls the more promising subjects as soldiers in the ranks, and admits another part of them into a special establishment, where it attempts to repair the defects of their moral and practical education, especially by teaching them a trade. From here they pass to the "elevators" and then into the employ of private individuals, or to the farm-villages, etc. The Army owns, besides, 84 bureaus for the unfortunate, the office of which is the direct and personal effort to conquer vice. In a year they visited about 58,723 poor families in private houses, 15,702 persons in public-houses, and 7500 in lodging houses, giving assistance to at least 3887 sick persons. The army also maintains special institutions for children, who are sent as speedily as possible to the country. For women the army maintains 9 special dormitories, and 13 Rescue Homes, which almost literally snatch women from public-houses and other doubtful resorts. They give employment to 1556 women, and

[1] White, Park, and Ferrari, "Truth about the Salvation Army," London, 1892; Booth, "Light in Darkest England," London, 1892.

after a certain time find places for them in private houses, or send them to their farms. It is remarkable to see how quiet a reception these new soldiers of charity meet with. Their houses, "elevators," and farms are open, and any one who wishes can go in or come out; and one who has left and comes back again is always received as a prodigal son, and enjoys complete liberty.

The principle of the work of the Wesleyans is not radically different. When Marcus, one of their leaders, had revealed the horrors of the condition of the poor of London, they threw themselves headlong into the work of converting the vicious and alcoholic.[1] Hughes, one of their great apostles, said in a sermon, "We must not be so wrapped up in saving the soul that we forget to save the body," and with the accents of the profoundest conviction he carried hundreds of persons with him, who professed themselves converted and confided themselves to his pastoral guidance. They choose the hours when men are most in danger, the social hours as they call them, between 9 and 11, invite them to evening gatherings, treat them well, and get them to sign the pledge. They visit the most infected places, where their sisters discover and save the women who are in danger. One of them one day saw a young girl being led into a public house by a libertine. Accosting her she said, "Remember that you are a woman," and kissed her on the forehead. The girl, much moved, replied, "I will never go into a public-house again; but take us in every evening, if you do not want us to fall into evil again."

In the "Protestant Association for the Practical Study of the Social Question," we find partisans of the idea of the participation of labor in the benefits of capital. Lord Shaftesbury, who transformed the condition of the miners in England, advocated also insurance against industrial accidents.[2]

The order of Good Templars, founded in New York in 1862, and that of the Blue Cross, founded in Geneva in 1877, number respectively 500,000 and 10,000 members, who are required to abstain for a certain time from all alcoholic drinks, and succeed

[1] "Revue du Christianisme Praticante," 1890–95; Malcolm Taylor, "Portraits and Pictures of the West," London, 1893; Marcus, "The Bitter Cry of the Outcast," London, 1893.

[2] "Travaux du Congrès de Montaubon," Paris, 1885.

in doing it. All this explains why it is that in Protestant countries, especially in Switzerland and England, alcoholism is decreasing, while it is increasing in Catholic countries.

Can we say that our Salesians and Sisters have accomplished more? Far from it! To attain similar results, or even to strive after them, there is necessary a degree of ideality not to be found in the old races, who shut themselves up within their ritual observances and reach their highest development in a dictator, whether he be pope, general of an order, or saint. This is a fact which I have directly demonstrated by putting side by side the work of Don Bosco and that of Doctor Barnardo. In Italy we see crime effectively combatted by rare individualities, but they are either dissenters, like Lazarretti, or at least have had for some time their center of action outside the orbit of the official church, like Don Bosco and St. Francis of Assisi. In either case they constitute, for the moment at least, a new religion, palpitating with life, and in a little time would form a schism, if the prudent statesmanship of Rome did not take precautions to draw them once more within the circle of her influence.

Hence it comes that saints like Don Bosco and Bartolo Longo do not arise without having obstacles everywhere placed in their way by those very ecclesiastical authorities who ought to build altars to them. It is for the same reason that when they wish to raise themselves up to the level of the advanced ideas of our own time they only half succeed; and instead of starting the children under their care in the more useful trades, on a large scale, by organizing emigration parties, or clearing the land, as Dr. Barnardo did, they succeed only in creating great monasteries, and in turning out priests and classical scholars for whom society has no place. They are saints, in short, of a time remote from our own, whose work, however vast it may be, is still necessarily short of the needs of the present, and rarely reaches the roots of crime. However admirable they may be for genius or sanctity, they must conform to the will of the higher authority and show that they have more at heart the triumph of the rites of Rome than that of virtue. If not, they are suppressed. Thus it is that Don Bosco had for his final aim the creation of Salesian priests; just as the object sought by Bartolo Longo was the worship of Our Lady of Pompeii. Now, even if, by giving to deserted children a trade and an education which was certainly moral, they prevented the occurrence of some accidental crimes, they could never in this way save the true criminaloid and criminal born.

We may conclude, then, by saying that ritual and liturgical formulæ are much more in evidence in institutions of this kind, than the rules necessary for a practical life.

On the other hand, in the Latin charities, the support of the public is almost never associated with that of the founder. It never manifests itself personally, and is consequently less interested and less efficacious; since the power of these great apostles lies completely in their own personality, they have all the merit and all the responsibility, and when they leave the scene they leave an empty place that cannot be filled. In the French orphan asylums, Joly tells us, for a long time only the religious interests of the children was thought of.[1] They were put into a brotherhood without being given any trade. Roussel also remarks that the church charities in France are all for young girls, so that neglected boys have no other refuge than the prisons and houses of correction; moreover, the Catholic orphanages almost never receive illegitimate children, and, unlike the Protestants, who try to throw as much light of publicity on their own organizations as possible, the Catholic institutions do all they can to escape it, and are never willing to report except to the bishop and to Rome. The pupils of the orphanages grow up without any knowledge of the world, and are consequently incapable of making a future for themselves.[2]

In conclusion we may say that Anglo-Saxon charity differentiates itself from the Latin still more fundamentally through taking particular care to preserve the self-respect of its beneficiaries, by making use of their services, by making itself, in fact, coöperative and mutual; and it concerns itself especially with the very young, to whom Latin charity pays little atten-

[1] Joly, "Le Combat contre le Crime," p. 91.
[2] Roussel, "Enquête sur les Orphelinats," 1882.

tion, feeding them at most. Among the Anglo-Saxons we see religious groups like the Salvation Army and the Baptists proposing, as their great aim in life, redemption from crime, the prevention of alcoholism, and the care of infancy. And if the influence of individual men, like Booth and Barnardo, through their inspiration and genius, counts for much in the search for better methods, they are not indispensable, for there is always a legion of fellow-workers, who by their numbers and enthusiasm ensure the support of the public.

Here then, it is not religion in general, that deserves the credit, but certain religions only, or, better still, the ideal tendency of certain progressive races. However, we must say of the operation of religion, as we have said of that of charity, that it is always individual, limited, and less effective than the economic influence, which alone is universally felt by the masses.

CHAPTER VI

THE DANGERS OF INSTRUCTION — EDUCATION — REFORM SCHOOLS, ETC.

§ 160.

TO say that the influence of mere instruction upon crime is beneficent is an exaggeration in which no one any longer believes. To instruct the criminal is to perfect him in evil, and to give him new weapons against society. It is necessary above all to suppress the schools in the prisons, which serve only to multiply recidivists, as I have shown in the first and second volumes of my "Homme Criminel." Let us seek, on the contrary, to extend education to the greatest possible number of honest persons; let us strengthen the body, occupying it pleasantly with gymnastics, marches, and dances in the open air;[1] let us prevent idleness and precocious lasciviousness, more by these means than by simple precepts. It would also be necessary to choose married teachers by preference, and to suppress the schools in monasteries and convents. When in the elementary schools a child is found who has the known marks of the born criminal, he must first of all be separated from the others and given a special training with the object of strengthening the inhibitory centers, always underdeveloped with this class, and of subduing or diverting the criminal tendencies by supplying them with a new outlet, while preventing the pupil from acquiring dangerous arts. Let us recall here the confession of born criminals themselves, that education was for them a powerful auxiliary to evil. It is the more to be feared nowadays when political conditions permit born criminals, who have received an education, to have easier access to political power than honest men have, because of the corrup-

[1] Physical training is a school of continence and chastity. A society for the cultivation of morals would attain its end better by giving the youth a taste for gymnastics, etc., than by sermons.

tion, violence, intrigue, and fraud which dominate in the political world. How many misfortunes, how much blood, would not Italy and France have been spared if Napoleon, Boulanger, and Crispi had been illiterate!

In order that the school may be useful, not negatively as now, but positively, we must change the basis of our education, which, at present, by its admiration of beauty and force, leads to idleness and violence. We must place in the first rank special schools for agriculture; and in the other schools we must give first place to manual work, in this way substituting something practical and exact for the nebulous mirages of the antique. This course, coupled with very heavy taxes upon universities, would relieve us of this deluge of the "declassé,"[1] which we increase daily by new university facilities.

"Up to the present," writes Sergi, "the school has debated upon the best way to teach the alphabet, how it is possible to learn to write soonest, and what is the best method of developing the intelligence; but it does not teach us any method of directing our feelings and impulses. Education, like hygiene, is designed to preserve sound health. Now any director or teacher of hygiene must necessarily know how to discriminate between normal and disturbed functions, must be able to recognize what causes disturbance and to prevent it. The same is true of the educator. He must know the nature of the human soul; how it works and acts individually and in society; what organic causes may alter its manifestations; and what external and social causes may disturb its normal functions. Our educators are not educated in this sense. They enter the schools to bring up the children, without any definite conception of the difficult end they are supposed to attain. Each little human being who goes to school is a problem with several unknown quantities, but he is treated as a problem already solved!

"In place of increasing the number of classical schools, reduce them to the minimum, and transform all the others into schools of business, arts, and trades, professional and practical schools corresponding to the demands of modern life. Introduce into these schools the cultivation of the intelligence and character needed for daily life; by these means you will inculcate the habit of working, which is in itself a very efficacious education.

[1] Any one who doubts the truth of this assertion has only to recall the classicism of the revolutionists of 1789, and to read Valles's "Le Bachelier et l'Insurge," in order to become convinced that this instruction, out of harmony with the times, results only in making rebels and "declassés."

When we have numerous schools of arts and trades, manual labor will be ennobled, whereas now any one who wants to learn a trade must serve under a master-workman, and learns it by practice more or less badly. The principal object of every school should be the education of the character, upon which all conduct depends. It should strengthen it where it is weak, create it where it does not yet exist, and direct it where it lacks direction."

§ 161. Family Education

In this regard the family can accomplish far more than the teacher. No one has ever set himself to investigate what relation there is between success in school, and success or non-success in life; no one has investigated the relations between the physical and ethnic energies, typical of a young man, and the unforeseen contingencies and accidents of the life of the future citizen.[1] It is to this especially that the family should apply itself. Yet with us the family relies upon the school for the care of education, while the schoolmaster, for his part, who in any case could do little because of the great number of pupils demanding his attention, counts upon what the family is supposed to accomplish. Thus both remain inactive just where crime could be most effectively prevented. The family-public does not realize that into the integration of the state and the destination of the child, vocation and aptitudes enter as exponents and the lack of intellectual preparation as a coefficient; and that to obtain the integration there is needed the union and the continuity of all forces, including those for whose developments the parents must earnestly strive.

Yet very little is necessary to bring about this reform in education.

"The children of a loving mother," writes Garofalo,[2] "affectionate or severe as the case demands, become accustomed to watch for the approbation or blame in her look. What penalty can be greater than the grieved reproof which the mother gives

[1] Francis Galton, "On International Anthropometry," "Bulletin of the International Institute of Statistics," 1890; "Idea Liberale," 1896.

[2] "L'Educazione in Rapporto alla Criminalità," Rome, 1896. See also Desmoulins, "A quoi tient la supériorité des Anglo-Saxons," 1897.

the child who has lied or maltreated a companion? Such a child will acquire, month by month and year by year, an instinct opposed to falsehood, theft, and cruelty, a physiological aversion, thanks to which crime will be for him no longer possible. Then the problem of education will be solved."

Criminal anthropology has taught us that, given the temporary criminality common to children, we need not be dismayed at their first criminal acts, nor visit them with too severe penalties, when these acts are not too often repeated, and are not accompanied with the anthropological marks of criminality. Evolution toward the good takes place in the normal human being gradually, like the transformation of the lower forms in the fœtus. Only a bad education, by stimulating the perverse instincts which are merely effervescent in childhood, can make them become habitual instead of being transformed. Spencer shows us in his admirable book upon Education how much evil too strict an education can do, by irritating the child without convincing him that he has done wrong, and by not fitting itself to his natural instincts; an education, in short, that tries to get more than the child can give, forgetting the immense influence of sympathy, on account of which even adults regret having injured a sympathetic person more than one unsympathetic.

We ought, then, to make punishments milder and at the same time render them more effective by always adapting them to the character. Thus when a child has injured a valuable object, let us buy another at the expense of some delicacy that he would have had, thus showing him the consequences of his fault. When he does not obey our orders let us show him less sympathy, but not give way to anger, which, however brief it may be, is always injurious to the father as well as the child — to the father, because it is at bottom but a relic of savage vengeance, and to the child, because it produces in him a dangerous reaction. The child ought to be persuaded without being constrained by violence. We should prevent, rather than encourage, as many do, the association of ideas between bad actions and punishment, on account of which, when the surveillance of parent or teacher is removed, children no longer fear to do wrong. This is why the children of persons who have been too strict, upon arriving at adult years, often commit more faults, and even crimes, than the children of parents who were not so strict.

§ 162. Application of Psychology to Reformatories

These reasons have double force when it is a question of a juvenile delinquent, naturally inclined to anger and revenge, and likely to take punishment in bad part. Cruel by instinct, he becomes still more so in the reform school from the example of others, from the glory attaching to misdeeds, and from the too often justifiable reaction against punishments that are too severe for the gravity of the offence and the age of the offender. What sympathy can the head of such an institution inspire in the child, to whom he has only a fleeting relation and then only to inflict punishment? How can he keep watch of him day by day, in such a way as to change his habits, when it is a question of hundreds whom he can hardly oversee? How, finally, can he avoid the greater danger of new opportunities for evil-doing, when the mingling of so many perverse beings, proud of their own perversity, would be corrupting even for an honest person, and when the juvenile criminal encounters this at an age when unhealthy ideas spring up and grow with most vigor? [1]

New subdivisions in the reformatories are too much to expect. It is much if the inmates are separated according to age and cause of imprisonment. How shall masturbators, choleric persons, sexual psychopathics, thieves, and tormentors of animals be separated? It is important, however, to improve these institutions by a special selection. It is necessary not only to separate the youths from the incorrigible adults, but to attempt to group them according to age, degree of depravity, etc., for, grouped together, their vices will propagate themselves, instead of being corrected. The evil tendencies must be combatted by hypnotic suggestion, which is especially effective at this age and when periodically renewed forms a kind of habitual inclination toward the good. This is a proceeding analogous to that of which Spencer speaks in his "Education."

[1] We shall see in the following chapter how Brockway, under the inspiration of these pages, created the reformatory at Elmira, thus giving to my work the greatest reward that a thinker can hope for.

"Some carp, having been put into an aquarium with smaller fish, were in the habit of eating them; being separated from the others by a glass partition, they at first threw themselves against it in their endeavor to seize their prey, but seeing the uselessness of their efforts they ceased their attempts, and when the glass was raised they lived with the smaller fish without trying to eat them. Habit made them harmless, if not innocent. It is thus that a dog, trained by habit and education, ends by not stealing."

It is by this method that born criminals ought to be treated, avoiding harsh punishments which can only irritate them.

The measure most necessary, preventive isolation of the criminal, is considerably facilitated by new advances in anthropology; for the characteristics of physiognomy and cranium, taken together with biological characteristics and the excess of tendencies to evil-doing, assist powerfully in distinguishing the dominant and always increasing criminality of the born criminal from that which is found temporarily in the case of all children.[1] It appeared from recent studies made in Italy upon this subject,[2] that of 333 pupils examined, 13% showed serious cranial anomalies. Now of these abnormal individuals 44% were insubordinate, while of the pupils of normal type only 24% were insubordinate. Of the former, 23% were dull, and 27% inert; of the latter, 11% were dull, and 10% inert. Among the abnormal there were 10% incapable of any progress, and only 2% among those of normal type. Of the 43 with cranial abnormalities, 8 complained of headache, or of a feeling of heat in the head, and of incapacity for continuous work; 12 were impulsive, irascible, and unable to restrain themselves, while 6, true criminals born, lacked moral sense and committed without compunction the most serious offences.[3] The isolation of the born criminal, in these cases, prevents his perfecting himself in evil;

[1] "Homme Criminel," Vol. I, chap. 2.

[2] Vitali, "Studi Antropologici in Servizio alla Pedagogia," 1896.

[3] Joly ("Le Combat contre le Crime," etc., p. 116) did not find any born criminals in the schools that he examined. "We have the weak and abnormal," the schoolmasters answered him, "but they are generally mild and inoffensive." But somewhat later Joly is obliged to admit that there were those who had committed homicide, and that they were not to be found in the schools because not tolerated there. Now where were they before they were expelled?

and, what is more important, prevents fruit, congenitally rotten, from tainting hundreds that are sound.

Does this idea, which I think is new as applied to the prevention of crime, amount to nothing in its practical application? In England, when a child plays truant from school or is refractory when he attends, he is confined, after a regular trial, in a truants' school. Here they endeavor to give him immediately, from head to foot, the sensation of a new life. To this end his hair is cut, he is bathed, disinfected, and clothed in suitable garments. He is then placed in his own division and obliged to keep silence all the week, except on Sunday. He has to do his part in the work of the establishment, as well in tailoring and shoemaking, which alternate with gymnastics and military exercises. The little recluses know that it depends upon themselves alone whether they regain their liberty in a longer or shorter period. The first time, they stay generally only 8 weeks or less, at the expiration of which they are released with the admonition to attend the ordinary schools. Of those set at liberty 25% or 30% offend again, and are confined in the school for 4 months, and if they commit a third offence, for 6 months. If, after this, they are found to require more prolonged moral treatment, they are sent to the reform school.

The industrial schools receive children who have not been convicted, but who, because of their environment, are in danger. The reform schools receive the young delinquents convicted by the magistrates, county court, or court of assizes. They are confined, for a term not to exceed 5 years, in authorized and inspected schools. In short, the industrial schools are preventive establishments, while the reform schools, as their name indicates, are repressive and at the same time educational institutions, in which delinquent children are carefully separated from those simply vicious, and where the dangers of promiscuity are avoided by a careful division into small groups.

§ 163. Associations among Children

For the same reason it is necessary to watch all the scholastic institutions in order to prevent turning them into criminal centers. This is the way to check the development of criminal tendencies, which exist already in germ. The associations of street-boys in the great cities appear inoffensive, but they are, on the contrary, greatly to be dreaded. It is these that we should try to suppress with the greatest energy. "The children who do the mischief," said a school teacher to Joly, "are never alone, and when they get together it is never for any good."[1]

We have already seen in the "Homme Criminel" and in Part I of this work, how men, when they form associations, lose in honesty, even when they are senators, deputies, or academicians. It is natural, then, that this law should manifest itself in the time of childhood, when dishonesty is a physiological characteristic. It is easy to understand how much more serious the danger from these associations is when the children are orphans, or belong to families that are immoral or incapable of training them.

"We can say," says Spagliardi,[2] "that the majority of young tramps and vagrants do not become such from perversity or poverty, but from defective education and because they were drawn away by evil associations. How many times have we not heard respectable families say something of this kind: 'As long as our son remained in the country he was an obedient young man and full of promise; but since we have been established in Milan he has lost his respect and affection for his parents, and has robbed the house several times.' A boy 8 years old, of a good and respectable family, disappeared from the house of his parents for several days and was able to evade the most diligent search. When he was found he was never willing to tell where he had hidden. To what shall we ascribe these strange changes taking place in children of respectable families? Where do they find the means of living lives independent of their families and emancipated from them, if not with bands of vagrants?

"But if the children who make an ideal of this kind of life, found, on the contrary, that the first step they took in that

[1] Joly, "Le Combat contre le Crime," etc., p. 127. "When some of the children go wrong," said another schoolmaster to him, "it is almost always due to friendships that become too intimate. Two children, previously good, make doubtful disclosures to each other and mutually corrupt one another. It is still worse where the children are naturally bad. They have a tendency to form bands which have all the criminal characteristics, and employ a sort of argot among themselves." (*Ibid.*)

[2] "The Monist," Chicago, 1895.

direction brought them hunger, isolation, and strict surveillance, would it not be better for the family, and could not the family by this means make its authority effective? There are already strict ordinances for public hygiene, for policing the streets, for preventing contagion . . . ; why should there not be one limiting these associations, which are a hidden menace to society? While they are children, a police officer would be sufficient to reduce them to subjection. Let them alone, and some day they will be resisting charges of cavalry."

§ 164. Reform Schools

Some years ago the reform schools admitted 7688 children: those in Italy, 3770, in Belgium 1473, in Holland 1615, and in America 2400, all with the ostensible purpose of preservation and amendment. But we have shown how far these institutions are from being able to realize good results under the actual conditions of their organization, which brings all these perverse natures into contact with each other. This promiscuity becomes still more dangerous when these young prisoners come to be more than a hundred in number. They cease then to be individuals and become a crowd, which cannot be watched and developed in detail, even by the most able director, so that the most stringent rules end in failure. I speak not theoretically but after a detailed inquiry into numbers of these institutions, while remaining an admirer of the rare philanthropists who are at the head of some of them.

If sometimes in these reform schools I have noticed young people who were industrious, trained, and without bigotry, I cannot say the same of many others, in which, under the mask of a jesuitical mildness, vice flourished worse than ever. I have even observed in one of the better establishments in Milan some of these juvenile delinquents who, when questioned as to the cause of their confinement, lied brazenly, even in the presence of the director, a fact which proves that they had neither repented nor had any realization of their offences. To assure myself with regard to this I have observed several of these delinquents after their liberation. I have questioned them, and their answers and autobiographies proved to me how full even the better establishments are of the most infamous vices, such as pederasty, theft, and the Camorra, just as in the case of the prisons. So bad indeed was it that it even disgusted my informants, though they made no pretensions to virtue, and soon fell again into crime.[1]

In some of these establishments, at G. and M. for example, there prevails unpunished the custom of compelling the new arrivals to masturbate all the adults that desire it. At Ascoli the inmates set fire to the establishment with petroleum. At Ambrogiana three of them stabbed one of the guards to death, with no other motive than the pleasure of doing evil. The ruses that they employ are unbelievable. One of them, taking advantage of his occupation as carpenter, hollowed out a piece of wood, in which he concealed cigars, sausage, etc., to sell to his companions. Another hid a dagger in his straw mattress. A third concealed a gold piece under his enrollment number, so that he always had it with him when he changed his cell, a trick that never would have been discovered without his own confession. Of the youths whom we interrogated at the "Generala," 8% manifested no desire to amend, although they had committed the most serious crimes. "If young people of our age," they said, "have money for amusements, why have not we the right to get some for ourselves by stealing either from them or from others." Others added, "Whatever crime we may commit will not equal what we have endured in the reformatory." 3% resolutely denied their offences; 11% declared that they repented, but did so with an air of indifference which proved their insincerity; 5% went so far as to insult their parents. We have seen[2] that in these institutions tattooing is very prevalent, 40% of the inmates being marked in this way. This is a very grave sign; but there is another worse still, if possible: this is the use of a special argot.

If, however, by the most assiduous pains the young prisoners are really improved, this improvement disappears when they go back among adults. More than this, there is but one rule not only for all parts of the country but for all ages, whereas

[1] For detailed proof see the autobiographies and dialogues at the end of the 2d edition of the "Homme Criminel," Turin, 1878.

[2] "Homme Criminel," Vol. I, p. 338.

what is needed is a tutor and a matron for the children, and for the adults a real martinet. Joly also tells of reform schools in France that seem at first glance to be like paradise, but which, in reality, are so many hells. The discipline is very severe but at the same time inefficacious. Thus, for example, there is a punishment room where the children have to march around in an ellipse from morning till night, covering as much as 25 miles over the rough floor before going to lie down on their plank beds. In revenge, when eight or ten of them get one of the guards in a corner, they threaten him with blows or with an accusation if he does not do what they wish.[1]

Would not total neglect be better than such a system of education?

There exist, it is true, certain rare establishments which have at their head men remarkable for their philanthropy and for their keen insight as teachers. Such men are De Metz, Ducci, Rey, Obermayer, Spagliardi, and Martelli, who by their devotion make up for every lack. But these are exceptions upon which the state cannot count.

It is certain that the bad results of these reformatories are much less when the number of the inmates is more limited. Thus in France the public institutions which almost always had as many as 400 pupils showed a recidivism over 19%, while the private institutions, having an average of 150 pupils, showed only 11% to 12%; and in Switzerland and in the Grand Duchy of Baden, where there are never more than 50 pupils, recidivism falls to 4% and 2.5%; while in England it is 4% for the boys and 1% for the girls.

However these figures do not satisfy me completely. In the United States they count upon 33% of recidivism in the numerous reformatories. Tocqueville, after praising them as the ideal of penal reform, declares that of 519 children released, 300 relapse into crime, including nearly all those addicted to theft and drink, especially in the case of the girls. Of 85 girls released only 11 had excellent conduct and 37 good. Out of 427 boys, 41 were excellent and 85 good. Everyone will recall the pompous eulogies of the colony of Mettray, which, accord-

[1] "Le Combat contre le Crime," p. 145.

ing to the statistics of some years ago, was able to reduce recidivism from 75%, which had been the figure, to 3.8% (Despine). Now, a few years afterward Du Camp informed us that recidivism had risen again to 33.3%, a fact which he explained by the aversion of the Parisians to the country, which is generally the delight of the young. Yet Mettray has the ideal system for a reform school, for the children are divided into groups or families of 16 or 17, each living in a cottage with its own head and assistant head. How shall we believe the miracles told of the cellular reform school of la Roquette, which is said to have reduced recidivism from 15% to 9%,[1] when we see that a few years afterward a government commission found it necessary to suppress it? And the French statisticians, while for the period 1866–68 they estimated the recidivists at 17% in the case of public reform schools and at 11% in the case of private ones, confessed that half of those released had a bad reputation.[2]

Even if these statistics were exact, they would prove absolutely nothing, because the private institutions are apt to get rid of their worst subjects by transferring the insubordinate and idle to the government reformatories; and when once they have got rid of these, those that are left make a relatively good showing. We know, moreover, that however useful the reformatories might be for effecting a moral cure, yet the enormous expense that they entail and their limited number, considering the need, must always make them insufficient.

We may add that the possibility of putting children into an institution when they become undisciplined, and this without expense, makes many parents less active in watching over them, and at times even interested in having them misbehave. I have observed at the "Generala" five youths of well-known families, two of whom had incomes of more than 100,000 francs, whom greedy guardians or guilty parents had had confined under more or less grave pretexts, keeping them there at a franc a day and refusing them even the money necessary to buy a musical instrument or a book with which to make their shameful imprisonment a little more bearable.

[1] Biffi, "Sui Riformatori dei Giovani," 1870.
[2] Bertrand, "Essai sur l'Intempérance," 1875.

"I must remark," says the former chief of police, Locatelli, "that the legislative measures with reference to refractory children are being wrongly interpreted by our people. While the legislators passed them with the intention of more effectually preventing crime, the people, following a system of interpretation taught by self-interest, persist in considering them exclusively philanthropic; so that fathers of large families consider themselves authorized by the law to have those children who cause them most trouble and expense confined and educated at the expense of the state. As soon as the persons interested perceived that their applications were received with circumspection, the attempts were made more craftily. Demands for the commitment of the children were supported by ample testimony, often from very high sources, proving the incorrigibility of the minor in question. What is still more deplorable, parents often even went so far as to force the child into idleness and vagrancy by all sorts of artifices, as by cutting down his food, for example, or disturbing his sleep, in such a way, however, that the authorities could get no proofs."

For those who believe that these reform schools are a benefit to deserted children and orphans, I would say that these schools have hardly 8% to 13% of orphans, and 8% to 12% of step-children. They can be useful only in those rare instances when they really teach the young prisoner a trade. We may add that in no reform school, or in hardly any, is the system of isolation at night or a rigid rule of silence applied — regulations which would hardly be applicable in institutions half didactic, half industrial, and which would be continually evaded by the tricks of the prisoners.

If any one is greatly concerned at the thought of the harm which some of these children would receive if left in their demoralizing homes, let him think of the effect upon honest but weak young people who are brought into contact with the vicious in the reform school. Those among them who come from the country, where they could not learn evil or form bad associations because of lack of opportunity, find in the reformatory evil associations all prepared for them. I would permit reform schools, then, only in exceptional cases and for a small number of individuals, these to be classified according to age, aptitude, and morality. They should be separated at night, but should enjoy relative liberty with no mark of infamy.

I would have these schools admit only those who for their poverty could not be received in military and naval schools. As for the rich who would like to have their children confined in such a place, they ought to pay a heavy tax, proportioned to their income.

§ 165. Educational Methods

If we sometimes meet with success in our reform schools, notwithstanding their defective organization, it is due to the fact that there the young man becomes used to regular and continuous work, something that the born criminal commonly refuses. This latter fact makes it easier to recognize such criminals and separate them from the others, and thus it is made easier to develop the physiological honesty of habit in the youth whose defect is only the physiological sub-criminality of the child.

Don Bosco[1] has traced for us an excellent system for the education of young delinquents who are capable of reformation.

"The greater part," he says, "have an ordinary temperament and character, but they are inconstant and inclined to indifference. They should be advised and warned briefly but frequently, and encouraged to work by small rewards and a great deal of confidence, though without any relaxation of surveillance. Effort and care must be especially directed toward the class of unruly pupils, of whom there is about one in fifteen. But the vice most to be dreaded is lubricity. Any one of the inmates who persists in this must be expelled. The young prisoners must not be allowed to keep any money or article of value; in this way we may prevent theft and the bargaining to which the children are inclined, being natural traders. . . . The repressive system is plainly capable of keeping down disorder, but it is powerless to make the soul better; for although children easily forget punishments inflicted by their parents, they always remember those of their teachers. Repression may be useful in the army and, in general, with persons who are mature and prudent; but what is needed with children is the preventive system. This system, based entirely upon reason, religion, and love, excludes any violent punishment. To understand the advantages of this system it is necessary

[1] Bonetti, "Cinque Lustri di Storia dell' Oratorio Salesiano," Turin, 1892.

to remember the instability of the child, which makes him forget disciplinary rules and the punishments that he incurs, often transgressing a rule and making himself liable to a punishment of which, at the moment of acting, he never thought at all. He would certainly have acted quite differently if a friendly voice had warned him. It is necessary to see that the pupils are never alone, and to give them ample opportunity to run, jump, and shout as much as they like. Gymnastics, vocal and instrumental music, declamation, amateur theatricals, walks, — all these are effective means of procuring good discipline, at the same time being useful for morals and health. The subjects for presentation in the improvised theater must be carefully chosen and only respectable characters depicted."

§ 166. Moral Training through Adoption

It is, above all, the example of the teachers that has influence; for we are led more by example than by persuasion. Every effort must be made to find the exceptional teachers that are necessary; and when these are wanting, when a mixing of the different classes cannot be avoided, because of crowding and because the frauds of parents cannot be prevented, when there is not a cubicle for each inmate, and when good workshops are lacking, as is unhappily the case in Italy, then it is preferable to entrust the children to moral and energetic families at a distance from the corrupting influences of the city. The deserted child little by little becomes fond of the family that adopts him, brings them his first earnings, generally never leaves the home that has received him, and finds there a stable moral environment, which directs him to rectitude.[1] Thus in France, of 11,250 children sent to families in the country, only 147 finally had to be sent to the reform school.

§ 167. American Reforms — Placing in the Country

Here philanthropy must assume new forms, abandoning the methods of the monastery and the barracks, as well as those of abstract morals, which have no hold on a being inclined to crime. What is necessary is to inspire the person with a desire for property, a love of work, and a feeling for the beautiful.

[1] Joly, "Le Combat contre le Crime."

This adoption must be supplemented by emigration to distant lands or migration to the country. This is the only effective remedy, as Barnardo, Bosco, and Brace have proved. In 1853 professors, judges, clergymen, and rabbis formed a society to help vagrant children,[1] and established philanthropic workshops, where they might be received. But the competition of the regular shops prevented the success of this enterprise, and the boys themselves, for their part, objected to being objects of charity and preferred their liberty. The plan of giving them lodging at a low price was then thought of. Beds were furnished at 6 cents, and a bath and dinner at 4 cents.

But there was as yet no way of making the lodgers work; as for asking them directly to do so, that would have been to empty the establishment at once. In order to awake neither repugnance nor suspicion, the director entered one morning and announced that some one wanted an employee at $12 a month. Twenty voices were raised to offer themselves. "Very well," said the director, "but a good handwriting is necessary." General silence! "Well, then, if no one knows how to write, we will teach it to you in the evenings." Thus it was that the night schools were started. In 1869 and 1870 8835 boys made use of the lodging-house. In 10 years the total had reached 91,326, of whom 7788 had become good workers. The poor women objected to mingling with the well-to-do in the industrial schools, and accordingly schools have been created expressly for them, and food and clothes are promised those who conduct themselves well. Since then the number of girls arrested for vagrancy has diminished, and from 3172 in 1861 fell to 339 in 1871. Only 5 out of 2000 pupils went to the bad. The number of female thieves fell from 944 to 572; and there were only 212 girls under age arrested in place of 405, the former number. Still more was done for the boys. Primary schools of carpentry were opened, in which hot meals were served. Entertainments were organized with admission costing 4 or 5

[1] Brace, "Reports upon the Questions of the Program of the International Penitentiary Congress at Stockholm, . . . According to what principles institutions for vagrant, mendicant, and deserted children should be organized," 1877; Brace, "Dangerous Classes of New York," 1875.

cents. At first the children broke the windows and shouted "We don't want any schools!" But the very fact that they were under no compulsion to go overcame the most unwilling; and the objective methods of Froebel ended by winning them over completely.

The institution supplemented this work by placing children on distant farms, where their work is best utilized, and, in consequence, preferred, where they are free from the bad influences of the large and small cities, and where the worker, being in direct contact with his employer, is better watched than he would be if he were living with his own family.

The continual contact with a good housekeeper makes good domestic servants out of the girls, and the boys learn from their employer to be good farmers. Living in an atmosphere of kindness, sympathy, and industry, stimulated at the same time by a new self-respect and the hope of a better position, and, on the other hand, having no bad companions nor any temptation to steal, they abandon with their rags many of their vices and find in the various activities of farm life an outlet for their energy. When they are too delicate, the society pays for their support until they gain strength enough to work; but if they finally prove not to be strong enough, the society takes them back again.

In this way the society in less than 23 years has placed more than 35,000 children who were deserted and without refuge, to say nothing of the large number received into the industrial schools (21 day schools and 14 night schools) and in the lodging-houses (more than 23,000 in 1875). After the children have contracted habits of order and sobriety in the night schools and Sunday schools, they are placed in the country, and the whole work has not cost more than $2,000,000.

Many of these children are adopted by their employers; others have started new farms by their work, or have entered some profession. Many of the girls have become excellent mothers of families. Some of these young people change their situations, as all employees do; but few return to New York, and very few indeed, not more than 6 in 15,000, get into the courts. In New York, in fact, in the ten years following the establishment of this work there was a decrease in the number of

Vagrants	from	3829	to	994
Thieves	"	1948	"	245
Pickpockets	"	465	"	313

This is, according to Brace, the only institution really useful for vagrant children, who, crowded together, could only corrupt each other, while by this means we use the boy to improve the land, and the land to improve the boy. This is surely a good cure for criminality, and how effective it would be in certain parts of Italy!

There remain the children who are sickly and otherwise incapable of farm work. For these separate beds have to be kept in the schools themselves, as is done in the "ragged schools" in England.

§ 168. Day Reformatories for Children

When it is not possible to bring about the creation of benevolent institutions like that described above, they may be replaced by the institution advocated by Spagliardi, a reform school for day pupils, which is much easier to establish. This is a compulsory day school for refractory children between the ages of 6 and 12, whom the neglect or incapacity of the parents have left unprovided with any education, and who cannot receive one in the ordinary asylums. With these are included the young vagrants found habitually together in the public places.

"Even the asylums for children," says this great philanthropist,[1] "do not get all the poor children, especially those of the very poor, ashamed of their poverty. But in any case, when the children come out of these institutions at an age when children are most inclined to evil, there is no longer any special refuge for them, and they become vagabonds."

In this way we may counteract the weakening of parental authority, which is one of the most serious causes of crime (not less than 20% among the children of the well-to-do), and this without taking them from home and shutting them up

[1] "Compte Rendu de la Réunion des Sociétaires de l'Œuvre Pieuse des Maisons de Réforme de la Province de Milan," 1872.

at just the time when they most need air and movement and the care and relationships of family life. In this way the child would be given a milder treatment and one better suited to his age, he would be spared fatigue disproportionate to his strength, while special attention would be given to his physical development.

This is not all. The reform school costs too much to be applied upon a large scale, while these day reformatories, better adapted to childhood, could readily extend their operations in direct proportion to the need. Moreover, even if the expense were greater, which is not the case, this would be largely compensated by the decrease in the number of criminals. We have a direct proof of this in the two institutions for children in Milan, which, out of the 700 children received since 1840, had not a single one convicted after leaving the school, while half the prisoners of the reform schools have been inmates of other asylums. It would certainly be sufficient, for the present, if the so-called oratories, where the children are assembled on Sundays (in Milan about 3000) for useless prayers interrupted by long and wearisome periods of idleness, should be secularized, conducted on rational lines, and utilized every day in the week.

§ 169. "Ragged Schools"

There exists in London an institution midway between the compulsory asylum of Spagliardi and the voluntary asylum of Brace. This is that of the "Home for Little Boys." These are real little villages or colonies given up to unfortunate children. The inmates are divided into groups like families, and are taught trades of shoemaker, farmer, valet, mechanic, etc.[1] We may cite also the "Ragged Schools," where the children are furnished with food and clothing as well as instruction, and where the poorest, the deserted children, and the orphans are also given lodging for the night. This institution, which costs the government nothing, was founded in 1818 with certain children picked up in the streets of London. These schools formed a noble bond between the higher and lower classes, and

[1] "Rivista di Disciplina Carceria," 1876, p. 197.

in them might be seen for thirty-four years a chancellor of England teaching the alphabet every Sunday. The children are allowed to enter and leave of their own accord, though many of them are brought to the schools in the first instance by the police. Numbers of them support themselves by their own work. Thus there were in 1860 368 bootblacks in the school, each of whom brought the society sixpence daily.

§ 170. Other English Measures for Children

Another English measure worthy of being imitated is that of obliging parents who are found to be responsible for a child's delinquency to contribute a penny out of every shilling of their wages toward his support while detained. Thus are they given an interest in taking care of their children, and do not consider their confinement an advantage. We have seen the miracles accomplished by the Society for the Prevention of Cruelty to Children. Another fine institution is that of the Boys' Brigade,[1] which enrolls the little vagabonds of the streets by hundreds. It was instituted in Glasgow by W. A. Smith in 1883, and in 1891 already numbered 20,000 boys, who drilled, marched, had common prayers, and sang in church.

§ 171. Barnardo's Institutions

To save, if not the born criminals, at least the criminaloids, it is necessary to take them in infancy.

"The attempts to reform unfortunate adults," writes Barnardo, "always come to nothing on account of the force of the criminal habit in the individual. The *vis inertiæ* of ignorance, vice, and crime is hardly to be overcome by the idea of reformation.

"It is quite otherwise when it is a question of children. Half the difficulties are smoothed away the moment that we have a plastic material in our hands. The influence of environment and circumstances in the formation of character is greater than would be believed. I have observed that a new and healthful environment is more powerful to transform and renew an individual, than heredity is to fix a blemish upon him. It is

[1] "Revue du Christianisme Pratique," 1892.

necessary, then, to cleanse and purify the atmosphere at once and thoroughly if perverse instincts are to be obliterated."

Barnardo cites triumphantly the careful examination that he made of the lists of the children received. This showed that 85% of the children were descended from drinking parents. Now we know how fatal an alcoholic heredity is; and yet, out of 9000 received and sent to Canada, who have grown up and whose history is known, only 1% have gone wrong. It is necessary, then, to take the child in the plastic state, if we want to change it. It is not a religious question simply, but one of economics. By spending $100 to take in and reform a child, society saves thousands of dollars necessary to defend itself against the adult criminal.

Barnardo receives all deserted children, looks carefully into their past, and keeps them for some time under observation, after which he chooses a trade for them and sends them to a farm or to Canada. One of his great secrets is to isolate the children as much as possible in small groups, leaving them full liberty to develop their different individual aptitudes, and thus avoiding as much as possible what he himself calls "the stamp of institutional uniformity," that curse of orphanages and children's homes in general. For this it is necessary not simply to avoid mingling children of different ages, but even to keep them in different buildings, having them pass from one to the other according to age and circumstances.

This intuition of the needs and capacities of each individual in relation to society Barnardo has carried into all his work, applying it systematically with profound penetration and truly humane feeling. He receives children of all ages; those between 3 and 5 go to the Tiny House, those from 4 to 9 to the Jersey House. Elsewhere he cares for children between 10 and 15. When they reach 13 years of age, Barnardo tries to accustom them to work, to harden them to fatigue, to prepare them, in short, for the life before them. But to the very little children, the nurslings, orphaned or abandoned, Barnardo wishes to give, if not luxury, at least the comfort of children brought up and cared for in their own homes. Their home is situated in the midst of gardens, they have young, strong nurses, rooms full of light and sun, white clothes, playthings, birds, little carriages, and good beds. If the Doctor cannot furnish complete comfort to all the children he takes in, he wishes at least to give it to the smallest. In his paper, "Night and Day," we see a photograph of one of the dormitories. Colored pictures cover the walls, in the background is a large rocking-horse, while bird-cages hang by the beds. The picture makes one think sadly of our orphanages and day nurseries, where the children are kept like cattle in a stable and everything goes on as if in tombs of the living. One of the branch homes is in the country because a little three-year-old country girl received into the institution could not accustom herself to it and cried continually. The case was brought before the council, and one of Barnardo's collaborators, Miss Blanche Watteley, at once found the solution: if the child could not get used to the city, they would establish a home in the country. This is how the "Bird's Castle" came into being.

After having snatched the children from misery and crime and taught them to work, Barnardo, to complete his task, sends them to Canada, where he has an agent to place them on farms and keep watch over them. Contracts are made with the farmers for three or five years, with food, lodging, and $50 or $100 a year in wages, according to the age of the ward. Thus they are rescued from the pernicious barrack system of crowded living, and at the same time transplanted into new surroundings, where the fevering stimulation of modern life cannot affect them.

It was with an equally true feeling for the needs and capacities of his wards that Barnardo organized the institution for girls. They have a little village all to themselves in a charming place a short distance from London. This village is made up of cottages, surrounded by gardens, having fanciful names, like "Pea-blossom," "Wild Thyme," etc. Each house holds 20 girls, watched over by house-mothers; for Dr. Barnardo says quite rightly that if the institutional stamp harms a boy, it stunts a girl completely, since her temperament demands for its complete development all the domestic details of the family life. The barrack system may very well under certain conditions be useful for boys, provided it is for a limited time only. But it would have no value whatever for girls, who would learn from it nothing that the wife of a poor man ought to know, — to make purchases, to quiet a crying child, to sew. All these are taught by the *cottage system*, and 200 girls trained in this way are annually sent to Canada, where they are very much sought after.

The benefits of this method of education cannot be doubted when one considers the list of the rescued that the delegates of the Salvation Army gave me. The histories cited by Barnardo also and backed up by photographs give us incontestable evidence of a transformation that is not only mental but also physical, so that the criminal, thanks to the Doctor, has become actually another man.

"Job, for example,[1] was 15 years old when he was admitted. His mother had died of cancer three years before in the hospital; his father was lazy, tuberculous, and a drunkard, and had often been imprisoned. Job, left to himself, on leaving the asylum had started out as a pedlar; being without shelter or resources he had been drawn away by evil companions and became a thorough vagabond, begging on the street corners under pretense of selling matches. He is now sober and does not smoke, and is a fine young fellow, well developed physically. For £8 for his education, and £10 for his voyage, he has become an independent citizen in a new country.[2]

"James, 14 years old, a Liverpool boy, lived with a married sister, the mother of three children, in a kind of cellar, which the police required them to leave. He had several times been put in prison for mendicity and for having been found in the company of known criminals. He was sent to Canada and placed upon a farm, and though at first there was some trouble because of his irregular conduct, he has now completely amended."

O noble souls of Don Bosco, Brockway, and Barnardo, take from these pages, across which crime has trailed its dark and dreadful lines, a greeting! for you alone have brought us light, have opened the only positive road to the prevention of crime.

[1] See "Homme Criminel," Atlas, XCII.
[2] "Night and Day," 1895.

§ 172. Medical Treatment

After attempts at moral suggestion the hypnotic cure should be tried. Although the effectiveness of this method has been exaggerated, it is certain that at least for the moment certain tendencies may be combated successfully by hypnotic methods, and the mind given the proper direction. This result has been obtained with paranoiacs. It ought to be still easier to attain success when the malady is in the incipient stage, and to produce by repetition the habit of right action. Further, we must not forget that the basis of criminal tendencies is always of an epileptic nature. According to Hasse and Esquirol, the epilepsies that manifest themselves shortly before the age of puberty frequently disappear when that age is reached. When epilepsy is hereditary it is frequently sufficient to remove the patient from the circumstances in which the parents lived; for example, to move him to another climate and to substitute for brain work muscular exercise in the open air. According to Bevan-Lewis and Clouston, the hydropathic treatment, coupled with a vegetarian diet, is very effective.[1] The internal treatment useful in such cases must also be applied. Bromides, opium, belladonna, etc., are given in various cases.

[1] Marro, "La Pubertà Studiata nell' Uomo e nella Donna," p. 438.

CHAPTER VII

PREVENTION OF POLITICAL CRIME

§ 173.

MANY of the economic measures that we have suggested for preventing parliamentary corruption and the excess of poverty and wealth would also be very efficacious for the prevention of the political crime that expresses the discontent of the masses, as ordinary crime expresses that of the individual.

§ 174. Racial Affinity

Historical experience, as Lanessen points out to us, shows that when a dominant people is inferior in power and culture the people ruled always end by freeing themselves completely. Of this Greece, Holland, and the United States are examples. Good politics, then, would consist in a voluntary abandonment of sovereignty in such cases; but vanity and immediate interests blind the ruling nation, and only rarely is this wise resolution taken. An easier method is a kind of incomplete detachment, like that of Austria and Hungary, and England and her colonies, a device that diminishes dependence, contacts, and dissensions, thus removing one of the greatest causes of rebellions and political crimes, the more so as the people, governing themselves, see the more serious evils and are able to remove them.

This device of detachment and autonomy is applicable at times within the nation itself, when there exists a great difference of race, as, for example, between the north and the south of Italy. Under these conditions, a uniform civil, penal, and political code provokes continual discontent, which manifests itself in insurrections. Among degenerate races showing great differences, as in the case of the castes of India and the fanatical

Mohammedan populations, the sole method of political conciliation consists in abandoning any attempt at civil or religious progress, and in preserving scrupulously the *status quo*, — this even to the smallest details, such as the respect for the ashes of manuscripts in Tonquin and for pork fat in India. This is the system of which the Romans were, and the English still are, masters.

§ 175. Decentralization

"The future of society politically lies in decentralization," says Spencer. If a people is treated like a child it loses all spontaneity and becomes incapable of contending against difficulties. Thus it comes that where the English have recourse to their mutual-aid societies, the French clamor against the government. They can no longer have a free government, for when they are free they lose all stability and give themselves up to anarchy. The imperial form of government, which is that best adapted to them, is naturally never liberal. On the other hand, by concentrating great powers in the hands of a few, great opportunity is given for corruption, the more so when parliamentary immunity protects the authors of it. If, however, you will allow the cities to administer their own affairs freely, according to their importance, to elect their own officers, to have charge of the courts of first instance, secondary education, the police, the prisons, the means of communication, you will eliminate a great cause of injustice and abuses, and in consequence will eliminate also the political crimes provoked by these abuses.

§ 176. Contest for Political Supremacy

In order that one class in exclusive possession of the political power may not proceed to excesses prejudicial to other classes, it is necessary that the people shall be represented somewhere among the multiplicity of historical constituent elements. Thus the tribunate preserved the Roman Republic for centuries and prevented popular uprisings.

§ 177. Universal Suffrage

Universal suffrage seems destined, in the course of time, to bring about the abolition of class distinctions, but turned over to the ignorant and corrupt it may easily be turned against liberty itself. The aristocracy of knowledge, which Aristotle believed impossible but which has nevertheless existed for centuries in China, would alone be fitted to counteract the power of money, acting through the bourgeoisie, and the power of numbers in the proletariat. But if we are to admit universal suffrage, like a torrent that cannot be stayed, it must be guided by the rational voices of men of higher worth and clearer sight.

§ 178. The Judiciary

The judiciary, for its part, ought to be freed from that subservience to the legislative power which, in Italy, paralyzes its forces. It is quite different in America, where popular election has given the judges a power and independence so great as to allow them, upon complaint of a citizen whose rights are infringed, to pronounce null and void laws which do not conform to the constitution. Noailles [1] shows how this judicial system, which comes directly from the English common law, protects the rights of the nation and of individuals against the power of Congress as much as it does the privileges of the federal government and individual rights against the power of the several states. When there is a conflict between a clause of the constitution and a legislative enactment, the judicial power steps in to see to it that constitutional liberty shall not be threatened by the weakness or the tyranny of legislative bodies.

§ 179. Poor Man's Lawyer — Legal Aid Societies

We see how the judiciary can prevent political crimes, which are committed in revenge for great injustices.[2] The internal peace of Rome was maintained for centuries by the influence

[1] Duc de Noailles, "Le Pouvoir Judiciare aux Êtats-Unis" (Revue de Deux Mondes, Aug. 1st, 1888).

[2] Lombroso and Laschi, "Le Crime Politique et Les Revolutions," 1891.

of the Tribunate, and that of Venice by the relative impartiality of justice. It is certain, on the other hand, that when tyrannical governments like that of Austria in Italy, and that of ancient Piedmont, survived so long without dissensions, they owed it to the equal justice which, except in matters concerning the king, prevailed there by means of the "advocate of the poor," and to the Senate, which had the right of abrogating any ministerial decree that did not conform to the laws.

This institution of a popular mediator to protect the poor and weak should again be established. I have observed that the voice of a single honest tribune (Jaurès, for example) often proves more powerful against the errors of the government than the entire chamber. Thus, in the recent banking scandals, without the Boulangist deputies in Paris and Colajanni in Italy, all parties would have united to hush the matter up.

§ 180. Ability to Change the Laws

If it is possible for a political form to endure, it is due to the flexibility of its constitution and laws, which must adapt themselves to new conditions. Switzerland is a striking proof of this. In the period between 1870 and 1879 the Swiss made 115 changes in the constitutions of the cantons and 3 in the federal constitution; and they were able to maintain their union notwithstanding great diversity of race and custom.

§ 181. Conservatism

But no change must be made too abruptly. "In order that the institutions of a people may be stable," says Constant, "they must keep themselves to the level of the people's ideas." The violent abolition of serfdom in Russia and of the ancient estates in France and Germany had become a necessity of justice; the same may be said of the secularization of the property of the church, when the accumulation of property in mortmain and the pretensions of the clergy to exemption from land-taxes had made all economic and political progress impossible. Yet these reforms were not brought about without immediate troubles, because there was a disregard of the law of conservatism, which does not permit too rapid an introduction of innovations, even for good.

§ 182. Referendum

The referendum, or appeal to the people, is able to show, where it exists, how far there exists a community of ideas between the nation and their representatives. It may be considered as the most powerful instrument for the education of a free people, because it forces them to study the laws submitted to them, and, by making them feel their whole responsibility, gives them a consciousness of the part they have in the political life of the country.[1]

§ 183. Archaic Education

If we are to protect ourselves from "occasional" revolutionists, who, however misguided and atavistic they and their measures may be, still do advocate reforms, we must strip ourselves of the unfortunate heritage received from our fathers, the rhetoric of Arcadia. Whoever will study the revolutions of 1789 and 1848, and the character of many mattoids, will see that one of the great causes for insurrection is the archaic system of education, which is in complete contrast with our positive needs. We bring up our young people in a hot-house instead of in the strong current of life, and we want them to be robust! In this way we get æsthetes, — I am willing to admit that, though some deny it, — but we do not get men capable of taking part in the contest of modern life.

§ 184. Economic Discontent

The sole remedy against our political criminals who are such from accident, from passion, from imitation, or from poverty, consists in remedying the economic uneasiness in the country, since this is the true basis for anarchy. We have to-day an economic fanaticism, as we formerly had a political fanaticism. It is imperatively necessary that we should open a vent for this economic fanaticism with economic reforms (see above), as we

[1] Brunialti, "La Legge e la Libertà nello Stato Moderno," Turin, 1888.

have opened one for political fanaticism with constitutional and representative government, and for religious fanaticism with freedom of worship. Now, we do nothing of all this; we permit taxes, recruiting, and penalties to affect the poor man most severely, and give him no compensation, except bright soap-bubbles under the names of national glory, liberty, and equality, which, by their contrast with reality, make his sufferings all the harder to bear.

CHAPTER VIII

PENAL INSTITUTIONS

§ 185.

MEASURES for the prevention of crime are unhappily, with our race at least, a dream of the idealist. The legal world that rules us, and for which the defense and the punishment of the criminal are sources of honors and rewards, has something to do besides preventing crime and devising a substitute for the almost always useless, and often positively harmful, penalties. It is just for this reason that we must consider these penalties carefully, particularly the institution of the prison, which, according to the common notion of our legal lights, is the only social defense against crime.

§ 186. Cellular Prisons

Once we have decided to inflict a prison penalty, the individual cell seems clearly indicated; for, if it does not reform the guilty, it prevents his sinking further into crime and removes, at least in part, the possibility of the formation of associations of evil-doers by interfering with the formation of that kind of public opinion in the prison that compels the prisoner to add the vices of his companions to his own. The cell seems also to reach the highest degree of perfection for the purpose of judicial investigation, isolating the criminal whose guilt is still to be proved; in the same way it is indispensable for the punishment of the delinquents still capable of correction, who have fallen for the first time and from whom criminal contact and association would soon take away all sense of shame. It offers, then, real advantages without the risk of grave danger to health, or at worst gives a somewhat greater opportunity for suicide.[1] But the advantages of the cellular prisons are in

[1] Lecour, "Du Suicide et de l'Aliénation dans les Prisons," Paris, 1876. According to this author, in America there was: 1 death to 49 prisoners in the common prisons; in those conducted on the Auburn system, 1 to

great measure neutralized by the great expense which makes their application on a large scale impossible; and even more objectionable is the fact that they favor inertia on the part of the prisoner and transform him into an automaton, incapable of taking part in the struggle of life.

"In the actual organization of the prisons," said Gauthier, "everything is combined to blot out the individual, to annihilate his thought, and destroy his will. The uniformity of the system that pretends to fashion all its 'subjects' upon the same model, the calculated severity of a monastic life where no room is left for the unforeseen, the prohibition of all intercourse with the outside world except through the banal monthly letter; everything, in short, even to the miserable, animal-like march in Indian file, is fitted to turn the prisoner into an unconscious automaton.[1]

"We want to make useful citizens out of these prisoners, and we force them to idleness. We accustom them to find food and lodging assured, without thought for the morrow, or any other concern than that of obeying the order given. We force them to be like the dog at the spit, who had only to raise his foot and turn the drum, like an unconscious machine. Is not this the ideal of the witless and the cowardly? It is Nirvana, the paradise of the Hindu.

"For many an honest man the struggle for existence is not only sharper, but much less safe. When the first repugnance is overcome, many — doubtless the majority — come imperceptibly to the point of preparing a prison future for themselves."

Gauthier knew a prisoner, a former army officer, who held the post of paymaster in the prison of Clairvaux and was serving his fourth or fifth term. Toward the end of 1883, being, to his great displeasure, near the end of his sentence, he begged that his place should be saved for him until he was sentenced again.

"And we may remark that, save for a few honorable exceptions, for nearly all the directors of prisons the ideal of a 'good

54. In France there is 1 to 14 in the cellular prisons. According to Alauzet, in 8 prisons on the Auburn system, in America, there is an average of 1 death to 50 with a minimum of 1 to 81. In Philadelphia the cellular prison gives 1 death to 83; in France 1 to 39. ("Essai sur les Peines," 1863.)

[1] "Le Mode des Prisons," Paris, 1888.

prisoner' is the recidivist, the veteran, the habitual criminal, whose prison experience and the docility he has acquired are guarantees of his orderly conduct.

"The unfortunate thing is that this 'good prisoner,' according to the formula, under this régime is not slow in becoming incapable of resisting his companions, criminals by birth or by profession. He has so little power of resisting unhealthy stimuli, the desire for unlawful gain, and the attraction of evil examples, that he is worse than the 'bad' prisoner.

"The only ambition that remains to him is for crime and wickedness, the result of the special education which he and other convicts have given each other. It is not without reason that in criminals' slang the prison is spoken of as 'the college.'"

To these things must be added the tale-bearing, quarrelsomeness, lying, and all the other special vices acquired or developed in prison.

"In the presence of the solitude and miserable formalism of the prison," writes Prins, the Belgian prison director, "we must ask ourselves whether the man of the lower classes can be regenerated only through solitude and formalism.

"Voluntary isolation may elevate the mind of the poet, but what effect can the solitude imposed upon the criminal have, other than to lower his moral level more and more? Do we teach a child to walk by putting difficulties in his way, or by filling him with fear of a fall and making him hang on to others? Shall we teach a man to take his place in society by shutting him up in a solitary cell, in a situation as unlike the social life as possible, and by taking from him even the appearance of any moral exercise, by regulating from morning till night the smallest details of his daily movements and even thoughts? If it were a question of making good scholars, good workmen, or good soldiers, should we be willing to accept the method of prolonged cellular confinement? If this method is condemned, then, by the experience of ordinary life, it will not become useful the moment the court pronounces sentence."

Other proofs of the evil effects of the prison may be found by consulting my "Palimpsestes de la Prison." See, for example, these lines written by a prisoner:

"I am 18 years old; misfortune has made me guilty several times, and each time I have been shut up in prison. But how have I been reformed in prison? what have I learned? I have perfected myself in wickedness there."

And this:

"To try to correct an idler and a thief by subjecting them to idleness is surely absurd.

" . . . Poor prisoners! They are regarded as so many animals; they are kept shut up like so many white bears, under pretense of reforming them. . . . In penal institutions a man learns to hate society, but not to make an honest man out of a thief. They are the universities of thieves, where the old teach the young their trade. To enter this hotel there is no need of money even to tip the servants. As for myself, I thank God I am happier than St. Peter. Here in my cell I am served by lackeys. What a Utopia! This is better than being in the country."

And another:

"Friends, do not try to escape from prison. Here we eat, drink, sleep, without the need of working."

I have even found a cryptogram in which a friend was urged to commit a crime in order to get into prison again. "For the two of us the time will pass more quickly, and when we are in the galley we can tell each other the story of our lives." Le Blanc, a notorious thief, said to Guisquet, the prefect of police: "If we are arrested, we finish by living at the expense of others; we are clothed, fed, and warmed, and all this at the cost of those we have despoiled."

What is still more serious, there are a great number who find prison life a real source of pleasure. We may say that in place of the complete isolation from the external world, that theoretically belongs to cellular prisons, there exist manifold means of information and communication, all the more harmful (especially for judicial investigations) from the fact that they are unforeseen and unknown.

"The walls of a prison," writes Gauthier again, "under the very eyes of the guards, offer a world of information and are marvelous instruments of correspondence. Thus, when I found myself at Chôlon-on-the-Saône, in the most secret cell, I learned of arrests that had been made in Lyons, Paris, and Vienne on my account, news which was of great importance to me. . . . There is first the little cord, stretched by the weight of a ball made of breadcrumb, and so thrown from one window to another, while one holds on to the bars of the window. There are books in the library which circulate covered with cryptograms. Then the pipes for water and hot air make excellent speaking-tubes. Another dodge, which needs persons with some instruction, is that by knocking on the wall. It is not necessary that the persons communicating by this method should be in contiguous cells. I once got valuable news in this way from a comrade 40 or 50 meters off." (*Op. cit.*)

Nothing is secret in prison. A judge having asked a certain prisoner at the Assizes how he communicated with his accomplices, the prisoner replied: "To keep us from communicating you would have to keep one of us in France and send the other to hell."[1]

But the aristocracy of crime, the rich or influential criminals, have no need of these expedients. The guards have nothing to lose by favoring their communication with the outside world, and the cellular system makes it easy to do this with impunity, for who can know what passes in a solitary cell? I have myself had direct evidence that facts are known in prison before they are published in the outside world. The removal of a procurator-general was announced to me in prison several days before it took place, and when no one, not even the official himself, knew of it. By studying the wall-inscriptions and documents of the prisoners in the great cellular prison in Turin,[2] I have become convinced that, while it is supposed that association and, above all, comradeship, are prevented by the cell system, in reality the "esprit de corps" is strengthened, where before it hardly existed. I have found in the writings of the prisoners how one of them affectionately salutes his successors, another leaves a crayon for his comrades that they may be able to write, a third advises comrades equally unknown to feign insanity in order to escape sentence. I have seen how the walls of the exercise yard, continually re-whitewashed, formed a kind of daily newspaper, carried on also, in summer, on the sand and the dirty windows, and in winter on the snow and in the books that the convicts are permitted to read. In studying the wall-inscriptions I have found that out of 1000,

[1] "Gazetta dei Giuristi," 42.
[2] "Palimpsestes de la Prison," 1889, pp. 21–56.

182 had reference to comrades, 900 were simple salutations, 45 contained news of trials, and 27 were encouragements to commit further crimes.

There is in the prisons a bureau connected with the administration department, called the matriculation office, in which there are always some prisoners kept, since here all are examined and observed when they enter and when they leave. This office is a center for imparting news, from which it is disseminated throughout the cells by the prisoners. Will it be believed that even upon audience days there are to be found collected in this ante-chamber a dozen or more convicts? Thus, at the very moment of judicial investigation, almost under the eyes of the judge, and for the very prisoner who is being examined, this system that has cost society so much is made futile.

I have not spoken of workshops. In the cellular prisons the efforts to prevent communication allow very little work to be done. From this there results, beside the injury to the state and to the prisoner who is kept in idleness, a still graver danger for the future. The active prisoners become accustomed to idleness, if they do not die of it, while the lazy ones are just in their element; consequently, when they go out they commit new crimes in order to return. But if work is allowed, it is impossible, even if those are excluded who have fellow-prisoners, to prevent new relationships from being formed with the foremen of the free workshops, the contractors, etc. The consequence of this is that the investigations which are kept secret from the public are no secret at all from the accused person himself.

"The object of cellular isolation," writes Prins,[1] "is to regenerate the guilty by checking the evil influence of fellow prisoners, in order that only the beneficent influence of respectable men may be operative. But see the real facts. Everywhere the guards, who are supposed to represent the good elements of society to the convict, are men devoted to duty, but they are recruited from the very sphere of society to which the convicts themselves belong; sometimes they are 'declassés' without employment, who for a ridiculously small salary, insufficient for the maintenance of a family, have to live very much as the prisoners do. Too few in numbers (scarcely 1 to 25

[1] "Les Criminels en Prison," 1893.

or 30 prisoners), they naturally are able to do little more than cast a glance into the cell or at the work, and see that the rules are observed. It is to these empty formalities and to the too hasty visit of an official or a chaplain that those charged with transforming or amending the guilty come to limit their efforts."

We see from all this how necessary it is to change our ideas about prisons.

§ 187. The Graded System

Everyone will understand why penologists, having only this mournful expedient of a prison, have tried to improve it as much as possible. It is as a result of such efforts that the Irish system has won so much applause. This system is as follows: The criminal passes the first period in solitary confinement, not exceeding nine months, which may be reduced to eight; during this period he has only a vegetable diet, poor clothing, and a monotonous task of oakum-picking. In the second grade there is collective work, rigidly watched, which is divided into four classes each more privileged and advantageous than the one below, into which the convict passes successively after having obtained by his work and good conduct a certain number of merit marks. In the first class the door of the cell remains open during the day; the work is not regularly paid for, but may perhaps be rewarded with a penny. After having received 54 merit marks the prisoner passes successively into the other classes, where he receives greater and greater compensation and also instruction, and finds himself more in contact with the public, and so on. This grade having been passed through, there commences for the convicts the grade of almost complete independence (intermediate prison) with work in the field. They wear their own clothing, receive wages, may be allowed to absent themselves, and are in continual contact with the outside world. From the conclusion of this grade until the end of their sentence they have provisional liberty under the surveillance of the police, who, in case they go wrong, send them back to prison. Before they go out they are registered, photographed, and warned that the first slip will bring them back to prison. When they first reach their destination they must report to the police, and monthly thereafter. The police look after them and help them get work.

This is a magnificent means of getting these rude and lazy beings into the notion of being virtuous, or at least of working. The criminal can in this way cut down his sentence (and the state its expense) by a sixth or even a third, and as every misdemeanor means being reduced to a lower grade, the most dreaded of penalties, all other punishments become unnecessary in the intermediate grades. The results obtained in Ireland by this reform were satisfactory, at least in appearance; since 1854, when the system was introduced, there has been a remarkable reduction in crimes. The following are the figures:

Year	Entered during year	Total convicts
1854	710	3933
1857	426	2614
1860	331	1631
1869	191	1325
1870	245	1236

We may add that this reform unites economy (upon which depends the possibility of applying any system) with the demands of criminal psychology, by permitting a gradual passage to complete liberty. It thus makes of the criminal's perpetual dream of freedom a means of discipline and reformation. It offers besides a means of overcoming the prejudice of the public against the liberated convicts, and inspires the convicts themselves with confidence.

In Denmark the convicts remain in their cells night and day, and work there for their own advantage. The incorrigible prisoners and the recidivists, after six years, live in common in a special prison, and have no other reward for their good conduct than the freedom of working in the fields near the prison. Those who are young and can still be reformed, or those who are convicted for the first time for a minor offense with a sentence of from three to six months at the most, remain in a special cellular prison. They are divided according to their conduct into different grades. In the first (from three to six months) there is absolute seclusion, instruction in the cell, work without pay, and only writing on the slate allowed. In the second grade (six months) they receive two shillings a day for their work, are taught in school but separated from others, can have paper on holidays and books every fortnight, may purchase with half their pay a mirror and an almanac, may write letters and receive visits every two months. In the third grade, which is twelve months at least, they receive three shillings a day, have books or paper every week, are allowed to buy many useful things, and send money to their families, receive visits every six weeks, and may have the portraits of their families. In the fourth grade they get four shillings a day, and, besides other advantages which are more and more conceded to them, they can go out of their cells, work in the open air, and have flowers and birds. Their sentence may be reduced for good conduct, a sentence of eight months to six, of three years to one, and of six years to three and one-half. Thus they pass from absolute solitude to solitude at night only, from absolute silence to work in the field and an almost complete liberty. Hardly 10% remain in their cells more than two years.[1]

Let us hail these institutions as a great step in advance, but let us not be under any illusion about them. There are other things to be remembered. In Ireland the statistics are affected by emigration, for liberated convicts, not finding work, went to America, where they peopled the penitentiaries.[2] Moreover, even with this system there are many recidivists in Denmark, and still more in England, where, as it appears, the paroled convicts easily change their residence, and notwithstanding the law go to places where they are unknown. There they do not act directly, but make use of the services of other criminals. According to Davis, chaplain of Newgate,[3] one sheriff had cases of prisoners released with ticket-of-leave, convicted a second time, again released on ticket-of-leave, and convicted a third time, all before the original sentence had expired. One of these, who was 36 years old, had been sentenced to a term of more than 40 years, and was free!

This is why the number of paroled prisoners in England,

[1] Pears, "Prisons, etc.," 1872; Beltrani-Scalia, *op. cit.*
[2] "Riv. di Disciplina Carceraria," 1877, p. 39.
[3] Cere, "Les Populations Dangereuses," 1872, p. 103.

which rose to 2892 in 1854, fell to 922 in 1857, to 912 in 1858, to 252 in 1859, and did not rise above 1400 in 1861–62–63.[1] In Germany, also, the number of those conditionally liberated fell from 3141, the figure for 1871, to 733 in 1872, and 421 in 1874. This lack of success is to be attributed to the imprudence with which released convicts are allowed to change their residence and to the practice of turning over to them their entire savings; also to the fact that many employers, more selfish than the philanthropists, seek only their own immediate profit from the convicts and do not further concern themselves with their conduct; and finally to a lack of active and continual surveillance, where a large number of individuals are concerned.

Together with gradations of punishments it is well to apply what I have called individualization of punishment, which consists in applying special methods of repression and occupation adapted to each individual, as a physician does in prescribing dietary rules and special remedies according to the temperament of each patient. Here is the secret of the success attained in Saxony (Zwickau), where there are special prisons for the old and for the young, for heavy penalties and for light ones, and where, according to the merits of each prisoner, his food, his clothes, and the severity of his penalty are changed. But these measures can be carried out only for criminaloids, and in small prisons, with very able directors. Otherwise the prize of liberty will fall to the worst criminals, who make the best prisoners, being the most hypocritical. For these reasons such reforms cannot be left to be administered by a short-sighted bureaucracy.

Besides these institutions it is necessary to seek to develop right feeling in the convicts. We must remember that virtue is not to be created artificially; and that the best results are to be obtained by basing it upon the interests and passions of men. A man may lose his life, but he cannot be stripped of his passions, and all men, even the most depraved, need an interest and an aim to guide them in life. They may be insensible to threats, to fear, and even to physical suffering, but they never are insensible to vanity, to the need of distinguishing themselves,

[1] Cere, *op. cit.*, p. 100.

and above all to the hope of liberty. This is why sermons and lessons of abstract morality are useless. We have to use the convicts' vanity as a lever, to interest them in the good by granting them material advantages, such as the gradual diminution of their penalty. Good results may be obtained by instituting a kind of decoration, and merit and demerit marks. The prisoners must be permitted to pass according to merit into the privileged classes, where they can, for example, wear ordinary clothing and a beard, ornament their cells with flowers and pictures, receive visits, work for themselves and their family, and, finally, catch a glimpse of the much-desired perspective of temporary liberty.

To gain liberty is the dream and constant thought of prisoners, and when they see a way open before them, more safe and certain than that of a surreptitious escape, they will take it at once. They will do right, it is true, only to obtain their liberty, not for its own sake, but as movements repeated become a second nature, so we may hope that they will form the habit of right conduct. This is why the right of pardon should be abolished, since it makes prisoners hope for liberty by the favor of someone else.

"It is necessary," says Despine rightly, "to elevate the criminal in his own eyes, by making him understand that he can reconquer the respect of the world; we must fill his soul with the need of becoming honest by utilizing the same passions which would make him still more depraved if left to himself."

Despine, Clam, De Metz, Montesinos, and Brockway have counted so much upon the influence of honor among the criminals that they have left them almost free upon their parole during their work; and fierce men, whom twenty guards could scarcely restrain, never even thought of escaping. Ferrus tells of a thief who was converted by a Sister in prison, who, with this end in view, trusted him with the care of the wardrobe. A convicted carpenter was unbearable because of his extreme violence; the oversight of other convicts was given to him, and he became the most docile of all. A prisoner of Citeaux, wearied by his labor, threw his mattock at the feet of the director, Albert Reey; the latter, without saying a word, took up the tool and went to work in the other's place. The unfortunate man, struck by this noble lesson of practical morality, took up his work, and did not offend again. These examples show us clearly how we must set about to reform these men. We must act upon them by example more than by word, by morality in action more than by theoretical teaching. Strict discipline is incontestably necessary with them, the more so since light punishments, having but a slight effect, have to be repeated more often and for this reason are less efficacious than severe punishments that are rare; but too great severity is certainly more harmful than useful. Severity bends but does not reform them, and it makes them hypocrites.

Adult criminals ought to be considered as children,[1] as moral invalids, who must be cared for at once with mildness and with severity, but more of the first than of the second, because the spirit of vengeance, the excitability which is the basis of their character, makes them consider even the lightest punishment as a persecution. It is for this reason that too strict a silence is detrimental to morals. An old prisoner said to Despine: "When you shut your eyes to our breaches of discipline we talked more, but we did not offend against morality; now we speak less, but we blaspheme and conspire." In Denmark, when the greatest severity prevailed in the prisons there were 30% of misdemeanors; now, with a milder régime, there are only 6%. Despine used an excellent method, by not inflicting punishment until some time after the offense, in order not to appear to yield to a fit of passion. The guilty prisoner was led to a meditation cell; the director went in only after an hour to tell him the penalty which the rule required; often the whole group to which the guilty person belongs was blamed and punished. This is a method used by Obermayer with great success.

Work ought to be the first care and the highest aim of every penal institution, in order to awaken the energy of the prisoner and give him the habit of productive labor, necessary after his liberation. It is, further, an instrument of penitentiary discipline, and also a means of indemnifying the state for the

[1] Miss Carpenter, who gave her life to them, said: "They are great children, whom society ought to govern as it governs children."

expense incurred;[1] but this last consideration is only secondary and should not be made the principal end, for many lucrative occupations cannot be used to advantage. We ought, for reasons above mentioned, to avoid the trades of locksmith, photographer, penman, etc., which prepare the way for other crimes. We should prefer, on the contrary, farm work, which shows the minimum of criminality in our statistics and gives an easy means of placing the discharged convicts; we may also use straw and wicker work, rope-making, typography, pottery-making, stone-cutting, etc.; and we should admit only as a last resort occupations like book-binding and cabinet-making, which require the use of tools that might become dangerous.

In every way the work ought to be proportioned to the forces and instincts of the convict, who, if he has accomplished as much as he is capable of, although that may be little, ought to receive a proportionate reward, if not in money, at least in the shortening of his sentence. For this reason I believe that it is necessary to eliminate the contractor from the prison system, since he seeks naturally to favor the most skilful and, nevertheless, in certain countries, even has control of the pardoning of the prisoners.

We must try to give criminals a love for work by making it a reward for good conduct and a relief from the boredom of prison. It is not best, then, to impose it upon them; they must be brought, by means of a cellular detention more or less prolonged, to want it and ask for it (Crofton). If we want to make the work profitable and to establish the spirit of comradeship

[1] Only the prisons of Charlestown, Chatham, Portsmouth, and Alipore, as far as I know, give returns nearly equal to their expenses. In 1871–72 Chatham and Portsmouth even showed a profit of £17,759. According to Garelli the Italian prisons cost the state 32,000,000 lire, and brought in only 1½ ("Lezioni sulla Riforma delle Carceri," 1862). According to Nicotera ("Relazione sul Lavoro dei Detenuti," 1876), there were in 1874–75 38,407 prisoners working, and 32,178 unoccupied. Of the workers one-fourth were weavers, one-sixth shoemakers, one-twentieth joiners, one-tenth agricultural laborers, and one-one hundredth employed in salt-works. The net profit for the administration in 1871 was 1,632,530 lire, and the prisoners received wages at the rate of 0.47 lire a day. This compares favorably with the wages paid in Belgium (0.26), Hungary (0.22), and Austria (0.41). In Austria a convict can be obliged to pay a certain sum for his detention. In Berne he must earn at least 75 centimes a day to get the benefit of his labor. In France he receives one-third of what he earns.

and emulation, which is one of the principal foundations of the reform of the prisoner, it is well, after the first period has been gone through, to mitigate the severity of the cellular system by allowing the prisoners to work together in small groups, according to the necessities of their occupation.

The work must not, however, be made a pretext for too many privileges, granted either generally or individually. Mareska attributes much recidivism to the privileges given to certain clerks in prison. He heard one day one of these say to a newcomer: "You fool, with a little scribbling you are better off in here than outside,"[1] — words which recall those of the Sicilian prisoner to the judge (Part I, Ch. XVII), and explain the fact, known by many prison directors, that the worst rogues are the most docile in the prisons, and in appearance the most repentant.

§ 188. Wages and Savings

A further means of moral reform has been suggested by De Metz and Olivecrona to prevent the recidivism of freed convicts. They advise that the money earned in prison, which is generally turned over to the prisoners when discharged and often becomes their capital for criminal enterprises, should be deposited as a guarantee of their good behavior and as a forced means of saving. It could be lodged with the government of the municipality to which they go or with the employer, and the interest alone paid to them. In Belgium and Holland seven-tenths of the wages of those condemned to compulsory labor is retained, six-tenths in the case of those sentenced to solitary confinement, and five-tenths in the case of those in the simple prisons; the rest is divided into two parts, of which one may be used in prison and the other on going out. In England the money is handed over to the released prisoner with his ticket, if it does not exceed £5. When it exceeds this amount it is paid in instalments upon certificate of good conduct.

§ 189. Homes, etc., for Released Convicts

Many advise also homes for the reception and employment of released prisoners, but, aside from the fact that they cannot

[1] "Des Progrès de la Réforme," 1838, III.

be applied upon a scale corresponding with the need, experience has shown to those who study these institutions in the world and not in books that they have no value in the case of adults, but, on the contrary, very often increase the tendency to idleness, and are rendezvous for criminal associations.

"Out of a hundred liberated convicts, twenty to forty years of age, received in the 'patronage' at Milan," writes Spagliardi, "only the youngest, and few even of those, responded at all to the immense efforts made for their restoration.

"The tendency to idleness and to libertinage, increased by the privations they had undergone, and the fact that they could come and go at pleasure decided them, after two or three months, to leave the asylum, the more so as they did not see in the director the man who was sacrificing himself for their good. He was to them only an enemy, and almost a tyrant. Hence there was a silent war against him carried on by insults, insubordination, violence, and threats."

This is why the statistics of these institutions are so limited and so deceptive. In France out of 16,000 convicts released from prison 363 were assisted. In England 48 societies extended aid to 12,000. In general it is considered unwise to establish institutions for more than temporary help or to give help in money. Instead, food and lodging should be given for future work, and the society should dismiss those who are lazy and also keep informed of the conduct of the persons whom they recommend to positions. For this purpose a special agent is necessary.[1] Maxime du Camp [2] also recognizes the uselessness of assistance rendered to born or habitual criminals, while it may be very useful with accidental criminals.

"Among the criminals," he rightly says, "there are those who become drunk on a glass of water; cashiers who make errors in figures; clerks who become confused about prices and end by committing irregularities, which appear dishonest and bring them before the courts, where they become still more confused and are convicted. These, once liberated, will not fall again into guilt, if they find an employment suited to their limited intelligence."

[1] Lemarque, "La Réhabilitation, etc.," Paris, 1877; Brown, "Suggestions on the Reformation of Discharged Prisoners," 1870.

[2] "Revue des Deux Mondes," 1889.

For these, I admit, assistance is necessary. Further, there are occasional criminals, who, having been tempted by some opportunity for pleasure, have stumbled the first time and robbed their employer. Such persons, if they are not assisted when they come out of prison, will look upon society only as an enemy, and one who was filled with remorse at having stolen twenty francs comes not to be dismayed at burglary and murder.

§ 190. Deportation

There is in Europe a party which see in deportation the only remedy against crime.[1] It has been asserted that a great part of the flourishing American colonies, and ancient Rome itself, owed their origin to a kind of penal immigration. This is an historical error. For Rome it is enough to recall the immortal pages of Virgil; and as for America, we must remember that if the third expedition of Columbus was made up of malefactors, among whom, however, were reckoned many heretics and adventurers, in the first and second only men of honor took part. Under James II deportation was forbidden; and on the other hand, many of the colonies of North America owed their origin to very respectable men, like the Quakers of Penn and Fox. From the influence of transported convicts in Australia Victoria, South Australia, and New Zealand must be altogether excluded; and if New South Wales and Tasmania owe their origin to transportation, it is a great error to suppose that they owe their prosperity to it. This is so true that the great philanthropists, Howard and Bentham, protested against transportation almost immediately, and shortly afterward the colonists themselves did the same; so that in 1828 its abolition was voted by Parliament. The prosperity of Australia is due to its fertile meadows and the trade in wool, which has brought in crowds of free men. The wealth of Melbourne and Sydney began just when the transportation of convicts ceased.

In New South Wales the population increased only at the

[1] Beltrani-Scalia, "Rivista di Disciplina Carceraria," 1872–74; Tissot, "Introduction au Droit Pénal," 1874.

rate of 2000 persons a year from 1810 to 1830, when transportation was at its height; while from 1839 to 1848 the exportation of wool increased from 7 to 23 million pounds, and the population from 114,000 to 220,000, although transportation had ceased in 1840. While it lasted, brigandage raged on a large scale. The convicts did not work, and those who were employed in the construction of roads had to be watched by guards and soldiers, who treated them worse than beasts, chased them with dogs, chained and flogged them. Those who had been set free sold the land the government had given them for the purpose of starting them at honest work, and joined their old accomplices in new crimes. We need not be astonished that the mortality of this part of the population reached 40%, while that of the free population was hardly 5%; and if the criminality in England was 1 to 850 inhabitants, in New South Wales it was 1 to 104, and in Van Dieman's Land 1 to 48. Finally, while the crimes of violence in England were to other crimes as 1 to 8, in New South Wales they reached 50%. In 1805–06 with an average deportation of 360 prisoners a year, there were 2649 convictions in England; and in 1853–56, with an average of 4108 deportations, there were 15,048 convictions. These facts show what sort of advantages are to be looked for from deportation, without counting the enormous expense and the crimes which criminals sometimes commit in order to be deported. In 1852, in fact, there were 3000 criminals in France who asked to be deported, and, what is worse, some of them committed new crimes to attain their end.[1] While in England the expense of supporting a delinquent is £10, this expense rises in the colonies to £26, £35, and £40.

In Guiana there is supposed to be a profit of £1511 with deportation; but dividing this by the number of days of work it is reduced to 54 centimes a head in 1865, and to 48 centimes in 1866; and there are 5% of escapes and 40% of deaths recorded. Each criminal costs 1100 francs a year, three times as much as a convict in prison; and the transportation cost reaches 400 francs.[2] By the French law of May 30, 1874, the

[1] Stevens, "Reg. des Établiss.," 1877.

[2] Bonneville de Marsangy "D'Améliovation des Lois Criminelles," II, 95.

deported convicts were to be employed at the hardest labor of the colony, while efforts were to be made to reform them. They were given the means of living honestly, something an honest man does not always get. A savings bank subsidized by the government was started for them; lands of the best quality, often cleared, were given them, which became their own after five years. While working the land they have a right to food, clothing, agricultural implements,[1] and hospital care; in the case of married persons, the wife has the same rights, besides 150 francs at the time of marriage, and complete furnishing. It is not only the environment that is changed, for everything that would occasion a relapse into crime is carefully removed. But we know that while a change of surroundings may reform an occasional criminal, it has no effect upon real born criminals, who make up the greater part of the deported convicts. In fact, according to official reports, — and the officials have an interest in concealing the truth — we see crime breaking out again in plain daylight, so that honest men, and the very officials themselves who send to the government their garbled reports, are often the victims of these pretended sheep returned to the fold. Thomas, an impartial foreigner, thus describes the situation from his own experience:[2]

". . . It is impossible to imagine the degree of infamy to which they have come. In 1884 one of the criminals tried to cut his wife's throat after having been married to her for 48 hours; surprised at the time, he afterward fled to the natives, who shot him. But the savages themselves are often the victims of these miserable men. Impunity and indulgence have given rise to real anarchy, to a veritable hell upon earth."

According to Mancelon,[3] criminals who had been condemned to death at least three times were finally set at liberty. A deported convict thus described to Laurent one of the marriages which the governor, M. Pardon, in his official capacity (1891), has mentioned with so much admiration:[4]

[1] "Circular of Ministers," Jan. 6, 1882.
[2] "Cannibals and Convicts," 1886.
[3] "Les Bagnes et la Colonisation Pénale," 1886.
[4] Laurent, "Les Habitués des Prisons," 1890.

"I was present on the Isle of Nou at a curious ceremony, the marriage of two of my fellow prisoners. The bridegroom was a man sentenced to five years at hard labor for a murder. To choose his wife he had gone to the convent of Bourail and selected an old prostitute, sentenced to eight years at hard labor, for giving aid in robbing and murdering a man in his own house. The marriage took place. After the mass the priest spoke to the newly married couple of pardon, redemption, and the forgetting of injuries, but the wife kept repeating in her argot, 'Ah, how he wearies me!'

"After mass a very 'wet' banquet took place. The witness drank so much that while he slept he was robbed of his pocket-book. The husband also became so intoxicated that the next morning he awoke without his pocket-book, with a black eye, and without news of his wife, who was absent until the next morning with another convict. He took it in good part, however, and even found it natural.

"Although married, this woman became the concubine of freed convicts, and of the prisoners themselves. One day she lured an Arab, whom she knew to be rich, into a secluded spot, where her husband robbed him and then killed him with a hatchet; but the wife, horrified, denounced the murderer, and he was condemned to death. Thus ended this happy match."

In the monograph, "Travaux Forcés Fin de Siècle,"[1] we are told of a certain Devillepoix, condemned to hard labor for life for two rapes upon minors followed by two homicides, who married as his second wife an infanticide. Some time afterward he set fire to the houses of his neighbors without reason, and also burned a plantation. He prostituted his wife to the first comer in order to live more comfortably. He was condemned to death.

"In 1881 the minister of marine complained that of 7000 persons, without counting freed convicts, only 360 could be employed upon the construction of the roads. All the others were wandering about at random, entirely unrestrained, nominally taking up land or working for private individuals. Thus there was no more discipline or prison. In 1880 there were only 640 to 700 escapes; in 1889 these had reached the constant figure of 800.

"The notorious bandit, Brodeau, who had escaped several times, killed an old woman and devoured a portion of her flesh.

[1] "Nouvelle Revue," 1890.

Under the knife of the guillotine he mocked at the law, and with a loud voice himself gave the signal for the knife to fall.

"Besides, who could restrain those depraved individuals, when they perceived that the prison, that scarecrow of the criminal codes, was nothing but a jest?

"The council of war loses its time with sentencing and re-sentencing convicts already condemned to life imprisonment. Additional sentences have been given of 10, 20, 100, and 200 years in prison.

"In Noumea there are individuals who have been condemned to death three times and afterwards pardoned and left at liberty for the rest of their lives.

"In 1891 the maritime tribunal of Noumea condemned to death a convict named Jamicol, who, in consequence of sentences incurred in the colony, would not have been freed before the year 2036, that is, in 145 years!

"A woman named Macè, sent to New Caledonia after having killed her two children, married, got a land grant, and killed another child. An old potter of Bourail, who had been sentenced for the rape of an older daughter, was rejoined by his wife, his victim, and by another younger daughter. He drove the older to the lowest prostitution, prepared the younger for the same mode of life, and went on with his flourishing pottery trade."[1]

The effects of such colonial organization are evident. A quarter of a century has already elapsed since the arrival of the first convoy of convicts in New Caledonia. Yet there are still no roads there; Noumea has neither sewers, embankments, nor docks; in a short time all the land will be in the hands of incendiaries and murderers. We can see from this how much confidence ought to be placed in reports of inspectors who maintain that "the holders of the land-grants are true farmers, some of whom might with perfect safety be pardoned and set at liberty."

I have reported the facts scrupulously in order that they may serve to counterbalance the assertion that is constantly being made: "Change the environment, and the criminal disappears." Now, here everything is changed, race, climate, conditions — all the causes of crime are removed — and in spite of everything the born criminal continues his series of crimes, while the honest man pays the expenses! What better

[1] Laurent, *op. cit.*

proof could we have of the supremacy of organic action over environment!

These facts show further a long series of deceptions on the part of bureaucrats, who represent the most deplorable measures as excellent. In fact, M. Pardon, the governor of New Caledonia, in his report for 1891, praised the system in use there, and stated that he had employed 1200 convicts upon the roads and placed 630 at agricultural labor with the farmers, declaring that they were watched by the guards without any danger. The holders of land-grants had increased to 123; the penalties were respected, and did not even arouse feelings of revolt; while industry prospered.[1] The truth, he should have added, is that, aside from the enormous expenses for the support of the criminals (not less than 900 francs a head), he fails to take into account the great proportion of the criminals who commit their crimes only to get themselves sent to this Eden.

In order to understand the economic harm done by penal colonies, it is necessary to note that the delinquents who are not peasants are more than half of the criminals deported. Now it is not at 25 or 30 years of age that one learns a new trade; moreover, the sluggishness, the repugnance to work, which is one of the characteristics of the born criminal, is something which we can hardly hope to see bettered in a hotter climate, itself an incentive to crime, nor in the neighborhood of savage populations, whose tendencies are so nearly allied to those of the born criminal. It is, then, natural that recidivism should increase instead of diminish; for we know that this is the rule and not the exception with the born criminal.

It is advantageous to sentence to deportation, therefore, only occasional criminals and criminals by passion.[2]

§ 191. Surveillance

All those of us who know anything of delinquents and of the police, know that surveillance occupies a large part of the time of the officers of public safety,[3] and this, with an expense

[1] "Bulletin des Prisons."
[2] See Chapters XII and XIII.
[3] G. Curcio, "Delle Persone Pregiudicate," in "Delle Colonie e dell' Emigrazione d' Italiani all' Estero" (Carpi), Milan, 1876.

of more than four millions, without any real advantage; for the crimes are in great part committed by the persons who are being watched. But the surveillance itself is a cause of new crimes, and it certainly is a cause of the distress of delinquents; for by denouncing them to respectable people through their personal visits, the police prevent their getting or keeping employment. Crime, as Ortolan has truly said,[1] leads to surveillance; and this prevents those who are watched from finding work, a circle that is even more fatal when they are sent to a residence far from their native country.

"The penalty of surveillance," says Fregier, "has accomplished nothing since its introduction, it offers no guarantee, and it holds out the promise of a security that does not exist."[2]

Add to this the enormous number of arrests, the loss to the government on account of the expense of imprisonment, the arbitrary arrests for forgetting to salute an officer, for addressing a suspect, or for being out a few minutes after hours, which reduce these unfortunates to the position of slaves in the hands of the police (Curcio.) "Enemies," says Machiavelli, "must be conciliated or exterminated." By surveillance we do neither the one nor the other, we only irritate them; and it is to this, or little more than this, that all our institutions for the repression of crime amount in the end.

[1] "Éléments de Droit Penal," chap. 7, tit. v.
[2] "Les Classes Dangereuses," 1868.

CHAPTER IX

ABSURDITIES AND CONTRADICTIONS IN CRIMINAL PROCEDURE

§ 192.

OUR methods and expedients in criminal procedure are no better than we have seen our penal institutions to be. Decisions in criminal cases are nothing more than a game of chance, where nothing is certain but the publicity which leads to new crimes.

§ 193. The Jury

The lack of uniformity in the verdicts brought in by juries in different years and in different countries shows the inefficiency of the institution. Thus, Cagliari reckons that there are 50% of acquittals, while upper Italy shows but 23%.[1] Venice shows a difference of 9% to 15% as we pass from the small towns to the large ones. "The cultivated classes," says Taiani, "are never represented on the jury," and in fact numerous cases prove to us only too clearly the complete ignorance of jurymen. Thus in a vote with regard to a homicide a ballot was found on which was written "Yes or no." It was counted in favor of the prisoner. When the juror was asked why he had written so strange a vote, he answered, "Because the ballot had printed on it, 'The juror must answer: yes or no.' "

There is no guarantee of the incorruptibility of the juryman, who, having no account to render and nothing to lose by an acquittal, often levies tribute upon justice, as is proved by numerous acquittals secured by bribery even after the criminal has confessed. More than this, the jury of itself is a cause of popular corruption. Borghetti[2] notes that many respectable peasants are corrupted by serving on the jury, and he adds: "It is the arena where the Mafia achieves its triumphs." More-

[1] Lavini, "Del Modo con cui e Amministrata la Giustizia," Venice, 1875.

[2] "Relaz. della Giunta per l' Inchiesta sulle Condizioni della Sicilia."

over the injustice towards the poor that springs from that corruption is a great cause of immorality, for the poor accused person, seeing that justice is quite other than equal for all, believes himself almost justified in indemnifying himself at the expense of a society which has condemned him, and regards his sentence as unjust, even when it is not.

In answer to those who maintain that juries are a guarantee of free government, we may recall that the history of England shows us how often juries change their opinion according to the will of the government. But besides, what has this argument to do with cases that are not political? Furthermore, in those cases where the government remains quite indifferent, public opinion, to which the most respectable juries are involuntarily subservient, is often easily misled by criminals and their defenders. And where will you find a greater tyranny than that of ignorance? "The jury," writes Pironti, "often acquits the man, who steals the public money, for the purpose of protesting against the government, or perhaps acquits a criminal because he was a brave soldier." I will add that this excessive mildness in dealing with criminals leads them to new crimes; and we may understand why in a brawl a comrade of the aggressor said to him, "Kill him, and you will have a jury trial. If you merely wound him, you will go to the police magistrate."[1] Where a matter must above all be decided on its merits without any reference to feeling, is it not the direct opposite of justice to leave it to be decided by popular instinct, by the feeling that happens to predominate in the crowd at the moment? And what can be done about the errors of the jury, springing often from causes that it is impossible to foresee, as in the Galletti case in Brescia, where a blot of ink upon the "Yes" of a juryman caused the acquittal of a man who ought to have been condemned to death?

It is vain to urge in support of the jury the necessity of modernizing the processes of justice, as well as other institutions. The jury existed already, though in rudimentary form, at the time of the Twelve Tables and the Germanic "Gerichte." It is just as modern as cremation, — that pretended innova-

[1] "Eco Giudiziario," 1878.

tion of the modern pseudo-hygienists, which was already ancient in the time of Homer — and quite as commendable in practice.

Have we not done everything to bind upon magistrates the duty of justifying and giving the reasons of their decisions and of not giving them in the form of oracles — this notwithstanding the guarantees offered by their past, by their special studies, by their experience, and by the fact that appeal may be taken from their decisions? And then we think we have discovered a new source of liberty and justice in permitting men without experience, without responsibility, to sentence by a simple *yes* or *no*, like children and despots, without giving any reason for their acts; and in Italy we aggravate the evil by decreeing that this irresponsible sentence shall be irrevocable when it is in favor of the criminal, and only subject to appeal when it is against him! Every magistrate must justify the condemnation or acquittal which he pronounces for libel, theft, or assault. But when it is a question of robbery or murder, the popular magistracy gives its decision without any other guarantee or reason than *yes* or *no*.[1] Worse than that, the juror may still more easily let the criminal go unpunished by casting a blank ballot, which, even if the law does interpret it as a definite expression, in the conscience of an ignorant juryman, who is inclined to make mental reservations, is always a compromise between truth and injustice.

If even those precautions prescribed by law to prevent the inconveniences of the jury system were only observed! One of the most important assuredly is that the jury shall communicate with no one until they have pronounced their verdict. They take an oath to observe this obligation, but in reality, as all the world knows, they do not keep it, and communicate, even publicly, with the counsel for the defense. Why, on the other hand, should the right of exclusion without cause be given to the defendant, who challenges the better jurors — just those who by their honorable character and their intelligence would be most capable of resisting seduction and rhetoric? How can we believe that an ignorant man could follow a trial like that at Ancona, in which 147 witnesses were interrogated

[1] "Eco Giudiziario," 1875.

and 5000 questions laid before the jury? Furthermore, how shall those who have nothing to lose by acquitting resist threats of death, when even responsible judges allow themselves to be intimidated? And, finally, if tried judges, if an assembly of experts, can in certain crimes hardly disentangle the truth, which can only be understood through a knowledge of toxicology, surgery, and psychiatry, how can it be done by individuals who are not only not specialists but quite ignorant of any science whatever? And this at a time when division of labor is required in things much less important than justice! Are we not abandoning to chance something that ought to be conducted according to the strictest rules?

Objection is made, it is true, that the average number of acquittals in jury trials is no larger than in those cases decided by the judge. But this objection is far from being exact, for the average in some regions is twice as great. Even if it were true, there is a great difference between the two cases. Before a case is brought to trial before a jury it has already been submitted to a long series of tests and judgments such as those of the prætor, the examining judge, the royal procurator, the section of accusation, the president of the court, the procurator general, experts, etc. After all these it is difficult for any proof of the innocence of the accused person to arise. Further, it is not so much in regard to number as to quality that the acquittals are at fault. They show a deplorable generosity toward murderers, homicides, and those guilty of insurrection; and also, by an unfortunate perversion, toward forgers and persons who steal public money, a fact which is certainly one of the causes of the constant increase of crimes of this kind.

The objection that in England and America the jury system works well has no weight. In the Anglo-Saxon race the feeling for justice and duty does not fail as often as it does with us. Further, they do not try by jury those who have confessed their guilt, while with us these cases, which amount to half the total number, give rise to the greatest scandals. Then there is a smaller number of criminals tried by jury in England, 1 to 132,770 inhabitants, while in Italy there is 1 for each 8931, — an enormous difference not sufficiently accounted for by our greater criminality. In England, moreover, in many cases such as insurrections, bankruptcies, etc., there are special juries, and the *habeas corpus* does not forbid (as some imagine) preventive arrests by the police, but gives the accused the right to secure within 24 hours the intervention of the magistracy (the High Court of London, or the County Court) to decide whether his detention should be continued or revoked. In all difficult cases the Coroner calls about him a veritable jury of specialists, physicians, or chemists. The jurors, moreover, take oath to conform to the instructions of the judge with regard to the law, and keep the oath scrupulously, thanks to their respect for the law. Public opinion in England, moreover, would revolt against a perjured verdict in which the instructions of the judge on points of law were disregarded. Besides this if the verdict appears unjust, the judge can suspend the execution of it, at least until it has been sanctioned by his colleagues.[1] We may add that the jury cannot leave the Court House until the verdict has been rendered, a measure that prevents many bad influences.

But even in England the jury system is not without its objectors. As early as the time of Elizabeth they used against the jury the words hurled by Cicero against corrupt magistrates: "Quos fames magis quam fama commoverit." [2] And in 1824 the "Westminster Review" attacked the jury system violently, and went so far as to call it the phantom of justice.

§ 194. Appeal

"Injustice makes judgment bitter," wrote Bacon, "delay turns it sour." As much may be said in our day, when, thanks to appeals, the penalty is no longer either prompt, certain, or severe. And whereas the judgment of the trial court is preceded by a regular and complete argument, that of the appellate court is based merely upon a written statement of the case often very irregularly and incompletely drawn up. This fatal edifice is crowned by the most ample right to reverse the decisions of the lower court, not based, as would be just (and as is

[1] Glaser, "Schwurgerichtliche Erörterungen," Vienna, 1876.
[2] Who are more influenced by hunger than by good repute.

the practice in America, England, and even France) upon substantial errors and errors of fact; but almost always upon matters of form, on account of which a very costly judgment may be reversed for a simple mistake in grammar made by an unfortunate clerk.

§ 195. Pardon

As if the right of appeal were not enough, we have also the right of pardon so profusely employed in Italy that pardons are here a hundred times as numerous as they are in France.[1] Now, how can we reconcile this clemency with the rarity of cases of moral reform? Who is not aware that criminals liberated after having passed through the graduated prison system (which is much more of a test than simple imprisonment) still give very poor results? How can we say that justice is equal for all, that it is destined to bring the disturbed juridical condition into equilibrium, and that it is based upon fixed, immutable laws, free from all personal influence, when all that is needed to blot out the whole thing is a simple stroke of the pen, — the signature of a man who may be the best man in the country, but is after all only a man? The system of pardons is founded upon the supposition that the right to punish exists only in the will of the ruler. "But we use it to mitigate justice when it is too severe," answers Friedrich. Very well, if that is so, you have not true justice, and you ought to change its methods. Says Filangeri:[2] "Every pardon granted to a criminal is a derogation of the law; for if the pardon is just, the law is bad, and if the law is just, the pardon is an attack upon the law. By the first hypothesis, laws should be abolished, and by the second, pardons." We may add as a last consideration that pardons are contrary to the spirit of equality that animates modern society; for when it favors the rich, as is too often the case, it makes the poor suspect that there is no justice for them. Rousseau's words in this connection may be remembered: "Frequent pardons announce that crimes will soon have no further need of them, and everyone knows whither that leads."

[1] "Relazione del Ministero di Grazia e Giustizia," 1875.
[2] "La Scienza della Legislazione," Bk. III, Pt. iv, Ch. 57.

§ 196. Criminological Prejudices

It is still worse that there should be instilled into judicial practice a series of prejudices which make every judgment useless. We deplore, for example, the principle that when there is a doubt as to the intent of the criminal, he must be presumed to have had the less evil intent; and that when we cannot prove which of two crimes he was aiming at, we must always presume that it was the less serious. Now it is the exact contrary of this that is the case with born criminals. The law, then, by following an hypothesis that is the direct opposite of the fact, endangers the safety of society.

But it is still worse when the law is more lenient with attempted crimes, when it denies the intention, even where the criminal has betrayed it by his threats and by the steps which he has taken to put it into execution. Thus, one who administers a substance that he believes to be poisonous, when it is not, is guilty from the point of view of common sense, which does not stop for the magic formulas of the old jurists; for he is as dangerous as if he had administered a real poison, the more so since we know the pertinacity with which poisoners repeat their crimes on a large scale. To take the opposite position is virtually to insist on seeing the victim quite dead before taking steps to protect him. This is to rob ourselves, through love of abstract theories, of a practical and concrete means of protection, — so much the more since we know the tendency of the born criminal to divulge his own crimes before committing them.[1] Further, it is absurd that our laws should be milder towards recidivists who do not fall again into the same crimes. They are no less dangerous on that account, but quite the contrary. The English statistics show that those who have committed crimes against persons, upon relapsing, commit more especially crimes against property, in order to escape justice. The criminal who always relapses into the same crimes is almost always a semi-imbecile, perhaps less dangerous. For such the increase of the penalty is less urgent; while the man, who at short intervals commits several kinds of crimes, shows greater intelligence

[1] "Homme Criminel," Vol. I, Pt. 3.

and greater versatility in crime. Such were Lacenaire, Gasparoni, Desrues, and Holmes, who knew how to combine theft, swindling, and poisoning, with forgery and assassination. Men of this sort are the most dangerous, and the hardest to recognize and arrest.

Again, the importance that is assigned to public trials is an error.

> "The public trial is almost always only a useless and often dangerous repetition of the recorded results of the preliminary investigation; for the witnesses simply repeat their depositions, which are already in the record. Now it is difficult for the memory not to become confused before an imposing tribunal, where the crowd is annoying and the lawyers ask captious, or even threatening, questions; while it is much easier to recollect and recount a fact exactly in a small room before two or three persons only."[1]

The same may be said of the arguments of prosecution and defence, — and this with the more reason because the written argument, which is an immense advance on the spoken one, is permanent, and the memory for words is much weaker than that for things. According to the experiments of Münsterberg and Bigham, the average of errors of memory is greater for the auditory series (31.6%) than it is for the visual series (20.5%). The vaunted oral trial is, then, absolutely contrary to modern progress, however much it may have been regarded as one of the pillars of justice.

Finally, when we cannot clearly prove that the person accused is a recidivist, or even when his crime has been committed in youth, we should at least take account of all his evil antecedents, in order to class him among suspects. What we want to arrive at is the degree of fear with which the individual must be inspired to keep him from doing harm, and if the legislator does not believe that anthropological and psychological characteristics may be of service to him in solving the question, he ought not, at least, to reject demonstrated criminological facts.

[1] Ferrero, "Les Lois Psychologiques de Symbolisme," 1890.

§ 197. Erroneous Theories

There are many jurists, who are deeply versed in scientific matters and in the current of the scientific movement with regard to the criminal, who have not been able to gauge its depth accurately for want of physiological ideas or of direct contact. These men have maintained that the great numbers of insane and feeble-minded to be found among criminals, and consequently the limited responsibility of many criminals for their crimes, lead inevitably to the reduction of the penalty. They do not understand that the new anthropological notions, while diminishing the guilt of the born criminal, imposes upon us at the same time the duty of prolonging his sentence, because the more irresponsible criminals are the more they are to be dreaded, since their innate and atavistic criminal tendencies can be neutralized only by selection and sequestration. These tendencies are like a swelling wave, which is turned back upon itself when it encounters a strong dike, but which sweeps on and becomes threatening if nothing checks it. Our jurists have not imitated the Dutch, but have thought that they check the evil by lowering the dikes more and more; hence the increasing tendency to give every opportunity of defense to the criminal and to facilitate pardons, while nothing is done to increase the security of society and the certainty of the repression of crime. Now, if a general, relying upon the power of philosophy, allowed himself to be guided solely by that, or by an abstract strategy, founded upon the history of ancient battles, without regard for modern ballistics, is it not certain that he would conduct his unfortunate soldiers to an inevitable death? Now, penal justice requires at least as much practical knowledge as does military strategy. Metaphysics in this matter can be only a negative resource, yet the practical results must often depend upon the opinion of persons, venerable indeed but inclined to substitute metaphysics for strategy, who dream with open eyes of free-will independent of matter and of a right to punish based not upon pressing social necessity but upon abstract violations of juridical order. Not only do they not think of eliminating the true causes of crime (such as alcoholism, associations of children, etc.), but, by introducing precipitately all the innovations that the civilized world has contrived in favor of the criminal, they forget the precautions necessary to mitigate the evil consequences of these (intermediate institutions for conditional liberation, etc.), and they forget, finally, the new means devised for the defense of society.

It is also to be deplored that the high-priests of justice regard the form of procedure of more importance than the protection of society; so that it has passed into a proverb that the forms more than the substance of the procedure are the supreme guarantee for both parties, and that "forma dat esse rei," — four words that are the greatest proof of human blindness in juridical matters.

§ 198. Causes of this State of Things

The cause of this fatal retrogession toward theory is to be sought, first of all, in that law of inertia and exaggerated conservatism by means of which a man, when he has been drawn along by extraordinary circumstances or by bold and fortunate rebels, turns back with terror from every change, however simple and logical; and if in some cases men submit to the change, notwithstanding their repugnance, it is because the time is so ripe, and the innovation so apt, that they are carried along in spite of themselves and forced to accept it. But here, as in religion and philosophy, the truth is hidden by formulas, whose mystic and imposing appearance prevents the discovery of their insubstantial character. Whoever, with uplifted religious feelings, hears for the first time rabbis or brahmins reciting mysteriously their Hebrew or Sanscrit prayers, attaches to them a profound significance, whereas if translated into the vulgar tongue they would appear quite simple. In the same way the public does not understand the legal vocabulary, and finds the jurist the more profound the less it understands him. Often jurists do the same, and think more of themselves, the more they entangle themselves in their hieroglyphics. We understand from this why it is that the public cannot take jurists seriously when they affirm, for example, that to authorize another person to commit a crime is not to be guilty of an overt act; or that when a convict's second offense is different from the first he is not a recidivist.

Ferrero finds another cause for these errors,[1] in ideo-emotional inactivity, in the tendency of the human mind to reduce to a minimum the number of mental associations necessary for any work whatever. In practice, then, the literal interpretation of the law prevails over all considerations of justice.

"This is the case with the bureaucrary of great governments. We know that the most common vice of this class of functionaries is the habit of applying literally the rules and laws given for their guidance; while these can be but the imperfect indication of the will of the law-makers, who, not being able to foresee everything, can only lay down general rules. The official ought to interpret these general rules according to the particular case, but, instead, the letter of the rule becomes standard, truth, and even reason itself. The employee of a private establishment, with an eye to his own interests, does not let himself so easily fall into the habit of carrying out a general rule without reflection, but interprets the directions he receives according to the circumstances of the case."

Now, what happens to codified laws, which are supposed to serve merely to guide the magistrate in particular cases, is that they become justice to him even when applied to the letter. To decide conscientiously the judge ought to make himself a personal criterion for the special case that he has under his eyes, and judge it according to the general spirit that emanates from the written law. The Roman jurisconsults also recognized that the civil law needed to be supplemented by what they called the natural law, which was nothing else than the expression of that feeling of justice that revolts against the application of general rules to particular cases to which they are not adapted. But all this requires an intense intellectual effort, a fatiguing labor accompanied by a tormenting sense of responsibility. It is much easier and more convenient to apply the general directions of the law by deducing their logical consequences. As soon as the mind has become accustomed to this way of working, a professional ideo-emotional stagnation is produced, which leads

[1] "Les Lois Psychologiques du Symbolisme," *supra*.

the judge to consider the literal application of the law as his whole duty. He soon comes to exclude every collateral idea that might lead to an equitable solution of the question. The amount of injury suffered by the victim and the causes which brought about the crime are not in any way taken into account.

These considerations help us understand why the sciences all began with the deductive method. Even the physical sciences, which from the nature of their subject would naturally hold themselves closer to nature, started with deduction. Primitive physics and chemistry, for example, consisted of a series of deductions drawn by force of logic from a principle established by the observation of facts at random. It was only later that men came to recognize the fact that to learn the laws of nature it is necessary to reason less and to observe more. In the beginning pure logic was preferred to observation and experience, because it was a less fatiguing psychological process, exacting the presence of a smaller number of intellectual elements in the mind.

"The employment of pure logic is, then, the effect of an ideo-emotional inactivity proper to the period of infancy, which appears in the period of old age by the well-known law of degeneracy and atavism. What is the science of the Middle Ages but an invasion of Greek subtilty into the field which the thought of antiquity properly submitted to the method of observation? Just so the absolutism of the deductive method in modern juridical science is a sign of decrepitude. The law of ideo-emotional inactivity explains to us why so often the law of rude and barbarous peoples is distinguished by a certain sound common sense, as compared with the marvelously logical but marvelously absurd subtilties of the law of the most civilized peoples." [1]

[1] Ferrero, "Les Lois Psychologiques du Symbolisme," Paris, 1894.

Part Three

SYNTHESIS AND APPLICATION

CHAPTER I

ATAVISM AND EPILEPSY IN CRIME AND IN PUNISHMENT

§ 199.

ALL that I have set forth in the present book and in those which preceded it (Vol. I and II of the "Homme Criminel") proves clearly the insecurity of the ancient criminological scaffolding. Have I succeeded in substituting a more solid edifice? If pride in a long and painful task has not blinded me, I think that I can answer in the affirmative. The fundamental proposition undoubtedly is that we ought to study not so much the abstract crime as the criminal.

§ 200. Atavism

The born criminal shows in a proportion reaching 33% numerous specific characteristics that are almost always atavistic. Those who have followed us thus far have seen that many of the characteristics presented by savage races are very often found among born criminals. Such, for example, are: the slight development of the pilar system; low cranial capacity; retreating forehead; highly developed frontal sinuses; great frequency of Wormian bones; early closing of the cranial sutures; the simplicity of the sutures; the thickness of the bones of the skull; enormous development of the maxillaries and the zygomata; prognathism; obliquity of the orbits; greater pigmentation of the skin; tufted and crispy hair; and large ears. To these we may add the lemurine appendix; anomalies of the ear; dental diastemata; great agility; relative insensibility to pain; dullness of the sense of touch; great visual acuteness; ability to recover quickly from wounds; blunted affections; precocity as to sensual pleasures;[1] greater resemblance between the sexes; greater incorrigibility of the woman (Spencer); laziness; absence of remorse; impulsiveness; physiopsychic excitability; and especially improvidence, which sometimes appears as courage and again as recklessness changing to cowardice. Besides these there is great vanity; a passion for gambling and alcoholic drinks; violent but fleeting passions; superstition; extraordinary sensitiveness with regard to one's own personality; and a special conception of God and morality. Unexpected analogies are met even in small details, as, for example, the improvised rules of criminal gangs; the entirely personal influence of the chiefs;[2] the custom of tattooing; the not uncommon cruelty of their games; the excessive use of gestures; the onomatopoetic language with personification of inanimate things; and a special literature recalling that of heroic times, when crimes were celebrated and the thought tended to clothe itself in rhythmic form.

This atavism explains the diffusion of certain crimes, such as the pederasty and infanticide, whose extension to whole companies we could not explain if we did not recall the Romans, the Greeks, the Chinese, and the Tahitians, who not only did not regard them as crimes, but sometimes even practiced them as a national custom. Garofalo has admirably summed up the psychical characteristics of the born criminal as being the absence of the feelings of shame, honor, and pity, which are those that are lacking in the savage also.[3] We may add to these the lack of industry and self-control.

To those who, like Reclus and Krapotkin, object that there are savage peoples who are honorable and chaste, we must reply that a certain degree of density of population and of association among men is necessary for crimes to develop. It is not possible for example, to steal when property does not exist, or to swindle when there is no trade. But the proof that these tendencies exist in germ in the savage, is that when they begin to pass from their stage of savagery and take on a little civilization they always develop the characteristics of criminality

[1] "Homme Criminel," Vol. I, pp. 136 to 579.
[2] Tacitus, "Germ.," VII.
[3] "Criminologie," 2d ed., 1895.

in an exaggerated form. As Ferrero has pointed out to us, even when honor, chastity, and pity are found among savages, impulsiveness and laziness are never wanting. Savages have a horror of continuous work, so that for them the passage to active and methodical labor lies by the road of selection or of slavery only. Thus, according to the testimony of Tacitus, the impulsiveness of the ancient Germans frequently resulted in the murder of slaves, committed in a fit of anger, an act which was not regarded as culpable. Tacitus notes also their lack of capacity for work.

"They have," he says, "large bodies, effective for sudden effort, but they lack the patience necessary for regular work. When they are not at war they do nothing . . . they sleep and eat. The strongest and most warlike live in idleness, leaving the care of the house and the field to the women, the old men, and the weak, becoming themselves brutalized in sloth."

At times, on the other hand, impulsiveness, rather than sluggishness, seems to ally itself with a ceaseless need of movement, which asserts itself in savage peoples in a life of incessant vagabondage. Thus the Andaman Islanders, as Hovelacque tells us, have so restless a disposition that they remain not more than two or three days in the same place, and their wanderings have no other reason than the need of movement. This attitude seems to be the result of a passage between physiopsychic inertia and an intermittent need of violent and unrestrained physical and moral excitation, which always goes with inertia and impulsiveness. Thus it is that those peoples who are normally most lazy and indolent have the most unrestrained and noisy dances, which they carry on until they get into a kind of delirium, and fall down utterly exhausted. "When the Spaniards," writes Robertson, "first saw the American Indians, they were astonished at their mad passion for dancing, and at the dizzy activity which this people, almost always cold and passive, displayed when they gave themselves up to this amusement." "The negroes of Africa," writes Du Chaillu, "dance madly when they hear the sound of the tom-tom, and lose all command of themselves." "It is," says Letourneau, "a real dancing madness, which makes them forget their troubles, public or private."

We may add that the atavism of the criminal, when he lacks absolutely every trace of shame and pity, may go back far beyond the savage, even to the brutes themselves. Pathological anatomy helps prove our position by showing in the case of the criminal a greater development of the cerebellum, a rarer union of the calcarine fissure with the parieto-occipital, the absence of folds in the passage of Gratiolet, the gutter-like shape of the nasal incisure, the frequency of the olecranial foramen, extra ribs and vertebræ, and especially the histological anomalies discovered by Roncoroni in the cortex of the cerebrum of criminals, that is to say, the frequent absence of granular layers, and the presence of nerve cells in the white matter, and immense pyramidal cells. In seeking for analogies beyond our own race we come upon the explanation of the union of the atlas with the occipital bone, the prominence of the canine teeth, the flattening of the palate, and the median occipital fossa, occurring among criminals as with the lemurs and rodents; [1] as also the prehensile foot, the simplicity of the lines of the palm, motor and sensory left-handedness. We recall also the tendency to cannibalism even without desire for vengeance, and still more that form of sanguinary ferocity, mingled with lubricity, of which examples are furnished us by Gille, Verzeni, Legier, Bertrand, Artusio, the Marquis of Sade, and others, with whom atavism was accompanied by epilepsy, idiocy, or general paralysis, but who always recall the pairing of animals, preceded by ferocious and sanguinary contests to overcome the reticence of the female or to conquer rivals.[2]

These facts prove clearly that the most horrible crimes have their origin in those animal instincts of which childhood gives us a pale reflection. Repressed in civilized man by education, environment, and the fear of punishment, they suddenly break out in the born criminal without apparent cause, or under the influence of certain circumstances, such as sickness, atmospheric influences, sexual excitement, or mob influence. We know that certain morbid conditions, such as injuries to the head, meningitis, and chronic intoxication, or certain physiological

[1] "Homme Criminel," Vol. I, pp. 160, 217, 176, 182.

[2] "Homme Criminel," Vol. I, pp. 449, 513; Vol. II, pp. 95, 96, 123, 139, 144, 147.

conditions like pregnancy and senility, produce derangements in the nutrition of the nervous centers, and in consequence atavistic retrogressions. We can see, then, how they may facilitate the tendency to crime, and when we take into account the short distance that separates the criminal from the savage, we come to understand why convicts so easily adopt savage customs, including cannibalism, as was observed in Australia and Guiana.[1] When we note, further, how children, until they are educated, are ignorant of the difference between vice and virtue, and steal, strike, and lie without the least compunction, we easily understand the great precocity in crime, and see why it is that the majority of abandoned children and orphans end by becoming criminals.[2] Further, atavism shows us the inefficacy of punishment for born criminals and why it is that they inevitably have periodic relapses into crime, so that the greatest variation shown by the number of crimes against persons is not more than $\frac{1}{25}$, and by those against property not more than $\frac{1}{50}$.[3]

We see, as Maury very truly remarks, that we are governed by silent laws, which never fall into desuetude and rule society much more surely than the laws inscribed in the codes.

§ 201. Epilepsy

The same phenomena which we observe in the case of born criminals appear again in the rare cases of moral insanity,[4] but may be studied minutely, and on a large scale, in epileptics, criminal or not,[5] as the table given below will prove. There we shall see that not one of the atavistic phenomena shown by criminals is lacking in epilepsy; though epileptics show also certain purely morbid phenomena, such as cephalea, atheroma, delirium, and hallucination. In born criminals also we find, besides the atavistic characteristics, certain others that appear to be entirely pathological, or which at first sight seem more nearly allied to disease than to atavism. Such are, for example, in the anatomical field, excessive asymmetry, cranial capacity

[1] Bouvier, "Voyage à la Guyane," 1866.
[2] "Homme Criminel," Vol. I, pp. 92 to 108.
[3] Maury, "Mouvemente Moral de la Société," Paris, 1860.
[4] "Homme Criminel," Vol. II, pp. 2–13.
[5] "Homme Criminel," Vol. II, pp. 50–201.

and face too large or too small, sclerosis, traces of meningitis, hydrocephalous forehead, oxycephaly, acrocephaly, cranial depressions, numerous osteophytes, early closing of the cranial sutures, thoracic asymmetry, late grayness of hair, late baldness, and abnormal and early wrinkles; in the biological field, alterations of the reflexes and pupillary inequalities. To these we may add peripheral scotomata of the visual field, which one never finds in savages, with whom, on the contrary, the field of vision is remarkably wide and regular, as we see in the case of the Dinkas. There is also to be added the alteration of hearing, taste, and smell, the predilection for animals, precocity in sexual pleasures, amnesia, vertigo, and maniac and paranoiac complications. These abnormalities, which are found in greater proportion among idiots, cretins, and degenerates in general, are to be explained by the fact that in these cases alcoholic intoxication is added to the effect of atavism, and still more to that of epilepsy.

However, the participation of epilepsy in producing the effect does not exclude atavism, since they equally involve characteristics at once atavistic and pathological, like macrocephaly, cranial sclerosis, Wormian bones, rarity of beard; and in the biological field, left-handedness, analgesis, obtuseness of all senses except that of sight, impulsiveness, pederasty, obscenity, sluggishness, superstition, frequent cannibalism, choleric and impetuous disposition, tendency to reproduce the cries and actions of animals; and especially the histological anomalies of the cortex, which we have noted among criminals, and which reproduce the conditions of the lower animals; and finally anomalies of the teeth. These latter might appear to have no connection with the brain, but are, on the contrary, intimately connected with it, since the teeth proceed from the same embryonic membrane as the brain does.[1]

We may recall here that Gowers, having often noted in epileptics acts peculiar to animals, such as biting, barking, and mewing, concludes from this "that these are manifestations of that instinctive animalism which we possess in the latent state." [2]

[1] "Homme Criminel," Vol. I, p. 232, n.
[2] "Epilepsy," London, 1880.

		Criminals	Epileptics	Atavism	Phenomena of Arrested Development	Morbid Phenomena	Atypical Phenomena
Cranium	Volume too great	+	+	...	...	...	+
	Volume too small	+	+	+	+	+	+
	Sclerosis	+	+	+	+	+	...
	Exostosis	+	+	...	...	+	...
	Asymmetry	+	+	...	...	+	...
	Median occipital fossa	+	+	...	+	...	...
	Cranial index too great	+	+	...	...	+	...
	Strongly arched brows	+	+	...	+	...	...
	Low, retreating forehead	+	+	...	+	...	...
	Hydrocephalous forehead	+	+	...	...	+	...
	Cranial osteophytes	+	+	...	...	+	...
	Numerous Wormian bones	+	+	+	+	...	...
	Frontal suture	+	+	+	+	...	...
	Early synostosis	+	+	...	...	+	...
	Oblique orbits	+	+	+	...	...	...
Face	Lemurine appendix	+	+	+	...	...	...
	Maxillaries too large	+	+	+	...	...	...
	Large and prominent zygomata	+	+	+	...	...	...
	Large, outstanding ears	+	+	+	...	+	...
	Facial asymmetry	+	+	...	...	+	...
	Strabismus	+	+	...	...	+	...
	Masculine face in women	+	+	+	...	...	...
	Dental diastemata	+	+	+	...	...	...
	Anomalies of bones of nose	+	+	...	...	...	...
	Anomalies of teeth	+	+	+	...	...	...
	Bones of face too large	+	+	+	...	...	...
Brain	Anomalies of fissures	+	+	+	+	...	...
	Small weight	+	+	+	+	...	...
	Hypertrophy of cerebellum	+	+	+	...	...	...
	Histological changes of cortex	+	+	+	+	...	...
	Traces of meningitis	+	+	...	...	...	...
Body	Asymmetry of thorax	+	+	...	...	+	...
	Prehensile foot	+	+	+	...	...	...
	Left-handedness	+	+	...	...	...	...
	Hernia	+	+	+	+	+	...
	Simplicity of lines of palm	+	+	+	...	...	+
	Visceral lesions	+	+	...	...	...	+

If fully developed epileptic fits are often lacking in the case of the born criminal, this is because they remain latent, and only show themselves later under the influence of the causes assigned (anger, alcoholism), which bring them to the surface. With both criminals and epileptics there is to be noted an insufficient development of the higher centers. This manifests

		Criminals	Epileptics	Atavism	Phenomena of Arrested Development	Morbid Phenomena	Atypical Phenomena
Skin	Abnormal wrinkles	+	+	+	...	...	...
	Sparse beard	+	+	+	...	+	...
	Yellowish tint	+	+	+	...	...	...
	Tattooing	+	..	+	...	...	...
	Crispy bair	+	+	+	...	...	...
Motor Anomalies	Left-handedness and ambidextry	+	+	+	...	...	...
	Abnormalities of reflexes	+	+	..	...	+	...
	Unequal pupils	+	+	..	...	+	...
	Abnormal agility	+	+	+	...	...	...
Sensorial Anomalies	Obtuseness of sense of touch	+	+	+	...	+	...
	Relative insensibility to pain	+	+	+	...	+	...
	Great visual acuteness	+	+	+	...	...	...
	Obtuseness of hearing, taste, and smell	+	+	+	...	+	...
	Sensorial left-handedness	+	+	+	...	+	...
	Peripheral scotomata of the field of vision	+	+	..	...	+	...
Psychic Anomalies	Limited intelligence	+	+	+	+	...	...
	Superstition	+	+	+	...	...	...
	Emotional obtuseness	+	+	+	...	+	...
	Lack of moral sensibility	+	+	+	...	+	...
	Absence of remorse	+	+	+	...	...	...
	Cannibalism, ferocity, lack of self-control	+	+	+	+	+	...
	Pederasty, onanism, obscenity	+	+	+	...	+	...
	Exaggerated religious beliefs	+	+	+	...	...	...
	Vagrancy	+	+	+	...	...	...
	Sexual precocity	+	+	+	...	+	...
	Vanity	+	+	+	...	...	...
	Simulation	+	+	..	...	+	...
	Laziness, inertia	+	+	+	...	+	...
	Improvidence	+	+	+	...	...	...
	Cowardice	+	+	+	...	...	...
	Passion for gambling	+	+	+	...	...	...
	Mania, paranoia, delirium	+	+	..	...	+	...
	Vertigo	+	+	..	...	+	...
Causes	Heredity (alcoholism, insanity, epilepsy, old age of parents)	+	+	..	...	...	...
	Alcoholism, etc.	+	+	..	...	...	...

itself in a deterioration in the moral and emotional sensibilities, in sluggishness, physiopsychic hyperexcitability, and especially in a lack of balance in the mental faculties, which, even when distinguished by genius and altruism, nevertheless always show gaps, contrasts, and intermittent action.

§ 202. Combination of Morbid Anomalies with Atavism

Very often, moreover, certain common characteristics of criminals and epileptics have been classed as abnormal or morbid and not as atavistic, entirely because of the insufficiency of our embryological and phylogenetic knowledge. Many of the characteristics given in the preceding table (which, however, is only schematic) are atavistic and morbid at the same time, such as microcephaly, cranial sclerosis, etc. Facial asymmetry would also appear to be atavistic when we recall, for example, the flat-fishes (Penta); so likewise the abnormally wrinkled face, taking us back to the Hottentots and the apes. Hernia, also, as Féré rightly remarks, recalls conditions that are normal in the lower vertebrates and in the embryo.

Very often morbidity and atavism go back to a common cause, as Wagner [1] observes in a magnificent dissertation.

"The idea," he writes, "that the atavism of criminals is associated with some specific disease of the fœtus has been completely confirmed by the discoveries of Ettinghausen. If, for example, we freeze the roots of an oak so as partly to kill it, the following year it will put out leaves that are not like the leaves of the modern oak, but like those of the oak of the tertiary period. This fact explains the reappearance of intermediate and indistinct fossil forms. We see very clearly, then, that influences capable of producing a disease can bring about atavistic morphological retrogressions."

The epileptic background upon which the clinical and anatomical picture of the moral lunatic and the born criminal is drawn (a picture that would otherwise be lost in vague semi-juridical, semi-psychiatric hypotheses) explains the instantaneousness, periodicity, and paradoxical character of their symptoms, which are doubtless their most marked characteristics. Note, for example, in this class, the coexistence and interchange of kindness and ferocity, of cowardice and the maddest recklessness, and of genius and complete stupidity.

§ 203. The Criminaloid

Criminaloids, while quite separable from born criminals, do not lack some connection with epilepsy and atavism. Thus

[1] Wagner von Jauregg, "Antrittsvorlesung an der Psychiatrischen Klinik," Vienna, 1895.

there are more epileptics among them (10% among pickpockets) than among normal men, and a greater proportion of criminal types (17%), but there are also certain specific anomalies, such as left-handedness, common among swindlers.[1]

In the biology of the criminaloid we observe a smaller number of anomalies in touch, sensibility to pain, psychometry, and especially less early baldness and grayness, and less tattooing. But, on the other hand, we meet with a larger number of strictly morbid anomalies, depending upon the abuse of alcoholic drinks, such as atheromata, paresis, and scars. Psychic anomalies are especially less frequent with the criminaloid, who has not the cynicism of the born criminal nor the passion for doing evil for its own sake; he confesses his fault more easily and with more sincerity, and repents more often. But he is more lascivious, and more often given to alcoholism; and the criminaloid women are more susceptible to suggestion. The criminaloid is more precocious and relapses oftener, — at least this is the case with pickpockets and simple thieves. They are often drawn into crime by a greater opportunity, although the lack of self-control which makes the epileptic commit crime without reason is sometimes found in the criminaloid also. We may recall how Casenova confessed that when he committed a fraud he never premeditated it, but "seemed to yield to a superior will." A pickpocket said to me, "When the inspiration comes to us we cannot resist." Dostojevsky depicts smugglers of the prison as carrying on their occupation almost without returns, notwithstanding the grave risks they run and in spite of repeated promises not to relapse. Mendel and Benedict describe the impulsive nature of the vagabond, which keeps him moving without object and without rest.

Criminaloids, then, differ from born criminals in degree, not in kind. This is so true that the greater number of them, having become habitual criminals, thanks to a long sojourn in prison, can no longer be distinguished from born criminals except by the slighter character of their physical marks of criminality.

Still less different from born criminals are those latent crimi-

[1] "Homme Criminel," Vol. II, pp. 216, 514, 518.

nals, high in power, whom society venerates as its chiefs. They bear the marks of congenital criminality, but their high position generally prevents their criminal character from being recognized. Their families, of which they are the scourges, may discover it; or their depraved nature may be revealed all too late at the expense of the whole country, at the head of which their own shamelessness, seconded by the ignorance and cowardice of the majority, has caused them to be placed. Even this strange species of criminal monomaniac, who seems to differ from the epileptic in the motive of his crime and the manner of carrying it out,[1] shows nevertheless the epileptic and atavistic origin of his criminality by obsessions, interrupted periods of ideation, lack of self-control, exaggerated importance given to certain details, exhaustion after his criminal crises, fondness for symbolism, excessive and intermittent activity, and finally by hereditary stigmata.

§ 204. Criminal Insane

Even among the true insane criminals those forms predominate which we may call the hypertrophy of crime, the exaggeration of the born criminal, not only in bodily and functional characteristics but also in the manner of committing the crime and in conduct afterward.[2] These serve to explain to us the extent of the impulsive, obscene, and cruel tendencies of the criminal insane, who are almost always obscure epileptics or born criminals upon whom melancholia and monomania have grafted themselves, according to the natural tendency of different forms of psychic disorders to take root together upon the corrupted soil of degeneracy. We have seen, likewise, how hysterical persons, alcoholics, dipsomaniacs, pyromaniacs, kleptomaniacs, the temporarily insane, reproduce many of the characteristics of the epileptic. Even the mattoid, who on account of his habitual calm and the absence of signs of degeneracy and heredity, seems far removed from epilepsy, yet shows at times this epileptic form, which we have seen to be the kernel of crime.[3]

[1] "Homme Criminel," Vol. II, pp. 94, 97, 418.
[2] "Homme Criminel," Vol. I, pp. 34 to 228; Vol. II, p. 213.
[3] "Homme Criminel," Vol. II, p. 646.

§ 205. Criminals by Passion

Criminals of this class form a species apart, and are in complete contrast with the born criminal, both in the harmonious lines of the body, the beauty of the soul, and great nervous and emotional sensitiveness, as well as in the motives of their crimes, always noble and powerful, such as love or politics. Nevertheless they show some points of resemblance with epileptics, such as their tendency to excesses, impulsiveness, suddenness in their outbreaks, and frequent amnesia.[1]

§ 206. Occasional Criminals

Occasional criminals, or better, pseudo-criminals, are those who do not seek the occasion for the crime but are almost drawn into it, or fall into the meshes of the code for very insignificant reasons. These are the only ones who escape all connection with atavism and epilepsy; but, as Garafalo observes, these ought not, properly speaking, to be called criminals.

§ 207. Causes

The study of the causes of crime does not lessen the fatal influence to be assigned to the organic factor, which certainly amounts to 35% and possibly even 40%; the so-called causes of crime being often only the last determinants and the great strength of congenital impulsiveness the principal cause. This we have proved in some cases by the continual relapses occasioned by very small causes, or even without causes, when not only the economic environment has been changed, but when all the circumstances that might encourage crime have been removed; and we have proved it especially by the increasing recidivism in London, notwithstanding the great efforts made by Great Britain to suppress the causes which produce crime. Finally, we have seen that certain circumstances have so strong an action upon criminaloids that they are equivalent to organic causes, and we may even say that they become organic. Among these circumstances should be noted the effect of excessive

[1] "Homme Criminel," Vol. II, p. 226.

heat upon rapes, assaults, assassinations, and revolts, and the effect of alcohol and heredity upon the whole gamut of crime; and to these must be added the effect of race, which in Italy through the Semitic race, and in France through the Ligurian race, increases the crimes of blood.

A fact of the greatest importance is that the same causes which diminish certain crimes increase others, making it difficult for the statesman to devise a remedy. Thus we have seen that education and wealth cause a decrease in certain brutal crimes, especially homicides and assassinations, but at the same time increase others, or even create new crimes, such as bankruptcy and swindling. And if, for example, too great a density is the cause of many crimes, such as frauds and thefts, a sparse population, in its turn, favors brigandage and crimes of blood. Scarcity favors thefts from the forests, forgeries, insurrections, and incendiary fires, while cheapness of grain multiplies the rapes, homicides, and crimes against persons generally.

Alcohol, which next to heat is the most powerful crime-producer, increases, when it is cheap, all the crimes against persons and against the public administration; and if it is dear, all the crimes against property. Yet it presents this strange contradiction, that the more serious crimes are least numerous where alcohol is most abused, doubtless because this abuse takes place in just those localities where there is a higher degree of civilization, and this, by favoring inhibition, decreases the more barbarous crimes.

The school, likewise is a cause of crime, but where education is most general it diminishes the number and seriousness of the crimes.

§ 208. Necessity of Crime

Statistics as well as anthropological investigations show us crime, then, as a natural phenomonon, — a phenomenon (some philosophers would say) as necessary as birth, death, or conception.

This idea of the necessity of crime, however bold it may appear, is nevertheless not so new nor so heterodox as one might believe at first sight. Centuries ago Casaubon expressed the same truth when he said, "Man does not sin, but he is coerced in various degrees"; and St. Bernard likewise said, "Which one of us, however experienced he may be, can distinguish among his own wishes the influence of the *morsus serpentis* from that of the *morbus mentis?*" And further: "The sin is less in our heart, and we do not know whether we ought to ascribe it to ourselves or to the enemy: it is hard to know what the heart does and what it is obliged to do." St. Augustine is still more explicit when he says: "Not even the angels can make the man who wills evil will the good." The boldest and most ardent defender of this theory is a fervent Catholic and a priest of the Tyrol, Ruf.[1]

The defenders of theories quite opposed to our own also affirm it indirectly by the contradictions into which they fall in their definitions. If we compare the different attempts at criminal codes we see how difficult it is for the legal expert to fix the theory of irresponsibility and to find an exact definition for it. "The whole world knows what a good or a bad action is, but it is difficult, even impossible, to tell whether the depraved act has been committed with a full, or only an incomplete, knowledge of the evil," says Mittermayer. Way[2] writes: "We have not yet any scientific knowledge of responsibility." And Mahring says:[3] "Irresponsibility is a matter which criminal justice cannot decide with certainty in any special case." In fact, there are men who are afflicted with incipient insanity, or are so profoundly predisposed to it that the slightest cause may make them fall into it. Others are driven by heredity to eccentricity or to immoral excesses. "Knowledge of the act," says Delbrück, "with an examination of the body and the mind before and after it, is not enough to clear up the question of responsibility; it is necessary to know the life of the criminal from the cradle to the dissecting table."[4] Now as long as the criminal is living it is hardly possible to dissect him. Carrara presumes "absolute responsibility where both intellect and will

[1] G. Ruf, "Die Criminaljustiz, ihre Widersprüche und Zukunft," Innsbruck, 1870.
[2] "Die strafrechtliche Zurechnung," 1851.
[3] "Die Zukunft der peinlichen Rechtspflege," p. 188.
[4] "Zeitschrift für Psychiatrie," 1864, p. 72.

combine in the accomplishment of a criminal action," but he adds immediately afterward, "upon the condition that the action of the will has not been lessened by physical, intellectual, or moral causes." Now we have seen that there is no crime in which these causes are lacking.

§ 209. The Right to Punish

Some one replies to us: "But if you deny responsibility, what right have you to punish? You proclaim that a man is not answerable for his conduct, and yet you exact a penalty. How inconsistent, and how harsh!" I shall never forget how a venerable thinker shook his head when he read these pages, and said to me: "Where will you arrive, with such premises? Must we let ourselves be pillaged and murdered by brigands upon the pretext that we cannot decide whether they know they are doing wrong?" I answer: nothing is less logical than to try to be too logical; nothing is more imprudent than to try to maintain theories, even those which are apparently the soundest, if they are going to upset the order of society. If a physician at the bedside of a patient, when there is grave danger, must proceed cautiously even with the best established system of medicine, the sociologist must observe still greater circumspection, for if he puts into operation innovations of an upsetting nature he will simply succeed in demonstrating the uselessness and inefficiency of his science.

Scientific knowledge, however, is happily not at war but in alliance with social order and practice. If crime is a necessary thing, so also is society's resistance to crime, and, consequently, the punishment of crime, which must be measured by the amount of apprehension with which it inspires the individual. Punishment thus becomes less hateful, but also less contradictory and certainly more efficacious.

I do not believe that any theory of punishment has a sound basis, except that of natural necessity and the right of self-defense. This is the old theory of Beccaria and of Romagnosi,[1]

[1] "Society has the right to make punishment follow upon crime as a necessary means for the preservation of its members." ("Genesi del Diritto Penale.") "Penalties which go beyond the necessity of preserving the public weal are unjust." (Beccaria, "Dei Delitti e delle Pene.")

of Carmignani, and, in part, of Rosmini, Mancini, and Ellero, and it has now valiant defenders in Ferri, Garofalo, and, above all, Poletti. In Germany we see this theory put forward by Hommel, Feuerbach, Grollmann, and Hottzendorff; in England by Hobbes and Bentham; and in France by Ortolan and Tissot. Tissot declares that it is impossible to find any moral relationship between crime and punishment.[1] In France a state prosecuting attorney has said:

"Man has no intrinsic right to punish; in order to have this right he would have to have the knowledge of absolute justice. If it were not in the name of the most absolute necessity, how could a man arrogate to himself the right of judging his fellow man? From the fact that man cannot defend himself without inflicting punishment, the conclusion has been drawn that he has the right to punish; but that he really does not have it may be seen from the fact that when this pretended right is taken by itself without reference to the concrete need it ceases to be valid."

Rondeau, governor under Joseph II, in his "Essai physique sur la peine de mort,"[2] denied the freedom of the will, repudiated the universally accepted notions of good and evil, merit and demerit, and in speaking of repressive justice he declared:

"Crime does not exist in nature; it is the law alone that imposes this unjust designation upon acts that are necessary and inevitable. The innumerable and diverse causes which produce the pretended criminality are all material and all independent of our will, like the miasma that produces fever. Anger is a passing fever, jealousy a momentary delirium, the rapacity of the thief and swindler an aberration of disease, and the depraved passions that drive men to sins against nature are organic imperfections. All moral evil is the result of physical evil. The murderer himself is a sick man like all other criminals. Why, and in the name of what principle, could they be punished, unless it is because they disturb the regular course of the social life and impede the normal and legitimate development of the species? On this ground society, or, better, the government,

"The reason for the state's calling a criminal to account is not to exact vengeance for the crime, but to bring it about that crime shall not be committed in the future." (Carmignani.)

[1] "Introduction Philosophique à l'Étude du Droit Pénal," 1874, p. 375.

[2] Frasati, "La Nuova Scuolo di Diritto Penale in Italia ed all' Estero," Turin, 1891.

had the right to place an obstacle in the way of the fatal consequences of their acts, just as a landowner has a right to build a dike against the flood which threatens to inundate his fields. The social power can, then, without scruple and without hesitation, deprive malefactors of their liberty; but the moment that all crime is recognized as the natural product and logical consequence of some disease, punishment must become only a medical treatment. We shall cure the thief and the vagrant by teaching them the joys of honest work. If by an exception, which is unhappily too frequent, they show themselves insensible to medical cure, they must be separated from their fellow citizens."

We see here that our boldest conclusions are already more than a century old.

One might question whether it is from wickedness or from the effect of their own organism that wild beasts devour man; but notwithstanding this doubt, no one would abstain from killing them and tamely allow himself to be devoured by them. Nor would any one, because of a belief in the right of domestic animals to life and liberty, refrain from harnessing them up for work, or slaughtering them for food. And what right have we to confine the insane, if it is not for self-defense? By what other right do we deprive the conscript soldier of his most holy and noble right of forming his own home and family, and send him, many times in spite of himself, to death?

It is just because the principle of punishment is based upon the necessity of defense that it is really not open to objection.

Formerly, punishment, which was made to correspond to the crime and like it had an atavistic origin, did not attempt to conceal the fact that it was either an equivalent [1] or an act of vengeance. The judges were not ashamed to carry out the sentence themselves, as the members of the holy *Vehme* did. Crime was considered not only as an evil, but as the worst of evils, which only death could pay for. If the guilty did not confess, torture was used. When torture was dispensed with,

[1] ποινή, poena, compensation. In the Iliad, Achilles killed twelve Trojans in return for the death of Patroclus. The compensation for the death of a Frank was 200 sous, and thefts also could be paid for. Slaves lost their lives for the same crimes which cost a free man only 45 sous. (Del Giudice, "La Vendetta nel Diritto Longobardo," 1876.)

witnesses sufficed. Later mere presumptions were sufficient, — and such presumptions! Not only did the judges kill the criminal, but they wanted him to taste death slowly. This cruelty did not diminish crime, but it was logical, nevertheless. The theory does not contradict the practice. The conception was that the criminal never improves, and that he begets children like himself. The death of the criminal alone prevented recidivism. Men of that day obeyed the instinct that impelled them to punish one offence by committing another; but they did not conceal this view. But our logic, our sincerity in penal matters, where is it?

We still have this primitive instinct. When we are trying a criminal, we have always a tendency to measure his punishment by the degree of repugnance and horror with which his crime inspires us and to be filled with indignation against the man who has confessed it. So we not infrequently see representatives of the law forgetting their abstract theories and demanding in loud tones that the vengeance of society be visited upon the offender. Yet the same men, when inditing a book upon criminal law or sitting to legislate on the same subject, would repudiate such an attitude with horror. And what logic is there in the theory, which is being brought into vogue again by Roeder, Garelli, Pessina, that punishment is for the purpose of reform, when we know very well that the reform of the guilty is always or nearly always an exception, while the prison not only does not improve him but even makes him worse. Besides, how, with such a theory, could one justify the punishments inflicted for political crimes, or crimes committed through excitement or passion, followed as they almost always are by spontaneous and complete repentance? Oppenheim, after having written that every crime should be followed by a proportionate penalty and that the penalty should not only be an evil but should appear as such, goes on to say (with Mohl and Thur): "Punishment should have for its only aim the reformation and employment of the criminal." But is not this an obvious contradiction? How can you reconcile the theory which has the criminal dishonored with that which pretends to improve him? How can you brand him upon the brow with iron, and say to him, "Make yourself better"? What are the theories of Herbert, Kant, Altomid, and Hegel, but the ancient ideas of vengeance and the *lex talionis* disguised in modern dress?

And with all this the State does not think of the morrow. It shuts the prisoner up, and when he has served the term of his sentence it sets him at liberty again, thus increasing the danger of society, for the criminal always becomes more depraved in the promiscuity of the prison, and goes out more irritated and better armed against society. With this theory it is not possible to justify the increase of the penalty in the case of recidivism nor the adoption of preventive measures.

Some legislators maintain that a criminal ought to be made to expiate his crime. But the conception of expiation is ecclesiastical, and how can we say that a criminal expiates his crime, when it is by force that we take away his life or his liberty?

The theory of intimidation in its turn offers numerous contradictions. Our predecessors cut off nose and ears, quartered, boiled in water and in oil, and poured melted lead down the throat. But they succeeded only in multiplying crimes and making them more horrible, for the frequency and ferocity of the punishments hardened men; in the time of Robespierre even the children played at guillotining.[1] But what do men expect to accomplish by intimidation nowadays, when penalties have been made so much milder and the prisons are almost like comfortable hotels? And then, what sort of justice is that which punishes a man, less for the crime he has committed than to serve as an example to others?

Further, the right to punish, based upon the nature of the deed itself, has nothing absolute in it, since we see the penalty varying according to the temper and habits of the particular judge. Breton affirms that a judge accustomed to deal with great crimes will inflict punishments relatively more severe

[1] The death penalty was visited in France as late as 1100 upon 116 kinds of crimes; thieves were broken on the wheel, murderers were hanged; later all were broken on the wheel. Between 1770 and 1780 a certain L. was broken on the wheel for stealing linen, and another thief for having stolen cheese. In 1666 in Auvergne there were 276 individuals hanged, 44 beheaded, 32 broken on the wheel, 3 burned, and 28 sent to the galleys. In a single province there were more persons executed than are now convicted in all France.

when he comes to deal with minor offenses; he will give months in prison instead of days. No judges, moreover, even in the same country and when it is a question of identically the same crime, agree exactly upon the sentence. Is it possible to believe in an eternal and absolute principle of justice among men when we see this pretended justice vary so greatly within a brief interval of space or time; when we see bigamy and rape punished so differently in England and in Germany; when we see that not so many years ago a Jew who accosted a Catholic prostitute was condemned to death, as was likewise a Catholic who allowed an involuntary blasphemy to escape him, while infanticide, incest, and rape were tolerated? Do we not even to-day see the right of pardon and the theory of limitations still in force, as if the favor of the king or the lapse of time could change the depraved nature of the criminal or make him less likely to relapse into crime?

CHAPTER II

PENALTIES ACCORDING TO CRIMINAL ANTHROPOLOGY — FINES — PROBATION SYSTEM — INSANE ASYLUMS — INSTITUTIONS FOR THE INCORRIGIBLE — CAPITAL PUNISHMENT

§ 210.

OF all the criticisms raised by punishment the most important is surely that which concerns its application, especially since the fruitful labors of Ferri, Garofalo, Van Hamel, Viazzi, and Sighele have not only corrected what there was irrational about repression, but have brought it into harmony with our juridical ideas. Now, when once it has been demonstrated that the penalty is not an equivalent of compensation to offended society, or a sort of excommunication inflicted by lay priests with more thought of the crime than of the criminal, we see that punishment must change its character. We must have in view the welfare of society more than the punishment of the criminal, and the criminal and his victim more than the crime. The fear inspired by a man who suddenly commits a murder for a question of honor, or for a political idea, is very different from the fear we have of a man who puts a climax on a life of crime with an assassination for the purpose of theft or rape. In the first case the punishment is almost useless, the crime itself being so grave a punishment that it is certain the offender will never repeat it. In the second case every delay and every mitigation of the penalty is a peril for honest men.

Thus in cases of assault it is absurd to establish, as the codes do, a great differentiation according to the seriousness and duration of the effects, especially since antiseptic methods now hasten the cure; for the murderer does not measure his blows, and it is only purely by chance if they are not mortal. On the contrary, in crimes of this kind we must observe carefully to see whether the guilty person is a respectable man and whether he had serious provocation. If this is the case, he belongs in the category of criminals of passion; while if the crime has a slight motive, or has been premeditated with accomplices, and the persons in question are habitual criminals, the slightest assault, the unsuccessful attempt, ought to be punished as a serious crime, in order to prevent fatal relapses into crime. In this case we ought to take no account of the quarrel of the two parties, who are not at all interested in what happens to others, for the State has the general welfare to care for.

"It is impossible," says Ferri, very rightly, "to separate the crime from the criminal, as it is impossible, in drawing up a penal code, to suppose an average criminal type, which, in reality, one never meets in any case. Now what does the judge do? Before him is a pair of scales. In one of the pans he puts the crime, in the other the penalty. He hesitates, then diminishes one side and adds to the other, expecting thus to measure the social adaptibility of the criminal. But, having once pronounced the sentence, the judge does not concern himself to know whether the person condemned falls again into the same crime. What does he know of the application of the penalty, and of the effect that it has upon the criminal to be deprived of his liberty? Further, when a criminal is sentenced for 20 years but reformed in 10, why keep him there for 10 years longer, when another, to whom it would be useful to remain in prison longer, is liberated at the end of 5 years? Crime is like sickness. The remedy should be fitted to the disease. It is the task of the criminal anthropologist to determine in what measure it should be applied. What should we say of a physician who, stopping at the door of a hospital ward, should say to the patients brought to him, 'Pneumonia? Syrup of rhubarb for 15 days. Typhus? Syrup of rhubarb for a month'; and then at the end of the time named turn them out of doors, cured or not?"

In order to avoid these faults the penalty should be indeterminate, and should be subdivided according to the principle of Cicero: "A natura hominis discenda est natura juris."[1] We must make a difference according to whether we have under our eyes a born criminal, an occasional criminal, or a criminal by passion. In the case of every criminal in whose case the crime itself and the personal conditions show that reparation

[1] "The nature of law is to be learned from the nature of man."

of the damage is not a sufficient social sanction, the judge should give sentence of imprisonment for an indeterminate time in a criminal asylum, or in the institutions (agricultural colonies or prisons) for occasional criminals, adults or minors. The carrying out of the sentence should be regarded as the logical and natural continuation of the work of the judge, as a function of practical protection on the part of special organs. The commission for carrying out penal sentences should include expert criminal anthropologists, representing the judge, the defense, and the prosecution. These men, together with administrative officers, would stand, not for neglecting and forgetting the prisoner as soon as sentence is pronounced, as happens now, but for a humanitarian work which would be efficacious for the protection, now of society against the liberation of dangerous criminals, now of the individual against the execution of a sentence which, in his case, has been proved to be excessive. It is apparent, then, that conditional liberation is bound up with the principle of the indeterminate sentence.

§ 211. Penalties other than Imprisonment

We ought as much as possible to avoid the short and repeated sentences to prison, which, as we have seen, is the school of crime, and especially of associated crime, the most dangerous of all. "They prevent any cure, they render impossible any continuous effort, and they give the criminal a sort of distinction, for there are many prisoners who mark on their caps the number of their sentences."[1] "We might say," writes Krohne,[2] "that most countries have adopted the principle of sending to prison as many men as possible, as often as possible, and for as short a period as possible." He might have added that they do this in a way to make the prison do as little good as possible and as much harm as possible. I have seen in prison 11 children arrested under the very grave charge of being a band of malefactors, for having stolen a herring, and 4 others, who had stolen a bunch of grapes. At the same time three ministers in the legislative chamber were defending a thief

[1] Aspirail, "Cumulative Punishments," London, 1892.
[2] "Handbuch der Gefängniskunde."

who had stolen 20 millions. According to Joly there have almost always been in France as many as 3,000,000 men who have passed at least 24 hours in prison. Each year more than 100,000 individuals step in to keep up or raise this formidable number by taking the places of those who die. Berenger reckons that the isolation (and we may add, the imprisonment) of half the persons sentenced might be dispensed with. Of 300,000 persons convicted 57,000 were for violation of police ordinances, etc.; 7000 or 8000 imprisoned for debt; 5500 foreigners expelled from the country, and 13,000 or 14,000 awaiting transfer; and 12,000 serving sentences of less than six days. The short sentences, almost always served in company with habitual criminals, can have no intimidating effect, especially with the ridiculously short sentences of one and three days possible under the penal codes of Holland and Italy. The effects, on the contrary, are disastrous, since they make it impossible for justice to be taken seriously. By taking away all fear from the minds of the persons convicted, they drive them irresistibly to new offenses, on account of the dishonor already incurred.

Accordingly, other repressive measures must be substituted for imprisonment for minor offenses, such as confinement at home, security for good behavior, judicial admonition, fines, forced labor without imprisonment, local exile, corporal punishment, conditional sentence. Let us look into these new means.

§ 212. Corporal Punishment — Confinement at Home

Corporal punishment for minor offenses would be an excellent substitute for imprisonment, if applied in a manner in harmony with our civilization. Fasting, the douche, and hard labor would be incontestably very efficacious, and at the same time less costly and easier to apply in varying degrees. In England whipping has been reintroduced, and, according to Tissot, with success. Not less useful would be the confinement of the guilty person in his own home, a measure already employed in the army.

§ 213. Fines

After corporal punishment the penalty which is most easily adjusted and most efficacious, provided it is guaranteed by bond, is a fine. Applied in proportion to the wealth of the culprit, it would contribute to diminish the enormous judicial expenses, while striking the criminal rich, who escape punishment most easily on their most vulnerable side, the side from which they are most often impelled toward evil. Bonneville de Marsangy truly remarks that a fine is the most liberal, the most divisible, the most economical, the most completely remissible punishment, and therefore the most efficacious. The more we advance, he says, the more value money has in this sense, that the number of pleasures it can buy becomes illimitable. Further, the number of those who use money for pleasure increases also, so that the more we advance the more useful a fine becomes. Fines ought aways to be employed for the punishment of those guilty of minor offenses, thus diminishing greatly the number of imprisonments. According to the code of criminal procedure in Holland, proceedings against a person guilty of a misdemeanor are not begun if the offender on being called is willing to pay the maximum fine. The case goes on only in the event of refusal to pay. For offenses for which the penalty would be not more than a month's imprisonment, this function could be exercised by the Chamber of Advice, which could stop the proceedings upon the payment of a fine by the defendant. Those who refused to pay would be sentenced to labor; and if they refused to submit to this, they would have to serve a prison sentence made as severe as was consistent with health and life.

As for the objection that the fine is difficult to proportion, it does not deserve to be taken seriously, for while a rich man does not care as little for one day in prison as a vagrant does, a fine of 10,000 francs from him would be the equivalent of a few francs from a poor man.

§ 214. Indemnity

A fine permits also the indemnifying of the victim, and in this way we strike at the root of crime, so much the more since the greatest number of criminals from cupidity are drawn from the professional and other well-to-do classes. The penal judges themselves should be obliged to fix the amount of damages to be paid, in order to avoid the delay and discomfort of a new trial in the civil court, and the public prosecutor by virtue of his office should call for the fixing of damages in cases where, whether through ignorance or fear, the victims take no action. Bonneville de Marsangy proposes to grant the victim a special lien upon the property of the convicted person. The indemnity should be collected by the state along with the expenses of the trial, and, if necessary, a part of the returns of the prisoner's labor should be retained in favor of the victim.

§ 215. Reprimand and Security

The judicial reprimand as substitute for punishment in the case of minor offenses is already admitted in the codes of Italy, Russia, Spain, and Portugal; also in the canton of Vaud, and in the Roman law which prescribed, "Moneat lex antequam puniat."[1] However, if admonition can be efficacious in cases of the pranks of the young, brawls, and insults, it is not serious enough for the offenses of criminaloids without security, which is really a suspended fine. The magistrate obliges the culprit to deposit a sum of money which shall guarantee society against his relapse. The deposit is made for a definite time, after which it is restored to him if his conduct has been irreprehensible. This practice is allowed in the United States and in Denmark, and it is certain that the obligation to deposit a sum of money and the fear of losing it in case of relapse are much more effective in preventing rioting and violence than a few days in prison.

The security for good conduct is no less useful. "When the magistrate, in place of inflicting punishment demands of the defendant a guarantee that he will not disturb the peace of another, or that he will maintain good conduct, or abstain from certain definite acts, he warns him that in case of a new offense he will be subjected to a more severe penalty than would have

[1] "Let the law warn before it punishes."

been inflicted for the first transgression." This measure has been adopted into the Spanish code; and in England it has been in operation from early times under the form of "recognizances to keep the peace," and of "good behavior," demanded by the justice of the peace from bad characters, or from a person who has threatened another, always upon the demand of the person threatened, supported by evidence. The same method has been authorized since 1861 as an accessory penalty in convictions for crime.

§ 216. Probation System — Conditional Sentence

The best preventive institution for minor or occasional criminals is the probation system, widely used in the United States, especially for young criminals. A young criminal, not a recidivist, is not put into prison, but receives an admonition from the judge, who warns him that at the first relapse he will be sentenced; and he is placed under the surveillance of a special officer of the state. If this officer finds that in his family he is not receiving a proper education or sufficient oversight, he is put into a special home for neglected children. If he commits a fresh offense he is again brought before the court and sent to a reform school.

This system has given such excellent results in Massachusetts that the idea was suggested of extending it to adult criminals, and the law of 1878 instituted a special official, the "probation officer." This officer is supposed to inform himself with regard to all persons convicted of misdemeanors by the courts of Boston, and to determine, by the aid of the information received, whether the offenders are capable of being reformed without the need of the infliction of a penalty. He is present at the trials of all those for whom repressive measures do not seem to be necessary, and after having made known the results of his investigations (of which the principal aim is to discover whether there has been a previous conviction), he asks that the culprit be released on probation. If the court consents to this the culprit is put on probation for a period which may vary from two months to twelve, under conditions imposed by the court. The probation officer formally undertakes to see that the conditions are carried out, and has the right at any time during the period of probation to arrest the culprit for any cause whatsoever, and to bring him before the court again in order to have him undergo the sentence which had been suspended. When the term of probation has expired, the probation officer asks that the sentence be annulled, but in certain cases he may ask that the time first fixed be prolonged.

The number of persons released on probation in the city of Boston, guilty of drunkenness, receiving stolen goods, petit larceny, and assault and battery, reached 2803 during the period from 1879 to 1883. Of these, 223 did not conduct themselves properly during the term of their probation, were brought to court again, and had to undergo the penalty; 44 took flight, and could not be apprehended. In 1888 out of 244 persons put upon probation, 230 appeared to be reformed. Many of these promises, without doubt, have not been kept, but on the whole the desired effect seems really to have been attained. The officer declared that nearly 95% of the persons under his charge the previous year had maintained good conduct and had been released; only 13, recognized as incorrigible, had had to undergo punishment. The experiment has been so successful that the law of 1880 extended the application of it to the whole state of Massachusetts.

An analogous system was put into operation in England by the "Probation of First Offenders Act" of 1887; but while in America the concurrence and coöperation of the probation officer guarantee the good conduct of the culprit, in England the pledge of the offender himself is required, or at least the concurrence of a bondsman whose assistance will be most efficacious, since he is stimulated by the thought that a fresh offense will forfeit the bond. Further, the English law demands special grounds for a release on probation, and allows the magistrate to fix the time without the intervention of any special officer. According to a letter of Colonel Howard published by Professor von Liszt, the number of persons conditionally released between 1887 and 1897 reached 20,000, with 9% of recidivisms.[1]

1 "Bulletin of the International Union of Criminal Law," May, 1897.

In Belgium this institution, introduced by law in 1888, bore immediate fruit. The minister of justice reported to the chamber in 1891 that of 449,070 persons convicted, 27,564 were conditionally released and only 2% relapsed into crime. These persons admitted to probation had been convicted for damage to property, blackmail, fraud, breach of trust, defamation of character, seduction of minors, marriage brokage, indecent exposure, threats, adulteration, unintentional injuries, appropriation of lost objects, mendicity, vagabondage, the carrying and sale of forbidden weapons, unintentional homicides, kidnapping, attempted rape, arson, and fraudulent bankruptcy. The crimes handled in this fashion, then, were mostly those that are committed by occasional offenders, and only a few such as born criminals commit.

In France also this new institution has been tried since the passage of the Berenger Law in 1891. M. Dumas, director of penal affairs, reported in 1893 upon the first nine months' experience with the law. The correctional tribunals had pronounced 11,768 conditional sentences, of which 7362 were for imprisonment and 4406 were fines. This was out of a total of 162,582, of which 97,245 were prison sentences and 15,337 were fines. Hence the sentences suspended represented 7.5% of the prison sentences and 6.7% of the fines.

In New Zealand and Australia in the first period of two years, according to the report of the minister of justice, the results of the experiment were excellent. Of 121 persons admitted to probation, 58 had conducted themselves properly, 9 had not fulfilled the obligations imposed, 1 had taken flight, and 53 were still in a state of probation at the end of the second year. From the 1st of October, 1886, to the 31st of December, 1888, in New Zealand, according to the report of Captain Hume, sentence was suspended and replaced by probation for 203 persons, of whom 70% appeared to be reformed and 5% were arrested again.

§ 217. The Reformatory at Elmira

Another method of applying the principle of which we have been speaking is found in the Elmira Reformatory, which was created by Brockway under the inspiration of my "Homme Criminel," as he himself says, and of which Winter, Way, and Ellis have given good descriptions.[1] To this establishment are regularly sent only young men between 16 and 30 years of age, guilty for the first time of a minor offense. The law grants unlimited authority to the board of directors,[2] who may set the prisoners at liberty at any time before the expiration of the sentence. The liberation is to be based upon a strong conviction that the culprit is reformed. The only formality which accompanies it is the word of honor that he gives the superintendent. However, though the board can shorten the sentence for the better prisoners, it cannot lengthen it for the others.

Brockway concentrates all his efforts upon gaining a knowledge of the young criminal, of his psychological conditions, of the environment in which he has lived, and of the causes which have contributed to debase him. From these he deduces the means to bring about his reformation. He sets himself to develop the criminal's muscular system by douches, massage, gymnastics, and by a proper dietary, and to strengthen his will by making him take part in procuring his own liberation. Immediately upon arriving at the prison the prisoner takes a bath, is then clothed in the uniform of the prison, is photographed, examined, and vaccinated. For two days he is shut up in his cell to meditate upon his crime and to prepare himself for reformation. The third day he is brought before the superintendent, who places him, according to his tendencies and schooling, in a school or industrial class; and he is made to understand his duties and the conditions upon which he may regain his liberty. He is instructed in a trade (more than 75% of the prisoners know none) which shall permit him to earn his living after his liberation. This is the first care of the management.

[1] Alexander Winter, "The New York Reformatory at Elmira," with preface by Havelock Ellis, London, 1891; "Fifteenth Annual Report of the Board of Managers of the New York State Reformatory at Elmira," Jan., 1891.

[2] The board of directors consists of the superintendent and five other members appointed by the governor of the state with the consent of the Senate.

The young prisoners are divided into three classes, — the good, the medium, and the bad or least corrigible. Each prisoner is marked monthly according to conduct, work, and progress in school, with a maximum of three for each; and to pass to the highest class he must obtain the maximum of nine marks each month for six months. Promotion to the first class carries with it certain advantages, especially with regard to correspondence; such as receiving visits, having books, and eating at a common table instead of in a separate cell. Finally the better prisoners are permitted to take walks together in the field, and responsible tasks are given to them, such as superintendence of the other prisoners. But just as they may win a place in the first class, so by negligence or bad conduct they may fall out of it. In this case they are put back into the third class, and must submit to harder work in order to regain their position. Brockway, taking account of the aptitude and physical strength of each prisoner, fixed at the beginning of each month the amount of work that he must accomplish in order to obtain the maximum number of good marks.

Each week there is published in the reformatory the "Summary," a paper conducted exclusively by the prisoners themselves. It contains a review of the political events of the week, taken from the better American newspapers; in addition there are items with regard to the life in the institution itself, lectures that have been held, promotions and degradations, and the liberation of prisoners. I have been receiving this paper for a year, and find that no juristic organ in Italy or France is so rich in news and especially in information as regards criminality.

All the work of the institution, even to the superintendence and guarding, is done by the prisoners themselves, so that the expense is reduced to a minimum. At the same time the work of the prisoners is chosen with a view to fitting them for life in society, and not to making the institution pay a profit. The prisoners in the first class are intentionally exposed to various kinds of temptations. After six months Brockway proposes to the board that they be given conditional liberty. The board has a right to refuse permission, but, as a matter of fact, always authorizes the liberation when Brockway considers it advisable. The release takes place, however, only after permanent employment has been found for the prisoner. After being liberated he must give account of himself regularly for the first six months at least, and receives complete liberty only at the end of a year of good conduct.

This is, then, the probation system perfected. No one is a warmer partisan than I myself of this reform, which is the first practical application of my studies. I believe firmly that the individual and physical study of each criminal, with practical, individualized instruction, can but have excellent results when applied to criminaloids. In these it will inculcate especially the habit of working.

But for born criminals this method does not seem to me equally efficacious. When I see that 49% of the inmates of the Elmira Reformatory are completely lacking in moral sensibility, that 12% have left home before they were 14 years old, that 37% come from drunken or epileptic parents, and that 56% show no signs of repentance, I do not believe that they can be reformed by hot and cold baths, great activity, and a sound education. I feel this the more since the more promising children are there in limited numbers and are mingled with the adults. In fact, if we examine the detailed statistics of 1722 prisoners set at liberty after remaining at Elmira for an average of 20 months, we find that 156 are settled in other states; 10 are dead; 128 have not yet finished the term of their probation; 185 could not be liberated until the expiration of their full sentence; 271 have been given partial liberty after having completed six months' probation satisfactorily; 47 were arrested for other offenses during the time of their probation; 126 did not furnish the reports required, and disappeared; 79 have had to be returned to the reformatory; 25 returned voluntarily, having lost their employment. Leaving out the 10 who died, we have 533 who were not reformed, that is to say 31%, a proportion closely approaching that which I have given for born criminals. Moreover, the supervision of the individuals under probation is so superficial, that if we count as recidivists those who have been lost sight of, we shall approach much more nearly to the reality than if we presume that they are reformed as Brockway does.

But notwithstanding these defects this system, together with the agricultural colony system, is the best possible substitute for the prison.

§ 218. Asylums for the Criminal Insane

There is another institution which we believe destined to promote harmony between humanitarian impulses and the safety of society; namely, asylums for the criminal insane. We might argue indefinitely upon the abstract theory of punishment, but the whole world is agreed upon one point: that among real or supposed criminals there are many who are insane. For these, prison is an injustice and liberty a danger to which in Italy we have opposed only half-measures, such as violate both morality and the social safety. The English, who have arrived at reforms by the practice of true liberty, have been trying for a century to fill up this most dangerous gap in the social structure, and have in large measure succeeded through the institution of asylums for the criminal insane. Beginning with 1786, dangerous lunatics were confined in a special ward in Bedlam, from which they could not be released except by the authority of the Lord Chancellor.[1] In 1844 this measure appeared to be insufficient, and the state resolved to confine 235 of the criminal insane in the private institution of Fisherton House. But the number of these unfortunates increased continually, and special institutions were finally erected at Dundrum in Ireland in 1850, at Perth in Scotland in 1858, and at Broadmoor in England in 1863. New laws ordered that not only those should be received there who had commited a crime in a state of insanity, or had become insane during their trial, but also all prisoners who, whether from insanity or from idiocy, were incapable of undergoing prison discipline. These last are separated from the others and placed in particular sections; if cured they are returned to prison; the others remain in prison as long as a royal order does not authorize their release. The

[1] Stat. 34 George III, ch. iv: "Whoever has committed manslaughter or high treason shall be kept in a place of safety during the pleasure of His Majesty."

number of these criminal maniacs in 1868 was 1244.[1] The character of the attendants, the attention to the comfort of the inmates, and the arrangements for their employment and entertainment are all excellent, yet many English philanthropists think that they have not yet done enough, and complain that there are many persons in the ordinary prisons who should be confined in these asylums instead.

In America there are similar institutions, including an annex to the great penitentiary at Auburn.

Now I ask myself: Is it possible that an institution, which has been found useful by the most oligarchical nation in the world and also by the most democratic, which in 24 years has been so greatly extended without yet fully meeting the demands upon it, — is it possible that this is a mere luxury, a caprice of Anglo-Saxon race? Does it not rather correspond to a sad social need, and ought not we, here in Italy, desire to see it take root and spread abroad in our land? If in Italy and in France the number of the criminal insane appears to be much smaller, this is because the public mind has not yet grasped the fact that a great number of criminal acts proceed from morbid impulses. If at times insanity is recognized as the sole cause of a crime and the trial is stopped, the authorities do not concern themselves further. Besides, many of these unfortunates

[1] On Jan. 1st, 1868, there were in Broadmoor 616, of whom 506 were men and 110 women. These had committed:

	Men	Women	Total
Capital crimes	188	69	257
Simple crimes	152	52	204
Attempted suicide	74	29	103
Already epileptic	43	6	49
" maniacs	81	20	101

From 1862 to 1868 there were 770 entries, 39 persons were cured, 55 died, and 5 escaped.

In Dundrum (Ireland), from 1850 to 1863 there were received 250 insane criminals, of whom 173 were men and 77 were women. Of these 38 were cured, 41 died, and 3 escaped. Their crimes were as follows:

Homicide	79
Burglary	72
Assault	30
Theft	12
Minor offenses	32

See Pelman, "Psychiatrische Reiseerinnerungen aus England," 1870; "Seventh Report on Criminal Lunatics," 1869.

have periods of rationality in the midst of their insanity, and are supposed on this account to be merely feigning.[1]

From another point of view the presence of these unfortunates in penal institutions is an offense to the moral sense, and it is not without danger, both for society and for discipline; they can neither be cared for nor watched properly because of lack of fit quarters and of a suitable organization. Further, they often act violently and without sense of shame toward the other prisoners, and are so much the more dangerous since they have sudden fits of excitement, often for the most trivial reasons. Thus an insane prisoner killed another of the convicts because he would not black his shoes for him. At the same time they obstinately resist the prison discipline, show themselves indifferent to punishment, discontented, and defiant, and make themselves the center and pretext of continual insurrections. If they are kept isolated and chained in cells, as is too largely the custom, inaction, and insufficient food and light soon make them the prey of disease, even if they do not themselves put an end to their unhappy existence. On the other hand, to send them to ordinary insane asylumns gives rise to other inconveniences. They take their vices with them, and become the disseminators of sodomy, flight, rebellion, and theft, to the detriment of the institution and of the other patients, who are terrified by their savage and obscene manners and by the unhappy reputation that has preceded them.

There is another class of the insane who, at a certain period of their lives, have been victims of a criminal impulse. These have not the depraved tendencies of the first class, but they are not less dangerous, for they are often irresistibly driven to savage and unforeseen acts. They wound persons and burn buildings, surmounting with remarkable clearness of mind all the obstacles that oppose them. There are those of them who feign the most perfect tranquillity in order to obtain their liberty or to combine secretly for an escape or a plot. They do not avoid society as other insane persons do, but tend to associate among themselves; and, as they preserve the restlessness of mind that

[1] Lombroso, "Sull' Istituzione dei Manicomi Criminali," 1872; Tamburini, "Sui Manicomi Criminali," 1873.

they had before they became criminal or insane, they continually imagine that they are maltreated or insulted, and succeed in inspiring others with their false ideas and in giving form little by little to plans for flight or rebellion. This again differentiates them from ordinary lunatics, who are quite incapable of such enterprises, but, like somnambulists, live isolated in an imaginary world.

All alienists are in agreement as to these facts, and I myself have had direct proof of them in the institutions of which I have been director. Thus Er., an insane person already imprisoned for receiving stolen goods, complained incessantly of the injustice of the courts and of our treatment of him, which he did not find sufficiently respectful. He wrote absurd letters of protest to the King and to the prefect. One day he appeared entirely changed, he had become humble and well-behaved; he had set himself to plotting with three other patients for a slaughter of the attendants, and a little later, while the attendants were engaged in distributing the soup at noon, he and his companions tore up part of the paving of the court and began to throw the stones in all directions. A few years later an epileptic homicide did the same thing and nearly succeeded in putting the whole force of attendants to flight. Another insane criminal, a homicide with hallucinations, was so intelligent, that although he was a poor shoemaker without education, he was able to write his autobiography in a style worthy of Cellini. This man conducted himself properly for two years, but one day there was discovered hidden in his bed a bar of iron which he had prepared for the express purpose of striking myself. Another day, having made a picklock of some pieces of wood, he opened two doors, let himself down from a window, and escaped. All investigators who have treated of this subject give examples of the danger of unexpected relapse into morbid tendencies on the part of individuals apparently harmless.[1] The burgomaster of Gratz some years ago became the victim of a religious monomaniac, who had already threatened the life of

[1] "Annales Medico-psychologiques," 1846, p. 16; Falret, "Sur les Aliénés Dangereux," 1870; Solbrig, "Verbrechen und Wahnsinn," Munich, 1870; Delbrück, "Zeitschrift für Psychiatrie," XX, p. 478.

another person. Hatfield, before making his attempt upon the life of George III, had attempted to kill his wife and three children. Confined in Bedlam, he there killed an insane person. Booth, the assassin of Lincoln, had once thrown himself into the sea, to speak, as he said, with a colleague who had drowned himself.

The harm of the unrestrained liberty given to insane criminals ends by extending itself to the whole nation. This is not simply because these unfortunates turn their homicidal thoughts towards the heads of the nation, but especially because, being endowed with a very clear mind and a tendency to form associations, they succeed, when the moment is favorable, in forming a partisan band. This is the more dangerous because the leaders, lacking balance of mind, are unable to control themselves, but act upon the mind of the mob by the very fascination of their strangeness, and succeed in drawing them blindly after them. They are, we might say, ferment germs, powerless by themselves, but terrible in their effects when they can act at a given temperature and upon a predisposed organism. Historic examples of this are to be found among the epidemics of insanity in the Middle Ages, among the Mormons and Methodists in America, in the incendiaries of Normandy in 1830, and in those of the Commune in Paris. We know now that, leaving aside the influence of certain rare idealists, the Commune was the effect of an epidemic delirium called forth by defeat and the abuse of absinthe, but especially by the great number of the insane, ambitious, homicidal, or even paralytic, freed too soon from the asylums, who, finding in this over-excited population a propitious soil, united and put into action their disastrous dreams. Laborde[1] cites at least eight members of the Commune who were notoriously insane. Such were Eude, Ferre, Goupil, Lunier, and Flourens, and such was B., who nevertheless was elected by 10,000 votes. The horrors of the French Revolution also were often provoked by the delirium of homicidal monomaniacs like Marat and Teroigne. The Marquis de Sade was president of the section of the "Pikemen."

[1] "Les Hommes de l'Insurrection de Paris devant la Psychologie," 1872.

The one remedy for all these evils is unquestionably the institution of asylums for the criminal insane. If these received legal recognition and their position were unequivocally fixed, the continual conflict between justice and public safety would cease, a conflict which now is renewed every time one of these unfortunates comes to trial and an attempt is made to determine how far he was driven by morbid impulses and how far by the perversity of his own will. In doubt the judges extricate themselves, now by an injustice, now by an imprudence — the latter when they lighten the sentence of a man who appears insane, or acquit him altogether; the former, when as, alas, too often happens, they condemn, perhaps to death, one whom an alienist would recognize at once as insane.

Many will object, it is true, that if we allow ourselves to be led by these considerations we shall end by punishing no one. But the same objections were raised against those who opposed the burning of those insane unfortunates whom men called witches.

This position should not be ascribed to a sentimental pity, dangerous to others, for the measure is preventive even more than humanitarian; since if those unjustly convicted are numerous, those imprudently acquitted are not less so. The thing to be done, then, is to prevent them from returning to society, to which they are a great source of danger, until we have every assurance that they have become perfectly harmless.

It may be objected again that it is easy to confuse those who feign insanity with those who are really insane; and, in fact, the number of these is very great among criminals. But the most recent studies have shown us that mistakes are made only because so many observers are ignorant of the connection between moral insanity and crime; and because, moreover, it is very difficult to make a true diagnosis, since many of the persons pretending insanity are really predisposed to it, so that in a short time they become actually insane, or are genuine insane persons who, ignorant of their true disease, easily pretend an artificial one. Further, these patients often present very rare forms of mental disturbance, and on this account the distrust of the physician is quite rightly aroused. Jacobi tells that he had to change his opinion four times about an insane person who appeared to be feigning insanity but proved to be really insane. A thief who was pronounced by Delbrück to be feigning insanity starved himself to death. Another pretended that he had in his right leg a disease that he had in reality in his left. A homicidal monomaniac imitated in prison a form of insanity which he did not have, and did this, as he told me, to escape sentence. But if some criminals really succeed in feigning insanity, the perpetual seclusion in a hospital for the insane will be punishment enough, even if modern society, not content with defending itself against them, still wishes to revenge itself upon them. Insane criminals, in fact, complain incessantly of being kept in the hospitals, and demand with loud cries to return to prison. There is, for example, the case of Trossarello, who would not allow his counsel to defend him as insane, preferring to be executed to being immured in an insane asylum. Would not the asylum for the criminal insane be the best means of making such criminals harmless? I do not know whether Vacher merely pretended to be insane, or was really so; but if he had been permanently confined in an insane asylum the lives of several men would have been spared.

Wiedemeister objects, further, that the asylums for the criminal insane in England are often the theater of sad scenes of blood, and require for their maintenance three times the expense of the others. This is true, for the tendency to make plots, very rare in the ordinary asylums, is, on the contrary, very frequent in the criminal asylums, since the inmates know that they will never be released, and furthermore, being conscious of their impunity, destroy clothing and utensils, attack the attendants, wound, and kill. In 1868 there occurred at Broadmoor 72 cases in which attendants were injured, two of them very seriously; and the daily expense, especially great because of the damage done by the insane and the high pay given the attendants, reached five francs for each insane person. There is nothing, however, to wonder at in that, nor should it cause any serious opposition, for it is natural that the bringing together of so many dangerous individuals should bring great dangers with it, especially to the poor attendants, who, notwithstanding their high wages, seldom remain long in the service.[1] But if it were not for the asylums for the criminal insane these things would occur in the ordinary asylums. Besides, the subdivisions recently introduced by Orange at Broadmoor have greatly improved conditions. First the convicts are separated from the others; then those who have been indicted but not convicted; finally the ordinary prisoners, who have been sentenced to short terms for crimes of little moment, are returned to the county asylums. The government has carried the reform to completion and removed all inconveniences by setting aside one wing of the Woking prison for convicts who become insane while in prison.

The statistics of asylums for the criminal insane show that they have a noticeably lower mortality rate than the general asylums. This is an encouragement to establish more of these institutions, and at the same time a proof that conditions in them are not as bad as has been represented.

The expense does not appear to be so excessive when one compares it with the cost of caring, not for ordinary insane persons, but for the violent insane, who, needing double watchfulness, occasion a considerable expense. It is necessary also to take into account the expense occasioned by escapes, frequent in the case of the violent. In Massachusetts this expense has been estimated at not less than $25 a day while the escaped lunatic is at large. This is even one of the reasons that led the state to erect an asylum for the criminal insane. We may add that the expense could be considerably diminished by transferring to the asylum a number of the better penitentiary guards at an advanced pay; in this way the frequent changes of attendants would be avoided, and at the same time men accustomed to this sort of danger and not easily intimidated would be secured. Finally, the number of inmates might be cut down by removing criminals who become inoffensive, by

[1] Attendants receive an average compensation of from £30 to £40, the head attendant from £150 to £175, his assistant from £40 to £60. Those who are married have a family apartment, a school for their children, a library, reading-room, and smoking-room. Yet in 1867 69 gave up their positions, and 64 in 1868. In Broadmoor there is 1 attendant to 5 patients, in Dundrum 1 to 12. The expense for clothing destroyed reached £512 in one year.

eliminating those who come from prison in an acute state of insanity and are therefore, as the experience of Gutch in Bruchsal shows, more likely to be cured, and also by retaining in the prison infirmary, under strict surveillance, those prisoners who are suspected of feigning insanity.

CHAPTER III

PENALTIES ANTHROPOLOGICALLY ADAPTED TO THE SEX, AGE, ETC., OF THE CRIMINAL, AND TO THE NATURE OF THE CRIME

§ 219. Sex

AS I have shown in Chapter XIV, and in my "Female Offender," we may conclude that the true born criminal exists among women only in the form of the prostitute, who already finds in her lamentable calling a substitute for crime. Most female criminals

"are only criminals from accident or passion, passing frequently from one to the other of these two classes. They very rarely show the type and tendencies of the criminal, and commit only from 11% to 20% as many crimes as men. They lead, it is true, in poisoning, abortion, and infanticide; but of the highway robberies only 6% to 8% are committed by women."

We may add that the crimes which are more essentially feminine, such as abortion and infanticide, are just those for which there is least need of punishment, being almost always committed at the suggestion of the lover or husband. It is often sufficient to separate the criminals.

The penalty for the greater number of female criminals could be limited to a reprimand with suspended sentence, except in the very rare cases of poisoning, swindling, or homicide, in which it would be necessary to confine the offender in a convent, where, on account of their great susceptibility to suggestion, religion could be substituted for the eroticism that is the most frequent cause of their crimes. I have had proofs of this in a cellular prison under my charge, where, however, the nuns in attendance were not especially well fitted for their duties. As for those who relapse two or three times into sexual crimes, the only method would be to enroll them in the official list of prostitutes, which would have the advantage of preventing clandestine prostitution, much the most harmful sort.

Recognizing the great importance which women attach to dress and ornament, we may often in minor offenses, such as thefts, brawls, and slanders, replace a prison sentence by penalties which will touch female vanity, such as cutting the hair, etc. In adopting special penalties for women we shall only be returning to usages of the ancients, the Jews, and the Germans. In Russia in the Middle Ages a woman who struck her husband had to ride upon an ass with her face toward the tail. In England women who quarreled among themselves had to go through the village with a weight chained to their foot; slanderers and busybodies had to wear a muzzle.[1] Konrad Celtes writes in his "De Origine, Situ, Moribus, et Institutionibus Germaniæ":

"Women who have been brought into disrepute because of witchcraft or superstitious practices, or have been guilty of infanticide or abortion, have various punishments inflicted upon them; being either sewed up in sacks and drowned, or even burned to death, or buried alive. Yet these cruel punishments are not sufficient to prevent their continually adding crime to crime."[2]

§ 220. Abortion

The crimes of abortion which do not have professional gain for their object ought to be punished only by reprimand or putting upon probation. It is to Balestrini that the credit is due for demonstrating that the procuring of an abortion ought not to be treated as a crime;[3] for the lawmaker cannot in this matter pretend to be protecting the family, since this crime is most often committed by unmarried mothers just with the object of not creating an illegitimate family. Regarded as a defense of the person, such a law would have no force except where the abortion was procured without the consent of the mother. The abstract legal object is equally without standing,

[1] "Revue des Revues," 1895.

[2] Lombroso, in "Proceedings of Second Penitentiary Congress," 1895; Moraglia, in "Archivio di Psichiatria," 1894–95.

[3] Raffaello Balestrini, "Aborto, Infanticidio, ed Esposizione d'Infante."

since society has nothing to gain from the birth of illegitimate children. The fiction of civil law which extends personality to unborn children cannot be carried over into criminal law. The legal existence of the fœtal life as a part of the social structure is, moreover, very contestable; an embryo does not represent a real human being, but a being still at the stage of animalism, or rather a lower animal, which, in the earlier months, it would take an embryologist to recognize as human at all. No right is injured, then, by an abortion produced by a woman upon herself, not even by the danger which she incurs, no one being able to prevent another from injuring himself.

We may add that indictments and, still more, convictions are very rare, and that there is the risk of an unjust conviction from the difficulty of obtaining certain proof except in very rare cases.[1] In Italy in 1863 out of 9 women tried 4 were acquitted; in 1870 there were 4 acquittals to 8 indictments, and in 1881 the same number to 13 indictments.[2] In England from 1847 to 1849 there were only 3 cases of abortion tried, in 1850 there were 5, in 1851 4, in 1852 9, in 1853 17, out of which number there were 12 acquittals. In 1853 there was not a single trial for abortion in Scotland, and the same was true in Würtemberg in 1853–54. And the rarity of convictions (28%) not only casts ridicule upon the law, but also makes it appear that there is injustice in the rare cases where the penalty is exacted.[3]

§ 221. Infanticide

All these arguments are applicable to infanticide also. Birth, the later development of the embryo, is only an unjust cause of infamy to the woman without being any advantage to society, to which on the contrary it becomes a charge; for if the infant is abandoned it is received into a foundling asylum, where it is legally assassinated, the mortality in these establishments being so great as to be like a permanent epidemic. Thus in Syracuse the mortality of foundlings reaches 73%, at Modica, 99%, and at Turin, 50%.

[1] Raffaello Balestrini, *op. cit.*
[2] "Statistiche Giudiziarie Penali."
[3] Beccaria, "Dei Delitti e delle Pene."

It may be objected that we ought not to interfere with the increase of the population, but in that case we ought to pass laws against onanism. All thinkers recognize that law is a relation of man to man, having for its object to make possible the existence of man in society; that it has two terms, man and society, but man only in so far as he is a member of society. In the case of the fœtus, and in the case of the newly born child as well, we can recognize only one of these two terms fully; we may even say that the social element is completely lacking. "It is evident, in fact, that both are rather under the guardianship of the mother, who constitutes their whole environment, than under that of society, of which they are still not directly a part." [1] The alarm of society for the life of an infant of whose existence it is still ignorant (for infanticide "honoris causa" must necessarily take place before the birth of the infant is known) ought to be much less than that for the loss of an adult in the flower of his age.[2]

We must, then, deduct from the theoretical evil caused by the murder of the new-born child, the amount of certain or probable evil which would come from the preservation of a life which exposes the father and mother to an irreparable loss of honor, compromises the peace of one family and sometimes of several, or, at least, in case the child is deserted, puts society in a perplexing situation; for, on the one hand, the imperious voice of charity imposes upon society the necessity of receiving the innocent foundling, while on the other hand reason and experience teach that, by constantly accepting the bringing up of these children as an obligation, it incurs the risk of encouraging desertion and makes charity degenerate into a reward of immorality.[3]

As for the direct harm caused by infanticide, it consists in the suppression of an existence so threatened, by the frequency of still-births and the great mortality of foundlings, that it does not all approach the harm done by an ordinary homicide.

It is hardly necessary to add that a penitentiary sentence

[1] Tissot, "Introd. Philosoph. à l'Étude du Droit Pénal."
[2] Balestrini, *op. cit.*
[3] Boccardo, "Dizionario di Economica Politica."

would have the infallible effect of depraving the woman, and of taking from her, together with the habit of housework, the means of rehabilitating herself when her term had expired. On the other hand, if we base the penalty upon the fear of a relapse, it can have no hold upon the infanticide, who is almost invariably a criminal by accident or by passion, rarely a recidivist. Probation, with security for good behavior, is here, then, very generally sufficient. Limiting in this way the repressive measures against women, we shall prevent those decisions of judges and juries which seem so unjust when we compare the treatment of women with that of men. Out of 100 of each sex who came to trial at the Assizes in Italy, 34 women and 31 men were acquitted; 31 women and 19 men before the Tribunal; and 8 women and 6 men before the justices of the peace. In France, 25 women and 50 men were acquitted at the Assizes; and in Russia, 31 women and 34 men.[1]

§ 222. Age — Youth

Prison is still less the proper expedient for the youth of either sex. I have shown that there are offenses which belong physiologically to childhood, such as cruelty to animals, theft of food, and cheating.[2] What is really useful in these cases is what we may call moral nurture, putting them into the care of respectable and kindly families, where the children will be well treated, and where they will be submitted to the proper sort of suggestion, so powerful at that age. Here they will be stimulated to continued activity for the satisfaction of their proper pride, and at the same time will be withdrawn from dissipation and idleness. Charitable institutions, agricultural colonies, and reform-schools like Barnardo's and that at Elmira, rendered more useful by the application of new ideas drawn from psychology and psychiatry and by emigration to agricultural centers, will prevent the occasional crimes so frequent at that age and will succeed in certain cases, if not in correcting, at least in usefully transforming, the born criminal, and in any case will prevent him from contaminating others.[3]

[1] Bosco, "La Statistica Civile e Penale," Rome, 1898.
[2] "Homme Criminel," Vol. I.
[3] I have read in the "Bulletin de l'Union des Sociétés de Patronage,"

For this purpose it is necessary to avoid the detention prison, which is the greatest source of corruption for youth.

"We speak," says Joly, "of the prisons of the Middle Ages, where they found a dead man between two sick men in the same bed. What we still do in our prisons is destined, I believe, to cause quite as much astonishment by and by. We put a person awaiting judgment, who is innocent or perhaps only an occasional criminal, in contact with hardened offenders. . . . France, with such promiscuities, transforms into malefactors children who have no tendency to crime."[1]

And all this has not even the advantage of making a selection, since, as Joly very well observes, the children acquitted are worse than those convicted.

It is for this reason that every violent correctional measure ought to be regarded as harmful and we should turn to milder measures. Especially, remembering the great precocity of criminals, the limit of age at which we begin their application ought to be set at some little time before nine years, and prolonged in the case of infantilism to a period considerably beyond that set by law. The limits should vary, also, according to climate, race, profession, etc. The Semitic and southern races are, for example, much more precocious in crimes of blood and in sexual crimes; and the poor and those who live in the country are slower to develop than the city dwellers and the rich.

§ 223. Old Age

The old man unable to do harm ought, like the child, to be spared the prison sentence. In his case the common refuge, the workhouse, is sufficient. Here such inmates should be kept in separate apartments, with special precautions to prevent the contagion of evil and also escape. Only when the crime shows an unconquerable perversity should the old man be incarcerated in a regular prison.

Oct., 1897, that the Tribunal of the Seine in passing judgment upon minors inquires into the character of the parents. If this is good the child is returned to them (25%); or he is sent (73%) to the temporary asylum for minors founded by the government in 1893, and thus all but a small proportion (2% to 5%) are spared a penal sentence. A circular of the Minister of Justice, May 13th, 1898, extends this measure to the whole of France. ("Revue Pénitentiare," 1898, p. 871.)

[1] "Le Combat contre le Crime."

§ 224. Criminals by Passion

For true criminals by passion remorse for crime is already the greatest of punishments. A fine, a judicial reprimand, or removal from the city or from the persons injured will be sufficient to protect society, to which they present no danger; and this treatment will leave them able to be useful, because of the great altruism which is characteristic of their class.

§ 225. Political Criminals

Much the same may be said of political criminals. If there is a crime which should be spared not only capital punishment, but even any severe punishment at all, it is that of the political criminal. This is especially true because many political criminals, if they are not criminals by passion, are insane and need the hospital more than the scaffold; and because even when they are criminals their altruism renders them worthy of the greatest consideration, and often by having their altruism given another direction they may be made useful to society. Louise Michel was called in New Caledonia "the red angel," so devoted was she to the sick and unfortunate.[1] Moreover, almost all political criminals are young, and it is in youth that heroism and fanaticism attain their highest degree. It is not possible to kill an idea by killing the man who has conceived it; on the contrary it grows and perpetuates itself better in the glow of the martyr's halo, all the more if it is true, while if it is false, it falls of itself. Furthermore, it is not possible to pass final judgment upon a man while he is alive, any more than a single generation can decide with certainty as to the falsity of an idea that has arisen under their own eyes. Russia has for a long time given us proofs of the uselessness of too severe laws against political criminals. Each of her terrible acts of repression by condemnation to a lingering death in the mines of Siberia has been followed by new and more violent reactions; and the same is true of France and Italy. Ravachol was not yet dead when

[1] Lombroso and Laschi, "Le Crime Politique," Paris, 1890.

he was turned into a demi-god, and hymns were sung in Paris in his honor instead of the Marseillaise.[1]

"There is nothing," writes one of our profoundest thinkers, G. Ferrero,[2] "more potent in exciting revolutionary tendencies than those legendary martyrologies that stir the imagination of the numbers of fanatics with whom our society is swarming, and who are always an important element in all revolutionary movements. In every society there is a crowd of persons who need a martyr. They enjoy being persecuted and believing themselves the victims of human wickedness. They enroll themselves in the political parties which offer the most danger, just as certain mountain-climbers choose the mountain that has the most dangerous precipices and the most inaccessible peaks. For all such there is no more powerful incentive to embrace revolutionary theories than violent persecutions; and nothing is more dangerous than to give these exalted imaginations the corpse of an executed leader."

That which characterizes these political criminals especially is a lack, which we might call specific, of adaptability to the form of government under which they are living; while born criminals show themselves unadaptable not only to the social environment of the nation in which they are found, but also to that of any nation of the same degree of civilization. For this reason, while born criminals must be eliminated from the civilized world, political criminals, who are such by passion, need simply be removed from the governmental and social environment of the people to whom they have proved unable to adapt themselves.

Exile, as it existed in Roman law and as it now exists in Abyssinia, and — in serious cases — deportation, are, then, the penalties most appropriate for this class of criminals. But these penalties ought always to be temporary and revocable every three or five years at the will of parliament;[3] for before the expiration of the sentence public opinion may very well have changed. It is just for this reason that our school, while opposed to jury trial for ordinary crimes, accepts it in the case of political crimes as the only means of diagnosis which permits

[1] Lombroso, "Les Anarchistes," Paris, 1896.
[2] "La Riforma Sociale," 1894.
[3] Lombroso, "Crime Politique," Pt. IV.

the recognition of whether the public opinion regards the offense in question as a crime. It was thus that formerly heresy was punished as the gravest possible crime, while to punish it to-day would seem ridiculous. It will be the same in a short time with crimes of leze majesty, strikes, and the pretended offenses of socialistic thought. By this means we shall prevent those rare cases of rebellion which are, as we have seen, the beginning of evolution; and this idea is neither revolutionary nor new, for it has already been applied in different countries and epochs, and under really free governments; in Florence under the form of admonition, in Greece under that of ostracism, and in Sicily as petalism. In the constitution of the United States it is Congress itself which fixes the penalty for political crimes; and the same situation prevailed in the Roman Republic.

But if the punishment for crimes provoked by political passion alone ought always to be temporary, in mixed political crimes, on the contrary, the penalty might be applied in a mixed form; that is to say, fixed for a certain term of years, corresponding to the legitimate social reaction, and indeterminate for another series of years, in order that it may be possible to interrupt it when the attack upon the political organization is no longer considered in the country as a crime.

§ 226. Occasional Criminals

The same crime calls for a different penalty according as it is committed by a born criminal, a criminaloid, or an occasional criminal, and even at times in this latter case for no punishment at all. In this case it is essential to recognize the true motive. An offense that is really occasional, and which excludes the thought of punishment, is the theft of food by persons who are famished.[1] Real punishment is equally inappropriate in all cases of involuntary offenses, according to the opinion of Puglia, Pinsero, and Capobianco,[2] the amount of the damages to be paid being left to the civil judges; for it would be unjust to regard a man as absolutely unfit to live in society,

[1] Cremani, "De Jure Criminali," 1748.
[2] "Scuola Positiva," III and VII.

simply for the reason that through negligence or thoughtlessness, or by a pure accident which could not be repeated, he has committed a harmful act. If the same thing occurs repeatedly, it is possible to add to the simple damages a fine, or suspension from the office, art, or profession which have been the cause of the blamable act.

§ 227. Aid to Suicide

Among the pretended crimes which the law punishes but which the public conscience absolves, are those which Garofalo calls "not natural" but juridical, and which we shall call conventional. Aid to suicide is an example.

"If, leaving aside pure abstractions, we interrogate the science of life, we shall see," write Calucci and Ferri, "that the interest of society in the existence of each of its members is not absolute, but that it decreases greatly, and even ceases altogether, in the case of voluntary death. On its side biology shows us that in the struggle for existence it is the weakest, those least adapted to the social life, who succumb. Suicide is one of the forms of this defeat. It is, according to Häckel, a safety valve for future generations, to whom it spares a fatal heritage of nervous diseases with their consequent misery. It is, says Bagehot, one of the instruments for the amelioration of the human race by the road of selection." [1]

Such is also the opinion of Morselli and of myself. I have shown with Ferri that suicide is opposed to homicide,[2] that it is a real safety valve, so that where the one increases the other decreases. On this side, then, suicide is of real advantage to the security of the state.

"Either," continues Ferri, "you maintain that a man has not a right to dispose of his own life, and then you ought to punish the suicide, or else you recognize that suicide is not a crime. In that case how can you punish the man who takes part in the suicide by aiding in it, just for taking part in what is no crime? For, even if we cannot deny that the state exercises its repressive function for the purpose of defending its citizens as individuals in the case of crime against their safety, who does not see that real and voluntary consent of the victim removes every excuse for interference on the part of the state?"

[1] Ferri, "L' Omicidio-Suicidio," 1884.
[2] "Homme Criminel," Vol. I.

Wherein do we feel our safety threatened when we learn that an individual has been killed at his own request? The Church alone can pretend to save the sinner in spite of himself.

§ 228. Defamation

The same may be said of the penalties decreed by the Italian code against defamation having a political or social object, the work most often of men better than the normal who have the courage to reveal to the public facts that pass for defamation only because the persons accused are powerful. These noble defamers are not to be feared, and they do no damage. They disobey the law only because it is imperfect. They are, then, pseudo-criminals,[1] more worthy of praise than punishment. It is enough to make them show their good faith by furnishing proof of the facts or by retracting if they are deceived, expecially since to lay bare our wounds is to begin their cure.

§ 229. The Duel

The situation is much the same with regard to the duel. Are we still subject to the tyranny of the custom which drove us to the duel in grave and exceptional cases when the services of the law became unavailing? If it is so, then we have before us, in persons guilty of duelling, harmless individuals, and we should be using an excessive and unjust zeal if we were to punish them in order to escape a danger which in reality does not exist. On the other hand, is it the office of the criminal law to correct morals? Assuredly not, for morals and laws follow the natural trend of things and are both determined by environment. It is enough to recall that duels raged most in the countries where they were punished most severely, and that from the Middle Ages to our own time the number has decreased in measure as the laws against them became milder. But who ever believed that prejudices could be overcome by penalties? Have not the prejudices already gathered enough victims without having these useless punishments coming in and demanding new ones? The penal code ought to aim at defending society

[1] "Homme Criminel," Vol. II.

by purifying it from the evil race of criminals. Now the duelist, at least in most cases, is rather a victim than a criminal, and if, on account of the means which science offers us, we are able to identify him as a criminal in those rare cases in which he is such, why should we offer him this honorable means of escape? If he is not a criminal, why should we punish him for being the victim of the very prejudices which we wish to eradicate? But the prejudice will either die, or it will be stronger than the law; and the penalties which, on account of their severity, will not be applied, will render the impotent efforts of the lawmaker all the more ridiculous.

§ 230. Adultery

In the matter of adultery, again, the situation is much the same. That it should be punished as a crime in the canon law is doubtless justified, but in the modern code it can be classed at most only as a contravention. Adultery is assuredly immoral, and it is certain that if a law could prevent it by punishment it would be welcome; but that it could do so is not the opinion of the majority. Moreover, in this kind of trial the victim suffers more than the culprit. It is useless, then, to have recourse to the law; and besides, the general and habitual impunity renders condemnation, in the rare cases where it takes place, all the more cruel. As Berenini rightly says in his magnificent monograph, "Offesa e Difesa," "The law cannot oblige a woman to love her husband or the husband his wife. It can only safeguard rights that may be exacted materially and by force. Love is not a right that either one of a married couple can require of the other, and the law cannot, in consequence, protect a right which does not exist for the person who claims to have been injured. Adultery, by dissolving the natural marriage, involves a moral divorce; why should it not also dissolve the civil marriage by a legal divorce? Why maintain forcibly the cause of the disturbance while aggravating its effects by the useless scandal of a trial and a condemnation?"

§ 231. Criminaloids

For criminaloids who are not recidivists and are without accomplices, it will be sufficient for the first time to suspend sentence, take security, and require the repayment of the damage, by work, where the culprit is not able to pay. This work should be in the fields when the offender is a peasant, or, in case of refusal to work, in a cellular prison.

§ 232. Homo-sexual Offenders

Homo-sexual offenders whose crime has been occasioned by residence in barracks, or colleges, or by a forced celibacy, plainly will not relapse when the cause has been removed. It will be sufficient in their case to inflict a conditional punishment, for they are not to be confused with the homo-sexual offenders who are born such, and who manifest their evil propensities from childhood without being determined by special causes. These should be confined from their youth, for they are a source of contagion and cause a great number of occasional criminals.

§ 233. Other Minor Offenses

Many other punishable acts could be transferred from the penal to the civil code for fines and payment of damages. In this class come the violation of private correspondence, damages caused to the property of another, and bad treatment of other members of the family when not habitual or proceeding from depraved and truly criminal instincts. To this treatment we may add, in the case of husband and wife, separation and divorce. These disciplinary measures would be sufficient in the case of a violation of the duties proper to a public employee, and could be carried to the extent of dismissing him from his position. Simple threats, violation of domicile without criminal intent, insult, arbitrary taking of satisfaction, abuse of pasturage rights, and trespass would be sufficiently punished by payment of damages, which could very well be estimated by a civil judge.[1] I would add to the list thefts of food of small value, provided that the small value of the articles stolen showed

[1] See Garofalo, "Riparazione alla Vittima del Delitto."

the occasional character of the offense. Is it not a flagrant injustice that petty thieves, most often quite inoffensive (children who have stolen fruit, for example), should be punished as severely as real criminals who steal upon a large scale, or even more severely, since the latter often escape punishment altogether? I shall never forget how upon the day when five ministers of the realm of Italy rose as one man in open Parliament to deny or to justify the thefts of Tanlongo and Company, running up to more than 30 millions, seven children were sent to weep for a month and a half in prison cells for having stolen a herring of the value of 35 centesimi.

In these last cases I should wish to make a distinction between the really criminal "gang" having a common understanding and a minutely detailed plan, and that accidental semi-complicity which often has nothing criminal in it, being the effect of a simple caprice. The former I would punish very severely, while for the latter a simple reparation to the person injured, with a reprimand or a conditional sentence, would suffice.

§ 234. Complicity

The least dangerous criminals, those who are occasional criminals or criminals of passion, having for their psychological characteristic always to act alone without accomplices, it follows that complicity, at least in thefts, highway robberies, and murders,[1] in the case of adults, must constitute by itself an aggravating circumstance; and in every case should not be looked into, as it is now, merely to determine what share in the guilt each member of the band had, but should be taken as a distinctive mark of criminals belonging to the most dangerous classes.[2]

§ 235. Habitual Criminals

As to recidivists and criminaloids who have become habitual criminals, they should be treated like born criminals but subjected to a less severe discipline, their crimes being almost always less serious (theft, swindling, forgery, etc.). Further,

[1] Sighele, "La Teoria Positiva della Complicità," Turin, 1894.
[2] Ferri, "Sociologie Criminelle," Paris, 1890.

while in the case of the born criminal the first crime, if serious, is sufficient to have him sentenced to perpetual confinement, in the case of the habitual criminal it is necessary, before determining upon this extreme treatment, to have the evidence of a number of recidivisms more or less great according to the kind of crimes and the circumstances under which they were committed. For the employment of these criminals there should be large workshops for those who come from the cities, and for those who come from the country agricultural colonies in the districts that need clearing, graded from the least to the most healthful according to the different categories of criminals. The colony of Castiadas, which has created an oasis in the most insalubrious district of Sardinia, and the miracles of the Trois Fontaines, prove how easy it is to put these organizations to practical use, diminishing the enormous expenses which respectable people have to pay for the punishment of criminals and at the same time making them of real service to the society which they have injured.

§ 236. The Criminal Insane

As for the criminal insane and the numerous born criminals in whom epilepsy and moral insanity manifest themselves clearly by fits of mental disturbance, the only proper treatment is confinement in a criminal asylum. By means of such an institution we take away from the criminal who might feign insanity all desire to do so; we prevent a criminal heredity derived from the inmates; we put an end to their forming criminal associations (the criminal bands having almost all a prison origin); we prevent recidivism, and cut down the enormous expenses of trials and the imitative crimes which often result from trials. Wiedemeister[1] objects that these asylums will do an injury to justice in case the patient becomes cured. In reply we will remark in the first place that these cases are quite rare. The statistics of Broadmoor record but 5.5%. However this may be, the inconvenience may be remedied by granting liberty to those patients only who have shown themselves to be cured during a long period of observation.

[1] "Zeitschrift für Psychiatrie," 1871.

"But as soon as a criminal has been recognized as insane," objects Falvet, "he is not to be considered as a criminal, but resumes his status under the civil law." To this we reply, that he cannot return to that status, because he has killed, ravished, and stolen, and cannot therefore be put on the same plane as the harmless insane; for as long as the danger persists, the right of defense remains. Aside from this, this method of reasoning is derived from a class of ideas which science will from now on eliminate; that is to say, that while insanity is a misfortune, crime is a perversity of the free will. Now, just as men came to recognize a century ago, contrary to the beliefs of the Middle Ages, that insanity did not depend upon free will, we must now recognize that neither does crime itself depend upon it. Crime and insanity are both misfortunes; let us treat them, then, without rancor, but defend ourselves from their blows.[1] On the principles of the positivistic school, the objection cannot be maintained that the insane "so-called" criminal comes under the civil law simply. He comes under the law of self-defense as much as the true criminal.

For this reason the objection falls that the insane person cannot be detained for an indeterminate time, and that when he is cured, even before the expiration of the term which he would have passed in prison in case of a conviction, he has the right to go free. This objection cannot be admitted, considering the great number of relapses which have been shown to occur in all forms of insanity. There are misfortunes that are inexorable, and grant only a short respite; since we cannot deliver the individual from them completely, let us try at least to prevent the family of the hapless wretch, and society in general, from being victims.[2]

Furthermore, all the more civilized nations show similar in-

[1] Ferri, "Sociologie Criminelle."

[2] Recently Christiani ("Archivio di Psichiatria," 1896) has shown that incurability (82%) and death (17%) are the most frequent results; while cures are more rare (5% to 8%), and that with almost all there is to be observed a predominance of anti-social tendencies (87%). Nicholson found that 75% of ordinary criminals are such from cupidity, 15% from hatred, and 10% from immorality; while in the case of the criminal insane the last figure becomes 71%. (Journal of Mental Science, Oct., 1895.) It is these who are, then, the fiercest and most dangerous.

stitutions. We have seen that in England they are already ancient. The criminal asylum exists also in Denmark; and it has been introduced into Sweden and Hungary. In France at the Prefecture of Police there is a permanent medical commission, whose duty it is to separate immediately from the other persons arrested those who appear to be insane. In 1870 a real asylum for the criminal insane was erected as a part of the central institution at Gaillon. This department is kept under the discipline of the prison except as to the compulsory labor, and also as to the punishments, which can be inflicted only with the permission of physicians. Only those who have been sentenced to imprisonment for more than one year are admitted here, and they cannot be discharged without the authorization of the minister.[1] All the other civilized peoples of continental Europe, if they have not regular criminal asylums, have laws and institutions which partly take the place of them. At Hamburg, Halle, and Bruchsal the penitentiaries have infirmaries which are reserved exclusively for the insane, with gardens, secure cells, and a special discipline, so that the insane can receive continual care there as in the regular asylums. In Belgium a law (1850) decrees that

"Persons arrested, proceedings against whom have been suspended for the cause of insanity, shall be consigned to asylums designated by the Public Minister. These asylums must have special wards for maniacal prisoners, accused or convicted, who cannot be mingled with the other patients without a special authorization from the minister of justice. The physician in charge is responsible for the escape of dangerous or criminal insane persons, and, in case of flight, must take all the necessary steps to recover them."

A new law, "la loi Lajeune" (1891), requires the appointment of three alienists as special inspectors of prisons, to discover, isolate, and care for the insane. In Hungary a kind of medical senate, composed of judges and physicians who are alienists, is charged with pronouncing upon doubtful cases.

We may say, then, in summing up, that in these asylums there

[1] Hurel, "Le Quartier des Condamnés Aliénés Annexé à la Maison Centrale de Gaillon," Paris, 1877.

should be received: 1st, all prisoners who have become insane, if they have criminal tendencies; 2d, all the insane who, on account of homicidal or incendiary tendencies, pederasty, etc., have been subjected to a judicial procedure which has been suspended upon the discovery of their insanity; 3d, all those charged with strange or atrocious crimes, committed without clear motive, in whose case has arisen the suspicion of insanity, or at least of a serious cerebral affection, as attested by three expert alienists;[1] 4th, in consideration of the extraordinary importance of epilepsy, all those who have committed crimes in a state of psychic epilepsy and criminals who have had epileptic fits; 5th, all those who, being of general good reputation, are driven to crime by an habitual and evident infirmity, such as pellagra, chronic alcoholism, and puerperal diseases, especially where they have insane or epileptic parents, or show numerous marks of degeneracy. In this connection we see the propriety of having special criminal asylums for the alcoholic, epileptic, etc.

The insane coming from the prisons must be isolated from the others and placed in separate wards in the infirmaries annexed to the prisons. The discipline should be severe for all, and the vigilance greater than in the common asylums, more like that of the prisons, but the work should be proportioned to the strength and alternated with long periods of rest and amusement. The direction should be medical, but the attendants should have prison training.

The individuals who are recognized as habitually dangerous and have already been several times arraigned ought never to be liberated. Those who are affected with a transitory or intermittent form of insanity and show signs of a perfect cure should be selected for discharge after one or two years of observation,

[1] At first sight this proposition appears absurd, and the absurdity has been made use of to refute those who uphold the criminal asylum. But proper attention is not paid to the fact that it is just the doubtful cases, intermediate between reason and insanity, in which crimes without cause are most frequent and in which, therefore, the criminal asylums are most useful and of most service in guaranteeing the public safety. We may recall here that a crime without reason is of itself a sign of insanity. Beccaria says that a sane man is not capable of useless cruelty not excited by hate, fear, or self-interest. (See "Homme Criminel," Vol. III.)

and subjected after their release to monthly medical visits for several years, as is done in Belgium.

§ 237. Incorrigible Criminals

We have seen that the best penitentiary system will not prevent recidivism, and that the individualized system has given unfortunate results in Denmark. On the other hand, we have seen that we have in the collective prisons the most frequent cause of repeated recidivisms and criminal actions.[1] Further, what can one hope for from individuals, like those described by Breton and Aspirall, returned to prison 50 or 60 times in a single year? Such persons evidently find themselves better off there than outside, so that for them prison is no longer a punishment but a reward and an encouragement to corruption? When no method is of service any longer, when the criminal is insensible to all the pains taken with him and relapses 10 or 20 times, society ought not to wait while he perfects himself in crime by a new sojourn in prison, but should keep him shut up until assured of his reformation, or, better, of his powerlessness to do harm. We should, for this end, establish special penal institutions, to which a jury composed of directors, physicians, and judges shall consign all the individuals who, having from infancy shown an inclination toward crime, have relapsed several times, especially if they present those physical and psychical characteristics which we have seen to be marks of the born criminal.

Even more important than the well-being of the inmates is the matter of making them useful that they may not occasion too great an expense, and also the matter of preventing the possibility of escape. For this reason islands or retired valleys offer the best locations. Here the prisoners may be occupied, if they come from the country, in work in the fields, which will be useful for their health and of advantage to the state, while those who come from the city may be provided for in workshops. Better still, disciplined military companies might be formed, as is the practice in Westphalia, and put to work to improve the

[1] See "Homme Criminel," Vol. I.

roads and drain the marshes. They should be permitted daily to spend some hours according to their own taste, but they should be set at liberty again only after extraordinary proof of reformation. The cellular system should be inflicted upon them only in the case of a new relapse. In this way the prison would become purged of those criminals who take pride in vice and render all attempts at reform there impossible. In this way we shall apply anew to society the process of selection to which is due the existence of our race, and also probably the existence of justice itself,[1] since it was the elimination of the more violent that gradually allowed justice to prevail. However high the expense of all this may be, it will always be less than the cost of new crimes and new trials. Thompson calculates that 458 Scotch recidivists cost £132,000, of which £86,000 was for the cost of the trials alone.

This proposition is not new, for in 1864 the House of Lords proposed to condemn criminals to penal servitude after a second recidivism. E. Labiste [2] proposes that after the expiration of his sentence, every individual whose total sentences exceed five years and who has relapsed for the tenth time, shall be permanently deported. The same reform is proposed by Bonneville,[3] Tissot,[4] and Doria Barini; [5] and it has already been put into operation in Belgium in the agricultural colony of Mexplas, which contains 4500 individuals. The buildings of this institution were all erected by the labor of the convicts themselves under the superintendence of 30 or 40 foremen. Everything was constructed little by little according to the needs and resources, so that this magnificent establishment, which in other countries would have cost millions, has cost Belgium only the price of the land. Live stock multiplies upon the place, since the farms have their own bulls and stallions. The workmen are occupied only with the production of such things as have an easy sale, and in the making of which they may be useful. The inmates are divided into four classes: 1st, those who are re-

[1] "Homme Criminel," Vol. I., Pt. I.
[2] "Essai sur les Institutions Pénales des Romains," 1875.
[3] "De l'Insufficiance Actuelle de l'Intimidation," p. 257.
[4] "Introduction Philosophique à l'Étude du Droit Pénal," p. 433.
[5] See "Rivista di Disciplinia Carceria," 1876.

fractory or dangerous, contact with whom might be harmful to the other inmates; 2d, recidivist convicts, under the surveillance of the police, those who have formerly escaped, and those who have had a bad record in the institution itself; 3d, men whose antecedents leave something to be desired, but who have never had to undergo severe punishment in the institution; 4th, those who have not been deported to the colonies more than three times and whose conduct might be considered as good. The communes sometimes send their paupers there, paying 65 centimes for those that are well and 85 for the sick. Those who refuse to work are kept in a cell three days upon bread and water. The inmates are paid for their labor in a currency which passes only in the institution but is exchanged for real money when they are discharged. In this way the danger of spending money in the neighboring hamlets is avoided.[1]

§ 238. The Death Penalty

But when, in spite of the prison, transportation, and hard labor, these criminals repeat their sanguinary crimes and threaten the lives of honest men for the third or fourth time there is nothing left but the last selection, painful but sure, — capital punishment. Just as the death penalty is too largely inscribed in the book of nature, so is it in the book of history; and like all other punishments, it has a relative justice. Capital punishment assuredly ought to be found in the penal system of barbarous peoples, among whom prison does not inspire sufficient terror; but among civilized people the delicacy of feeling which wishes to abolish it is too respectable to be brushed aside, to say nothing of the fact that the singular prestige produced by a death inflicted in cold blood by judges, and at times met with bravado, often multiplies crimes by imitation and creates among the rabble a sort of worship of the unfortunate victim.

But the opponents of this form of punishment do not think of asking: What means of defense is left to society against a man guilty of repeated murders who keeps his guards in constant danger of violence or death? Would it be more just or more humane to keep him bound hand and foot for life?

[1] Joly, "Le Combat contre le Crime."

Let no one advance the objection, with Ferri, that in order to make capital punishment effective it must become a regular butchery, a thing repugnant to modern thought. To retain the death penalty is not the same as multiplying it. It is enough that it should remain suspended, like the sword of Damocles, over the head of the more terrible criminals, when, after having been condemned to imprisonment for life, they have several times made attempts upon the lives of others. Under these conditions there is no longer any weight to the otherwise fundamentally sound objection which is so often put forward, namely, that this penalty is irreparable. I should also wish to have this punishment retained when the social system of a country is menaced by associated crime under the forms of brigandage, the Camorra, etc. From this point of view it seems to me that the civil conditions are absolutely equivalent to the conditions for which this penalty is reserved in time of war. What! shall we be unmoved when by the right of conscription we condemn in advance thousands of men to an early death upon the battlefield, often for dynastic caprice or demagogic madness, and shall we hesitate when it is a question of suppressing some few criminal individuals, a hundred times more dangerous and fatal than a foreign enemy, in whose ranks a chance bullet may strike a Darwin or a Gladstone?

Assuredly if we take the point of view of strict abstract right, we do not believe ourselves to be God's vicars and therefore have no absolute right over the life of our fellows. But unless this right comes to us with the necessity of self-defense, neither have we any right to deprive men of liberty or to hold them accountable for the least misdemeanor. To claim that the death penalty is contrary to the laws of nature is to ignore the fact that this law is written in the book of nature in letters only too clear, and that the very progress of the organic world is entirely based upon the struggle for existence, followed by savage hecatombs. The fact that there exist such beings as born criminals, organically fitted for evil, atavistic reproductions, not simply of savage men but even of the fiercest animals, far from making us more compassionate towards them, as has been maintained, steels us against all pity. Our love for animals (except among the fakirs of India) has not reached such a point that we are willing to sacrifice our own lives for their benefit.

Here I can but recall the vigorous lines which Taine wrote to me shortly before he died:

"When in the life and in the intellectual, moral, and emotional organization of the criminal the criminal impulse is isolated, accidental, and transitory, we can and even ought to pardon; but the more this impulse is bound up with the entire fabric of the ideas and feelings, the more guilty is the man and the more ought he to be punished. You have shown us fierce and lubricious orang-utans with human faces. It is evident that as such they cannot act otherwise. If they ravish, steal, and kill, it is by virtue of their own nature and their past, but there is all the more reason for destroying them when it has been proved that they will always remain orang-utans. As far as they are concerned I have no objection to the death penalty, if society is likely to profit by it."

Many of the measures which I have advocated may appear contrary to certain ideal principles which, while more noble than practical, are regarded by short-sighted intolerance as unassailable axioms. Further, they may be regarded, by those who are frightened at the first cost, as difficult to put into practice; but this is to lose sight of the economies which they would make possible in the future, especially if we should suppress, at least for recidivists, the costly and useless judicial proceedings based solely upon errors in form.[1] In any case they cannot be accused of endangering that public safety which is the ultimate aim of all penal systems.

[1] In France, where, as De Foresta observes, the person has no right of appeal for merely technical errors, and each new trial or decision may bring an increase of the penalty, appeals are very rare and taken only for grave reasons. Out of the money thus saved it would be possible to support three criminal asylums and a large institution for incorrigibles.

CHAPTER IV

PRACTICAL PROOFS OF THE UTILITY OF THESE REFORMS — ENGLAND — SWITZERLAND

§ 239.

THE utility of these reforms is proved by the recent statistics of London and Geneva, where there has been a perceptible decrease in criminality, while, on the contrary, crime is increasing in countries like Italy and Spain, where such reforms have not been applied.

In the period between 1829 and 1838 there were recorded at Geneva, for each 100,000 inhabitants, 79 criminals convicted by the Criminal Court and 1000 by the correctional tribunal, while between 1872 and 1885 there were recorded 12 of the former and 300 of the latter; that is to say, between the two periods the serious crimes decreased by five-sixths and the minor offenses by two-thirds. This is certainly a great honor to the city, and the facts are even stronger, for the crimes committed by the Genevese themselves have decreased nearly nine-tenths in the last 80 years.[1]

What are the causes that make Geneva an oasis of morality in the midst of Europe? Guénoud attributes it in the first place to the fact that foreigners who have been for some time residents in Geneva have taken up the customs and morals of the natives; and the observation of Joly[2] is to the same effect, namely, that the immigrants at first contribute largely to the criminality, but as they become established in their new country they gain in morality and honesty. But Ladame urges by way of objection,[3]

"The assimilation of foreigners to the natives does not prevent immigration; the same causes consequently continue to

[1] Guénoud, "La Criminalité à Genève au XIX Siècle," Geneva, 1891.
[2] "La France Criminelle."
[3] "Journal de Genève," Feb. 4th, 1891.

be active, and if, on one side, the population of Geneva annually assimilates a certain number of foreigners, the resultant moral influence is neutralized by new immigrants whose influence is the other way."

Nor can we look for the cause in education, since we have seen that this very often increases at least the minor forms of criminality.

The sole reason remaining is, then, that Geneva (see Pt. II, Ch. VI) is certainly that place in central Europe where there have been established the greatest number of institutions for mutual aid, which without degrading the recipients remedy the greatest evils of poverty, and also preventive institutions for children, for degraded women, against alcoholism, etc.

The proof of this conclusion appears more clearly still in England, especially in London. If we compare the criminality there in the years 1892–93 with those of the ten years preceding, we find an increase of 28% in the offenses against persons and 18.9% in those against property, caused by a desire for vengeance and taking the form of arson or the destroying of crops. But in other crimes (theft, receiving stolen goods, forgery, offenses against the public order, etc.) the decrease was respectively 8.8%, 36.3%, 34%, and 22.2%, with a *total* absolute *decrease* of 8%.[1] Now it must be noted that in these ten years the population *increased* 12%; so that even if there had been as much as an absolute increase of 12% in the criminality it would mean that relatively to the population crime was not on the increase in England.

"The decrease there in the criminality of minors, which in Italy continues to increase, is still more remarkable. In 1868–69 there was recorded the conviction of 10,000 children less than 16 years of age; in the succeeding years the figures fell to 9700, and finally to 4000. Thus we find that, taking account of the increase in population, England recorded in 1868–69–70 46 juvenile criminals to the 100,000 inhabitants; in 1893 there were only 14, a real decrease of 70%; while it appeared that in France in 1889 the number of juvenile offenders had increased 140% in 50 years. The criminal classes of England are composed of individuals at liberty, known to be thieves

1 Joly, "La Revue de Paris," Paris, 1891.

or receivers of stolen goods, and of persons under suspicion. Here also there is an improvement. In 1867 this last category comprised, taking prisoners and those at liberty together, 87,000 individuals. This figure fell later to 50,000; in 1881 to 38,960; and finally in 1891–92 to 29,826. The suspected houses fell from 2688 to 2360."[1]

We do not have here those accidental variations in figures common in statistics, for they show such a decided difference that no doubt can remain,[2] and they extend even to unpunished crime.

This great decrease in criminality is actually due to preventive measures, especially those which have to do with children, and to the moral and religious fight against alcoholism. We find an incontestable proof of this in the great diminution of crime in London as compared with the smaller cities and with the country. This is exactly the opposite of what is observed elsewhere, since the general rule is the greater criminality of the principal cities. Now, while the city of London, which has the largest population of any city in the civilized world, records 15 suspected persons to 100,000 inhabitants, the country shows 61 and the other cities 50. Further, while London has 3.4 suspected houses to each 100,000 inhabitants, the country has 3.9 and the other cities 8.4.

We have another proof of the influence of preventive measures in the diminution of alcoholism which has taken place in just those districts of England and Switzerland where the religious and purely ethical societies vie with the state in striking at

[1] Joly, "La Revue de Paris," 1894.

[2] However, one remark must be made here: in the statistics for juvenile offenders in England we see —

JUVENILE OFFENDERS (UNDER 16)

	1864–68	1889–98
Sent to prison	8,285	2,268
" to reform schools	1,228	1,163
" to industrial schools	966	8,737
Sentenced to be whipped	585	3,028
	11,064	13,806

We see that if the juveniles sent to prison or to the reform schools have decreased enormously (over 6000) the number sent to the industrial schools or sentenced to whipping has increased by 9300.

the evil at its very source. While in France the sales of alcoholic drinks increased from 365,995 in 1869 to 417,518 in 1893, and from 1.82 litres to each inhabitant in 1830 to 4.20 in 1893, in England, on the contrary, the consumption per capita has fallen in recent years from 7 liters to 5, and in Switzerland from 11 liters to 7.[1]

§ 240. Born Criminals

It would be a mistake, however, to imagine that the measures which have been shown to be effective with other criminals could be successfully applied to born criminals; for these are, for the most part, refractory to all treatment, even to the most affectionate care begun at the very cradle, as Barnardo finally became convinced. Such was Jac——, whom he placed in conditions best fitted to reform him, but who escaped repeatedly to live a life of vagabondage. While the less advanced peoples are lingering over the utopias of the old jurists and, believing that reform is possible for all criminals, are taking no measures against the continually rising tide of crime, the English, more provident, have recognized that although they have been able by their efforts to eliminate the accidental criminal almost entirely, the born criminal still persists. They are the only nation to admit the existence of criminals who resist all cure, the "professional criminals," as they call them, and the "criminal classes."

It will not be useless, for the benefit of those who limit the causes of crime to education and environment, to verify this with figures. While crime in England has decreased by 8%, recidivism among male criminals has remained stationary or nearly so. The English statistics, in fact, show 41.7% of recidivism in 1892–93 and 45% in 1894–95.[2] In the case of the women recidivism has increased from 54.6% to 60.4%, and this notwithstanding the fact that the preventive institutions for women in London are much more numerous than those for men; but all efforts break down against the corruption encouraged by prostitution and against the increasing alcoholism of

[1] "Revue du Christianisme Pratique," Nov., 1894.
[2] Paolucci, "Revue des Revues," May, 1896.

women. "No one ever knew of a man," says Paolucci, "who has reached 500 convictions for drunkenness, like Tessie Jay, or even 250, like Jane Cakebreade." We have seen, in this connection, how the introduction of agricultural colonies has lessened theft and vagabondage in Westphalia.

We must say, however, that this system can be of use only for occasional criminals, or for vagrants who are such from lack of work, while it is of no value for born vagabonds. We have a proof of this in an experiment which was tried in Paris. According to the "Économiste Français" (1893), a certain person arranged to obtain positions in stores, factories, etc., at 4 francs a day, for all persons presenting a letter from himself. In 8 months he offered this letter to 727 beggars who complained that they were starving because of lack of work. More than half (415) of these did not even call for the letter; 130 got the letter but did not present it to any employer. Others worked for half a day, drew their two francs, and did not return. In short, out of the whole 727, only 8 continued at work. Taking simply those who took the letter, we see that out of every 40 beggars able to work, only 1 had a sincere desire to do so.[1] Even if the young people whom Barnardo sent to Canada were reformed, out of those who emigrated to the same country from the reform school at Redhill 42% returned worse than before, notwithstanding the £1000 spent for their reformation (Joly).

[1] See also Paulien, "Paris qui Mendie," 1890.

CHAPTER V

PRACTICAL APPLICATION TO THE CRITICISM OF CRIMINAL LAW, TO EXPERT TESTIMONY, PEDAGOGY, ART, AND SCIENCE

§ 241.

ALL these facts prove abundantly that criminal anthropology not only solves the theoretical problems of law, but suggests useful lessons in the struggle of society against crime; while ancient penal science, the more it rose into the exalted regions of jurisprudence, the more it lost touch with practice and the less it knew how to protect us.

§ 242. Political Crime

One of the newest and at the same time most practical applications of criminal anthropology is that which takes into account the fact that men's hatred of the new is the juridical basis of political crime. From the study of the physiognomy and biology of the political criminal it establishes the difference between a real revolution, a useful and productive thing, and mere revolts, which are always sterile and harmful.[1] It is a fact now definitely recognized, and one of which I have given proofs in my "Crime Politique," that those who start great scientific and political revolutions are almost always young, endowed with genius or with a singular altruism, and have a fine physiognomy; and far from presenting the insensibility common in born criminals, they are, on the contrary, marked by a real moral and physical hyperesthesia. But if from the martyrs of a great social and religious idea we pass to rebels, regicides, and "presidenticides," such as Fieschi and Guiteau, to the promoters of the massacres of 1793, such as Carrier, Jourdan, and Marat, and to the anarchists, we see that all, or nearly all, are of a criminal type. These are rebels.

[1] See "Homme Criminel," Vol. II, p. 255.

§ 243. Application to Psychiatric Expert Testimony

Medical experts and practical penologists who have studied criminal anthropology have become convinced of the value of this science in recognizing the real culprit and in deciding how far an accomplice has participated in a crime. Hitherto these things have had to be determined from unreliable indications, such as prison confessions and vague official information.

I will cite as proof of this the following examples: 1. Bersone Pierre, 37 years of age, well known as a thief, had been arrested under charge of having stolen 20,000 francs upon the railroad. In prison he feigned madness, pretending that someone had poisoned him. It was soon plain that he had committed many other thefts, since he was found in possession of a number of documents and passports, among others that of a certain Torelli. The result of an anthropological examination was as follows: mean cranial capacity, 1589 c. c.; cephalic index, 77; type of physiognomy, completely criminal; touch, nearly normal — tongue, 1.9 mm. (between points perceived separately), right hand, 2–3, left hand, 1–2 (with sensorial mancinism); general sensibility and sensibility to pain, very obtuse — 48 mm. and 10 mm. respectively, on the adjustable Rhumkorff coil, as against 61 mm. and 24 mm. for the normal man. An investigation with the hydrosphygmograph [1] confirmed me in my observation of his great insensibility to pain, which did not change the sphygmographic lines. The same apathy persisted when he was spoken to of the robbery on the railroad, while there was an enormous depression — a fall of 14 mm. — when the Torelli theft was mentioned. I concluded, therefore, that he had had no part in the railway robbery, but that he had certainly participated in the Torelli affair; and my conclusions were completely verified.

2. Maria Gall —— of Lucera, 66 years of age, was found dead in her bed, her face to the mattress, and her nostrils bloody, bruised, and lacerated inside. Suspicion at once directed itself

[1] An instrument by which tracings of the pulse and of alterations in the volume of the members under the influence of emotion may be obtained, and which expresses in millimeters the psychic reaction.

against her two step-sons, M—— and F——, men of bad reputation, who had been seen roaming in the neighborhood during the day and alone had an interest in the death of the victim, since she was about to purchase a life-annuity which would have disinherited them. At the autopsy there were shown to be all the internal marks of advanced putrefaction and of asphyxiation; and in the œsophagus was found an intestinal worm resting upon the opening of the glottis. Two experts pronounced it to be a case of asphyxia, produced by violent suffocation through the victim's being held with her face against the bolster, the worm having been drawn there only through a fit of coughing. Another expert admitted the asphyxia, but was not willing to deny the possibility of its having been caused by the worm. Called in, in my turn, as a consulting expert, I was able at least to observe that death from asphyxia produced by intestinal worms are found only in infants and insane persons, and that then marked phenomena of reaction appear, which in this case were completely wanting; further, that the witness C—— declared he had heard stifled cries and the sound of blows on the night of the crime in the direction of the chamber of the victim; and especially that M——, the accused person, was juridically and anthropologically suspected of the crime, of which he had been openly accused by his brother, who, much less criminal than he, was less obstinate in his denials. M—— was, in fact, the most perfect type of the born criminal: enormous jaws, frontal sinuses, and zygomata, thin upper lip, huge incisors, unusually large head (1620 c. c.), tactile obtuseness (4 mm. right, 2 mm. left) with sensorial mancinism. He was convicted.

3. A rich farmer, S——, returning from market with 2000 francs about him, was asked by an unknown man seeking work to take him into the carriage with him. From then on this person did not leave him. They supped together and were seen towards evening going along the high road, where the following night the unfortunate farmer was found assassinated, bearing the marks of strangulation, his head shattered with great stones, and his purse empty. Four witnesses called the judges' attention to the sinister physiognomy of the unknown

man, and a young girl declared that she had seen in the evening, sleeping near the murdered man, a certain Fazio, who was observed the next day hiding himself when the gendarmes approached the neighborhood. Upon examination I found that this man had outstanding ears, great maxillaries and cheek-bones, lemurine appendix, division of the frontal bone, premature wrinkles, sinister look, nose twisted to the right — in short, a physiognomy approaching the criminal type; pupils very slightly mobile, reflexes of the tendons quicker on the right side than on the left, great tactile obtuseness, more in the right hand (5 mm.) than in the left (4 mm.); motor and sensorial mancinism; a large picture of a woman tattooed upon his breast, with the words, "Remembrance of Celina Laura" (his wife), and on his arm the picture of a girl. He had an epileptic aunt and an insane cousin, and investigation showed that he was a gambler and idler. In every way, then, biology furnished in this case indications which, joined with the other evidence, would have been enough to convict him in a country less tender toward criminals. Notwithstanding this he was acquitted.

§ 244. Proof of Innocence

Criminal anthropology can not only help us to discover the real culprits, but may also save, or at least rehabilitate, innocent persons accused or convicted.

Such a case occurred where a little girl, three and a half years old, was violated and infected by an unknown man, and her mother accused successively six young men who lived on the same staircase and were familiar with the child. They were arrested, but all denied the crime. I picked out immediately one among them who had obscene tattooing upon his arm, a sinister physiognomy, irregularities of the field of vision, and also traces of a recent attack of syphilis. Later this individual confessed his crime.

A case observed in my clinic and published by Rossi in "Una Centuria di Criminali" revealed the innocence of a convict. A certain Rossotto Giacinto, as a consequence of a series of false declarations and a letter received from his brother-in-law begging him to give false testimony, was condemned to imprisonment for life for highway robbery. Examining this man before my students, I found to my great surprise that this was the most normal individual I had ever investigated. He was 50 years old; his height was 1.73 meters; he weighed 74.5 kilograms; his hair and beard were abundant; mean cranial capacity, 1575 c. c.; cephalic index, 84; and he was without facial anomaly. His sense of touch was very fine, 1.1 mm. for the right hand, 1.0 for the left, and .5 for the tongue; his general sensibility was normal (50), and sensibility to pain 30. He was ignorant of thieves' slang and was not cynical. He showed the condition of mind common to the average man; he was fond of work, which had been his only consolation during the long years of his captivity. His conduct had always been exemplary; even in prison he had shown no vexation except at his unjust condemnation and at his separation from his family. Married at 19 years, he had never had intercourse with any other woman than his wife; and his family included neither insane persons nor criminals. While I was examining him, not yet knowing anything of his antecedents, I said to my students, "If this man had not been sentenced for life, he would represent to me the true type of the average honest man." It was then that the unfortunate man quietly answered, "But I am an honest man and I can prove it." He put into my possession numerous documents proving his perfect honesty, such as death-bed declarations of the real authors of the crime with which he had been charged, who swore before the justice of the peace that he had no part in the crime, attestations of prison directors, etc. His neighbors, of whom I made inquiries with regard to him, declared that he was a perfectly honest man.

§ 245. Pedagogy

To our school is owing still another application, direct and no less useful, namely, the application to pedagogy. Anthropological examination, by pointing out the criminal type, the precocious development of the body, the lack of symmetry, the smallness of the head, and the exaggerated size of the face explains the scholastic and disciplinary shortcomings of children thus marked and permits them to be separated in time from their better-endowed companions and directed toward careers more suited to their temperament; and sometimes it may even point the way to a cure, through emigration, moral education, and medical treatment.

§ 246. Art — Letters

In literature itself we can see a last application of this new science, not only in the interpretation of masterpieces in which genius has already anticipated some of the results of criminal anthropology, as Shakespeare in "Macbeth" and "Lear," and Wiertz in the "Enthaupteten"; but also in suggesting new forms of art, as in the admirable works of Dostojewsky, "Totenhaus" and "Schuld und Sühne," in Zola's "Bête Humaine," Garbarg's [1] "Kolbrottenbro og Andre Skildringer," Ibsen's "Hedda Gabler," and d'Annunzio's "Innocente."

And why should we not count among our triumphs the new applications that have been made to the most distant branches of science? Thus Max Nordau has found in our science a basis for the criticism of artistic, philosophical, and literary creations; [2] in the same way Ferri and Le Fort have made an application of it to the criticism of the great masters of painting and the drama; and now Sighele, Ferrero, and Bianchi have applied it to modern history and politics.

When a collective crime rises suddenly as a strange, inexplicable phenomenon in modern society, the researches into the special crime of mobs explain it for us admirably. At the same time they teach us to defend ourselves against such crimes by the preventive measures counseled by philanthropy. Otherwise a cruel reaction would certainly follow with universal approval, and the wound would be poisoned instead of healed.[3]

[1] See Ferri, "Les Criminels dans l'Art," 1897; Lombroso, "Le piu Recenti Scoperte," 1893; Le Fort, "Le Type Criminel dans l'Art," 1891.
[2] "Degeneracy," Vols. I and II.
[3] Sighele, "La Foule Criminelle," 1889; Ferrero, "Le Symbolisme du Droit," 1889.

CHAPTER VI

THE UTILIZATION OF CRIME — SYMBIOSIS

§ 247.

HAVING arrived at the end of my long labor, like the traveler who finally touches the shore, I cast a glance over the space that I have traversed; and among numerous omissions, of which there is no lack in the most carefully executed work, I perceive that I have too much neglected that side of crime which concerns its utility, proved, at least indirectly, by its long continuance.

If we try to apply the Darwinian law (according to which only those organisms survive which have utility for the species) to the fact that crime does not cease to increase, at least under the forms of swindling, peculation, and bankruptcy, we are driven to believe that it must have, if not a function, at least a social utility.

It is known, in fact, that in ancient times, and still to-day among the less civilized peoples, the greatest crimes were, and still are, utilized as a political weapon. We even possess a code, that of Machiavelli, which is only a long series of criminal projects with a political end, in which Borgia was the model. Do we not see, from the time of the Council of Ten in Venice, who hired assassins for political purposes, to the massacre of St. Bartholomew, crime reigning as sovereign in the most remote as well as in the most recent epochs? No one has forgotten the parliamentary corruption of Pitt and Guizot, or the treasons of Fouché and Talleyrand. More recently the Panamists and the Crispists have shown us that political morality differs widely from private morality, and that ministers may be criminals even though highly esteemed; while the anarchists, in their turn, have declared that they regard crime as a weapon of war. The man of integrity, moreover, whose love of justice and truth prevents his telling a lie necessary to surmount an obstacle, to lure distrustful persons, or to flatter princes with whom flattery is the highest virtue, will always find insurmountable difficulties barring his way. We see then that vice becomes almost necessary for parliamentary government of uncivilized and civilized peoples alike. Buckle has shown in his immortal work how much more dangerous it is to have statesmen ignorant than to have them criminal; for if they are ignorant they leave the nation exposed to all the rascals there are, while if they are rascals themselves they alone commit crime. It was the worst minister that Italy has had who declared, "We shall be incapable, but honest"; yet history has shown that not even he was honest. In our time the lie is no less necessary to specialists, physicians, and lawyers; it is even the basis of their operations. The pious lie which comforts the last moments of the consumptive, is often used not simply for the hysterical and chlorotic, but even for those who are perfectly well; just as the defense of the orphan and the widow is easily used also on behalf of their persecutors. Further, is there any greater crime than war, which is only an accumulation of theft, arson, rape, and murder, provoked by causes similar to those of common crimes, such as personal ambition and cupidity, and excused only because they are committed on a large scale? However, we must recognize that if war is an evil in civilized countries, it is in semi-barbarous countries the starting point for immense progress. Beginning with the primitive tribe, men are welded by war into small groups, then into larger groups, and finally into nations. Furthermore, military conquest has obliged savage men, who are naturally idle, to endure privations and to overcome the natural disinclination to work; it has initiated the system of gradual subordination under which all social life has been established (Spencer). War, on the other hand, has often contributed to popular liberty. It is doubtless for this reason that the indignation against war is not sufficiently general to prevent men from provoking it. Prostitution, which we have seen to be the equivalent of crime, can, in its turn, prevent a number of sexual crimes, as is proved by the relatively greater number of rapes in country districts. We know that the creation of houses of prostitution brought Solon eternal gratitude, when it was recognized how useful they were for checking the increasing number of rapes at Athens. Usury itself was not without utility: it was from this that the *bourgeoisie* arose, with the first accumulations of capital capable of giving birth to the most potent enterprises of humanity. Novikow has shown us that the expulsion of the Jewish merchants and usurers from Russia impoverished the very peasants on whose behalf it was carried out; for it had as its result the lowering of the price of flax, for want of able speculators to sell the product. We know, also, that the officials of the communes in the Middle Ages, after having expelled the Jews, soon had to recall them, because their expulsion had paralyzed all the industries.[1]

I have shown [2] that many of the penalties against crimes in barbarous times were themselves only new crimes, such as codified vengeance, cannibalism, etc. The *tabu* was a series of prohibitions, often absurd, introduced by the priests nearly always for their own self-interest; but there are found among these some which are useful, such as those which protected the crops and the fisheries from exhaustion by a premature gathering. Compensation for homicide, which barbarous chiefs imposed upon their subjects and bishops and popes continued during the Middle Ages, was nothing else than simony and peculation under different forms. But it was a check upon homicide, and fixed the principle of a less barbarous codification having a principle of gradation.

I believe, then, that the modern tolerance toward so many criminals is due to the tendency to a love of the new which they very often bring into the industries and even into politics, — a tendency totally opposed to the temper of the average man. In the writings of criminals,[3] among innumerable things that are shameful I have at times observed traces of a

[1] Lombroso, "L'Antisemitismo," 1894; Id., "Le Crime Politique," 1892.
[2] "Homme Criminel," Vol. I.
[3] Lombroso, "Palimpsestes de la Prison," Lyons, 1894.

genius which is not met with in the average man. In criminals as in men of genius, with whom they have in common an epileptoid basis, degeneracy is not productive of evil alone. Just as in the man of genius the excess of intelligence is compensated for by a lack of moral sense and practical energy,[1] so in the criminal the lack of feeling is often compensated for by energy of action and the love of the new, the organic anomaly destroying the exaggerated conservatism habitual to the normal man. Their abnormality, their love of the new, impel them to enroll themselves in the extreme parties. Cæsar and Catiline at first found partisans only among rascals, while the ancient consular party drew only respectable persons.[2] History teaches us that the nucleus of almost all great rebellions is criminal. Moreover, criminals play such a part in parliamentary life that it would be impossible to eliminate them from it without great harm; just as it would not have been possible to expel the ancient tyrants, who were criminals, but useful criminals. Even forgers and swindlers, though they work entirely for their own advantage, set in motion so many different activities that they give a powerful impulse to progress. Their lack of scruples, their violent impulsiveness, and their blindness to obstacles cause them to succeed where honest men would inevitably fail.

This fondness for innovations which they carry out by crime is at times the starting point for immense enterprises. The construction of the Suez Canal, for example, is due to a colossal swindle, accomplished by the same artifices which were employed in connection with Panama. Similarly the English navy had its origin in the piracy of Drake and his contemporaries. The colonization of Venezuela by the Italians is due to an officer expelled from our army for cheating. Mimande[3] mentions two swindlers, an incendiary, and two thieves who introduced into New Caledonia the cultivation of tapioca and potatoes on a large scale, and also the tanning of leather; while another thief, formerly a distiller, discovered the means of

[1] Lombroso, "The Man of Genius," Pt. IV.
[2] Lombroso and Laschi, "Le Crime Politique," 1890.
[3] "Criminopolis," 1897.

extracting perfumes and liquors from the indigenous plants. Among semi-barbarous nations, where crime is rather a common activity than a misdeed, the criminals often become popular justices and, as it were, political tribunes. They exercise and put in practice, for their own benefit, it is true, but also for the benefit of others, a kind of violent communism, which permits them to enrich themselves while despoiling the rich and powerful; but they apply at the same time a summary justice which supplies the lack of official justice. In Sardinia, in Corsica, and for a long time in Sicily under the Bourbons, the real judges, the true protectors of the oppressed, were, and still actually are, the brigands, who often divide their booty with the poor, becoming their leaders in revolts. In Naples, and in Sicily in part, the Camorra and the Mafia, although they are criminal associations, for a long time administered a relative justice upon the people, expecially in the haunts of vice, in the inns, and in the prisons. They were able to offer property owners and travelers a kind of security against malefactors which it was far from being in the power of the government to guarantee. It was for this reason that they were tolerated, and even aided, by honest men. Thus it was that under Louis XIV during nearly a century, the poorer people of France owed to brigands and smugglers, associated and organized almost into an army, the fact that they were able to have salt, which was then so heavily taxed that it had become an article of real luxury.

In the midst of too corrupt a civilization, when the extreme of legalism has come to encourage crime by impunity, lynching, which is itself a crime, becomes a barbarous but efficacious means of self-defense. In California, for example, all the public offices, including the judgeships, were in the hands of a band of real malefactors, who stole with impunity and were acquitted when accused. The majority of the people, becoming disgusted, rose up and lynched them. Since then California has been the quietest state in the Union. Without this means justice would never have succeeded in extirpating the criminals, any more than now in Italy it succeeds in reaching great rascals if they are under the shelter of their high offices.

All this explains why, among barbarous peoples as among the most civilized, many crimes are not only not punished but are even encouraged, and why the reaction against certain crimes is so weak and insufficient.

Besides, the objections, revisions, appeals, and counter-appeals for the purpose of securing the impartiality of the verdict are so numerous that, when sentence is finally pronounced, men have forgotten the crime, or they are so wearied by waiting that the most unjust verdict awakens no opposition. And if sometimes the judgment is unjust and severe, pardons and amnesties remedy the matter, so that a criminal must be very poor and very stupid if he is to undergo the whole of the punishment that he deserves. Criminal trials too frequently serve only to allow lawyers to transfer to their own pockets the money which criminals have stolen from honest men; such trials are after all only a pretext for us to lull ourselves into a feeling of security which new crimes daily prove false.

We may add that if the ancient criminal trials, juridical cannibalism, the public copulation of persons guilty of adultery, and the combats with wild beasts were wretched and criminal amusements, modern trials, in their turn, are no less immoral, thanks to the theatrical character of the assizes and of the infliction of the death penalty. At these the worst criminals congregate, finding them their best amusements, as well as a means of learning more evil and increasing the number of their misdeeds. It results that the penalty itself and the means of executing it are another form of crime, of which the whole cost is borne by honest men. Thus Italy, having lost 20 millions by the evil devices of criminals, loses four times as much in having them arrested and tried, and six times as much for their support in prison. It is not too much to say that a good share of honest men's earnings are paid out for the benefit of criminals, for whom an ill-conceived pity always finds extenuating circumstances, and the more so the worse they are.

All this would not have persisted through so many centuries, if the fundamental usefulness of certain crimes among barbarous or semi-barbarous peoples had not been great enough to prevent a really decided reaction from arising in the hearts of honest men.

§ 248. Symbiosis

But, this temporary function of crime being admitted, does it follow that the supreme end to which this book is directed, the contest against crime, is useless, and perhaps even harmful? If it were so, I myself, in whom desire for the good and hatred of evil surpass any theoretical conviction, would be the first to tear up these pages. But happily we can, even at present, already catch a glimpse of a less discouraging way, which, without abolishing the struggle against crime, will admit of less harsh means of repression.

The new way which is open before us is only in part pointed out by our pitiless criticism of present penal methods and our praise of preventive measures as the most direct and effective helps against crime. The new method requires, as one of the principal measures, the creation of institutions for utilizing the criminal in the same degree as the honest man, to the great advantage of both; and this so much the more since very often crime (for example, the crime of anarchy) reveals the most infected seat of the social diseases, just as cholera points out the quarters of the city that most require sanitation.

We aim at this end in proportion as we lay aside the ancient repressive cruelty, in accordance with the change in the times and the amelioration of social conditions. If it is true that crimes are increasing in number, it is also true that they are being stripped of their ancient atavistic ferocity and clothed in new, less repugnant, and less savage forms, — like forgery and swindling, against which culture and foresight are a better safeguard than repression. As the times change we see harsh social inequalities become less and less, and just as our most urgent social needs have been met by collective means, in public lighting, education, and road-making, so now we begin to see that similar means will repair our greatest social injustices, and that in this way one of the most powerful causes of accidental crime, the insufficiency of work, may be eliminated and the excess of wealth, another potent cause of crime, prevented.

There exists, it is true, a group of criminals, born for evil, against whom all social cures break as against a rock — a fact which compels us to eliminate them completely, even by death. But we comprehend that this deplorable necessity will end by disappearing, — at least for the less dangerous criminals, the criminaloids, — and that the means of adapting them to social life will become more and more frequent, thanks to medical cure and to their utilization in occupations suited to their atavistic tendencies. Such would be war or surgery for homicides, the police or journalism for swindlers, etc., and finally colonization in wild and unhealthy countries for vagabonds, where they would be at least subjected to a fixed abode.

If, on the one hand, natural history has shown us the existence of murderous organs even in plants (carnivorous plants),[1] it shows us also, almost as a symbol of human charity, numerous cases of symbiosis, *i. e.*, instances where plants, harmful in themselves, become useful and beneficial when united together, while increasing their own vigor. Thus the richness of nitrogen in leguminous plants is due to a schizomicete, the *Rhizobium leguminosarum* of Frank, which collects in the roots of these plants and penetrates by their rootlets in the earth into their very cells, where it multiplies. The cells, in turn, being irritated, divide, giving rise to another tubercle, where the germ is formed, part of which is utilized by the plant, and another part spreads in the soil, increasing its richness in nitrogen. In the animal world we see the medusa *Combessa Palmipes*, which attacks everything that approaches it, defending the *Caranx melampygus* against the large fishes; and in the same way the hermit crab, in place of devouring the *Actinia*, allows it to fasten itself upon its shell, and, while carrying and protecting it, makes use of its brilliant color to attract its own prey. If science has shown us that the fusion of two useless or harmful plants may be useful, as when the fungi and the algæ together produce the lichens, the time is not far distant when society will find the means, with an appropriate symbi-

[1] "Homme Criminel," Vol. I, Pt. I.

otic culture, to acclimate the criminaloid to the environment of the most fully developed civilization, not only tolerating him but also utilizing him to its own advantage. The time is doubtless not far distant when we shall see in human civilization the carnivorous plants being eliminated, while the symbiotic plants go on increasing.

But we shall attain this end completely only upon the basis of the new science of anthropology, which, by individualizing its work, can give us powerful aid in discovering the special tendencies of criminals, in order to direct them and utilize the less anti-social of them.

Nino Bixio is a striking example of the possibility of this reform. Criminal and impulsive from his childhood, he was the terror of his companions, whom he struck on all occasions. A vagabond and deserter, he seemed entirely incorrigible; yet he became a famous man when he was brought into the navy, where he could expend his excess of activity. In the same way men are not rare whom Garibaldi transformed from vagabonds into heroes. Very often in prisons I have heard thieves and assassins declare that they had committed their crimes only in order to get the means to become comedians or bicyclists; protesting, with that accent that does not admit of doubt, that if they had been able to attain their ideal they would have become famous and forever escaped from crime. I am the more convinced that they were right, since I have observed born criminals occupying high positions in the world, who satisfied their evil propensities in the exercise of their profession, becoming very often, instead of the anti-social beings they once were, useful members of society. There is a certain celebrated surgeon who presents upon his face and skull and even in his talk all the marks of congenital criminality, of which he has also the ætiology. He has found an outlet for his cruel energy in surgical operations which, while doubtless sometimes dangerous, have nevertheless always the signs of genius. I have also known a certain Trinis, an athletic workman, who was well-behaved as long as he could spend his energy upon his work, but became dangerous as soon as sickness kept him idle. This is the type of the murderer from superabundance of force, which he discharges against someone else, especially against the police. I have known another criminal, analgesic and afflicted with vertigo from birth, who remained honest as long as he could satisfy his fondness for the sight of blood in his trade of butcher. When he became a corporal, however, he beat the soldiers to whom he had to teach the manual of arms. Out of work he became a swindler, thief, and murderer. Tolu, the Sardinian brigand, many times a murderer, was in the last years of his life very useful for the public safety in Sardinia against certain bands organized to steal cattle, whom he kept in order by the terror of his name alone, while soldiers and gendarmes could do nothing against them. Tiburzio did the same for more than a quarter of a century in the Roman campagna, and prevented all thefts by other criminals; but Tolu did still more, for he introduced the prevention of crime by having cattle lent to those who would otherwise have had to steal them, and persuaded the people that honest labor pays better than theft.[1]

I have shown in my previous studies [2] that genius, like moral insanity, has its basis in epilepsy. It is not absurd, then, to see moral insanity united with genius, and by that very union made not only harmless but sometimes even useful to society. This occurs in the case of great conquerors and leaders of revolutions, so that the criminal marks escape notice, even with contemporaries, although they may be even more striking than the marks of genius. When we study the lives of the great pioneers in Australia and America we see that they were almost all born criminals, pirates, or assassins, whose excessive fondness for action, strife, carnage, and novelty, which would have been an immense danger for their country, found a useful outlet in the midst of tribes of savages. All this proves that we must profit by the change which epileptic insanity sometimes brings on, impelling born criminals to excessive altruism and even saintliness, which, in its turn, draws along not only individuals but whole masses in an epidemic of virtue. Such were the cases of Lazzaretti, of Loyola,

[1] Costa, "Il Brigante Tolu," 1879.
[2] "Man of Genius," Pt. III.

and of St. John of Ciodad. Their insensibility to pain and their recklessness make heroes of them in the face of danger, as we have seen in the case of Hollen, Fieschi, and Mottini, who had gained medals for valor in war, and the Clephtes, who were the first heroes of the Greek war of independence. Many are criminals from an impulsiveness which drives them as irresistibly toward good as toward evil. It is thus that we may explain the heroism of the convicts at the time of the cholera at Naples and Palermo, and the similar heroism which saved the whole village of Kotscha from burning.

It is for this reason that the state, instead of using repressive measures, ought to attempt to direct to great altruistic works that energy, that passion for the good, the just, and the new, which animates the criminal by passion and the political criminal. A great people ought to aim at the utilization of these forces, which, left to themselves, would certainly become dangerous; for they can be utilized, and may even succeed in transforming the apathetic masses. Revolutions are the result of energies entirely polarized toward the new and the useful, but often the immaturity of the innovations which they set themselves to introduce makes them, for the time being, unsuitable and dangerous. It follows, then, that the punishment of the authors, if it is at all possible to punish them, ought not to be made painful; and if it is necessary to prevent the new movement from starting prematurely, it is not necessary to prevent it from taking a direction which might be advantageous at a more propitious time.[1] If the ball which struck Garibaldi had killed him, many great works would never have seen the day; and if death had not so soon snatched him from us, who knows whether he would not have realized his dream of turning the marshes of Italy into fertile fields, in place of our throwing ourselves headlong into the barren moors of Africa. In a nation like Russia, exhausted by an all-powerful bureaucracy, we have seen the energy of persecuted sectaries transform almost uninhabitable regions into fruitful fields with prosperous and populous cities.

Here are the results of symbiosis. This is the sublime goal

[1] Lombroso, "Le Crime Politique et Les Revolutions," 1894.

which the great Redeemer and the prophets foresaw when they prophesied, "The wolf and the lamb shall feed together, and the lion shall eat straw like the bullock. . . . They shall not hurt nor destroy in all my holy mountain, saith the Lord"; and it is what Madame de Staël, that saint of a newer time, divined when she declared: "To understand is to pardon."

BIBLIOGRAPHY OF THE WRITINGS OF CESARE LOMBROSO ON CRIMINAL ANTHROPOLOGY[1]

1863 Prelezione al Corso di Clinica di malattie mentali (*Gazzetta Medica Lomb.*, Chiusi, Milano).

—— Cenni di geografia medica italiana. Ai medici militari d'Italia (*Giornale di Medicina militare*, pag. 481).

—— Memoria su un tumore del cervelletto (Letta alla conferenza scientifica dell'Ospedale militare di Pavia) (*Id.*, pag. 1080).

1864 Sul tatuaggio degli Italiani (*Id.*).

—— Rivista Psichiatrica e Psicologica (Bibliografie pubblicate negli *Annali Universitari di Medicina*, marzo, luglio e ottobre).

1865 La médecine légale des aliénations mentales étudiée par la méthode expérimentale. Rapport à la Société de Marseille (*Bulletin des Travaux de la Société Imperiale de Médici de Marseille*).

—— *La medicina legale nelle alienazioni mentali studiata col metodo sperimentale.* Pag. 49 (con 2 tav.). Padova, Prosperini edit.

—— Studi clinici sulle malattie mentali. Torino (*Giornale della Regia Accademia di Medicina*, N. 13, 14).

1866 Ancora sulla medicina legale delle alienazioni studiata col metodo sperimentale. Risposta. Pag. 36. Padova (*Gazzetta Medica Italiana Provincie Venete*, Anno IX, N. 5, 6, e 7).

—— Diagnosi psichiatrico-legali eseguite col metodo sperimentale (*Archivio ital. per le malattie mentali e nervose*, Milano).

1867 Algometria elettrica nell' uomo sano ed alienato (*Ann. Universali di Medicina*, Milano).

—— Diagnosi psichiatrico-legali eseguìte col metodo sperimentale (*Archivio italiano per le malattie nervose*, Anno IV, pag. 50, Milano).

—— Sull'orina nei pazzi (*Riv. Clinica*).

—— Sul peso dei sani e dei pazzi (*Id.*).

—— Craniometria nei sani e nei pazzi (*Id.*).

—— Mania epilettica da cisticerco nel cervello e nei reni (*Accademia di Medicina*, Torino).

—— Sulla medicina legale delle alienazioni (*Gazz. Med. It.*, Padova).

[1] This Bibliography was kindly prepared by Professor Lombroso's daughter, Signora Gina Lombroso-Ferrero.

1867 *Azione degli astri e delle meteore sulla mente umana.* Pag. 110. Premiato dall'Istituto Lombardo (*Archivio italiano per le malattie nervose,* Milano).
—— Dinamometria nell'uomo sano e nell'alienato (*Id.*).
1868 Sull'algometria elettrica. Risposta. (*Rend. dell'Istituto Lombardo,* serie II, vol. I, fasc. VIII, Milano).
—— Diagnosi psichiatrico-legali. Parte II. Studiate con metodo sperimentale (in collaborazione con Platner). Stabilimento Redaelli, Milano (*Archivio italiano per le malattie nervose,* pag. 28).
—— Sulla relazione tra l'età ed i punti lunari e gli accessi delle alienazioni mentali e dell'epilessia (*Rendiconti dell'Istituto Lombardo,* serie II, vol. I, fasc. VI).
—— Di alcuni studi statistici ed anatomo-patologici dei psichiatri di Olanda, Germania ed Inghilterra (*Archivio italiano per le malattie nervose,* Milano).
—— Azioni del magnete sui pazzi (*Rivista Clinica,* Bologna).
—— Studi clinici psichiatrici (Gangrena polmonare. Mania acuta. Demenza pellagrosa. Mania pellagrosa). (*Gazzetta medica italiana,* anno XI, N. 46, 47, 48, 49. Padova, Prosperini).
—— Influenze delle meteore sulle tendenze criminali (*Arch. italiano,* Milano).
—— Documenti per la storia della meteorologia applicata alla medicina e psichiatria (*Archivio italiano per le malattie mentali e nervose*).
1871 Sulla pazzia criminale in Italia nel 68, 69, 70 (*Rivista Discipline Carcerarie*).
—— Circonvoluzione cerebrale soprannumeraria di un omicida e satiriaco (*Archivio italiano delle malattie nervose,* Milano).
—— Osservazioni meteorologiche-psichiatriche dell'anno astronomico 1868 nella clinica psichiatrica di Pavia (*Rivista clinica,* Bologna).
—— Dei pazzi criminali in Italia (*Riv. Discipline Carcerarie,* Roma).
—— Diagnosi medico-legale di un uxoricida (in collaborazione con Scarenzio) (*Gazzetta medica italiana,* Milano).
—— Osservazioni di psicologia patologica (*Morgagni,* Napoli).
—— Caso di un tricoma circoscritto in un monomaniaco (*Rendiconti dell'Istituto Lombardo*).
—— *Esistenza di una fossetta cerebellare mediana nel cranio di un delinquente* (*Rendiconti dell'Istituto Lomb.,* vol. V, fasc. 18).
1872 Rivista psichiatrica (Bibliografie). Milano, Tip. Sociale.
—— Verzeni e Agnoletti (*Riv. di Discipline carcerarie,* Roma).
—— Sull'istituzione dei manicomi criminali in Italia (*Rendiconti dell'Istituto Lombardo*).
—— Antropometria di 400 delinquenti veneti (*Id.,* vol. V, fasc. XII). — (Nucleo dell'*Uomo delinquente*).

1872 Cranio (*Enciclopedia medica Vallardi*).
—— Antropofagia (*Id.*). — Cretinismo.
—— Quattro casi di microcefalia (*Rendiconti dell'Ist. Lomb.*, vol. IV. fasc. XX; vol. V, fasc. I).
1873 Sulla Teorica dell'imputabilità e la negazione del libero arbitrio di Ferri. (*Archivio Giuridico*, XXI, fasc. 3°, Pisa).
—— Sulla statura degli italiani in rapporto all'antropologia e all'igiene (*Rendiconti dell'Istituto Lombardo*, serie II, vol. VI, fasc. VI). Milano, Tip. Bernardoni.
—— Diagnosi medico legali eseguite col metodo antropologico sperimentale. Pag. 63 (*Annali Universali di medicina*, vol. 223). Milano, Fratelli Rechiedei.
—— Studi clinici e antropometrici sulla microcefalia ed il cretinesimo. Pag. 57 (*Rivista Clinica*, Bologna, Fava e Garagnani).
—— Rivista Psichiatrica (*Rivista di Medicina, di Chirurgia e di Terapeutica*, Milano, Tip. Sociale).
—— Sui rapporti del cervelletto colla fossetta occipitale mediana (in collaborazione con Bizzozzero) (*Archivio d'Antropologia*, v. III, Firenze).
—— Verzeni ed Agnoletti studiati col metodo antropologico. Roma.
1874 Casuistica medico-legale. Pag. 63. Milano, Rechiedei editori.
—— *Affetti e passioni dei delinquenti* (2° nucleo dell'*Uomo Delinquente*). Pag. 22. Nota letta all'Istituto Lombardo.
—— Raccolta di casi attinenti alla medicina legale (*Id.*).
1876 Sulla trasfusione del sangue comparato agli innesti animali. Memoria di 120 pagine premiata all'Ist. Lombardo (*Morgagni*, fasc. ott.-nov.-dic., Napoli).
—— Della fossetta occipitale mediana in rapporto collo sviluppo del vermis (*Rivista sperimentale di freniatria e medicina legale*, anno I, fasc. II).
—— Behandlung der Eczemate und Chloasmat von verdorbenem Mais (*Centralbl.*).
—— *Uomo Delinquente*, 1ª ediz. Pag. 252. Milano, Hoepli.
—— Seconda risposta verbale al dott. Biffi (*Rendiconti dell'Istituto Lombardo*, 4 maggio 1876).
—— I veleni del maiz e della pellagra (*Id.*, 23 marzo 1876).
—— Sull'abolizione dei riformatori dei minorenni (*Rivista di discipline carcerarie*, Roma).
—— Il cervello dell'assassino Leopoldo Frend (*Rivista di discipline carcerarie*, VI, 8, Roma).
1877 Sulla statistica della pellagra in Italia. Roma-Torino, Eredi Botta.
—— Sui veleni del cadavere e sulla pellagra (*Gazz. Medica Italiana*, Padova, 1877).
—— Sulle condizioni economiche-igieniche dei contadini dell'Alta e

Media Italia. Pag. 50. Estr. dall'*Italia agricola*, Milano, Tip. Bernardoni.

1877 *I veleni del maiz e le loro applicazioni all'Igiene ed alla Terapia* (*Rivista Clinica di Bologna*). Pag. 377. Tip. Fava e Garagnani, Bologna.

—— *Sulla medicina legale del cadavere*. Pag. 200. Torino, Baglione editore.

1878 Dell'influenza dell'orografia sulla statura (*Arch. di Statistica*, anno II, fasc. III). Roma, Tip. Elzeviriana.

—— Note di Antropometria sulla Lucchesia e Garfagnana (*Annali di statisitca*, vol. I, serie II. Roma).

—— Sulla Trossarello-Sola. Relazione. Torino (*Rivista di discipline carcerarie*, anno VIII, fasc. 8).

—— Alcuni cenni sull'assassino Alberti (in coll. con Maffei). Torino.

—— Su Giovanni Cavaglià omicida e suicida (coll. Dr. Fiore) (*Rivista di discipline carcerarie*, anno VII, fasc. 8).

—— Sul cranio di Volta (*Rendiconti dell'Istituto Lombardo*, serie II, vol. XI, fasc. 7).

—— Mnemosine. Poesia. 20 maggio 1878. Tip. Bortolotti.

—— Su alcuni prodotti del maiz guasto. Strassburg, di Husemann.

—— *L'Uomo Delinquente*. 2ª edizione. Vol. unico. Pag. 740. Torino, Bocca.

—— Del maiz in rapporto alla salute (*Rassegna settimanale*, giugno 1878, Firenze).

—— Rapporto sull'opera: "De la cause réelle de la pellagre" (*Giorn. Accad.*).

—— Relazione sull' opera "Ueber einige Producte des gefaulten Mais" (*Id.*).

1879 Studi su 106 cranii piemontesi (in coll. con Manuelli) (*Giornale dell'Accademia di Medicina di Torino*).

—— Studi sui segni professionali dei facchini e sui lipomi delle Ottentotte, camelli e zebù, e sullo stricnismo cronico. Pag. 46 (in collab. con Cougnet) (*Id.*).

—— Sullo stricnismo cronico.

—— Prolusione al corso di medicina legale (*Giornale internazionale di scienze mediche*, anno I, genn., Napoli).

—— *Sull'incremento del delitto in Italia e sui mezzi per arrestarlo*. Pag. 157. Torino, Bocca.

—— Considerazioni al processo Passanante. Pag. 60 (*Giornale Internazionale delle scienze pratiche*, anno I, n. 4).

—— Su Passanante: risposta alla Nota del prof. Tamburini (*Id.*, anno I, fasc. 9).

—— La pellagra nella provincia del Friuli (*Giornale della R. Accademia di Medicina di Torino*).

—— Parere medico-legale sullo stato di mente di G. Berton nel momento in cui dettava il suo testamento 4 aprile. Udine, Lavagna.

1879 La pellagra in rapporto alla pretesa insufficienza alimentare (*Giorn. Acc. di med. di Torino*).
— Su alcune nuove forme di malattie mentali (*Id.*).
— Cinque casi di divisione dell'osso malare (in collaborazione con Amadei) (*Id.*).
1880 Il vino nel delitto, nel suicidio e nella pazzia. Conferenza. Ermanno Loescher edit., Torino.
— Sulla Trossarello-Sola. Relazione (*Archivio di Psichiatria*, Torino).
— Scrittura ideografica di un monomaniaco (in collaborazione con Toselli). Con 2 tav. (*Id.*).
— Del lavoro dei carcerati nelle opere di bonifica. Comunicazione al Congresso Internazionale d'Igiene (*Annali Universali di medicina*, 7–11 settembre).
1881 La nuova proposta di legge sui Manicomii criminali (*Archivio di Psich.*, vol. II, fasc. 2).
— Delinquenti d'occasione (*Id.*, II, 313, Torino).
— Sfigmografia dei delinquenti alienati. Torino.
— Sull'incremento del delitto in Italia e sui mezzi per arrestarlo (*Rivista sperimentale*).
1882 Imbecillità morale in donna ladra e prostituta (*Id.*, volume II, fasc. 2).
— Sul delitto e le meteore. Studi critici (*Rivista Clinica*, Milano, Vallardi).
— Sull'azione del magnete e sulla trasposizione dei sensi nell'isterismo (*Arch. di Psichiatria*, III, 3).
— La reazione vasale nei delinquenti e nei pazzi (in collaborazione con Cougnet) (*Id.*, V, pag. 1).
— Gasparone (con fig.). Torino, Loescher edit.
— La reazione vasale nei delinquenti (con Couguet) (*Arch. Psich.*, Torino).
— Pazzia morale e delinquente nato (*Id.*).
— Sul mancinismo nei sani, pazzi e ciechi (*Id.*).
— Denti a sega negli idioti (*Id.*).
— Processo Spada (*Id.*).
1883 Sull'analgesia ed anestesia dei criminali e dei pazzi morali (in collaborazione con Pateri) (*Id.*).
— Sui caratteri fisionomici di criminali e di 818 uomini viventi in libertà (in collaborazione con Massimino) (*Archivio di Psichiatria*).
— Fossa occipitale mediana delle razze umane (*Gazzetta degli Ospedali*, 24 giugno, n. 50, Milano).
— Capacità cranica di 121 criminali (*Arch. di Psichiatria*).
— Delitti di libidine e di amore, con 2 fig. (*Id.*).
— Omicidio e furto per amore pazzesco (*Id.*).
— *L'amore anomalo e precoce nei pazzi* (*Id.*).

1883 La fisionomia di donne criminali (in collaborazione con Marro) (*Arch. di psichiatria*).
—— Riflessi tendinei nei criminali (Id.) (*Id.*).
—— Processo Pelzer (*Id.*).
—— L'orecchio nelle atrofie degli emisferi (*Id.*).
1884 Pazzo morale e delinquente nato (*Id.*).
—— Misdea (in collaborazione con Bianchi). Torino, Fr. Bocca.
—— Pro schola mea (*Arch. di psichiatria*).
1885 L'identità dell'epilessia colla pazzia morale e delinquenza congenita. Pag. 29 (*Archivio di psichiatria*, Torino).
—— Epilessia larvata (con Morselli) (*Id.*).
—— Del tribadismo nei manicomi (*Id.*).
—— Ninfomania paradossa (*Id.*).
—— Del tipo criminale nei delinquenti politici (con R. Laschi) (*Id.*).
—— Nuovi dati sull'identità dell'epilessia e pazzia morale (*Id.*).
1886 Del tribadismo nei manicomii (*Arch. di psichiatria*, vol. VI).
—— I processi Pel e Zerbini e la nuova scuola criminale (*Id.*, v. VI).
—— Epilessia larvata. Pazzia morale (Perizia in collaborazione con Morselli) (*Id.*, vol. VI, fasc. 1).
—— I delitti di libidine, 2ª ediz. Pag. 57. Torino, Fratelli Bocca.
—— La prima esposizione internazionale di antropologia criminale (in collaborazione con Severi) (*Arch. di psicologia*, vol. VII, pag. 19). Torino, Bocca.
1888 Nevrosi vasomotoria in un truffatore (in collaborazione coll'Ottolenghi) (*Id.*).
—— I pazzi criminali (*Archivio di psichiatria*, Torino).
—— I gesti dei criminali (in collaborazione col Pitrè) (*Id.*).
—— Il manicomio criminale e la forza irresistibile (*Id.*).
—— L'arte nei delinquenti (*Id.*).
—— Omicidio e suicidio (*Id.*).
—— Influenza della civiltà e dell'occasione sul genio (*Id.*).
—— *L'homme criminel.* II Vol. 1ª ediz. Pag. 580, con atlante di XXXIX tavole. Paris, Alcan.
—— *Troppo presto! Appunti al nuovo Codice Penale.* Torino, Bocca.
—— *Palimsesti del carcere.* Torino, Bocca.
1889 Studi sull'ipnotismo e sulla credulità (in collaborazione con Ottolenghi). Unione Tip.-Torinese. Estratto dal *Giornale della R. Acc. di Medic.*, anno 1889, n. 1.
—— *Uomo delinquente.* I Vol. 4ª ediz. Delinquente nato e pazzo morale. Pag. LV-660. Torino, Bocca edit.
—— Uomo delinquente. II Vol. 4ª ediz. Delinquente Epilettico, d'impeto, pazzo, criminaloide. Con 16 tav. Pag. 581. Torino, Bocca ed.
—— Cranî di Torinesi ignoti (in collaborazione con Ottolenghi) (*Giorn. Accad. di medicina*, Torino).

1890 *Il delitto politico e le rivoluzioni* (in collaborazione con Laschi). Pag. x-550. Torino, Fratelli Bocca editori.

— Rapport au Congrès pénitentiaire international de Saint-Pétersbourg.

— *Medicina legale del cadavere.* Pag. 190. Pinerolo, Chiantore e Mascarelli, 2ª ediz.

— *Das Politische Verbrechen*, ecc., II Vol. Pag. 250.

— *Le crime politique et les Révolutions* (in collaborazione con R. Laschi), t. 1°, pag. XIII-293. Félix Alcan, Paris.

— *Le crime politique*, tomo II, pag. 423.

— *Nouvelles recherches de Psichiatrie et d'Anthropologie criminelle.* Pag. v-180. Félix Alcan, Paris.

— *L'uomo di genio.* Traduzione in russo di Mad. Tekukenova. St-Pétersbourg.

— Forma nuova di follia del dubbio (*Giorn. dell'Acc. di Medicina di Torino*, 1892, Num. 8 e 9).

1891 Petites et grandes causes des révolutions. Paris.

— Les passions dans les révoltes (Id.).

— Tatto e tipo degenerativo in donne normali, criminali e alienate (*Arch. di Psichiatria*).

— La definizione del delitto politico (in collab. con Laschi) (*Id.*).

— Due genii nevrotici femminili (*Id.*).

— Infanticidio in pellagrosa (*Id.*).

— Assassinio epilettico (in collaborazione con Albertotti) (*Id.*).

— Feritore epilettico (*Id.*).

— Il processo del Cav . . . (in collaborazione con Marro) (*Id.*).

— Educazione anticriminale (*Id.*).

— Un autografo di Seghetti (*Id.*).

— Un'applicazione pratica dell'antropologia criminale (*Id.*).

— Educazione dei criminali (*Id.*).

— *L'Antropologie criminelle et ses récents progrès.* Paris, Alcan.

— The physionomie of Anarchists. The Vorth.

— Die Sinne der Verbrecher. Berlin.

1892 Relazione a S. E. il Ministro dell'Interno sulla ispezione dei manicomi del Regno (in collaborazione con Tamburini e Ascenzi) (*Arch. di psichiatria*).

— Criminelle d'occasion et criminelle-née (*Id.*).

— Pazzo e simulatore falsario (*Id.*).

— Processo Bonaglia (*Id.*).

— Palimsesti del carcere femminile (*Id.*).

1893 Les corrupteurs actuels (*Nouvelle Revue*), Paris.

— Psychologie des Wirtes (*Du Zukunft*) Berlin.

— Sui recenti processi bancarii di Roma e Parigi (in collaborazione con G. Ferrero) (*Arch. di Psichiatria*, vol. IV, fasc. III, pag. 191).

1893 *Le più recenti scoperte ed applicazioni della Psichiatria ed Antropologia criminale.* Pag. VII-435, Bocca ed., Torino.

— *La donna delinquente, la prostituta e la donna normale* (in collaborazione con G. Ferrero). Pag. XI-640. Roux ed., Torino.

— Un'inchiesta americana sull'Uomo perfetto (*Gazzetta Letteraria*), Torino.

— La longevità delle peccatrici (*Tavola Rotonda*), Napoli.

1894 *Gli anarchici.* Pag. 95, Fr. Bocca editori.

— *L'uomo di genio.* 6ª ed., pag. 739. Fr. Bocca edit.

— *Das Weib als Verbrecherin und Prostitute* (con G. Ferrero) Pag. 587 (*Verlagsanstalt und Druckerei*). Hamburg — Kurella trad.

— *Neue Fortschritte in den Verbrecherstudien,* Wilhelm Friedrich, Leipzig.

— Il delitto e il genio negli animali (*La Piccola Antologia*), Roma.

1895 *L'homme criminel.* 2ª ed., vol. I, F. Alcan, édit., Paris.

— *L'homme criminel,* vol. II. Criminel né — Fou moral-Épileptique — Criminel d'occasion — Par passion. Pag. 580. Félix Alcan édit., Paris.

— *Die Anarchisten* (trad. tedesca di Kurella) (*Verlagsantalt und Druckerei*). Hamburg.

— *The female offender* (con G. Ferrero). Fisher Unwing edit., London.

— Sei cranii di criminali abissini (in collaborazione col Dott. Carrara) (*Atti dell'Acc. di Medicina di Torino*).

— *La donna criminale e prostituta,* trad. in polacco. Varsovia, Cohn.

— Nevrosi vasomotoria in un truffatore istero-epilettico (in collaborazione con Ottolenghi) (*Giornale Accademia di Medicina,* Torino).

— Criminal Anthropology applied to Pedagogy (*The Monist*), Chicago.

1896 *Les anarchistes.* Pag. XX-258. Ernest Flammarion, éditeur, Paris.

— La funzione sociale del delitto. Pag. 31. Remo Sandron editore, Palermo.

— *L'uomo delinquente.* 5ª ed., vol. I, pag. XXXV-650. Fr. Bocca, Torino.

— *L'uomo delinquente,* vol. II, pag. 576. Fr. Bocca edit.

— Histoire des progrès de l'Anthropologie et Sociologie criminelles pendant les années 1895–1896 (*Comptes-Rendus du IVe Congrès International de Genève,* 1896).

— Le traitement du criminel d'occasion et du criminel-nè selon les sexes, les âges et les types (*Id.*).

— The origine of tattooing (*Pop. Sc. Month.,* avril 1906, New-York).

1896 Il cervello del brigante Tiburzio (*Nuova Antologia*, vol. LXVI, serie IV, 16 dicembre 1896, Roma).
—— *La race dans l'étiologie du crime. L'humanité nouvelle*, Paris.
—— Religion und Verbrechen (*Zukunft*, Berlin).
1897 Contributo all'Antropologia dei Dinka (in collaborazione col prof. Carrara) (*Atti della Società romana di Antr.*, vol. IV, fasc. II, pag. 24).
—— Criminal Anthropology (*Twenty Century Practice of Medicine*, vol. XII, pag. 372-433. New-York).
—— *L'uomo delinquente*. Vol. III, pag. 677 con atlante. Fr. Bocca edit., Torino.
—— *Genio e degenerazione* (Nuovi studi e nuove battaglie). Pagine v-318. Remo Sandron, Palermo.
—— La delinquenza e la rivoluzione francese. Conferenza (Estratto dalla *Vita Italiana durante la Rivoluzione Francese*, Treves edit., Milano).
1898 I precursori dell'Antropologia criminale (*Arch. di Psichiatria*).
—— Simulazione di pazzia (*Id.*).
—— Homicides aux États-Unis (*North American Review*, New-York).
—— Die Epilepsie Napoleons (*Deutsche Revue*, januar, Stuttgart).
—— Le cause dell'anarchia (*Id.*).
—— Luccheni et l'anarchie (*Revue des Revues*).
—— Mr Place e l'omicidio nelle donne (*The World*, New-York).
—— La dismaternité chez la femme (*Revue des Revues russes*, St-Pétersbourg).
—— Discorso inaugurale al Congresso di Medicina Legale. Torino. Atti del I Congresso Medicina Legale (*Rivista di Medicina Legale*, 1898). Torino.
—— Anarchistic crimes and their causes (*Indipendant*, Nuova York).
1899 Il delinquente e il pazzo nel teatro moderno (*Nuova Antologia*, 16 febbraio 1899).
—— *Luccheni e l'antropologia criminale*. Fr. Bocca, Torino.
—— *Le crime, causes et remèdes*. Pag. 572, con tavole. Schleicher et C. édit., Paris.
—— *Kerker Palimpsesten*, 5 Trad. di Kurella. Hamburg.
—— Anarchici-monarchici con doppia personalità (*Archivio di Psichiatria*, ecc., Torino).
—— Casi di ferimenti ed assassinii per accessi epiletici ed alcoolistici (*Id.*).
—— Una semiguarigione di criminale-nato (in collaborazione con Alva) (*Id.*).
—— Los hermanos Mangachi y la antrop. criminal (*Criminologia moderna*). Buenos-Ayres.
—— La dismaternidad en la mujer delincuente (*Id.*).

1899 Caractères spéciaux de quelque dégénérescence. Relazione letta al Congresso medico a Mosca.
—— I regicidi (*Die Woche*, Berlin).
—— Un anarchico paradosso (Appleton's *Popular Science Monthly*, New-York).
—— L'omicidio agli Stati Uniti (*North Amer. Review*, New-York).
1900 Les peines des femmes. Torino.
—— Le nozioni dell'Antropologia criminale nei pensatori antichi (*Archivio di Psichiatria*).
—— Danneggiamento per vendetta paranoica (*Id.*).
—— Il delitto col biciclo (*Nuova Antologia*).
—— Bresci (*Forum*, New-York).
—— La polizia in Italia (*L'Adriatico*).
—— Il sistema carcerario in Italia (*Id.*).
—— *Lezioni di medicina legale*. 2ª ediz., pag. 573. Fr. Bocca edit., Torino.
—— Les conquêtes récentes de la Psychiatrie (*des Comptes-Rendus du Congrès d'Anthropol.*).
—— Perchè i grandi criminali non presentano il tipo.
1901 Il delitto nel secolo XIX (*Nacion*).
—— Les anarchistes aux États-Unis (*Independent*, New-York).
—— Le traitement des criminels (*Revue scientifique*).
—— Sulla cortezza dell'alluce negli epilettici, nei criminali ed idioti (*Archivio di Psichiat.*, vol. XXII, fasc. IV–V, Torino).
—— *Nouvelles recherches d'antropologie criminelle*. 4ª ediz., Alcan édit., Paris).
—— Le pieghe laterali ed i solchi vestibolari della bocca (*Archivio di Psichiatria*).
—— Der Selbstmord der Vebrecher insbesondere in Zellen (*Der Tag.*, N. 397, 1901).
1902 Giuseppe Musolino (*Arch. di Psich.*, vol. XXIII, pag. 1).
—— Enrico Ballor detto il martellatore (*Id.*, pag. 121).
—— La critica alla nuova scuola in Germania (*Id.*, pag. 592).
—— *El delito. Sus causas y remedios*. Pag. VI-650. Madrid, Libreria de Victoriano Suares.
—— *Die Ursachen und Bekämpfung des Verbrechens*. Bermüheler. 1902, Berlin.
—— *Delitti vecchi e delitti nuovi*. Pag. IV-335. Torino, Fr. Bocca.
—— Innocenza di gravissima imputazione dimostrata dall'antropologia criminale (in collaborazione con Bonelli) (*Id.*, fasc. VI, vol. XXIII).
1903 *La donna delinquente, la prostituta e la donna normale*. Nuova edizione economica (in collaborazione con Guglielmo Ferrero), Torino, Frat. Bocca.
—— La psicologia di un uxoricida tribade (*Archivio di Psichiatria*, vol. XXIV, fasc. I-II).

1903 Sul vermis ipertrofico e sulla fossetta occipitale mediana nei normali, alienati e delinquenti (*Id.*).
—— Razze e criminalità in Italia (*Id.*).
—— La psicologia criminale secondo Melchine e le riforme penitenziarie (*Revue des Revues*).
—— La libertà condizionale e la magistratura in Italia (*La Scuola Positiva*).
1904 Notre enquête sur la transmission de la pensée (*Annales des sciences psichiques*, N. 5, 1904, Paris).
—— Rapina di un tenente dipsomane (*Arch. di psichiatria, neuropatologia*, Vol. IV.)
—— Ladro pazzo morale (*Id.*, Vol. IV).
1905 *La perizia psichiatrico-legale coi metodi per eseguirla e la casuistica legale.* Pag. 640. Torino, Fr. Bocca.
—— *Il caso Olivo* (in collaborazione con A. G. Bianchi). Pag. 271. Milano, Libreria Editrice Nazionale.
—— *Il momento attuale.* Milano, 2ª ed.
—— Come diventerà il delitto adottandosi la nuova scuola (*Berliner Tageblatt*).
—— L'armée des crimes et le combat contre le crime (*Le Journal*, août).
—— I geroglifici dei criminali (*Varietas*, gennaio).
—— La psicologia dei testimoni (*La scuola positiva*).
—— La causa della genialità negli Ateniesi (*Congresso di Psicologia*, Roma).
—— Mattoide falso monetario (*Arch. di psichiatria, antropologia criminale*, fasc. 4-5).
1906 *Problèmes du jour.* Paris, Flammarion.
—— Dell'anarchia in Spagna. (*N. Antologia*).
—— *Crime; Causes et remèdes*, 2ª ed. Alcan, Parigi.
—— Il mio museo criminale. Torino. Arch. Psich. vol. XXVIII.
—— Ossessione isterica di paternità causa di omicidio (*Archivio di psichiatria, ecc.*, fasc. 1° e 2°).
—— Psicologia dei testimoni (*Id.*).
—— Du parallélisme entre l'homosexualité et la criminalité innée. Relaz. al VI Congresso di Antropologia criminale (*Id.*, fasc. 3°).
—— *La femme criminelles* (in collab. con Ferrero), 2ª ediz., Parigi, Alcan (600 pag. con fig.).
1907 *Genio e degenerazione.* 2ª ediz., Remo Sandron. Palermo.
—— *Neue Fortschritte der kriminellen Anthropologie.* Marhold (Halle). Trad. Jentsch (pag. 110).
—— Ueber die neuen Entdeckungen krimineller Anthropologie (*Nord u. Süd*, Berlin).
—— Una truffatrice simulatrice (*Arch. di psichiatria, antropologia criminale*, fasc. 1-2).

1907 *Neue Studien über Genialität* (*Schmidt's Jahrbücher der gesammten Medizin*). Trad. Jetsch (90 pag.).
— Come nacque e come crebbe l'antropologia criminale. Ricerche e studi di psich., neurop. Vol. dedicato al prof. E. Morselli.
— Anomalie in cranî preistorici (*Arch. di psichiatria, antropologia criminale*, fasc. 1-2).
— La mortalità e la moralità in Italia. Comunicazione fatta alla R. Accademia di Medicina di Torino, 22 febbraio.
— I delitti coll'automobile (*Pall Mall Magazine*).
— Processo Thaw (*New-York World*), 1907.
— Id. (*Id.*) 1908.
— La precocità nel delitto (*Mitt. Straffrecht*).
1908 *Genio e degenerazione*. Nuovi studi e nuove battaglie. 2ª ediz. con molte aggiunte. Remo Sandron. Palermo.
— Ueber die Entstehungsweise und Eigenart des Genies (*Schmidt's Jahrbücher der gesammten Medizin*. Bd. CCXCIV, p. 125).
— *Neue Verbrecher-Studien*. Trad. Jentsch, Halle, edit. Marhold.
— Perchè i criminali aumentino malgrado le mitezze delle pene (*Rivista di discipline carcerarie*, 1908).
— Psicologia di Nasi (*Neue Freie Presse*).
— La criminalité nord-américaine (*New-York World*).
— La felicità nei pazzi e nei genii (*Archivio di Psichiatria*, ecc., vol. XXIX, pag. 381).
— Criptomnesie (*Id.*, pag. 291).
1909 Pensieri sul processo Steinheil (*Archivio di Psichiatria*, ecc., vol. XXX, pag. 87).
— Nuove forme di delitti (*Id.*, pag. 428).
— I delitti e la nevrosi di Grete Beyer (*Id.*, pag. 442).
— Alcoolismo di Stato (in collab. con Antonini) (*Id.*, pag. 462).
— Le cause della criminalità spagnuola (*Id.*, pag. 545).

INDEX

INDEX

[References are to Pages]

CPSIA information can be obtained
at www.ICGtesting.com
Printed in the USA
BVHW030212200720
584109BV00001B/151

9 789353 977139